THE LOCKEAN THEORY OF RIGHTS

STUDIES IN MORAL, POLITICAL, AND LEGAL PHILOSOPHY

General Editor: Marshall Cohen

A list of titles in the series
appears at the back of the book

THE LOCKEAN THEORY
OF RIGHTS

A. John Simmons

PRINCETON UNIVERSITY PRESS
PRINCETON, NEW JERSEY

Copyright © 1992 by Princeton University Press
Published by Princeton University Press, 41 William Street,
Princeton, New Jersey 08540
In the United Kingdom: Princeton University Press,
Chichester, West Sussex

Library of Congress Cataloging-in-Publication Data

Simmons, A. John (Alan John), 1950–
The Lockean theory of rights / A. John Simmons.
p. cm.—(Studies in moral, political, and legal philosophy)
Includes bibliographical references and index.
ISBN 0-69-10378-17
1. Locke, John, 1632–1704—Contributions in political science.
2. Locke, John, 1632–1704—Contributions in human rights.
3. Locke, John, 1632–1704—Contributions in natural law.
I. Title. II. Series.
JC153.L87S56 1992
323'.01—dc20   91-36773

This book has been composed in Linotron Palatino

Princeton University Press books are printed on acid-free paper
and meet the guidelines for permanence and durability of the
Committee on Production Guidelines for Book Longevity of the
Council on Library Resources

Printed in the United States of America

3 5 7 9 10 8 6 4 2

CONTENTS

v

CONTENTS

ABBREVIATIONS

Two Treatises of Government—I or II, followed by paragraph number

An Essay Concerning Human Understanding—E, followed by book, chapter, and section number

Essays on the Law of Nature—ELN, followed by page number

A Letter Concerning Toleration—L, followed by page number

Two Tracts on Government—First Tract or Second Tract, followed by page number

The Reasonableness of Christianity—R, followed by page number (and paragraph number)

An Essay Concerning Toleration—ECT, followed by page number

Some Thoughts Concerning Education—Education, followed by paragraph number

ACKNOWLEDGMENTS

This book benefited greatly from the contributions and support of many individuals and institutions. The University of Virginia and the University's Center for Advanced Study generously provided research time and other resources several times during a period of six years. The National Endowment for the Humanities also supported a semester of research in 1980. It was Nick Sturgeon's incisive lectures on Locke and the British moralists that first turned my mind to the project finally completed here (some fifteen years later). During the intervening years, many colleagues, students, and academic audiences have bravely endured my presentations of earlier versions of the ideas developed here, and they have made many valuable suggestions for the improvement of my work. My failure to acknowledge them individually indicates no lack of gratitude for their help, but only the (considerable) limits of my memory. More recently (and within the limits of my memory), Julian Franklin and George Klosko kindly read and offered many helpful comments on the first four chapters of the book. Discussions with Ken Kipnis added much to my understanding of issues I treat in chapter 4, and Josh Cohen and Warren Quinn provided extensive comments that have much improved the arguments of chapter 3. Finally, I must thank the staff of the Bodleian Library for their help with my research, and Eusebia Estes and Anne Cox for typing large parts of the manuscript. My greatest debt, however, is owed to my friend and wife, Nancy Schauber. She contributed much in the way of substantive philosophical insight; but more important, she rekindled my interest in completing this project at a time when I had nearly given it up.

One chapter of this book contains material that has been previously published. Chapter 3 (excluding section 4) is a longer, slightly altered version of "Locke and the Right to Punish," *Philosophy & Public Affairs* (Fall 1991).

THE LOCKEAN THEORY OF RIGHTS

INTRODUCTION

This is a study in Lockean moral and political philosophy. The theory of rights employed and (to some extent) defended by John Locke in his *Two Treatises of Government* is, for all its gaps, ambiguities, and confusions, the most thorough and extensive conception of the natural moral rights of persons presented by any of the classical philosophers. Much of the enduring value and appeal of the *Treatises* rest on this fact. Yet surprisingly little attention has been paid specifically to the structure and logic of Locke's theory of rights, or to the arguments he advances in support of various aspects of that theory. Much has been written about Locke's political philosophy generally, with references to but no thorough examination of the theory of rights on which that philosophy rests. There have also been substantial studies of Locke's moral philosophy generally, and of his theory of property specifically, but again without careful analysis of the full body of rights with which Locke was so centrally concerned, or much thought about the potential for developing his insights in fruitful directions.

Part of the reason for this lacuna in the literature on Locke may be the belief that rights in Locke follow fairly simply from his theory of natural law. Rights in Locke, some have claimed, are the mere shadows of the duties we owe to God. This view, I will argue, is far too simple to take account of the variety of arguments Locke advances for specific rights. And even if this view were correct, it is still far from easy to see how specific duties in Locke are meant to follow from his general claims about God's law. Another reason for the paucity of literature on Locke's theory of rights is no doubt the widespread belief that all rights in Locke can be understood by understanding property rights. Since all rights are characterized by Locke as property, once one has explicated the theory of property, one has said all that need be said about rights. I will suggest, however, that this approach also fails to do justice to the full scope of Locke's views on rights. To try to characterize as "maker's" or "laborer's" rights (and thus as foundationally identical to the rights we have in external goods) the general rights of self-government all persons are born to, their executive and des-

3

potical rights, and even their contractual or parental rights will lead to serious distortion of Locke's position. Finally, a third reason for its neglect is no doubt the simple fact that Locke's theory of rights is offered by him primarily in support of an attractive project in political philosophy: a defense of a particular conception of political obligation and its limits, and of the authority of legitimate limited government. It is, as a result, quite natural to pass over the details of the theory of rights in order to focus on Locke's more distinctly political views. But Locke's theory of rights has value independent of its political employments; and it must, in any event, be properly understood before the political philosophy based upon it can be fully appreciated.

This book, however, is not intended simply as a study of Locke's theory of rights. It aims, rather, at a more general exploration of what I will call "the Lockean theory of rights." By "the Lockean theory of rights" I mean not Locke's own theory, as he presented it, but instead the *best version* of that theory—a theory close enough to Locke's own to be considered "Lockean," but improved by certain departures from the letter of Locke's theory. The departures and modifications I will suggest are primarily those motivated by concerns Locke himself expressed (but failed to act on) and those dictated by (or at least consistent with) the *spirit* of Locke's project in moral and political philosophy. Explicating the Lockean theory of rights will thus inevitably involve taking a stand on the quite controversial question of what the spirit of Locke's project really is. Was he an uncharitable apologist for capitalism or a leveling social revolutionary, a radical voluntarist and libertarian or a social welfare theorist, a secular humanist or theological ethicist?

My intention in this work, then, is to offer the reader both a systematic interpretation of Locke's theory of rights and an estimation of the potential for a Lockean approach (and for natural rights approaches generally) to some central issues of moral and political philosophy. I will examine a distinctive set of problems about moral rights and their relevance to political philosophy, trying to solve these problems where I can and to point in the appropriate directions for dealing with them when I cannot. In doing so I will say a great deal about the general character and internal logic of a particular kind of moral viewpoint and try to illuminate one way of understanding the relation between moral and political philosophy. I am not unaware of the dangers of attempting to combine in this way scholarly and philosophical tasks. In under-

4

taking two tasks at once, it is easy to muddle both; one may err either in finding more in the texts than is there, or just as badly in binding oneself too firmly to the texts. I attempt here to negotiate the path between these mistakes.

I take both the interpretive and the philosophical portions of my task to be badly in need of doing. The interpretive lacuna I have already described. But in some ways the philosophical project seems more urgent, partly because the philosophical discussion of natural rights has been left too long to people often more interested in the conclusions than in the arguments that might support them, and partly because current communitarian and pragmatist thought seems to proceed far too quickly in dismissing the insights of the natural rights tradition. The language of natural rights and natural law is, of course, not much in fashion today, the rights being stressed primarily by libertarians and the laws primarily by neo-Aristotelians and Thomists. I will argue in chapter 2, however, that taking seriously the possibility of natural law and natural rights requires far less of a theoretical commitment than is normally supposed, and that many popular communitarian arguments for dismissing the natural rights tradition are confused or otherwise unpersuasive.

The many philosophers who reject altogether the idea of natural or objective moral rights (not all of them communitarians or pragmatists by any means) are far from the only thinkers who will be skeptical in advance about the philosophical ambitions of this book. "Commonsense Lockeans," who accept Locke's moral principles but take them to be self-evident or otherwise in no need of argument, will no doubt anticipate that my treatment of Locke will be too harsh or analytical. By contrast, those who believe that Locke's theocentric perspective can only produce in his works arguments and positions irrecoverably distant from our own contemporary theoretical enterprises, will probably expect my study of Locke to wrench his claims from their true intellectual foundations, badly distorting everything in the process. I hope to say enough in the course of this volume to convince all of these skeptics that the approach here employed is more fruitful than it might seem to promise to be.

The general strategy pursued in this work is simple. I begin with Locke's own theory of rights, outlining both its general structure (chapters 1–2) and the arguments for specific rights and specific features of rights (chapters 3–6). Throughout I pursue both constructive, analytic interpretation of Locke's texts and active criticism of his positions and arguments. Where Locke's claims are unconvincing or incomplete, and where his arguments are antiquated or otherwise philosophically suspect, I try to develop the Lockean position in ways consistent with Locke's ambitions. My aim is always the presentation of the most plausible, philosophically respectable Lockean stance, driven by a desire to do the best that can be done for Locke—that is, an elaboration and improvement of his ideas that will put Lockean insights in a fair light for contemporary eyes. Finally, I ask how persuasive the resulting Lockean position really is. An evaluation of this best version, what I call the "Lockean theory of rights," should give us the truest measure of the tradition in moral and political philosophy of which Locke's philosophy is paradigmatic.

The Lockean theory of rights that must emerge from any such analysis utilizes a largely "protective" conception of natural moral rights, one that gives special emphasis to rights of self-government and to associated rights to make property, to make contracts and promises, to punish moral wrongdoers, and to make and rear a family. The defense of these "protective" rights gives the Lockean position in moral and political philosophy much of its distinctive flavor, for these rights are subsequently used to justify an essentially voluntaristic conception of the proper moral relation between citizens and their governments. But however compelling this picture may be, I will argue, it is important not to lose sight (as so many have done) of the limits to this protective, voluntaristic view of moral and political relations, both in Locke's theory and in the best Lockean theory. Locke, as we will see, was sensitive to the limits on our private pursuits and acquisitions, set not only by the direct harm we may do to others, but also by considerations of fairness and the needs of others. Similarly, any Lockean position that would take seriously its own moral foundations must be sensitive to these limits.

In attempting to reveal the character and force of Locke's theory of rights and its role in political philosophy, I aim at what I take to be the heart of Locke's normative philosophy. But I should stress my awareness that this is not to address the whole of Locke's thought even in this area. The theory of rights (and of their logically correlative and equally important duties) is only one (the deontic) part of Locke's moral theory. I say very little in this volume about Locke's theory of virtue and its relation to his deontic theory. Locke stresses his theory of rights and duties in his later work, of course, because he intends to apply his moral theory to politics. And politics is chiefly concerned with the same essentially interpersonal relations as is deontic moral theory. But much of interest remains to be said about Locke's theory of virtue, independent of his (and our) preoccupation with his political philosophy. Similarly, I address only briefly problems in Locke's moral epistemology (and problems at the foundations of his moral philosophy generally) that were central to his philosophical concerns. And while I discuss here many questions about the moral basis of Locke's (and Lockean) political philosophy, I make no attempt to do a complete study of his political philosophy. Very little is said about the details of Locke's theory of government, especially where these details seem not to be directly determined by aspects of Locke's theory of rights.

I do not, then, deal in this work with the whole of Locke's philosophy, or even the whole of his normative philosophy. But the strategy of this volume does involve assumptions about the best way to read the whole of Locke's philosophical work. I read this work throughout as argument, as Locke's attempts to address enduring questions of philosophy in an almost unremittingly analytical fashion. I take Locke's *Treatises*, for instance, not as primarily apology or ideology or code or dogma, but as philosophical theory aimed at resolving questions asked many times both before and since Locke asked them.[1] This is not to say that Locke did not try to advance other aims as well in his work. Locke had a practical political purpose in writing the *Treatises*, a purpose that largely squared with his philosophical views. But this *is* to say that we should not take Locke's case in the *Treatises* to be wholly guided by the current needs of his political cause, to be an unconnected hodgepodge of attempts at persuasion, with no deeper philosophical concerns underlying his arguments. The *Treatises*, I will try to show, reveal a coherent theory of rights that is largely consistent with the philosophical positions Locke advances in other, less polemical works. The author of the *Treatises* is, after all, the same man who wrote the *Essay*, a "man of letters" concerned to satisfy "the demands solely of truth" (as Locke asserted in his epitaph), a man with a well-documented and insatiable thirst for knowledge and system. Locke made lasting contributions in metaphysics, in the philosophy of mind and action, in epistemology, in the philosophies of religion and education. Throughout he addressed the great problems of philosophy and responded by reasoning, with

---

[1] Regardless of his political (and other special) concerns, Locke clearly wrote the *Treatises* with his philosophical vision firmly fixed on both his predecessors and his successors. See, for example, Waldron, *Private Property*, 134–36; Grant, *Liberalism*, 10–11; and Pangle, *Republicanism*, 277.

bodies of philosophical argument.[2] The idea that Locke did not have similar intentions in the *Treatises*, with their straightforwardly theoretical concerns, is, on its face, simply not at all plausible, regardless of what Locke's practical, nonphilosophical agenda may have been.

No doubt Locke had clear ideas about the conclusions that he wanted his arguments to support, and these conclusions were undoubtedly those to which he was committed in his practical political affairs. This fact, however, should not incline us to view Locke's approach in the *Treatises* as unphilosophical. Philosophy seldom begins in anything like a social vacuum; normative philosophy never does. Locke was deeply concerned with how we (and he) ought to live our lives and the kind of society in which we (and he) ought to live. He entered the philosophical arena with opinions on these questions that he did his best to defend, opinions that obviously squared as well with many of those who shared his political affiliations. Indeed, the most striking difference between the *Treatises* and other, less celebrated Whig works of the period (including many that preceded the *Treatises*) lies not in their main conclusions or assumptions. In these the *Treatises* are far from original.[3] What makes the *Treatises* a great work is their successful blend of practical and theoretical appeals. The *Treatises* are (where pamphlets of the period are not) a thorough and systematic effort to produce a coherent political philosophy, evidenced largely by their careful articulation of the theory of rights on which the theories of society and government are based.

Philosophers typically approach their subjects with views about what a proper answer will probably look like. Locke was no exception to this rule (although this influenced just as much the content of the *Essay* as it did that of the *Treatises*). The test of Locke's work, then, should not be whether or not he had conclusions in mind in advance that he hoped to defend (he did), or where these ideas originated (whether from abstract reasoning or from practical political involvement), but rather how effectively Locke succeeded in justifying his views and whether his arguments for them have any enduring force as rational, philosophical appeals.

[2] This work will try to show that not only are there *more* arguments in Locke's *Treatises* than are usually noticed, but that there are more *interesting* arguments, more components of a coherent theoretical structure. Many have disagreed with this view of the *Treatises*. See Ashcraft's remarks on this subject in *Locke's Two Treatises*, 3.

[3] See, for example, Ashcraft, *Revolutionary Politics*, 164–65.

I will read Locke's texts as works that not only *do* speak to us, but that were *intended* to speak to us—to later generations of thoughtful men and women, interested in the same philosophical questions. The *Treatises* were clearly intended to be "more than an occasional political tract in favor of the Glorious Revolution."[4] The theory of rights advanced in the *Treatises* is one that can, in my view, be evaluated and improved without distortion by the application of contemporary standards of argument. With this in mind I will try to do here what has not often been done in scholarly work on Locke—to apply contemporary philosophical insights and methods to the analysis of Locke's theory of rights (and his arguments for that theory).

This does not mean, of course, that I believe there is no intellectual distance between Locke and ourselves, or that we can understand his claims without understanding a good deal about the intellectual and historical setting in which he wrote. Much of what Locke takes for granted will be questioned or denied by a modern reader; many arguments, acceptable in his day, are not acceptable in ours. Nor can we even hope to appreciate the content or meaning of many of Locke's claims without appreciating first the political and philosophical climate to which Locke responded in the *Treatises* (as the careful scholarship of Dunn, Tully, Ashcraft, and others ought by now to have convinced us). But to take Locke as first and foremost a philosopher is to suggest that the gulf between us and Locke is not unbridgeable, that his work need not be taken to be only of purely historical interest to us. It is to claim a continuity across time in the project of moral and political philosophy; it is to assert that Locke's questions and Locke's reasons overlap in important and productive ways our own questions and reasons. Consequently, I try in this study to advance a reading of Locke that is faithful to his texts and historically plausible; but I search as well always for that in his work which is of continuing philosophical interest. No doubt this approach runs the risk of reading too many of our own contemporary worries back into Locke. But this is a risk that must be accepted, while making every effort to avoid serious mistakes; for to do otherwise is to run the much more serious risk of losing the insights with which Locke's texts can illuminate our present philosophical concerns.

[4] Rapaczynski, *Nature and Politics*, 15. As Rapaczynski notes, Locke compared his *Treatises* to Aristotle's *Politics*; and he plainly thought of the *Treatises* as comparable in character to the great theoretical treatises of Grotius and Pufendorf (see De Beer, "Locke and English Liberalism," 36, 41, 43; and McNally, "Locke, Levellers," 38).

My belief that Locke's arguments should still be of interest to us three hundred years later is, however, based on more than the simple observation that Locke had philosophical concerns prominently in mind in his writings. It is based as well on the diverse styles of argumentation Locke actually employed in defending his views. The diversity I claim to find in Locke has, of course, been denied. John Dunn, for instance, has argued for "the intimate dependence of an extremely high proportion of Locke's arguments for their very intelligibility, let alone plausibility, on a series of theological commitments." The uniformly theocentric approach Locke embraces in his arguments, Dunn claims, means that none of the arguments of the *Treatises* can still "be interesting as a starting point for reflection about any issue of contemporary political theory."[5] Now while I agree with Dunn that Locke's theology must be taken very seriously as his starting place in ethics and political philosophy, that Locke's theological commitments are not mere "packaging" for his real secular interests,[6] I do not think we should conclude from these facts that Locke's moral and political arguments have no lasting philosophical interest. Locke was not only a theologian; he was a philosopher, and his styles of argument are predictably diverse, given the many levels on which he engaged philosophical theories and opponents.

Few will disagree, I suspect, that Locke often seems more interested in establishing his positions than in precisely *how* he establishes them. Many of Locke's arguments concerning rights are purely conceptual. Many are simple appeals to common sense, as we might expect from a great champion of commonsense philosophy. These arguments are logically independent of and detachable from the theological foundations with which Locke begins, and are as a result arguments that should be of interest even to those whose perspective is perfectly secular (including, it seems, the majority of contemporary moral and political theorists). Indeed, they are not only detachable, but are often presented by Locke quite apart from any reference to his theological presumptions. We will see, for example, that one of Locke's arguments for the natural freedom and equality of persons, and many aspects of

[5] Dunn, *Political Thought*, xi, x. From the existence of God, Dunn claims, "all else follows" for Locke (ibid., 24). For a more qualified version of this view, see Ashcraft, *Locke's Two Treatises*, 67–69. Dunn has more recently "repudiated" the second sentence quoted above ("What Is Living?" 9, 13–14), but he continues to hold (even if less unqualifiedly) that little in Locke's moral and political theory (other than his ultimately indefensible contractarianism) can be properly understood or be thought to be defended by Locke independent of his theological commitments (ibid., 12).

[6] Dunn, *Political Thought*, 222.

his arguments for property, the right to punish, and familial rights, have this character. Such arguments are intermingled with others that more obviously refer to or rely on Locke's theology. Even, then, if Locke thought of his arguments as uniformly depending for their intelligibility on the existence of God, the logical detachability of many of them assures their relevance to contemporary philosophy. They can still have force and be evaluated relative to quite different foundational commitments than Locke's. But the diversity of Locke's arguments suggests a more interesting possibility as well: that even at its foundations Locke's project in moral and political philosophy is fundamentally pluralistic.[7]

It would not be surprising if Locke had been interested in arguing for his conclusions in more than one way in the *Treatises*, for, I will claim, Locke was at the center of many crossroads in moral and political thought. He wrote during a transitional period, when the religious and secular components of his central concepts of rights and property were no longer simple to delineate. While he came to his project armed with serious theological views and faced by opponents who required a response in those terms, Locke did relatively little in the *Treatises* to expound upon those views. He may well have taken for granted that his audience would share his views. But he may also have believed that his arguments ought to convince even those readers who did not share them. I will urge a reading of Locke's moral theory that regards it as pluralistic at a variety of levels. First, it is a theory that is neither right-based, nor duty-based, nor virtue-based, but that takes seriously all three categories. Second, within the deontic portion of the theory, it appeals to both consequentialist and deontological considerations to justify the rights and duties it defends. And finally, it is pluralistic in that at the foundations of the theory arguments proceed from both theological and secular starting points.

Locke's pluralism does much to explain the incredibly wide range of interpretations of his moral and political philosophy offered in the scholarly literature. One can hardly read Strauss, Macpherson, or Nozick and believe they are discussing the same texts that interest Dunn, Tully, and Ashcraft. But all of these authors can find in Locke some real support for their readings, simply because Locke argues in so many different ways.[8] Locke's conclu-

---

[7] See, for example, Waldron, *Private Property*, 142; Ryan, *Property and Political Theory*, 22, 24; Monson, "Locke's Political Theory."

[8] Neither camp, I will suggest, decisively wins the day. In this I agree with Shapiro: "We can accept as conclusive much of the revision in Locke interpretation undertaken by Dunn, Tully, Riley, Ashcraft, and others and recognize with them

sions are often "overdetermined," as we will see, following from quite different styles of argument, all aimed at showing the same thing. Such an argumentative strategy invites interpretive controversy. It is not, then, only the preinterpretive ambitions of various authors that determines the diversity of their readings of Locke.

The reading of Locke's theory of rights presented in this volume aims at sensitivity to the pluralistic aspects of his thought. In this regard, the interpretive portions constitute a reading that is intermediate between two broad classes of interpretation: those that stress Locke's secular concerns and ascribe to him a radically individualist position (including, among the many strange bedfellows, libertarian, Marxist, and Hobbesian interpretations) and those that emphasize Locke's theocentric perspective and his communitarian or majoritarian sides. I believe that a part of Locke's genius and a major source of the enduring interest and appeal of his thought, lay in his ability to identify and defend an at least apparently coherent position between these extremes. Locke's moral and political theories are moderately, not radically, individualistic; his moral arguments utilize both theological and secular first premises. Locke is throughout a blender and compromiser, drawing together many disparate theoretical concerns and reconciling these with his practical political interests. His was a complex task and one that he dealt with if not brilliantly, then at least more coherently than his many detractors have allowed.

The basic orientation of this study is guided by two Lockean distinctions: that between moral and political philosophy and that between (what H. L. A. Hart has much more recently called) general and special rights. The former distinction is really only between a whole and one of its parts. As Locke puts it, "true politics I look on as a part of moral philosophy."[9] Political philosophy is the application of (logically nonpolitical) moral principles to the realm of politics—that is, the study of how states and societies ought (morally) to be, how citizens and governors ought (morally) to behave, the moral rights and duties of persons qua political beings. To understand political morality, we need only understand natural morality (the law of nature) and the facts of political life, seeing how the former evaluates the latter. More precisely, Locke distin-

---

the centrality of Locke's theology to his political writings. The implications of this for Locke's place in the liberal tradition, however, are not so devastating to older conventional wisdom as Tully and others seem to suppose" (*Evolution of Rights*, 108).

[9] Letter to Lady Peterborough, in King, *Life*, 1:9.

guishes between two parts of politics, "the one containing the original of societies and the rise and extent of political power, the other, the art of governing men in society."[10] The first part of politics—political philosophy proper—is the subject of Locke's *Treatises*. It is also the subject of many portions of this study. The bulk of the book, however, is devoted to the moral principles (those defining rights and duties) that are to be applied in political philosophy.

A further division in my discussion of these principles is determined by the distinction between general and special rights (and duties), a familiar distinction in contemporary theories of rights and one clearly anticipated by Locke (as we will see in chapter 2). Chapters 1 and 2 concern the basic structure of Locke's moral theory and the natural moral condition of humankind (the general rights and duties to which all persons are born). My concerns in these chapters are primarily interpretive. Chapters 3 to 6 take up the most important of the special rights in Locke and their roles in his project in the *Treatises*, and my treatment there is more philosophical in nature. The rights discussed in these latter chapters are "special rights" in the sense that they all arise from special performances, transactions, or relationships, and their importance to Locke's political theory and any related Lockean project is plain. The defense of these rights gives Locke's and the Lockean theory of rights their real character as distinctive theories. I have tried to compose chapters 3 to 6 to be as much as possible "free-standing" discussions, accessible (without extensive reading in the remainder of the book) to those with special interests only in the particular topics of those chapters.

Throughout this book I try to take seriously and to respond frequently to existing literature on Locke's moral and political theory, on rights generally, and on the specific rights with which I deal here. There are, of course, limits to this task, set by both my own energy and my exegetical and philosophical ambitions, so this task is often confined to footnotes. This relegation should not be taken to indicate my assessment of the importance of the literature in question. Those interested in a reasonably complete (but by no means exhaustive) list of prominent books and articles in these areas will find one in "Works Cited."

[10] "Some Thoughts Concerning Reading and Study for a Gentleman," 400. See Tarcov's discussion of this distinction in *Locke's Education*, 5–6.

O N E

THE STRUCTURE OF LOCKE'S MORAL THEORY

1.1. The Demonstration of Morality

Most people in the English-speaking world (and many outside it) have a practical, nonacademic acquaintance with the Lockean theory of rights. A commitment to (parts of) that theory grounds many of their social and political practices and institutions, and, as a result, guides many of their commonsense judgments about right and wrong, just and unjust. It provides prominent and comforting landmarks in their moral world. American school children learn by rote (or, at least, used to learn) some of the content of the Lockean theory: "that all men are created equal, that they are endowed by their Creator with certain unalienable rights, that among these are life, liberty and the pursuit of happiness."[1] But they learn at the same time to regard these claims as "self-evident." They are claims not to be questioned, standing in need of no clearly articulable justification. Few ever discuss or even remember the reference in the Declaration to "the Laws of Nature and of Nature's God." We "know" and live by much of the specific content of the Lockean conception of rights, without having bothered to explore its foundations or its theoretical superstructure.

The readers for whom Locke wrote the *Second Treatise*, of course, were not interestingly more inquisitive or "philosophical." While "the Laws of Nature and of Nature's God" were much more central to their moral landscape than to ours (and the specific Lockean rights rather more controversial), Locke's audience was just as confident and secure in their moral beliefs. That we ought to obey our Creator's law was, we might say, "self-evident." Why we ought to do so was a question, then as now, left to one side for

[1] "There remains a very real sense in which Americans can say that Locke is *our* political philosopher" (Tarcov, *Locke's Education*, 1).

14

philosophers and theologians. How one determines the nature of God's intentions for humankind and derives from them the specific content of God's law was similarly an issue on which Locke's audience was unlikely to have much dwelled. Such questions were for them largely rendered moot by revelation. These facts about Locke's readers in part explain much of the disturbing paucity of foundational work in the *Second Treatise*. The content of parts of the natural law and the rights defined by it receive considerable attention; but very little is said about why these are our duties and rights (or about how we are to discover the remainder of the law's content). Our being God's creatures will not seem to a modern reader a plausible explanation of why we must obey His laws, nor are we so sure that we can know of either God's existence or His will for humankind. Locke's readers were more confident on these points, obviating the requirement of presenting a more elaborate foundation for the moral theory that guides the arguments of the *Second Treatise*.[2] Indeed, in none of Locke's writings is there a clear and systematic presentation of the whole of his moral theory.

My object in this chapter will be to very briefly explore the foundations of Locke's theory of rights. I begin with an attempt to piece together certain aspects of Locke's moral theory, drawing on claims he makes in a variety of published and unpublished works. At least partly because Locke provides us with so patchy a framework for such discussion, we must try throughout to be more careful than is usual to distinguish the various levels of Locke's (and Lockean) theory. It is, for instance, confusing to see Locke described as an egoist or a utilitarian (or even an intuitionist or proto-Kantian) while noticing at the same time his commitment to a divine will or divine command theory of morality. I will, accordingly, distinguish in this chapter the foundations of Locke's moral theory (sections 1–3) from the theoretical superstructure (section 4) and the specific content (section 5) of that theory. My discussion of all of these matters will necessarily be brief, but I hope nonetheless convincing and adequate for my purposes in the remainder of this volume (which will be more concerned with the content of Locke's theory of rights than with its foundations).

The rights defended by Locke in the *Second Treatise* are grounded in a familiar and largely traditional natural law theory.[3]

---

[2] See, for instance, Gauthier, "Why Ought One Obey God?" 426, 431–32. Locke can thus characterize his arguments as mere appeals to "common sense" (in the preface to the *Treatises* and, e.g., in I, 137) without obvious impropriety.

[3] See Laslett, "Introduction." I take Locke's commitment to this theory to be sin-

CHAPTER ONE

The law of nature (and the duties and rights it defines) is God's law for man, a law for beings with reason and free will, binding them to perform (often contrary to their inclinations) as God wills and as their rational status demands. Natural law is "the decree of the divine will discernible by the light of nature and indicating what is and what is not in conformity with rational nature" (ELN, 111).[4] It is not natural law in the descriptive sense, that is, rules according to which things in God's universe actually operate, although Locke, like so many others, is not always entirely clear on the distinction.[5] It is the *moral* law (R, 14 [23], 152 [219]); "the law is the eternal, immutable standard of right" (R, 162 [232]). More precisely it is *divine* law that is "the only true touchstone of moral rectitude" (E, 2.28.8). When divine law is given to man by revelation, as in the Bible, it is *positive* moral law.[6] When it is discovered

---

cere, to be neither a use of Macpherson's "facade" (*Possessive Individualism*, 270) nor an embracing of Strauss' Hobbesian "partial law" (*Natural Right*, 219–21, 227–28; see also Kendall, "John Locke Revisited," 228). Strauss maintains that Locke's law of nature is not *true* law, differing from revealed law in both source and content. I argue below against these claims. For effective criticisms of Strauss' position, see Seliger, *Liberal Politics*, 58; Dworetz, *Unvarnished Doctrine*, 126–31; and Von Leyden, *Hobbes and Locke*, 134–36. I will not try to add here to the already considerable literature on the history of natural law theory and Locke's place within it. Locke's theory of natural law can be positioned at least largely within the Thomist tradition. The influences on his views that are most apparent (and most frequently commented on) are the writings of Hooker, Grotius, Pufendorf, and Cumberland. See, for example, Tully, *Discourse*, 5–6, 48; Tuck, *Natural Rights Theories*, 172–73; and Colman, *Moral Philosophy*, chapter 2, for recent discussions of Locke's position within various natural law traditions. General discussions of natural law theory can be found in, for example, Gierke, *Natural Law* (and Barker's Introduction to Gierke); d'Entreves, *Natural Law*; and Sigmund, *Natural Law*.

[4] It is "that rule which was suitable to his nature . . . the law of reason, or, as it is called, of nature" (R, 9 [14]).

[5] On these two kinds of natural law, see White, *Philosophy*, 150–60. Best argues (unconvincingly) that for Locke natural law really *is* descriptive ("Innocent," 174). The argument seems to be: the law of nature is the law of reason, "rational men act rationally," therefore the law only describes. But of course rational persons (in Locke's sense of *minimal* rationality) do *not* always act rationally. Colman seems to get Locke right on this point (*Moral Philosophy*, 30–31). The primary sense in which natural law is natural for Locke, is simply that it is a law we "may attain to the knowledge of, by the use and due application of our natural faculties" (E, 1.2.13). While Locke does mention "the rule of living according to nature," he makes it clear that he means living "in conformity with *rational* nature" (ELN, 111; my emphasis—see also I, 58), which we by no means do automatically. The natural law is also natural for humans because they are naturally sociable, and the law guides us to peaceful coexistence, and because it is not a law *made* by people, but one that applies to them simply by virtue of their rational nature. See Drury, "John Locke," 535–36; and 1.4. below.

[6] "There needs no more, but to read the inspired books to be instructed; all the duties of morality lie there clear, and plain, and easy to be understood" (R, 180 [243]).

16

by man without revelation through the use of reason (the "light of nature"), the divine law is the *law of nature* (ELN, 187). But the content of divine law is in the two cases the same, as is its binding force.[7]

We learn only a little about the law of nature in Locke's *Two Treatises*. There is a sketch of the kinds of duties it places on us (II, 6) and extensive discussion of certain rights it defines. The law binds us, we are told, because we are all God's "workmanship" (II, 6), although no real explanation of that claim is offered. The law of nature is the law of reason (e.g., I, 101; II, 6, 57, 96). But Locke never tells us just what this means. And while the natural law is "as intelligible and plain to a rational creature, and a studier of that law, as the positive laws of commonwealths, nay possibly plainer" (II, 12), the *Treatises* do not show us how to discover or "study" the rules of morality.[8]

Locke's readers fare slightly better in *An Essay Concerning Human Understanding*. In books 1 and 2, for instance, Locke clarifies the relations between law and morality and the meaning of moral good and evil. And he offers further claims about why we ought to obey God's commands (E, 2.28.8). But certainly the best known argument concerning morality in the *Essay* is that designed to show "that morality is capable of demonstration, as well as mathematics" (E, 3.11.16; first suggested at 1.2.1). We seem here to be promised by Locke exactly what we want—a step-by-step "demonstration" from clear and certain premises to the rules of natural law as conclusions.[9] Few readers, however, are inclined to think that Locke makes good on this promise, when he finally discusses the demonstration directly (E, 4.3.18). He seems there to present

---

[7] So the rational demonstration of morality is for Locke perfectly consistent with the acceptance of revelation. "The divine law is that which, having been delivered to men by God, is a rule and pattern of living for them. And according as it either becomes known by the light of reason which is natural and implanted in men, or is made manifest in divine revelation, it is in turn divided into natural and positive law. And each of these I describe under the same head as 'moral' since each is exactly the same in its content and matter and they differ only in the manner of their promulgation and the clarity of their precepts. For this is that great rule of right and justice and the eternal foundation of all moral good and evil" (Second Tract, 222). Whatever is not required or forbidden by the law is morally indifferent. Locke also distinguishes between God's particular commands (for example, to Moses) and His general commands (to all persons at all times). Only the latter are "the moral part" of God's law, the part that is "of eternal obligation" (R, 12 [20]).

[8] This makes it rather misleading to characterize the *Second Treatise* (with Grant) as a *demonstration* of Locke's theory of rights and duties (see *Liberalism*, 198).

[9] For Locke a "demonstration" involves an "uncovering of conceptual connections" (Yolton, *Compass* 92).

little more than a couple of simple "analyses" of moral terms: "Where there is no property there is no injustice"; "No government allows absolute liberty." While these propositions may be true, the demonstration of their truth seems a project quite remote from the grounding of the moral law.[10] We want to know how we should act, and why. How do we discern God's will? Why are we obligated to obey His commands? What makes moral law the law of reason? How can we prove the specific precepts of natural law?

The best we can do in answering these questions for Locke is to draw together bits from his various works that suggest a coherent position. Opinion among philosophers and political theorists is sharply divided on the issue of whether Locke's texts reveal a consistent moral theory. And on the question of morality's demonstrability, we know that by the time Locke wrote *The Reasonableness of Christianity*, he himself was no longer very confident in his (or anyone's) ability to produce a "full" demonstration of morality: "it is plain, in fact, that human reason unassisted failed men in its great and proper business of morality. It never from unquestionable principles, by clear deductions, made out an entire body of the 'law of nature.' "[11] But even if we can nowhere in Locke find a thorough proof or justification of the moral theory at work in the *Second Treatise*, we can, I think, find a sketch of a position that

[10] See Gough's complaint that "the examples he gave amount to no more than defining the meaning of certain terms and then drawing tautologous conclusions from their logical incompatibility" (*Political Philosophy*, 7); and the similar criticisms of Locke's "blunder" in White, *Philosophy*, 177–78; Herzog, *Without Foundations*, 94–95; and Aaron, *John Locke*, 262–63.

[11] R, 171 (241). Note that Locke does not here say that *none* of morality can be demonstrated. And even the *whole* of morality is never said to be beyond demonstration. No one ever undertook to "give it us all entire" (174 [242]), "in *every* part demonstrable" (178 [243]); only "*some* parts of that truth lie too deep for our natural powers *easily* to reach" (177 [243]; my emphases throughout). This is perfectly consistent with the possibility of demonstrating the core or basic requirements of morality. Indeed, it is also perfectly consistent with the possibility of a *full* demonstration of morality. In the passages at issue, Locke is primarily discussing the "demonstrations" of the "heathen philosophers" before Christ (169–71 [241]; 173–74 [242]). And Locke never asserts that it is "too hard a task" for reason to produce a full demonstration; he says only that "it should seem, by the little that has hitherto been done in it, that it is too hard a task for *unassisted* reason" (170 [241]; my emphasis). After the "assistance" of revelation (which shows us what needs demonstrating), "reason *confirms*" the truths of morality (178 [243]; my emphasis). It is only "the greatest part of mankind" that lacks the leisure and skill for producing a full demonstration (170 [241]; 178 [243]; see also E, 4.20.2–6). Locke is far too often taken to be admitting in the *Reasonableness* that the project of the *Essay* is impossible. For more reasonable and accurate accounts of the true significance of his claims there, see Yolton, *Compass*, 171, 180; Colman, *Moral Philosophy*, 138–40; Ashcraft, *Locke's Two Treatises*, 267; and Grant, *Liberalism*, 4, 22–23. See also note 99 below.

remains substantially the same throughout his works (nearly all of which are concerned in one way or another with morality).[12]

The key to understanding Locke's remarks in the *Essay* on the demonstration of morality is to avoid being misled by the examples he offers in discussing it.[13] His analyses of moral ideas like "property," "injustice," and "government" (in E, 4.3.18) are not (as it might at first appear) badly misguided attempts at examples of the demonstration of rules of natural law, nor does Locke suggest that they are.[14] The propositions in question are obviously not rules for action at all. These analyses are meant only to make a simple point about moral ideas generally—that they have clarity and "adequacy" sufficient to make a demonstrative science of ethics possible. The connections between moral ideas (e.g., property and injustice) that Locke's analyses reveal are simply examples of the *kinds* of connections that he thinks will be employed in the demonstration of morality. The demonstration itself must begin with the ideas of a "a supreme Being" and of "ourselves, as understanding, rational creatures" (as Locke, too subtly, suggests earlier in E, 4.3.18) and end with the precepts of natural law.[15] But it is only the clarity and adequacy of moral ideas which will permit such a demonstration, which will make possible moral certainty.

Let me explain these points more carefully. According to Locke, a systematic, demonstrative science is possible only where we can

[12] Moral theory was Locke's single most enduring concern (see Ashcraft, *Locke's Two Treatises*, 234). Colman has convincingly defended the consistency of Locke's various efforts in moral philosophy (*Moral Philosophy*, 235–43) against the charges of inconsistency advanced by, for example, Aaron (*John Locke*, 256–57, 266–67). Grant (*Liberalism*, 22–23) and Rapaczynski ("Locke's Conception of Property," 305) argue for the (more limited) view that we should read the *Essay* and the *Treatises* as parts of one, coherent project; and Ashcraft correctly points out that we should expect consistency between at least the *Essay* and the *Treatises*, given that Locke spent at least a decade working on them simultaneously (*Locke's Two Treatises*, 232–34). While Locke's moral views seem to have stayed reasonably constant from the 1660s on, his political thought clearly underwent some substantial shifts during the period between 1660 and 1681. See Ashcraft, *Revolutionary Politics*, 75–76; and Parry, *John Locke*, 11–13.

[13] The discussion that immediately follows owes much to Mattern, "Moral Science"; Colman, *Moral Philosophy*, chapters 5–6; Tully, *Discourse*, chapter 1; Yolton, *Compass*. I will for the most part not note below the many points of contact between these works and my own discussion.

[14] Locke seemed perfectly aware that mere analysis would be inadequate for his purposes in demonstrating morality. See "Of Ethics in General," one of whose main focuses is precisely the distinction emphasized in this paragraph. The criticism that ethics for Locke amounts to pure analysis of terms, and that no real obligations can be derived in that way (Aaron, *John Locke*, 263–64), thus seems misguided.

[15] "Of Ethics in General," section 10.

reveal the necessary connections between the real essences of things. But, of course, we can do this only if we can *know* the real essences.[16] We cannot, for instance, have a demonstrative science of nature since, as Locke famously claims, we cannot know the real essences of natural kinds (or "substances"). Our substance ideas are inadequate (they are imperfect "ectypes") because they are intended to represent external things whose true constitutions are not known (or knowable) to us (E, 2.31.11). Thus, certain knowledge in this area is denied us. In mathematics and morality, however, things are rather different. Our mathematical and moral ideas are "modes" that concern not natural kinds but purely conventional kinds. These ideas are not made after any pattern of real existence in nature; they are themselves the patterns that "the mind of man has arbitrarily put together" (E, 3.11.15) (modes and relations are "archetypes" [E, 2.31.14]). Mode ideas cannot be inadequate to their natural subject. Truth is here not a matter of correspondence with the states of external things, nor are the real essences hidden from us. Rather, the real and nominal essences are "the same" (E, 4.6.4). Since our moral and mathematical ideas are adequate, "real knowledge" in these areas is possible (E, 4.4.7), as is demonstrative science (if we can reveal the general logical structure of [necessarily connected] ideas, as Locke seems confident we can [E, 4.3.20]). These facts also address in part Locke's familiar worries about our knowledge of universal propositions (which will, of course, be part of a moral science). Many universal propositions (those about substances) are not certain, because certain knowledge requires either direct experience of all members of the kind referred to in the proposition (an experience we generally lack) or knowledge of that kind's real essence (which, in the case of substances, is denied us).[17] We can, however, know the real essences of moral kinds, making universal, instructive, certain propositions in morality (and mathematics) possible.

All of this, of course, only shows how a demonstration of mo-

[16] The "real essence" of a thing is (roughly) that which makes a thing what it is (in the case of a body, its internal constitution). The "nominal essence," by contrast, is that by which we name and classify a thing, by which we "know it" (see E, 3.6.2; and Yolton, *Locke*, 103–5).

[17] There is, of course, also the problem of whether such propositions will be "instructive" or only "trifling" (true by definition). Locke seems to believe that many universal propositions in mathematics and morality will be necessary but also instructive (E, 4.8.8). On the significance of this claim for Locke's moral science and on the inevitable comparison with Kant's class of synthetic-a priori propositions or judgments, see Colman, *Moral Philosophy*, especially 157–62.

rality is *possible*. Locke may have been (or have become) skeptical about our (and his) ability to actually produce without great difficulty a full demonstration of the whole of morality. But he certainly had an idea of the form that demonstration would take and of some of the connections between ideas that could be established (even if he thought a full demonstrative science of ethics to be a problem). In fact, Locke offers us a fairly substantial sketch of the basis of his demonstration in essay 4 of his *Essays on the Law of Nature*.

Strictly speaking, the heart of the demonstration of morality is "hypothetical" in form—that is, Locke can first establish conclusions exclusively from the relations of ideas, without any concerns about whether the ideas in the demonstration are ideas of any real things in the world. This, after all, is the form of mathematical demonstrations, which "concern not the existence" of their objects; a demonstration involving a square or circle proceeds "the same, whether there be any square or circle existing in the world or no." Similarly, Locke believes, we can display the necessary connections between ideas that lead to the rules of morality (which forbid or enjoin action) without concern for "real existences," since we know these rules "will be true in reality of any action that exists conformable to" them (E, 4.4.8). Our senses will then inform reason about the real application of moral rules that can first be derived strictly through the use of reason (the "voice of God in man" [I, 86]).[18]

When Locke sketches his argument in the *Essays*, the evidence of our senses and the operations of reason are presented together, but we can separate them for clarity's sake. Suppose, first, a "powerful and wise creator," who creates brute beasts, mortal, rational beings, and an environment to support their lives. It follows simply from the ideas of these things, Locke believes, that the beings created are rightly subject to the authority of the creator ("for who will deny that the clay is subject to the potter's will" [ELN, 157]). We can conclude further that the creator has intentions with regard to his creatures, for being "wise, it follows from this that he has not created this world for nothing and without purpose" (ELN, 157). The mortal beings ("so curious and wonderful a piece of workmanship" [I, 86]) would not have been given reason, for

---

[18] Here, of course, we speak only of the logical order of the demonstration, not the historical or psychological order. Our ideas of objects and actions in the world to which the demonstration applies will obviously precede historically their employment in any proof of morality.

instance, unless they were intended to use it (it being unwise to decorate creations pointlessly) (ELN, 117). But if we know that the creator is a rightful superior who wills that his creations perform in certain ways, this is sufficient to conclude that the creator's will is a law for those creations (since a law is simply "the decree of a superior will," laying down "what is and what is not to be done," which "binds men" and is "sufficiently known" to them [ELN, 111–13][19]). The specific rules of this law are whatever rules must be followed to best achieve the creator's intentions for his creatures.

All of this, Locke believes, can be shown by reason, through the discovery of the connections between the ideas employed in the demonstration. But the demonstration is thus far only hypothetical, logically independent of the real existence of things in the world. *If* such a creator and such creatures exist, *then* the creatures have certain obligations. The evidence of our senses then completes the proof.[20] This evidence reveals the natural world and ourselves as mortal, rational beings. From the regularity and perfection of nature and from human nature "it is undoubtedly inferred that there must be a powerful and wise creator of all these things" (ELN, 153; see also, e.g., I, 53).[21] We have only to follow the remainder of the hypothetical proof to reach the conclusion

[19] The last of these features of law—that it be promulgated—can be inferred from the terms of the demonstration if we add (as Locke clearly wishes to) that reason is sufficient for the creatures to know their creator's will. Every person (rational individual) is capable of employing reason to discover at least the basic content of God's will: "the same spark of the divine nature and knowledge in man which, making him a man, showed him the law he was under." Reason is the "candle of the Lord," although one can "put out" or "neglect" the light of reason (R, 162 [231]). Reason is humankind's "only star and compass," which makes them "almost equal to angels" (I, 58) and distinguishes them from the beasts (E, 4.17.1). All of this suggests, of course, that Macpherson's reading of Locke as defending differential rationality based on social class, cannot be correct (see Ryan, "Locke and the Dictatorship," 240–41; Ashcraft, *Locke's Two Treatises*, 249–53). See note 99 below.

[20] The *Essays* are concerned to argue that the law of nature is known by reason through sense experience (and not by inscription or tradition). See Yolton, *Locke*, 48.

[21] God "hath left so many footsteps of himself, so many proofs of his being in every creature, as are sufficient to convince any who will but make use of their faculties that way" ("Knowledge, Its Extent and Measure," 166–67). The proofs of God's existence employed here are familiar, conforming to standard versions of the "argument from design" and the "anthropological argument" (which is closely related to Descartes' "causal argument"). (See Tully, *Discourse*, 38–39; Herzog, *Without Foundations*, 91–93.) These are the arguments (Locke claims) that rely most directly on sense-experience. In other places, Locke suggests other paths to knowledge of God. Locke's main discussion of these issues, of course, is in E, 4.10.1–19.

that man is in reality bound to follow God's will, which is the law of nature. Thus, "our faculties . . . plainly discover to us the being of a God, and the knowledge of ourselves, enough to lead us into a full and clear discovery of our duty and great concernment" (E, 4.12.11).[22] The form of the demonstration of morality,[23] then, is as follows:

(1) Our senses (with reason) reveal the existence of God.

(2) Our senses (with reason) reveal the existence of man ("ourselves, as understanding, rational creatures") and that man was created by God.

(3) The relation of God to man grounds a duty for man to do God's will.

(4) The nature of God and human nature together reveal the "principle" of God's will for man (ELN, 157).

(5) From the principle of God's will and the empirical conditions of human life (revealed by our senses), our specific moral duties follow.

On the strength of this style of argument, Locke feels able to assert:

It seems to me to follow just as necessarily from the nature of man that, if he is a man, he is bound to love and worship God and also to fulfill other things appropriate to the rational nature, i.e., to observe the law of nature, as it follows from the nature of a triangle that, if it is a triangle, its three angles are equal to two right angles. (ELN, 199)[24]

I will ignore here many of the obvious problems faced by Locke's demonstration.[25] Two problems, however, must at least be

[22] From which, together with our inability to know the "real essences of bodies," Locke concludes "that morality is the proper science and business of mankind in general" (E, 4.12.11).

[23] This same "style" of demonstration is suggested by Locke in other, later works. As we have seen, the *Essay* makes passing reference to the basic elements of the demonstration (E, 4.3.18). So does the *First Treatise* (e.g., in I, 86), with gestures in similar veins in the *Second Treatise*.

[24] "The duties of that law, arising from the constitution of his very nature, are of eternal obligation; nor can it be taken away or dispensed with without changing the nature of things, overturning the measures of right and wrong, and thereby introducing and authorizing irregularity, confusion, and disorder in the world" (R, 136 [180]).

[25] Steps (1) and (2) of the demonstration are, of course, highly controversial (at the very least); but I cannot address them here, beyond noting that a secular foundation for Locke's moral theory (if possible) would have the advantage of avoiding

mentioned in passing. First, it may seem that Locke's employment in the demonstration of substance ideas like our idea of "man" must undermine his strategy. For will not our knowledge of our obligations (the goal of the demonstration) be as uncertain as our knowledge of man generally (whose real essence we cannot know)? The problem here relates to a common worry that natural law theory lacks a convincing account of the essential features of human beings, from which to derive moral law (a worry I will address more directly in 2.5). Locke's reply to such concerns seems to be that in the demonstration of morality we use not the *natural* idea of man, but rather a conventional, *moral* idea: "when we say that man is subject to law, we mean nothing by man but a corporeal rational creature: what the real essence or other qualities of that creature are in this case in no way considered" (E, 3.11.16).[26] This move, of course, preserves the "certainty" of Locke's moral conclusions. While we may be unable to decide whether some unfortunate creature counts as a man in the natural sense,[27] we need only know that the creature is corporeal and rational for the conclusions of Locke's argument to hold. The obvious consequence of this point, of course, is that the precepts of natural law that conclude Locke's demonstrations can be taken to apply not to human beings (of which we have no clear idea), but only to rational, corporeal beings—a class that neither includes *all* human beings nor is confined *solely* to human beings (in principle, at least).[28] This is,

---

these thorny steps. Steps (1) and (2) were not, as I noted earlier, as controversial for Locke's audience; indeed, the first sentence of the *Essays* finds Locke saying "I assume there will be no one to deny the existence of God" (ELN, 109). I will also say not much more about problems in the demonstration caused by Locke's use of questionable epistemological assumptions.

[26] See Grant's discussion of Locke's concept of "man" in *Liberalism*, 28–31.

[27] Children, changelings, and monkeys (E, 3.11.16) are Locke's examples of this uncertainty about man "in a physical sense." Elsewhere Locke poses the following question: "if a woman should bring forth a creature perfectly of the shape of a man, that never showed any more appearance of reason than a horse, and had no articular language, and another woman should produce another with nothing of the shape, but with the language and reason of a man, I ask which of these you would call by the name man?—both or neither" (King, *Life*, 1:162). The answer, for Locke's purposes in the demonstration, must be that the *true* man (in the *moral* sense) is the latter.

[28] On the face of it, alien rational beings would appear to fall under natural law, for the same reasons that Locke's monkey "would no doubt be subject to law, and in that sense be a *man*" (E, 3.11.16). Whether or not angels (noncorporeal rational beings) are within the province of the law is unclear. I should note here that lack of knowledge of the real essence man is not the only problem of this sort in the demonstration. We also lack clear and certain knowledge of the real essence of God.

as we shall see, of considerable importance in trying to understand the moral status of children, the insane, and others who seem to lack the rationality that would make the precepts of natural law apply to them.

A second problem is this: Locke's argument for the certainty of moral knowledge turns importantly on his claim that moral ideas (like mathematical ones) are purely conventional, not patterned after any real object in nature. His derivation of the content of natural law, on the other hand, proceeds from objective facts about the nature of God and human nature. What, we may ask, is to bring these two strands of the argument together? That is, while we can discern the connections between our moral ideas in a way sufficient to produce certain demonstrations, why mightn't our ideas (and the moral conclusions we generate) turn out to have nothing at all to do with the objective will of God or with facts about human nature? Locke's answer can only be that while this *could* have happened, it did not. Our moral ideas, although purely conventional, are not silly or arbitrary. They are framed concerning those matters that are central to the peaceful and happy living of our lives. And this, of course, is God's concern for us as well. The two strands of the argument, then, will come together; "it is no wonder" that our moral ideas "everywhere correspond" to the requirements of "the law of God" (E, 4.28.11). As far as I can see, however, it was neither logically nor physically necessary that this be the case.[29]

Of the many remaining problems facing Locke's demonstration, I will focus in this chapter only on those involved in steps (3)–(5) of my sketch of the argument. It is in this part of the demonstration that we can find revealed the distinctive character of Locke's divine will theory of morality, and the method of applying this theory to the specific moral and political problems with which I am chiefly concerned. I begin with a query about step (3) of the demonstration: why are we bound to do God's will?[30]

[29] Colman seems to think that these strands *are* necessarily connected: "The law and our moral notions are . . . bound together" (*Moral Philosophy*, 136). Baier worries about these aspects of Colman's argument in her review of his book (616–17). For suggestions about this problem similar to my own, see Tully, *Discourse*, 18, 23–24, 26; and Grant, *Liberalism*, 27–39. Notice however, that if our moral notions are in fact patterned on divine law, as Locke sometimes suggests (e.g., King, *Life*, 1:370–71), there will be difficulties in portraying these notions as archetypes.

[30] This is a question about which Locke and others clearly *were* concerned, contrary to Finnis' contention that for such theorists the question "has no bite" (*Natural Law*, 405).

1.2. Why We Ought to Obey God

Suppose we could show that God exists and that humankind is His creation. The next step of the demonstration is in a way even harder, for it makes the move from "is" to "ought." What is it about the relation of God to persons that makes it obligatory that we do as God wills? In the *Essays*, Locke mentions three grounds of our obligation to obey God. He begins by saying only that "this obligation seems to derive partly from the divine wisdom of the law-maker, and partly from the right which the Creator has over His creation" (ELN, 183). But God's power to punish offenders (those who break the law of nature) also seems to have a role as a third source of obligation: "*not all* obligation seems to consist in . . . that power which can coerce offenders and punish the wicked" (ELN, 183; my emphasis[31]). These same three sources of God's authority over us (and of our duty to obey) are repeated in the *Essay*.[32] Of God's "right of creation" (ELN, 185), wisdom (and goodness), and power, only the first of the three seems to be emphasized by Locke in the *Treatises*: human beings "are his property, whose workmanship they are, made to last during his, not one another's pleasures" (II, 6).

How seriously should we take these various suggestions? It might be natural to suppose that Locke's special emphasis in the *Treatises* on God's property in humankind (His right of creation) indicates that this was his considered view on the ground of our duty to obey God. On the other hand, Locke's remarks on law and duty in his other works strongly emphasize the power to impose sanctions: "what duty is, cannot be understood without a law; nor a law be known or supposed without a lawmaker, or without reward and punishment" (E, 1.2.12); "moral good and evil, then, is only the conformity or disagreement of our voluntary actions to some law, whereby good or evil is drawn on us, from the will and power of the lawmaker; which good and evil . . . is that we call reward and punishment" (E, 2.28.5). Passages like these may suggest to many that God's law is obligatory for persons only (or

[31] The "not all" construction suggests that at least *some* of the obligation derives from God's power, contradicting Pangle's claim that mentions of divine reward and punishment are absent from all of Locke's works but the *Essay* (*Republicanism*, 204).
[32] God has the right to make law for us because "we are his creatures: he has goodness and wisdom to direct our actions to that which is best: and he has power to enforce it by rewards and punishments of infinite weight and duration in another life" (E, 2.28.8).

largely) because of God's power to impose sanctions on us. Is Locke here embracing a sanction theory of obligation, of the sort associated with the classical legal positivists (e.g., Hobbes, Austin, Bentham)? According to the (most basic) sanction theory, "obligation" is simply defined as "liability to a (significant) threat of sanction for nonperformance." Is this Locke's view?

There are several good reasons to suppose that it is not. In the first place, the (simple) sanction theory of obligation is not even remotely plausible, and Locke seems to see this. As Hart has argued in this century, the sanction theory blurs the distinction between being merely "obliged" (compelled) to perform (as when you are obliged to surrender your wallet to a gunman) and being "obligated" to do so (as we certainly are *not* in the gunman case).[33] Locke similarly compares the situations of a captive "constrained to the service of a pirate" and a subject "giving obedience to a ruler," arguing that "fear of punishment alone" imposes no obligation in the former case (ELN, 185). In the second place, a sanction theory of obligation has political implications that would be unacceptable to Locke (and which would run directly counter to the teachings of the *Second Treatise*). Locke cannot espouse a theory of obligation one of whose consequences is that any powerful maker of civil law can obligate us to obey simply by threatening punishment for disobedience. The consent of the governed, not the power of the governor, must be the ground of our obligation to obey civil law.

There is, of course, other (more direct) textual warrant for rejecting any reading of Locke as a sanction theorist. For instance, the definition of "obligation" Locke accepts concerns only "rendering what is due," with no mention of sanctions (ELN, 181). And while Locke distinguishes three kinds of laws "with their three different enforcements" (divine law with God's sanctions, civil law with legal sanctions, and the law of opinion with social sanctions), only one of these laws, divine law, determines moral obligations (E, 2.28.6–8).[34] The other laws, even though they are backed by very real sanctions,[35] obligate us only insofar as God's

---

[33] *Concept of Law*, 80–81.

[34] In the *Second Tract* (221) Locke had distinguished four kinds of law: divine (moral), political (human), fraternal (the law of charity), and monastic (private) law.

[35] The sanctions of the law of opinion, however informal, are a very serious matter for Locke. "The principal spring from which the actions of men take their rise," Locke wrote in 1678, "seems to be credit and reputation" (King, *Life*, 1:203). This same point is emphasized elsewhere in Locke (e.g., *Education*, 56, where esteem and disgrace are described as "the most powerful incentives to the mind"; and E,

will allows it. Other lawmakers, no matter how powerful, can only "borrow" the authority that is delegated by God (ELN, 187).[36] There is clearly meant to be something special about God's commands and the divine sanctions attached to them. The most plausible explanation of this is that we have an antecedent obligation to obey God's commands, based on something other than His power to compel compliance, which explains why we are bound to obey God, but not other powerful lawmakers. Locke, for instance, maintains (clearly distinguishing the right to command from the power to compel) that a lawmaker "has a superiority and right to ordain, and also a power to reward and punish."[37] A lawmaker is a "superior power to which [one] is *rightly* subject" (ELN, 151; my emphasis; see also ELN, 153–55, 181–83, 189; and Second Tract, 223):

> A man can never be obliged in conscience to submit to any power, unless he can be satisfied who is the person who has a right to exercise that power over him. If this were not so, there would be no distinction between pirates and lawful princes, he that has force is without any more ado to be obeyed, and crowns and scepters would become the inheritance only of violence and rapine. (I, 81; see also II, 134, 176, 184)

God's sanctions are necessary to give divine law a "point" or "purpose" (E, 2.28.6; ELN, 173); but they are not what makes divine law obligatory.[38]

2.28.12, where people are said to worry more about reputation than about the sanctions of God or the magistrate). See Parry, *John Locke*, 45; and Tarcov, *Locke's Education*, 101–2.

[36] It is God "from whose authority all laws do fundamentally derive their obligation, as being either immediately enjoined by him, or framed by some authority derived from him" (First Tract, 124). See also Second Tract, 226.

[37] "Of Ethics in General," section 10.

[38] Those familiar with the work of Hobbes (or of Pufendorf) may recognize there a parallel problem of interpretation. Hobbes, of course, has a long-standing reputation as a sanction theorist of obligation; but this reputation seems in one way undeserved. For while in Hobbes all laws obligate us and are commands backed by sanctions, a law is not just "a command of any man to any man, but only of him whose command is addressed to one *formerly obliged* to obey him" (*Leviathan*, chapter 26, paragraph 2; my emphasis). Thus, our obligation to obey civil law derives not from its threat of sanctions, but from our consent to the authority that makes the law (which grounds our antecedent obligation to obey). Of course, in the end Hobbes' theory may just be extensionally equivalent to a simple sanction theory, for A's power to coerce B (at least in cases of extreme disparity of power) seems in Hobbes to entail B's consent to A's authority over him (which in turn entails B's obligation to obey A). Hobbes writes (claiming that the child's obligation to obey

28

What are our possible alternative explanations of God's author-ity over man? Perhaps it is God's wisdom (and goodness) that makes His will obligatory for us, or His wisdom combined with His great power. But again we can ask whether Locke would be happy with the earthly consequences of such a view. Could he accept the implication that any very wise (and good), or wise and powerful person has natural authority over and can make binding law for the rest of us? On the face of things, this is a kind of claim that Locke's consent theory seems to preclude: nothing is able to put a person "into subjection to any earthly power, but only his own consent" (II, 119). Locke does, of course, mention a "just precedency" that virtue and "excellency of parts and merit" (among other things) may give some persons; but he hastens to add that this is not meant to deny that we are all equal "in respect of jurisdiction or dominion, one over another" (II, 54). And Locke even refers to "God-like" princes or rulers (II, 42, 166), but again without suggesting that their authority is based on anything but the consent of their subjects.[39] Locke could, of course, argue that

his parents is based in "the child's consent" [*Leviathan*, chapter 20, paragraph 4]): "For it ought to obey him by whom it is preserved, because preservation of life being the end for which one man becomes subject to another, *every man is supposed to promise obedience to him in whose power it is to save or destroy him*" (chapter 20, paragraph 5; my emphasis). Perhaps, then, our obligation to obey God is also based in our consent, providing further support for Hobbes' claim that there is "no obligation on any man which arises not from some act of his own" (chapter 21, paragraph 10).

Nothing like this, however, goes on in Locke. Coerced consent for Locke is not consent at all (II, 186). So while in Locke all genuine laws must involve the threat of sanctions, it is not this threat that explains their binding force: "We should not obey a king just out of fear, . . . but for conscience' sake, because a king has com-mand over us by right" (ELN, 189). The command of a superior is the "formal cause" of law's obligation, which is *not* to say that the obligation is constituted by the fear of punishment (see Tuck, *Natural Rights Theories*, 93). It is possible, of course, that Locke believes that not just *any* liability to sanctions constitutes an obligation, but only liability to sanctions of infinite weight and duration. To qualify the sanction theory in this way, however, deprives that theory of its real force, and amounts to little more than the unhelpful claim that liability to sanctions imposed by God constitutes obligation. One might as well just say, without explanation, that we are obligated to obey God. Interestingly, in light of the comparison I am drawing between Locke and Hobbes, Hobbes seems to have thought that the "in-finite" character of God's sanctions did connect them to obligations in some im-mediate fashion: "To those whose power is irresistible, the dominion of all men adheres naturally by their excellence of power; and consequently it is from that power that the kingdom over men, and the right of afflicting men at his pleasure, belongs naturally to God Almighty—not as creator and gracious, but as omnipo-tent" (Hobbes, *Leviathan*, chapter 31, paragraph 5).

[39] Locke is, admittedly, less than clear in II, 166. But I gather that since Locke rejects "that argument, that would prove absolute monarchy the best govern-ment," he cannot be intending to support the claim that "God-like princes indeed

only *perfect* wisdom or virtue gives dominion, so that only God, not any God-like person, has natural authority. But, as in the case of God's infinite power, this would amount more to simple assertion than to argument or explanation (its being unclear why sufficient, rather than perfect, wisdom or power would not be enough).

It seems, then, that we are naturally driven back to our first suggestion: that God's special authority over us (and our antecedent obligation to obey His commands) derives from His property in us, from His right of creation.[40] This is, as we saw, the only claim about God's authority that is clearly emphasized in each of Locke's major treatments of the problem. And there may seem to be good reason for Locke to opt for this line of argument, given his apparent desire to establish the uniqueness of our obligations to God. Mortal lawgivers can be powerful and impose terrible sanctions; they can also be extremely wise and virtuous. But they cannot claim to have created us or to have a creator's property in us. If our obligation to obey God stems from His right of creation, there will be no (possibly objectionable) earthly parallel obligations. Locke's claim for the ground of our obligation to obey God would not, then, conflict in the ways we have seen with his consent theory (which accounts for all obligations to mortal superiors). The only plausible candidates for mortals with the right of creation over other mortals would be parents, who might claim to have created their children. But Locke is clear that God's "fatherhood is such an one as utterly excludes all pretence of title in earthly parents; for he is King because he is indeed maker of us all, which no parents can pretend to be of their children" (I, 53). God's right of creation, then, seems to be perfectly *sui generis*; and this fact would appear to serve well Locke's project in political philosophy.

Things are not, however, so rosy for Locke as they seem. Let us recall the structure of Locke's argument (in II, 6). All persons are bound by natural law to preserve themselves and others, and forbidden "to harm another in his life, health, liberty, or possessions." This is because "men being all the workmanship of one

---

had some title to arbitrary power." It is worth mentioning that when Locke quotes Hooker at length (II, 5), he does *not* include the portion of the passage in which Hooker acknowledges a right to rule for those who are most rational. Sigmund comments on this fact (*Natural Law*, 84).

[40] This is a reasonably common claim in recent literature on Locke. See, for example, Colman, *Moral Philosophy*, chapter 2; Tully, *Discourse*, chapter 2; Gauthier, "Why Ought One Obey God?"; Lenz, "Locke's Essays"; Ashcraft, *Revolutionary Politics*, chapter 2.

omnipotent, and infinitely wise Maker . . . they are his property, whose workmanship they are, made to last during his, not one anothers pleasure." We must not harm ourselves or others. Why? Because we are all God's property, and everyone knows that one mustn't harm or destroy another's property. But how does everyone know this? Presumably, according to Locke, only because it is one of the precepts of natural law that we must not harm others ("in their possessions"). And here we have at least the appearance of a very tight circle. Part of the conclusion of the argument (that portion of natural law that includes the rules of property) seems to also function in it as a premise (to explain why we must do God's will).

There are several ways out of this predicament. Locke could withdraw the rules of property from the list of precepts of natural law in need of justification. He might then treat them as self-justifying rules and use them at the foundation of his theory, to explain why we must obey God. But aside from the implausibility of regarding such rules as self-justifying, however, this strategy would seem to involve setting certain principles of right above (or independent of) God (a problem to which I will return momentarily). A second tactic Locke might employ could wedge open the circle by claiming that the rules of human property justified by Locke's argument are not the same rules as the rules of divine property that explain our general obligation to obey God. When Locke says we must respect God's "property," on this line, he would use the word "property" differently than when he says humans must not harm one another in their "property." This strategy, of course, would also involve acknowledging independent principles of right; but worse, it makes the nature of our obligation to God utterly mysterious. And whichever strategy we employ on Locke's behalf, the argument of II, 6 looks confused.

The problems for Locke (and for many divine will theories of morality) that I have thus far identified can perhaps be summarized as follows. One might wish to explain our obligation to obey God in a convincing fashion by showing it to be a species of some familiar and believable kind of obligation, an obligation we will take to be particularly clear and easy to understand from our everyday lives. Thus, we might say we are obligated to obey God because of His wisdom, goodness, or power, or out of gratitude for the benefits He provides us, or out of respect for His property in us. But all of these kinds of obligation (if, indeed, they *are* all kinds) are themselves requirements of the very natural law whose obligatory character Locke is seeking to explain, as well as being (in many cases) obligations whose instantiations in earthly cases would be unacceptable to Locke. And if Locke responds by making the obligation to obey God utterly *sui generis*, he will puzzle his audience and leave them unconvinced. His answer will seem to amount to a simple assertion of a special and unexplainable obligation to obey God (or to obey "beings" with characteristics only God could possess), and his efforts to justify his position will then seem wasted.

These difficulties, of course, also relate to some other problems faced by divine will theories of morality that are perhaps more familiar (and about which I will accordingly say rather less). We have seen that for Locke moral right and wrong presuppose the existence of a law (divine law), and that law is the command of a rightfully superior will (in this case, the will of God). But in specifying the relation of God's commands to morality, Locke must deal with what is sometimes called "the dilemma of voluntarism."[41] Are acts right (or wrong) simply because they are commanded (or forbidden) by God? Or does God command us to perform these acts because they are right? If the former is the case (the voluntarist position), of course, there can be no morality without God; but, unhappily, what morality there is *with* God seems perfectly arbitrary. God could have made anything at all right or wrong, or changed right and wrong as He pleased (since there is no independent standard of rightness by which to assess His commands or distinguish them from the commands of an imposter). Mere will seems insufficient as the basis of morality. On the other hand, if the latter is the case (the intellectualist position), there is some external standard of morality (like those referred to above) to which God must conform His will and which is both independently obligatory and (in principle) discoverable independent of any knowledge of God's will. While God may *see* the right more clearly than we (so that we do well to take His commands as good advice), and add His threat of sanctions to help enforce the right, His will or command does not *make* the right. In that case, of course, the project of grounding morality in God's will seems (as Kant argues) to have short-circuited itself (although this is not the intellectualists' intention). God becomes superfluous in the dem-

---

[41] For a clear statement of this dilemma (along with a rejection of religious morality), see Nielsen, "Some Remarks." The problem here is, of course, closely related to that of Plato's *Euthyphro*.

onstration of morality, as Grotius (notoriously, if reluctantly) concedes:

> Whatever is clearly at variance with [a well-tempered] judgment is understood to be contrary also to the law of nature, that is, to the nature of man. . . . What we have been saying would have a degree of validity even if we should concede that which cannot be conceded without the utmost wickedness, that there is no God, or that the affairs of men are of no concern to him.[42]

Where Locke stands on these questions is again far from clear. He most frequently speaks like a voluntarist, urging (as we have seen) a necessary connection between morality and (divine) law. The "true ground of morality . . . can only be the will and law of a God, who sees men in the dark, has in his hands rewards and punishments, and power enough to call to account the proudest offender" (E, 1.2.6); "The taking away of God . . . dissolves all" (L, 156). On the other hand, Locke seems disinclined to admit that morality is, as a result, perfectly arbitrary. Indeed, he goes so far as to assert that "God himself cannot choose what is not good"; God's will is "determined by what is best" (E, 2.21.50).[43] And Locke argues (seemingly with Grotius) that since "what is proper now for a rational nature . . . must needs be proper forever . . . , certain duties arise out of necessity and cannot be other than they are" (ELN, 199). If morality is derivable from an immutable (rational) human nature, God would seem to be superfluous to the demonstration of morality.

It is easy to become convinced by such passages that Locke is simply confused and inconsistent on these issues, or at best ambivalent.[44] But while this view may be largely true, I think it would be a mistake to be led in this way away from the predominant strain of voluntarism in Locke's writings.[45] Even when Locke is

---

[42] *De Jure Belli ac Pacis*, prolegomena, sections 9, 11. For discussions of the proper reading of these claims in Grotius, see Tuck, *Natural Rights Theories*, 76–77; Finnis, *Natural Law*, 43–44.

[43] God "cannot err, and will not deceive" (E, 4.18.8). See Dworetz, *Unvarnished Doctrine*, 153–54.

[44] See Von Leyden, "Introduction," 51–56; Aaron, *John Locke*, 265–67; Soles, "Intellectualism," 64, 70, 78.

[45] Among those who favor an intellectualist reading of Locke, Herzog argues that our duty to obey God's commands is explained in Locke by an independent principle of gratitude (*Without Foundations*, 101–7). But, as we have seen, Locke's most explicit pronouncements on the subject deny this. Soles urges an Intellectualist reading of the *Second Treatise*, primarily on the strength of the kinds of arguments

busy claiming that morality is derivable from "rational nature," for instance, he feels obliged to remind us that this is not meant to imply that "God . . . could not have created man differently" (ELN, 199). God might have made morality different by making humankind different; morality is only necessary for us given that God chose to make us as He did. Even if God's choice was uniquely (and constrainingly) wise and best, Locke seems always to emphasize the choice over the determination. This is not meant to assert that Locke was particularly clear in confronting these problems; indeed, his texts seem to reveal a decided lack of clarity. I mean only to claim that where Locke expresses firm convictions, they seem to be voluntarist in character. The one position from which he seems never to (consciously) waver is that the source of all moral obligation is God's will, that an attempted derivation of morality that ignores God's commands (and sanctions) can never arrive at any obligations at all.[46]

But if Locke's position is intended by him to be staunchly voluntarist, he seems still obliged at least to deal with the one problem on which we have focused in this section. Why ought we to obey God? What is the ground of our obligation to do as He wills? As we have seen, Locke's answer seems to be that we must obey God's commands not because of their character as wise or power-backed, but because we have an antecedent obligation to obey, correlative with God's right of creation. But with the "dilemma of voluntarism" in mind, we are entitled to ask whence came this right of creation. What moral code or system includes this right and how is it justified? The right of creation cannot be part of a morality independent of God, but neither can it be a part of God's

we will consider below in 1.3. ("Intellectualism"). But while it is impossible to deny that many of Locke's arguments in the *Treatises* are logically independent of his theological commitments, a purely intellectualist reading of the *Treatises* simply cannot be convincing in the face of passages like I, 86.

[46] This is Colman's view of Locke as well (*Moral Philosophy*, chapter 2), a view shared by (among others) Ashcraft, *Locke's Two Treatises*, 39–40; Shapiro, *Evolution of Rights*, 103–5; Riley, *Will and Political Legitimacy*, 86–87; Abrams, "Introduction," 88–91; Rogers, "Locke," 148, 151–52; Drury, "John Locke," 535–36, 543–44. That the issues here are not especially clear (due largely to the ambiguity of terms like "voluntarist") can be seen in the fact that from virtually the same textual data, Colman finds Locke to be a consistent voluntarist, Singh finds him *not* to be ("John Locke and the Theory of Natural Law," 113), and Tully finds in Locke a compromise between the voluntarist and the intellectualist (rationalist) positions (*Discourse*, 41). While Tully seems right about what Locke's texts actually *say*, I think Locke's most basic commitment was to voluntarism. For other discussions of these issues, see Dunn, *Political Thought*, chapter 14; Mabbott, *John Locke*, chapter 12; Yolton, *Compass*, especially 167–69.

moral law (even God could not make the law that gives Him authority to make law, even if the law were somehow a "metalaw" that applied only to Him). On the face of it, this seems to exhaust the possibilities.

But perhaps Locke would not be distressed by this apparent predicament. The right of creation seems for Locke to simply be the end of the explanatory chain, the one moral fact for which no further justification can be given. It is simply and finally true that "all things are justly subject to that by which they have first been made and also are constantly preserved" (ELN, 185); we are subject to God "in perfect justice and by utmost necessity" (ELN, 187).[47] We must just *see* the obvious truth of these claims; they are meant to be self-justifying or in need of no justification at all. That we will see this seems to be taken for granted by Locke in roughly the same way that he takes for granted a general acknowledgment of God's existence. Modern readers, of course, are bound to be less than satisfied here, and Gauthier takes this to simply be the measure of the vast gulf between our perspective and Locke's:

> From our standpoint the derivation of man's obligation to obey God from God's creation of man requires argument. Creation and obligation are not intrinsically or necessarily connected. But this is the fundamental measure of the difference between Locke's conceptual framework and our own. His framework is theocentric; everything depends on God. . . . No argument from creation to obligation is needed from Locke's perspective.[48]

But the troubling aspects of Locke's position are perhaps even more severe than Gauthier's remarks suggest. The problem is not only that the modern reader sees no necessary connection between creation and obligation. Even if we *did* see this connection as Locke sees it, we would want to apply this connection in earthly cases. The parents who "create" a child, or a scientist who "creates" one in a test tube (or on a laboratory table, for that matter)

[47] In the manuscript "Ethica B" (MS c28, fol. 141), Locke suggests "dependency" as the source of all law and obligation.
[48] Gauthier, "Why Ought One Obey God?" 431–32. Colman seems completely untroubled by these problems, seeing God's right of creation as the perfect tool to answer the intellectualist objections: "the right of creation . . . is both independent of law and intrinsic to God" (*Moral Philosophy*, 46). What is not clear from Colman's argument, however, is why it would not be just as appropriate to claim that the right of creation shows that "Locke held a standard of right independent of God's will" (Lenz, "Locke's Essays," 110).

will seem to someone convinced of the connection between creation and obligation to have authority over "their creatures" (we can even imagine, if we wish, fiendish, science-fiction arrangements by which the creations are "constantly preserved" by their creators, to extend the parallel with God's right of creation). But this apparent consequence of the position will never do for Locke. Only God *really* creates living beings; it is only by God that things have *"first* been made"; so only God can have the right of creation over living beings. And now Locke comes dangerously close to simply asserting God's authority without any further substantial comment. It is not "creation" or "dependency" in our familiar, ordinary senses that explains God's authority. It is only God's kind of creation that will do. His right over us is thus utterly *sui generis,* grounded in traits or capabilities that only God could possibly possess.[49] We must obey God because He is God.

1.3. The Secular Strain

God's law for man (the law of nature) is the law of reason (II, 6).[50] Just how are we to take this prominent claim in Locke?[51] In its strongest form the claim would be that the acts required by the law are somehow inherently rational (such that their nonperformance would amount, say, to a kind of "practical contradiction").

[49] Whether or not Locke *intends* to claim that the right of creation is just "self-evident" in (e.g.) E, 4.3.18 (as Tully claims in *Discourse,* 40–42) is unclear. What Tully seems not to see is the problems in regarding this right as anything but *sui generis.* God makes humankind; but He also makes the lower animals and the inanimate world, over which persons can have (virtually) absolute authority. We no more make a chair (from God's tree) than we make the child, in the sense of "making" as God does. Of course, we can design a chair (but can we now, or soon, design the child too?); and God gave the earth and animals to us (in a more obvious sense than He gave us children?) I return to these problems in 4.2.

[50] Reason is the voice of God in us, and to be moral (to do God's will) is thus to be rational (Yolton, *Locke,* 35). God gave us "reason and with it a law, that cannot be otherwise than what reason should dictate, unless we should think that a reasonable creature should have an unreasonable law" (R, 193 [252]).

[51] It is *not,* I think, to be taken as a simple restatement of the claim that morality is *demonstrable.* The content of the law is, of course, discoverable by reason, because the law is rational for mankind. But to prove the law's rationality is not to demonstrate that it is obligatory. And even if God did *not* will what was most rational from our viewpoint, we might still be able to demonstrate the content of morality (e.g., by inference from the evidence of our senses to the nature of God's will for us). Von Leyden—unfairly I think—accuses Locke of a quite basic confusion on this point ("John Locke and Natural Law," 27–29). Locke also cannot mean (as he sometimes seems to) that the law is *identical* to reason ("it is only the object of reason, not reason itself" [ELN, 149]), nor is the law even properly a "dictate of reason" (ELN, 111). See Hancey, "John Locke and the Law of Nature," 442.

Thus, a Kantian could say that the moral law is "the law of reason." In a weaker form, the claim might be that the acts required by the law are those that best advance the agent's interests (so that nonperformance would be "irrational" in the weaker, prudential sense of the word). Hobbes, for instance, describes a law of nature as "a precept or general rule, found out by reason, by which a man is forbidden to do that which is destructive of his life or takes away the means of preserving the same and to omit that by which he thinks it may be best preserved."[52] On either the Kantian or the Hobbesian (egoistic) interpretation of the claim, it is natural to go on to say that moral wrongness consists precisely in the irrationality of noncompliance with the law. That is, it is true not only that wrongdoing *is* irrational, but that conduct is wrong solely *because* it is irrational. And on either the Kantian or the Hobbesian interpretation, natural law would then not only be independent of God's will, but be derivable without reference to God at all.

Such consequences are clearly anathema to Locke's voluntarism. The natural law cannot be the law of reason in the sense of binding us *because* it commands what is rational; it binds us because it is commanded by God.[53] No derivation of morality could, without consideration of God's will, move beyond what is merely rational to what is obligatory.[54] But God's commands might still be commands to do what is in fact either inherently rational or prudent, and thus the law of nature might still be the law of reason in one of these weaker senses (where the rationality of the law does not ground its obligatoriness). Morality as prudence may seem to be what Locke has in mind in the *First Treatise*, when he argues that the "strong desire of preserving his life and being having been planted in [man] as a principle of action by God himself, reason . . . could not but teach him and assure him, that pursuing that natural inclination he had to preserve his being, he followed the will of his Maker" (I, 86). Perhaps *this* is the sense in which "there necessarily result from his inborn constitution some definite duties for him" (ELN, 199).[55]

[52] *Leviathan*, chapter 14, paragraph 3.

[53] Locke's thoughts here, of course, depend in part on his belief that the threat of God's sanctions is necessary to motivate us to do what is right. While either reason or revelation can inform us about what is morally good or right, the mere rational recognition of rightness cannot be counted on to create the force of obligation. See Yolton, *Compass*, 146–47; and *Locke*, 34–35, 51.

[54] See Von Leyden on the parallel positions of Grotius and Suarez ("John Locke and Natural Law," 32).

[55] It is undoubtedly passages like this that motivate the view that natural law in

But Locke elsewhere (most prominently in essay 8 of the *Essays on the Law of Nature*) rejects such suggestions. Morality cannot consist solely in doing what is in our own best interest, for "a great number of virtues, and the best of them, consist only in this: that we do good to others at our own loss" (ELN, 207).[56] And of the dictates from our "inborn constitution," Locke writes: "principles of actions indeed there are lodged in men's appetites; but these are so far from being innate moral principles, that if they were left to their full swing they would carry men to the overturning of all morality" (E, 1.2.13).[57] It seems that morality is not chiefly concerned with rational self-interest, but rather with the interests of all persons, taken together. As we shall see, the fundamental law of nature is that *mankind* is to be preserved. The law prescribes not what is to the advantage of each individual separately, but what is "universally useful" (R, 174 [242]).[58] God has "by an inseparable connexion, joined virtue and *public* happiness together, and made the practice thereof necessary to the preservation of society" (E, 1.2.6; my emphasis). It may on some occasions be irrational (in the prudential sense) for individuals to obey the law of nature, assuming (as I am here) that it is possible to rationally advance one's interests by doing what is wrong.[59] God's sanctions, of course, complicate this argument, since throwing their infinite weight into the calculus (a la Pascal) guarantees that moral conduct will always be in our best interests (with the afterlife included) (E, 2.21.72).[60] I take it, however, that this is not what is supposed to make natural law the law of reason, since on that argument the law of nature could have any content whatsoever and still be the law of reason.

In what sense, then, *is* natural law the law of reason? I think

---

Locke is essentially concerned with *self*-preservation—a view defended by Strauss and others (e.g., Cox, *Locke on War and Peace*, 84–89, 138; Goldwin, "John Locke," 484–85; Medina, *Social Contract Theories*, 33).

[56] "An Hobbist, with his principle of self-preservation . . . , will not easily admit a great many plain duties of morality" (King, *Life*, 1:191).

[57] *Education*, 33, 45, 52, and 200 strongly suggests that virtue and morality consist in reason's denying, tuning, controlling, and crossing our selfish desires, *not* in finding the means to their satisfaction. See Tarcov, *Locke's Education*, 85–93, 189–90; Yolton, *Locke*, 22–23; and Yolton and Yolton, "Introduction," 21.

[58] On Locke's opposition to ethical egoism, see Tully, *Discourse*, 103–4; and ELN, 181, 211.

[59] Locke frequently uses "rational" in the prudential sense we are discussing. See Colman, *Moral Philosophy*, 223.

[60] "Virtue and prosperity do not often accompany one another" if only this life is considered; but virtue is "by much the best bargain" if we "put into the scales on her side an exceeding and immortal weight of glory" (R, 82 [245]; 184 [245]). See Dunn, *Political Thought*, 195–96, 230.

what Locke has in mind is simply this: natural law commands
what is in the best interests of mankind as a whole, and is in this
sense rational for *Man* (although not for each person on every occasion). It will, of course, benefit each person for *others* to obey the
law (E, 1.2.6), for each profits from a secure and peaceful environment; and compliance with the law is often necessary as a means
of securing similar compliance from others. But it will also be possible (and rational, in the prudential sense) to reap personal advantage from clever "free-riding." Morality forbids such behavior,
so morality is not always rational for each person. Locke distinguishes less clearly than Hobbes between what is rational for each
person and what it would be best for all people to do together. But
I think we make the best sense of his texts if we ascribe to him the
view that the moral law is only the law of reason for Mankind, not
for persons taken separately.[61] Presumably, this is one reason why
Locke argues that atheists are not to be tolerated in society: "the
taking away of God, though but even in thought, dissolves all" (L,
156). The atheist cannot be counted on to fear God's sanctions. But
even worse, without knowledge of God and God's will, the atheist
"can never be certain that anything is his duty" (E, 1.2.13), and so
will be unmoved even by the ideas of right and wrong. All that
will command the atheist's attention will be personal interests
(and fear of the sanctions of civil law and public opinion). This is
not enough for Locke, since private advantage so often leads away
from the achievement of "public happiness."[62]

The law of nature, then, is "rational" (in the sense of commanding what is best) only for mankind as a whole, and demonstrable
by reason only given a knowledge of God's will for man. Occasionally, however, we see a hint of a different position at work in
Locke's arguments, a position more amenable to intellectualism
and to the secular moral theories of the Enlightenment than to the
dominant strain of voluntarism in Locke.[63] In Kantian terms, of
course, Locke's law of nature (as I have thus far presented it) commands only hypothetically. While its form is categorical, the law
gives us reason to act only insofar as we share the ends the law is
designed to advance.[64] If we care about the well-being of human-

---

[61] See Pangle, *Republicanism*, 190–91, 211.
[62] In *A Letter Concerning Toleration* only atheists, and not, for example, polytheists, are considered "intolerable." In the *Essays on the Law of Nature*, however, atheists and polytheists are taken to be equally bad (ELN, 175).
[63] See Soles, "Intellectualism," 70–81.
[64] On the difference between categorical form (which is shared by, e.g., rules of

kind as a whole (which many of us will), or about our personal well-being, threatened by God's sanctions (which all of us will), the natural law's imperatives will apply to us. Its imperatives may be "assertorical" (to use Kant's term[65]), but they are nonetheless hypothetical only, concerning the advancement of contingent ends. The true moral law, according to Kant, commands categorically, independent of the subjective ends of persons. Moral action is inherently rational, giving all rational agents reason to conform their conduct to the demands of the moral law.

And it may sometimes seem as if Locke agrees with Kant. Indeed, in the only substantial passage concerning the justification of natural law that he presents in the *Second Treatise*, Locke quotes approvingly and at length from Hooker, deriving our obligations from human equality:

The like natural inducement, hath brought men to know that it is no less their duty, to love others than themselves, for seeing those things which are equal, must needs all have one measure; If I cannot but wish to receive good, even as much at every man's hands, as any man can wish unto his own soul, how should I look to have any part of my desire herein satisfied, unless my self be careful to satisfy the like desire, which is undoubtedly in other men, being of one and the same nature? To have any thing offered them repugnant to this desire, must needs in all respects grieve them as much as me, so that if I do harm, I must look to suffer, there being no reason that others should show greater measure of love to me, than they have by me, showed unto them; My desire therefore to be loved of my equals in nature, as much as possible may be, imposeth upon me a natural duty of bearing to themward, fully the like affection; From which relation of equality between our selves and them, that are as our selves, what several rules and canons, natural reason both drawn for direction of life, no man is ignorant. Eccl. Pol. Lib. 1. (II, 5)

---

etiquette or club rules) and deeper notions of categoricality, see Foot, "Morality as a System"; and Goodpaster, "Morality as a System."

[65] An assertorical hypothetical imperative is one that says "the action is good to some [actual] purpose" (Kant, *Foundations of the Metaphysics of Morals*, 414). All "dependent beings" (including humans) have happiness as a purpose, but it is not a necessary end for a rational being as such. In the rather rough-and-ready characterization of Kant used in this paragraph, and far more so in those below, I express views that are not precisely Kant's own, but are only Kantian in some extended (but I hope still recognizable) sense.

Note that here the duties of natural law are derived, *without* reference to God's will or His commands,[66] from the fact that "those things which are equal, must needs all have one measure." And the argument strongly suggests that it is the irrationality (or inconsistency) of treating others as if they were different from ourselves that establishes its immorality. There is a kind of "practical contradiction" involved in harmful conduct toward others.[67] The state of nature has a law to govern it; "and reason, which is that law, teaches all mankind . . . that *being all equal and independent*, no one ought to harm another" (II, 6; my emphasis).

Let me briefly sketch a parallel argument that is perhaps sufficiently Kantian in character to highlight the similarity between a Kantian position and the Hooker–Locke argument quoted above.[68] We can begin with Kant's second (or third) formulation of the categorical imperative: "Act so that you treat humanity . . . always as an end and never as a means only" (or "not merely as a means to be arbitrarily used by this or that will").[69] One way of understanding Kant's words is this: we stand under both negative and positive duties with respect to others, duties that derive from the same roots. Negatively, our (fundamental) duty toward others is not to use them, not to treat them merely as means to our own ends. As Locke says, we are not "made for one another's uses" (II, 6). We must treat other persons as what they manifestly are[70]—beings like ourselves, "persons" in Kant's sense, beings of independent worth (on Locke's similar concept of "person," see 2.2. below); we

[66] See Soles, "Intellectualism," 73.

[67] The Hooker argument could, I suppose, be pushed to read as a causal argument to a good egoistic rule of thumb: don't treat others badly because, being just like you, they will treat you badly in return. This reading seems to me neither true to Hooker's intentions nor accurate as a way of capturing the spirit in which Locke borrowed from Hooker (see Soles, "Intellectualism," 72). While this is not the place for an extended discussion of Hooker, two points can be quickly made to show how implausible an egoistic reading of this passage is. First, in the section from which Locke quotes (*Of the Laws of Ecclesiastical Polity*, 1.8.7), Hooker is clearly attempting to state the underlying justification for the "Golden Rule" of morality. It would be most odd to suppose that this justification was believed by Hooker (or Locke) to be egoistic. Second, far from assuming that the egoistic advantage of obedience to the laws of nature has been demonstrated in this passage, Hooker goes on to discuss the benefits of keeping the law in a separate chapter (1.9) (and he emphasizes not egoistic considerations, but the good that is done for "the whole world").

[68] See the similar argument discussed in Fressola, "Liberty and Property," 316.

[69] *Foundations of the Metaphysics of Morals*, 429, 428.

[70] "Man necessarily thinks of his own existence this way; . . . Also every other rational being thinks of his existence by means of the same rational ground which holds also for myself" (*Foundations of the Metaphysics of Morals*, 429).

must not treat them as objects or tools to be used for our purposes, as we use the inanimate world (the world of "things"). Positively, we must take the lives and life plans of others to provide us with reasons for acting on their behalf. We must recognize their ends as having the same kind of value our own ends have, and work honestly to advance both.

When the soap-opera heroine condemns her ex-lover by saying, "All along he was only using me," she criticizes him for his failure to value her feelings and projects. He treated her as a mere means to his ends, as a tool or an object. In doing so, however, he did more than break her heart; he acted "inconsistently." For, on the one hand, he recognized that she was a person like himself, with a perspective on the world like his own, and with desires and plans as intimately connected with her happiness as his own plans are connected to his own happiness. On the other hand, however, he treated her not like a person but like a thing. In short, he treated her as other than he acknowledged her to be, as other than she manifestly was. And a perfectly familiar form of irrationality in action (although a weaker sense than Kant had in mind) is that of treating something as other than it clearly is. To treat others as things is to act in a way that belies one's own beliefs, to pretend a significance and a priority one cannot in good conscience affirm. It is also to fail to show the respect that is an appropriate response to beings who are not things (an idea to which I will return in 2.2 and 2.4). The *equality* of persons in nature makes special treatment of some persons irrational. The *personhood* of persons makes using them (in Kant's sense) irrational. Each of us has a duty to do what commands rational nature as such (what commands categorically). Just as we must for Locke respect God's property, whether in ourselves or others, the Kantian strain in Locke requires us to respect humanity (personhood), whether in ourselves or others.

In offering this reconstruction of the Hooker–Locke argument, I mean neither to defend the line of argument as unproblematic[71] nor to suggest that it was especially central in Locke's thought. I intend only to point to a certain affinity between one strand of Locke's argument and one kind of Kantian position (a position divorced from Kant's metaphysics and much else that was important to his ethical theory).[72] The most obvious affinities between the

[71] On the vagueness of commonsense notions of "using people" and the difficulties in employing them in systematic moral philosophy, see Davis, "Using Persons."

[72] Kant was, of course, another participant in the voluntarist, legalist tradition in

Lockean and Kantian theories, however, are not here at the foundations of the theories, where the Kantian must argue for a ground of obligation that Locke would never have acknowledged as the sole ground. More obvious are similarities in the contents of the moral theories flowing from these foundations. For theories that begin with something like the second formulation of Kant's categorical imperative seem to naturally yield a body of rights and duties that is recognizably Lockean.[73]

---

moral theory, albeit only in a secularized form. And he defended a form of natural law and natural rights (see, e.g., Sigmund, *Natural Law*, 162–63). The autonomous, legislative will takes God's place in Kant's theory; but for Locke too the value of rational self-government is a central concern (see Rapaczynski, *Nature and Politics*, 161; Parry, *John Locke*, 13–14; Wood, *Capitalism*, 140). And just as the rightfulness of other commands (e.g., those of our earthly sovereigns) is determined in Locke by their conformity to God's will, so in Kant their rightfulness is measured by their conformity to the rational will (i.e., according to what rational agents would will for themselves). Nor is the (prominently placed) Hooker argument the only point in Locke's writings where his claims resonate with a Kantian tone. We shall see in subsequent chapters other examples of this "leaning" or "strain" in Locke's thought. For instance, in Locke's views on punishment (3.5) and property (5.4), we will see a focus on natural fairness, which is often noted as a condition for showing equal respect for persons in contemporary Kantian moral theory.

One text that I will not consider in any detail later, however, should at least be mentioned here. The central argument of Locke's short manuscript on "Morality" begins, like the Hooker argument, with the recognition that natural equals must be "equally under one and the same rule"; it then uses a Kantian-style universalization argument to establish the obligation to keep one's word ("Morality" [MS c28, fol. 140]). Here I disagree with Dunn's claim that the argument of "Morality" is "purely utilitarian" (*Political Thought*, 50n). It is rather, I think, evidence of Locke's mixture of rule-consequentialist and deontological reasoning that I stress in the next section of this chapter. Other Kantian aspects of Locke's claims have been noted from time to time in the secondary literature on Locke, most often in the writings of Raymond Polin (see his *La Politique Morale de John Locke* and papers cited below). Grant (*Liberalism*, 192–94) and Riley (*Will and Political Legitimacy*, 81) have noted the similarities between Locke and Kant in their accounts of freedom as subjection to reason and law; to be free for Locke is to be governed neither by another's will nor by one's own unchecked desires (see 6.2 below). Richards has rightly pointed out the Kantian aspects of Locke's views on autonomy and toleration (*Toleration*, 80). And many have noted the possible place of synthetic a priori judgments in Locke's moral theory.

[73] The same is true, of course, of the rule-consequentialist theory I discuss in 1.4, explaining the ease with which Locke moves from one style of reasoning to another. A familiar example of a Lockean project with Kantian foundations can be found in Robert Nozick's writings on moral and political theory. Nozick's avowedly Lockean enterprise in *Anarchy, State, and Utopia*, insofar as it has explicit moral foundations at all, has straightforwardly Kantian ones. The "inviolability of the person" necessary for Nozick's view of rights as "side constraints" is derived directly from the second formulation of the categorical imperative (*Anarchy*, 32–33). Now Nozick's reading of Locke in that work, of course, is (wishfully) libertarian, and it is not even remotely clear how a libertarian moral theory can be drawn without violence from Kantian foundations. Nor does Nozick even really attempt to show how this might be done, a fact made more disquieting by his Rawlsian rivals'

To say that such theories are fully consistent with the "spirit" of Locke's moral theory would, of course, be misleading. God is too much at the center of Locke's work for such secular, Kantian arguments to capture its essence. But we can fairly say, I think, that such projects touch a *part* of what is going on in Locke (explaining their popularity as a way of "carrying on" the Lockean tradition). Locke is moved (as I will argue in chapter 2) both by a conception of humankind as God's property and part of God's plan and by a conception of the dignity of persons in their equality and independence as moral agents. We are made by God, curious and wonderful pieces of workmanship (I, 86) invested with "dignity and authority" (I, 44). Our dignity calls for and makes obligatory certain kinds of treatment, just as does our status as property of God. Certain conduct is "suitable to the dignity and excellence of a rational creature" (*Education*, 31).[74]

---

also claiming Kantian foundations for their quite different social-welfarist views. A properly Lockean moral theory, I suggest, will support a political philosophy that falls somewhere between libertarian minimalism and Rawlsian egalitarian liberalism (see 6.2 and 6.3 below).

But in his more recent work, *Philosophical Explanations*, Nozick seems (without comment) to abandon his spartan libertarian moral theory for a position more compatible with genuinely Lockean views (Nozick's least libertarian moments occur at 468–69, 498–503) and to present a much clearer account of the Kantian foundations for a more moderate liberalism, in terms of what he calls "moral responsiveness":

Ethical behavior somehow recognizes or acknowledges the [basic moral] characteristic, it treats the bearer of the characteristic as having that characteristic. On the supposition that the basic moral characteristic is being a value-seeking I, the fundamental ethical principle is: Treat someone (who is a value-seeking I) as a value-seeking I. This has kinship with Kant's principle: treat everyone as an end-in-himself and not merely as a means. (*Philosophical Explanations*, 462)

The similarities between Nozick's strategy and that of our reconstruction of the Hooker–Locke argument are, I hope, obvious. (I will return to them in 2.2.) My point here is only that in the "recentering" of Nozick's moral theory, we can see the natural tendency for this kind of Kantian foundation to yield a body of moral rights and duties similar to those defended by Locke.

A central charge in Shapiro's *Evolution of Rights* is that there is a kind of "incoherence" in trying "to combine a substantive appeal to the arguments of the early English contract theorists with a methodological appeal to Kant's ethics." Modern writers leave "crucial premises" behind (ibid., 5–6; see also Shapiro's "Resources," 55–56). I can see nothing in his work that justifies so general a claim. Since Shapiro acknowledges that Locke himself employed both rationalist arguments (which facilitate dropping God from the picture [146]) and religious ones, it is hard to see how the modern project can involve any *new* incoherence not already present in Locke (or in Kant, who did *himself* embrace many of the same claims made by "English contract theorists").

[74] Our rational agency is as much a part of the "inborn constitution" on which duties are based as is our desire for self-preservation. See Murphy's discussion of the parallel strategies in Locke and Kant for marking out "the special kind of treat-

I do not think Locke saw these secular and religious conceptions of humankind and morality as inconsistent. As a result we find in Locke a variety of styles of argument for moral conclusions, sitting side by side and without any explanation of their differences. Some arguments appeal directly to God's will; others appeal to it indirectly by rule-consequentialist reasoning (of the sort I outline in 1.4); still others appeal to it not at all.[75] Of this third (secular) class, some of the arguments are purely conceptual,[76] while others appeal for their moral force to a particular view of the person as free and equal, rational and valuing. The force of these last arguments is best captured in Kantian terms. Locke seems not to want to explicitly explore their potential for a nontheological ethics, emphasizing throughout his work that only God's will can make actions obligatory. But it is precisely this potential that makes intelligible claims to be pursuing a secular, but nonetheless Lockean project in moral and political philosophy.[77] To a certain extent, what Locke is doing is detaching some of his derivations of the specific content of morality from his view of what makes that content obligatory.[78] But seen in another way, Locke is simply working from more than one foundational stance at a time. The result of this is that in his political philosophy we find Locke employing

ment (called 'respect' by Kant) which is particularly fitting or appropriate to *autonomous, rational persons*" ("Rights and Borderline Cases," 230–31).

[75] Herzog claims (against Dunn) that Locke's political philosophy has "conceptual working room for a fairly secular approach" (*Without Foundations*, 106n). Others who have noted the secular strain in Locke's thought (in addition to those mentioned above) include Parry (*John Locke*, 13–14), Rapaczynski (*Nature and Politics*, 117), and many of the more "traditional" writers on Locke, such as Sabine (*History of Political Theory*, 518).

[76] Tully discusses the argument for "conceptual connections" between certain acts (and the relationships they establish) and the obligations and rights that arise from them (*Discourse*, 34). If *moral* properties are really related to human acts (e.g., begetting a child) as the properties of a triangle are related to its real essence, then these conceptual connections can be employed in secular moral argument.

[77] I have in mind here the kind of "Lockean, secular morality" that Gauthier (rightly) claims "modern moral philosophers have wanted," but (mistakenly, I think) claims "is not to be found" ("Why Ought One Obey God?" 428; a position similar to Gauthier's is defended in Replogle, *Recovering the Social Contract*, 180–81). Dunn, who emphasizes the theological side of Locke's argument, does mention the "purely secular" strain of Locke's thinking about morality. But he identifies this with a concern for "terrestrial utility," similar in some ways to Hobbes (*Political Thought*, 257–58). I argue below that the "utilitarian" aspects of Locke's thought are really the final stage of his reasoning in theological terms. The *genuinely* secular aspects of Locke's thought are not utilitarian, but Kantian.

[78] As Colman allows: "Locke is not a voluntarist with respect to the content of the moral law. His voluntarism is strictly a theory of moral obligation" (*Moral Philosophy*, 32).

arguments that are designed to appeal both to those who see the secular ends of the state as good in themselves and to those who see them only as means to religious ends. Not only, then, do secular, Kantian enterprises in political philosophy have the machinery to produce the content of Locke's theory. They capture some of its spirit as well.

1.4. The Superstructure of Locke's Theory

Recall the final steps of Locke's demonstration of morality:

(4) The nature of God and human nature together reveal the "principle" of God's will for mankind.

(5) From the principle of God's will and the empirical conditions of human life (revealed by our senses), our specific moral duties follow.

We have already seen part of the point of Locke's claim in step (4). A study of human nature alone may reveal for persons the "fixed law of their operations and a manner of existence appropriate to their nature" (ELN, 117), but it cannot reveal a moral obligation to act in ways "appropriate to their nature" (as, e.g., some modern Aristotelians suppose). It is only from human nature and the nature of God together that we can derive our moral obligations, for it is God's will that makes acts obligatory (or so the dominant strain in Locke's thought suggests). Human nature, in other words, can reveal the substance of God's will for us, but *that* He wills anything for us is derivable only from God's nature. Specifically, "it does not seem to fit in with the wisdom of the Creator to form an animal that is most perfect and ever active, and to endow it abundantly above all others with mind, intellect, reason, and all the requisites for working, and yet not assign to it any work" (ELN, 117).

Knowing God's wisdom we are free to assume that human nature reveals God's will for man (and thus, our obligations). We know, for instance, that He would not have endowed us with reason if He did not wish us to follow the "law of reason." But in what does following reason consist? As we have seen, it is initially tempting to suppose that Locke means rationally advancing the end of the "first practical principle"—self-preservation (as Locke seems to suggest in I, 86, and again in II, 149, where he calls self-preservation the "fundamental, sacred, and unalterable law").[79] The principle of God's will would then be that we are to (rationally) preserve ourselves. But (as we have also seen), Locke in fact argues *against* the view that "the basis of natural law is each man's own interest." It is true that *general* "observance of this law gives rise to peace, harmonious relations, friendship, freedom from punishment, security, possession of our property, and—to sum it all up in one word—happiness."[80] But it is true as well that morality requires one "to stand by one's promise, though it were to one's own hindrance" and requires "the restitution of a trust that diminishes our possessions" (ELN, 215).[81] In short, Locke is no ethical egoist.

[79] "But if any law of nature would seem to be established among all as sacred in the highest degree, which the whole of mankind, it seems, is urged to observe by a certain natural instinct and by its own interest, surely this is self-preservation, and therefore some lay this down as the chief and fundamental law of nature" (ELN, 173). It seems clear, however, that Locke is not *himself* claiming self-preservation as the fundamental law in this passage. And in II, 149, the self-preservation that is said to be "fundamental" is the preservation of the *society*, not of each individual. Only I, 86 really suggests the egoistic reading of Locke.

[80] The relation between Locke's hedonistic theory of good and evil (E, 2.20.2; 2.21.42–44; 2.28.5) and his nonhedonistic moral theory is complex (and not always consistently presented by Locke). Briefly, while "things . . . are good and evil, only in reference to pleasure or pain" (E, 2.20.2), it is open to us to determine what will give us pleasure or pain (to "tune" our desires). Moral conduct brings personal happiness only if this determination is the correct one ("morality, established upon its true foundations, cannot but determine the choice in anyone that will but consider" [E, 2.21.72]). See Yolton, *Compass*, 144–46; and Rapaczynski, *Nature and Politics*, 144–59.

[81] Locke concludes this argument by stating (correctly): "And thus the rightness of an action does not depend on its utility; on the contrary, its utility is a result of its rightness" (and more clearly: "Utility is not the basis of the law or the ground of obligation, but the consequence of obedience to it" [ELN, 215]). (By "utility" here Locke clearly means *personal* utility.) The argument of essay 8 of the *Essays on the Law of Nature* (from which these passages are drawn) is still, however, troubling for several reasons. Locke never adequately distinguishes between the *natural* consequences of obedience to natural law (how one would fare simply in a natural society of equals) and the *artificial* consequences (which include the imposition or withholding of sanctions by God and civil authorities). It is, as a result, never clear which kinds of consequences are being considered in the claim that obedience to natural law results in (personal) utility. Since Locke acknowledges that the law sometimes requires us to act contrary to our present interest, he must mean one of the following: obedience to natural law (a) results in longer term natural advantages, (b) avoids legal punishment, or (c) avoids God's punishment (or some combination of the three). But (a) is true only when others are also obeying the law, and not always even then (as Hobbes saw more clearly, I think, than Locke). And (b) is true only when the law of the land rewards virtue and punishes vice (which it does not always do). This leaves (c). The problem is that Locke does not refer centrally to God's sanctions in the argument, but seems to have in mind a (bad) argument using only (a) and (b). Elsewhere, Locke acknowledges that only God's sanctions can establish a convergence of private and public utility (i.e., make self-

The principle of God's will is not that persons are to preserve themselves, but that mankind as a whole is to be preserved. We cannot simply read off the content of God's will from facts of human psychology or physiology of the sort (and in the fashion) Locke confusedly suggests in I, 86.[82] Accordingly, Locke writes in the *Essay* that morality necessarily promotes *"public* happiness" and "the preservation of society" (E, 1.2.6; my emphasis); and in the *Second Treatise*, he repeatedly claims that "the fundamental law of nature" is "the preservation of mankind" (e.g., II, 7, 16, 134, 135, 149, 159, 171, 183).[83] It is this fundamental law that I have referred to as "the principle of God's will"; for Locke seems clearly to intend that all the specific rules of natural law are somehow derivable from this quite general statement of what God wills for man.[84] Locke also refers to this fundamental law as "the basis of natural law":

> By the basis of natural law we mean some sort of groundwork on which all other and less evident precepts of that law are built and from which in some way they can be derived, and thus they acquire from it all their binding force in that they are in accordance with that, as it were, primary and fundamental law which is the standard and measure of all the other laws depending on it. (ELN, 205)

interest and morality consistent): "If there be no prospect beyond the grave, the inference is certainly right—'Let us eat and drink,' let us enjoy what we delight in, 'for tomorrow we shall die' " (E, 2.21.56; see also E, 2.21.72). See Herzog, *Without Foundations*, 90–91.

[82] I, 86 has led Macpherson to suppose that Locke's method is simply to "deduce" rights and duties from our "strong desires" ("Natural Rights," 229). That this is not his method can be seen in the simple fact that, according to Locke, God gave us a desire to preserve ourselves (and our offspring), but not a desire to preserve all mankind (which morality nonetheless requires). It is not "strong desires" but reason that provides the best evidence of God's intentions. Reason enables us to see what is best for mankind as a whole and to see that achieving this end requires cooperation of various sorts, not just rational pursuit of self-interest. God wills that we use our reason in this wider manner. See Tully, *Discourse*, 46–47.

[83] Similarly, Locke writes in *Education*, 116 that "the preservation of all mankind" is "the true principle to regulate our religion, politics and morality by."

[84] Colman argues that the preservation of mankind could not really be the fundamental law of nature (despite Locke's repeated claims to this effect) because the virtue of "liberality" could not be derived from it (*Moral Philosophy*, 199). This seems a weak argument in at least two respects. First, Locke's insistence that liberality is a virtue is considerably less frequent than his insistence that preservation is the fundamental law. But second, as we will see below (and in 6.3), given the rule-consequentialist method of deriving specific precepts of natural law from the fundamental law, there is no obvious reason why Locke could not derive a duty of liberality (and similar "soft" duties) from the rule of preserving mankind (even leaving aside further Kantian derivations).

We have seen a number of reasons why Locke claims that the preservation of mankind is the fundamental law (or basic "principle" of God's will). We can infer that God wills our preservation both from His having bothered in the first place to create such intricate and interestingly endowed creatures as ourselves and from the supportive environment He created for us to live in (I, 86). Preservation (peace, happiness) is the rational end for mankind, and God can be assumed to wish us to employ our reason. And finally, God has property in each of us, and no one must interfere with the preservation of another's property.

The last of these reasons (God's property in us) seems problematic in more than one way in its role as the source of all natural law (and it is, as we have seen, both problematic in other respects and, unfortunately, frequently emphasized by Locke). First, it is unclear how the property argument can yield anything more than negative moral injunctions (explaining, perhaps, why Locke is so often read as a libertarian). For while we know that we must not harm or destroy another's property, there is no familiar rule of the institution of property that says we must *preserve* the property of others in positive ways. (Am I morally bound to patch your roof when it starts to leak?) Yet Locke clearly wishes to argue for positive duties as well as negative ones (as I will argue in chapter 6); and if all duties must be derivable from the fundamental law, a property-style defense of that law seems inadequate (we must not destroy God's holdings, but must we help him maintain them—as a duty of property?) Second, on this line of argument, God's property in us must really be understood not so much as property in each specific person, but rather as property only in humankind as a whole (an odd notion). For the fundamental law of nature is not exactly that *each and every* person must be preserved:

> By the fundamental law of nature, man being to be preserved, as much as possible, when all cannot be preserved, the safety of the innocent is to be preferred [II, 16]; the first and fundamental natural law, which is to govern even the legislative itself, is the preservation of society, and (as far as will consist with the public good) of every person in it [II, 134]; [we may do what tends] to the preservation of the whole, but cutting off those parts, and those only, which are so corrupt that they threaten the sound and healthy. [II, 171]

We may justifiably harm (or even kill) another human being (who is God's property) if this is necessary for the more effective pres-

CHAPTER ONE

ervation of mankind as a whole.[85] The purpose of law is "the *general* good of those under that law" (II, 57; my emphasis), and when a "nobler use" (i.e., the preservation of mankind) than the "bare preservation" of some individual (or lower animal) calls for harming him (it), we may do so (II, 6). Locke clearly has in mind here harming individuals who are threats to the rest of humankind. But it is still hard, on the face of it, to see how God's property in the dangerous person is any less substantial (and less protective) than His property in the innocent.[86]

Supposing that the "principle" of God's will is indeed the preservation of mankind, how are we to proceed with the derivation from our fundamental law of the specific rules of natural law (step [5] of Locke's demonstration of morality)? There is, unfortunately, very little textual evidence to support an interpretation in this area. And we have seen that Locke clearly had doubts about his (and our) ability to produce a demonstration of the whole content of natural law. But we can make a "best guess" at Locke's (undoubtedly inchoate) intentions; and in this case I believe there is one position that sits most easily within the text. Specifically, the fundamental law of nature is, I think, meant to function in Locke's moral theory much as the principle of utility has been thought to function in some rule-utilitarian schemes. The superstructure of Locke's moral theory, then, is a kind of rule-consequentialism, with the preservation of mankind serving as the "ultimate end" to be advanced.[87] The fundamental law specifies this end, and all of the specific rules of natural law are members of that set of rules

[85] See Windstrup's discussion of this point in "Locke on Suicide," 170–72.
[86] Perhaps the principle at work here (although I doubt Locke thought much about the problem) might be that another's (God's) property becomes more vulnerable to interference when it threatens our own (as when I "pull down an innocent man's house to stop the fire, when the one next to it is burning" [II, 159], or shoot your rabid dog when it attacks me). Since people have (a sort of) property in themselves (in addition to God's property), when God's property (other people) threatens this, perhaps it loses its protected status. Or perhaps God "gives up on" those who threaten others, throwing away His property in them. As I argue below, there are good rule-consequentialist grounds for allowing the innocent to dispose of the dangerous. But these concern simply "maximizing" the preservation of man, not respecting all of God's property claims. If each person were thought of as an entrusted custodian of all of God's property (not obviously an intelligible notion), then each person might be (morally) able to decide to sacrifice some of God's property to better preserve the rest. Mere bystanders seem to have no right to make such decisions concerning another's property without prior authorization; but perhaps Locke takes us to be authorized by God to make such decisions in the same divine trust that gives us the right to punish others (the "executive right," which is the subject of chapter 3).
[87] As I first argued in "Inalienable Rights," 199–200.

obedience to which best promotes the preservation of mankind. More formally, we could characterize the law of nature as follows: an act A is contrary to natural law if and only if A violates one of that set of rules (the specific precepts of natural law) general conformity to which would more effectively preserve mankind than conformity to any alternative set. The precepts of the law of nature are the "ideal rules" (the most rational means) for preserving mankind. (God being perfectly wise, His law must be "ideal" in this sense.)[88] Our moral duty is to follow these ideal rules, and to respect the rights they define.

A set of rules that is ideal will not often generate conflicts of duties or rights. But considerations of simplicity and memorability of rules will limit the power of an ideal set to eliminate moral conflict. When occasionally the rules yield conflicting claims, conflicts are to be resolved by direct appeal to the fundamental law—which tells us that whatever solution best preserves all involved parties is to be pursued. For instance, in discussing the conflict between a just conqueror's right to the vanquished's property and the right of the vanquished's wife and children, Locke states:

> Here then is the case; The conqueror has title to reparation for damages received, and the children have a title to their father's estate for their subsistence. For as to the wife's share, whether her own labour or compact gave her a title to it, 'tis plain, her husband could not forfeit what was hers. What must be done in the case? I answer; The fundamental law of nature being, that all, as much as may be, should be preserved, it follows, that if there be not enough fully to satisfy both, viz. for the conqueror's losses, and the children's maintenance, he that hath, and to spare, must remit something of his full satisfaction, and give way to the pressing and preferable title of those, who are in danger to perish without it. (II, 183)

---

[88] Being a member of the set of ideal rules, of course, must involve (as in developed rule-utilitarian theories) being a good rule for human beings, with their defects in wisdom, memory, disinterestedness, and so on. So the ideal rules will be ones which are easy to follow and remember, which do not require calculations that our self-interested biases (or other limitations) will render impossible, and so on (and for these reasons, of course, *ideal* rule-consequentialism of this sort is not simply extensionally equivalent to *act*-consequentialism). The ideal rules for more perfect beings might be rather different. Above all, the ideal rules are not mere "rules of thumb"; they have positive normative force within a real rule-consequentialism.

51

In cases where the specific rules generate no conflicts, we are to scrupulously follow the rules (rather than try to advance the end directly, in an act-by-act fashion). As Mill puts it, "only in these cases of conflict between [specific rules] is it requisite that first principles should be appealed to."[89]

Why read Locke as a rule-consequentialist, instead of an act-consequentialist? Why not a single basic rule of natural law ("preserve mankind") with associated rules of thumb (analogous to the single act-utilitarian principle: "maximize utility")? Obviously, the texts can support no such reading of Locke's intentions, for everywhere that Locke speaks of morality and natural law, he clearly has in mind a set of binding rules. Ethics is, for Locke, "those rules and measures of human actions, which lead to happiness and the means to practise them" (E, 4.21.3). Indeed, it would be surprising if the possibility of an act-consequentialist stance ever entered Locke's mind. The natural law tradition within which he wrote, of course, emphasized a multiplicity of binding rules. The project of showing that God's revealed (positive) law has the same content as natural law obviously requires these multiple rules for natural law. And it is perfectly natural to think that the best way to get fallible human beings to promote the end of morality is by directing them to follow a set of simple, memorable rules. Act-consequentialist reasoning, by contrast, would be significantly impaired by our "short sight," "there being so many actions . . . and so many nice circumstances and considerations to be weighed . . . , we cannot secure ourselves from being in the wrong."[90]

Furthermore, there are good reasons to think that a rule-consequentialist superstructure will "fit" better than any form of act-consequentialism with Locke's most firmly entrenched positions.[91] Few can have failed to notice that while Locke often writes like a consequentialist, his strongest commitments concerning the con-

[89] *Utilitarianism*, chapter 2, paragraph 25.

[90] Locke, letter to Grenville, in Fox Bourne, *Life*, 1:391.

[91] Whether or not any rule-consequentialist positions are ultimately defensible, of course, is another question (and one with which I will not attempt to deal here). Their viability is being reaffirmed by the emergence of "two-level" utilitarian theories (as in R. M. Hare's recent work); but they must ultimately deal with charges that they either require a kind of "moral schizophrenia" (by recommending the adoption of dispositions inconsistent with philosophical reflection) or else involve a blind and irrational "rule-worship" (that is, as Smart argues, they advocate, with no theoretical justification, obedience to rules even where disobedience would more effectively promote the good). On rule-utilitarianism's (only apparent?) ability to generate commonsense judgments about rights, see Lyons, "Utility and Rights."

tent of natural law (e.g., to basic liberties, the sanctity of reparation, individual rights generally, etc.) seem distinctly deontological.[92] The natural position for squaring these elements of Locke's
thought is some kind of rule-consequentialism. Indeed, the primary motivation in this century for the reemergence of rule-utilitarian theory seems to have been precisely a desire to square utilitarian foundations with commonsense, deontological views of
what acts are right and wrong. And Locke's commitments to such
deontological views seem extensive. For instance, Locke strongly
believes in what we can call a "robust zone of indifference"[93] or
wide "domain of autonomy."[94] Locke believes that our conduct in
a large part of our lives is "up to us," or outside of the realm of
required and forbidden actions (it is, in Locke's language, "indifferent").[95] Doing our duty does not occupy the whole of our lives,
but only occasionally limits our conduct. We enjoy a significant
sphere of moral liberty within which we can pursue our own
(harmless) goals and desires. As Locke writes in a well-known series of letters to Denis Grenville, morality does not demand anything of us "in the greatest part of the actions of our lives wherein
I think God out of his infinite goodness considering our ignorance
and frailty hath left us a great liberty."[96] As long as we obey the
law, we may do as we wish with the rest of our lives.[97] This "zone
of indifference" figures prominently in Locke's defense of religious toleration.

By contrast, of course, act-consequentialism seems to dissolve
this sphere of indifference or moral liberty. A familiar objection to
act-utilitarianism has been that, by advancing the single require-

[92] The distinction between consequentialist (or teleological) and deontological
theories is drawn most prominently by Rawls in *A Theory of Justice*, 24–30, and
much more exhaustively in Scheffler, *Rejection* (although Scheffler does not discuss
rule-consequentialism). For a recent attack on this way of classifying moral theories,
see Piper, "Distinction."

[93] Fishkin, *Limits of Obligation*, 23.

[94] Nozick, *Philosophical Explanations*, 501–2.

[95] "What doth not lie under the obligation of any law is . . . indifferent" (First
Tract, 124).

[96] "There is a great latitude, and, therein we have our liberty which we may use
without scrupulously thinking ourselves obliged to that which in itself may be
best"; "the grounds and rules on which the right and wrong of our actions turn
. . . lie possibly in a narrower compass, and in a less number, than is ordinarily
supposed" (Fox Bourne, *Life*, 1:391, 393, 395).

[97] See Shapiro, "Resources," 50. We should live in peace with our fellows and
worship God. But we are also free to pursue our own "ease, safety, and delight"
and "a plenty of the good things of this world" (King, *Life*, 1:165–68). The mandatory and optional features of the law of nature are discussed below (2.1) in the
context of Locke's theory of rights.

ment that we always maximize expectable utility, it seems to leave nothing morally indifferent. In even our most trivial and common-place activities, there is some course of action that maximizes utility (and is thus morally required).[98]

Similarly, Locke's apparent commitment to the "sacredness" of individuals would seem to sit uneasily with his consequentialist concern for the good (preservation) of the whole of mankind. For another familiar objection to act-consequentialist theories has been that they seem bound to allow that individuals may be sacrificed when this is necessary in order to most effectively advance the good. But Locke, while he is (as we have seen) willing to allow that a specific class of individuals (those who are threatening serious harm to others) may have to be sacrificed for the common good, limits this implication of consequentialism by embracing rule-consequentialism. The sacredness of the individual is (in virtually all cases) affirmed as a matter of *rule*, not simply as a contingent matter of how the consequences of actions happen to balance out.

Reading the superstructure of Locke's moral theory as rule-consequentialist also enables us to make sense of some central but puzzling passages in the *Second Treatise*. For instance, Locke's (aforementioned) claim that "when all cannot be preserved, the safety of the innocent is to be preferred" (II, 16) makes little sense on its face. Which party in a conflict is "innocent" would seem to be a matter of what the law of nature says about such situations; but it is only by knowing who is innocent, we seem to be told, that we can determine what the law of nature requires in cases of conflict. This seems to help us about as little as we could possibly be helped. If, however, we understand the "innocent party" not as the "party favored by the law of nature" but in a rule-consequentialist way, things may be easier to fathom. We can read "innocent party" as "that party who is of the type more likely to promote the preservation of mankind." For instance, the party laboring on and holding the goods is less likely to destroy mankind than the party trying to take them, so the former's position is to be preferred in cases of conflict between them.

Interpreting Locke as a rule-consequentialist can also help us to see, for example, why acts that appear not to have any direct life-threatening properties are nonetheless morally wrong. If the pres-

[98] "If we were never to do but what is absolutely best, all our lives would go away in deliberation" (Fox Bourne, *Life*, 1:393).

54

ervation of mankind is the fundamental law of nature, it is initially difficult to see how, say, a petty theft (which in no way threatens the victim's preservation) can be wrong. But if we understand the theft's morally significant property not to be its direct consequences, but rather its being of a type that (as a rule) "tends against" the preservation of mankind, its classification by Locke as wrong seems more sensible. Indeed, Locke's "rule orientation" is nowhere clearer than in his primary statement of the content of natural law: we may not "take away, or impair the life, or what *tends to* the preservation of the life . . . of another" (II, 6; my emphasis).

But if rule-consequentialism makes sense of much in Locke, it also renders preposterous his claim that the content of the law of nature is "as intelligible and plain to a rational creature, and a studier of that law, as the positive law of commonwealths, nay possibly plainer" (II, 12). How difficult it would be to determine the set of ideal rules that follow from the fundamental law of nature can, perhaps, be best seen by noting how little of the "ideal code" contemporary rule-utilitarians have been able to convincingly articulate. Little wonder that Locke later lost faith in our ability to do the whole of the job. But perhaps certain of the ideal rules are sufficiently obvious that they will serve for the project in political philosophy that Locke undertakes in the *Treatises*.[99]

[99] I cannot take up here more of the complexities of Locke's (possibly changing) views on our knowledge of natural law (who can know it, how easily, etc.). While this is clearly an important subject (since natural law is properly only a real law for those who know its particulars), the only claim I wish to make here is that in the *Treatises* (my primary concern) Locke clearly believes us all capable of a knowledge of (at least the basics of) natural law: "reason teaches *all* mankind, who will but consult it" what the law of nature requires (II, 6; my emphasis). Some refuse to think about it, and others (out of bias) refuse to apply it in their own cases (II, 124, 136). But it is promulgated to all rational persons (see ELN, 113–15, 187–89; note 19 above; Seliger, "Locke's Natural Law"; Grant, *Liberalism*, 184). I believe this is also Locke's view of matters in the *Essay*, although this is not as clear. Abrams argues (with Strauss) that Locke in fact does not consider the law of nature a *real* law either in the *Essay* or (apparently) for most of his life after 1667 ("Introduction," 88–90). How one can deal with the *Treatises* on this view, I cannot see. And notice that Locke allows that *after* Christ, at least, people do have "clear knowledge of the lawmaker and the great rewards and punishments that await us" (R, 176 [243]). See Yolton's decisive rejection of Abrams' position in *Compass*, 178–80; Grant, *Liberalism*, 24–26, 39; Riley, *Will and Political Legitimacy*, 86–90; Herzog, *Without Foundations*, 96–101; Monson, "Locke's Political Theory," 180–82; and note 3 above.

Locke seemed confident that ordinary folk could see the basics of what the law required, even if they could not do the complex reasoning required to prove the principles of natural law: "A ploughman that cannot read, is not so ignorant but he has a conscience, and knows in those few cases in which concern his own actions, what is right and what is wrong. Let him sincerely obey this light of nature"

The similarity between the view I am attributing to Locke and those of certain utilitarian philosophers is, I think, too striking to ignore.[100] In particular, there is a very close structural parallel between (the superstructure of) Locke's moral theory and that of John Stuart Mill.[101] Like Locke, Mill begins with a "first" or "fundamental" principle (the principle of utility), from which we can derive a set of "corollaries," "secondary principles," or "subordinate principles."[102] These are the ideal rules for advancing the end set by the fundamental principle (happiness) and make up the body of morality: the "standard of morality" Mill tells us, may be defined as "the rules and precepts for human conduct, by the observance of which an existence [exempt from pain and rich in enjoyments] might be, to the greatest extent possible, secured to all mankind."[103] We are (as we have already seen) to follow the secondary principles, appealing directly to the first principle as a principle of resolution only in cases of conflict between secondary principles. As a consequence in Mill, some actions which fail to maximize utility are nonetheless not morally wrong (those which are "simply inexpedient"—i.e., not serious enough for us to think "a person ought to be punished in some way or other for doing [them]");[104] Mill's theory thus allows a "zone of indifference" within which our choices are not morally constrained.

These similarities between Locke and Mill, of course, do much

---

(King, *Life*, 2:78). The greatest part of mankind has no time or inclination for proofs (E, 4.20.2); but "God has furnished men with faculties sufficient to direct them in the way they should take" (E, 4.20.3). Perhaps Locke is thinking here as Mill was when the latter wrote: "mankind must by this time have acquired positive beliefs as to the effects of some actions on their happiness" (*Utilitarianism*, chapter 2, paragraph 24). We may be able to know what we *need* to know, even if the rest of natural law remains "secret and hidden" (ELN, 115). While most people cannot be "perfect in ethics" and must sometimes "believe" because they "cannot know" (in the sense of not being able to follow a long "train of proofs") (R, 179 [243]), this does not rule out their use of commonsense analogues of the "scientific" demonstrations of morality philosophers strive for (see Grant, *Liberalism*, 41), nor does it rule out proofs (demonstrations) of morality for those capable of following them.

[100] Locke's basic position is, for instance, very like the "theological utilitarianism" later defended by William Paley. I discuss below the similarities to the better known views of J. S. Mill.

[101] Aaron refers to Mill as Locke's "disciple" (*John Locke*, 361). My reading of Mill follows some of the main lines of the interpretation offered by David Lyons in, for example, "Mill's Theory of Morality," and "Human Rights." I will not try to defend the reading here.

[102] Humankind, according to Mill, is constantly (if not altogether consciously) engaged in the long-term enterprise of trying to articulate these ideal rules (*Utilitarianism*, chapter 2, paragraph 24).

[103] *Utilitarianism*, chapter 2, paragraph 10.

[104] Ibid., chapter 5, paragraphs 14–15.

to explain the occasional claims that Locke is a utilitarian.[105] There is, as we have seen, some basis for such contentions. But, in the first place, it is not at all clear that Locke's consequentialism specifies the same "proper end of conduct" as does utilitarianism. Utilitarians, of course, identify as the good happiness or utility. And while there is no denying that Locke often ties morality to the promotion of happiness (indeed, he frequently *defines* morality in these terms), he just as often specifies "peace" or the "preservation of mankind" as the end of morality. This is not to say that there is any inconsistency involved in aiming at peace, preservation, and happiness together. Peace and preservation are obviously necessary means to happiness. But Locke does *not* seem to have in mind that moral rules should be thought of as aimed at *maximizing* the total amount of happiness in the world (as utilitarianism is often characterized). Rather, Locke seems to believe that the rules of morality aim at insuring a decent, comfortable existence for all persons (period), without allowing for tradeoffs between persons designed to maximize total happiness. While some who threaten mankind may have to be eliminated, more mundane utilitarian tradeoffs seem to have no place. The common good is conceived of not additively, but distributively: society's laws must be "made conformable to the laws of nature, for the public good, i.e., the good of *every particular member* of that society, as far as by common rules, it can be provided for" (I, 92; my emphasis).[106] I leave it to others to decide whether or not this is sufficient for ascribing to Locke a utilitarian theory of the good.[107] Much more important, however, no moral theory (like Locke's) can be called genuinely utilitarian which rests on divine will or divine command foundations.[108] No utilitarian can say "utility is not the basis of the

[105] See, for example, Brogan, "John Locke and Utilitarianism." Others who have commented on utilitarian elements of Locke's thought include Murphy, "Paradox," 268n; Seliger, "Locke's Natural Law," 337; Drury, "Locke and Nozick on Property," 40; Wood, *Politics*, 136–37; Ryan, *Property and Political Theory*, 22, 30; Macpherson, *Possessive Individualism*, 194; Strauss, *Natural Right*, 235n. For counterarguments, see Sidgwick, *Outlines*, 178; White, *Philosophy*, 43–45.

[106] The magistrate's goal ("the safety of all") is "the preservation, as much as is possible, of the property, quiet, and life of *every individual*" (ECT, 185; my emphasis). On Locke's distributive view of the common good, see Tully, *Discourse*, 162–63; Tarcov, " 'Non-Lockean' Locke," 134.

[107] I by no means intend to argue here that the classical utilitarians might not also have held to a distributive conception of happiness. Indeed, Mill, in yet another striking similarity to Locke, can quite plausibly be read in this fashion.

[108] Brogan seems to see this, and quotes John Gay's remark that "the happiness of mankind may be said to be the criterion of virtue but once removed" ("John Locke and Utilitarianism," 80). As Gough argues, Locke "anticipates" utilitarianism

law or the ground of obligation, but the consequence of obedience to it" (ELN, 215).[109] Insofar as Locke's moral theory is utilitarian at all, it is only utilitarian in its superstructure. The end of morality is set by God. Locke's consequentialism concerns only the advancement of that end.

But we can see at work in Locke the same consequentialist strategies that allow utilitarians their defense of liberal individualism. By employing ideal rule-consequentialisms, both Locke and Mill (in chapter 5 of *Utilitarianism*) can combine their consequentialism with strong theories of individual rights. And Mill (in *On Liberty*), like Locke, can defend the sanctity of the individual and individual pursuits, and preserve a sphere of morally indifferent activity within which we are all our own masters. It is the rule-guided character of their theories that make these commitments at least coherent (if not, perhaps, ultimately defensible), at the same time explaining why both Locke (e.g., when discussing punishment) and Mill (both between and within *Utilitarianism* and *On Liberty*) can seem to be speaking one moment the language of consequentialism and the next moment that of deontology. Because Locke stresses the preservation of mankind *as a whole* as the end of natural law, and the *common* good as the end of civil law, it is tempting to dismiss Locke's individualist moments as misleading (as, to use one extreme example, Kendall has done[110]). But this is to ignore both Locke's distributive conception of the good and his ideal rule-consequentialist employment of it. Both facilitate the brands of individualism traditionally associated with Locke and Mill.[111]

But because there is more to Locke's moral theory than the rule-consequentialist superstructure I have been describing, there are more sources of Locke's individualism than my remarks above suggest. The sacredness of individual persons follows for Locke from their being special beings made by God in His image (I, 30); they are not just *parts* of God's creation, the whole of which is to be most efficiently preserved. Similarly, the "Kantian" respect for the dignity of equal and independent moral agents, evinced by Locke in the ways described above, motivates an individualist stance. And finally, the fact that mankind is best preserved (and

in certain ways, but he lacks the "secular outlook" required by that theory (*Political Philosophy*, 45).
[109] By "utility," of course, Locke here means *personal* utility. But the same point holds for general utility. It is God's will, not the utility of His commands, which makes natural law obligatory.
[110] *Majority-Rule*.
[111] Locke's individualism is especially well documented in Parry, "Individuality."

so God's will most dutifully followed) when individuals enjoy the rights and liberties individualists espouse, provides one more source to complement the others. The styles of arguments for individualist conclusions suggested here can be found working together in many places in the *Treatises*.[112]

The various styles of argument at work in Locke create several problems. At the interpretive level, they allow interpreters to find almost whatever they are looking for in Locke (and to conveniently dismiss the rest as unimportant or confused), accounting for the astonishingly wide range of interpretations of Locke's "real position" over the years. Theoretically, they raise concerns that Locke's project may ultimately be incoherent, heading in many different directions at once. I will suggest in 2.4 that Locke's positions are frequently "overdetermined." But whether or not this amounts to theoretical incoherence is much the same as the question of whether ethical pluralism in general (what Rawls unhappily calls "intuitionism"[113]) is incoherent. My own view is that while such theories are certainly "unconstructive,"[114] they are not at all obviously inadequate simply in virtue of embracing a plurality of irreducible moral principles. (I shall not argue for that view here.) Nor need the diverse grounds of moral duty and right obviously point in conflicting directions, requiring a higher principle or intuition to legislate between them. Locke's arguments suggest that he believed (as we might well) that there are many different kinds of equally good moral reasons all backing one individualist position.

1.5. The Content of Natural Law

We have discussed the foundations of Locke's moral theory and the theoretical superstructure that is supposed to generate the specific content of natural law. But as yet we have seen no more than the most general view of the kinds of duties and rights the law

---

[112] For instance (as I argue in 2.1), Locke argues for the *moral* equality of persons (i.e., for equal natural rights) both in terms of how we are best preserved and in terms of persons' natural, nonmoral equality as rational, valuing beings. And (as I argue in 3.5) Locke's defense of the natural right to punish is derived not only from God's authorization and our right to preserve mankind, but as well from a (quite secular) theory of forfeiture. Similarly, I find in Locke's theory of property (in 5.2) justifications both in terms of God's intentions and in (what I will argue are) the perfectly secular terms of the argument from labor-mixing. I will discuss other examples in other chapters.

[113] Rawls, *Theory of Justice*, 34.

[114] Ibid., §§7–8.

defines. Unfortunately, Locke (as usual) had nothing very systematic to say on the question. Perhaps his best effort to provide a general structure for our duties is found where the content of natural law is briefly sketched in II, 6. Initially, the law of reason is described only as teaching that "no one ought to harm another in his life, health, liberty, or possessions";[115] but this account is immediately expanded and further specified. I believe we can ultimately distinguish in II, 6 four categories of duty (or "natural obligation" [II, 118]) that bind all persons:

(1) Duties to preserve oneself (i.e., not to kill or endanger oneself)

(2) Duties to preserve others (when this does not conflict with self-preservation)

(3) Duties not to "take away the life" of another

(4) Duties not to do what "tends to destroy" others (by, e.g., interfering with or "impairing" their "liberty, health, limb or goods")

These are far from surprising as derivations of general categories of duty from the fundamental law of nature—the preservation of mankind. For they amount only to the following: (1) Preserve mankind in yourself; (2) Preserve the rest of mankind *positively* (i.e., by giving positive aid to others); (3) and (4) Preserve the rest of mankind *negatively* (i.e., by refraining from harming others). The more specific "ideal rules" for preserving mankind, then, will fall under these general headings, with the least controversial duties (e.g., not to murder, assault, rape, steal, etc.) falling in categories (3) and (4).

Obvious questions abound concerning each of the four categories and the relations among them. Libertarian interpreters of Locke, for instance, typically disregard category (2) (the class of positive duties toward others), maintaining that when Locke says we must "preserve the rest of mankind," he means only (reiterating his earlier claim) that we must preserve them by the *negative* means he goes on to mention immediately after.[116] These libertar-

[115] This description, given in terms of simply *not harming* others, is clearly inadequate, in its failure to account for both duties toward oneself and duties to positively assist others. A description intermediate between this one and that given in the text below, is Locke's early definition of vice as "nothing else but doing of harm," "either to oneself or others" (Fox Bourne, *Life*, 1:162–63).

[116] See, for example, Mack, "Locke's Arguments," 58, 60. Nozick seems simply to ignore this side of Locke (*Anarchy*, 10). G. A. Cohen (no libertarian) also finds in II, 6 only negative duties of forbearance ("Marx and Locke," 383). Tully, on the

ians are moved, I'm afraid, more by their search for philosophical forbears of suitable respectability than by close attention to Locke's texts (as we will see in 6.3). Similarly, category (2) is usually either questioned or ignored by those who wish to find in Locke not a friend but a target—for example, an apologist for laissez-faire capitalism and defender of the rights of the propertied classes.[117] I reserve my arguments against these views for chapters 5 and 6 (where I also take up the question of the relative stringency of the various categories of duty [6.4]).

Category (1) (duties of self-preservation) is also controversial for a variety of reasons. Again, libertarian interpreters of Locke will either ignore this category or argue that Locke was mistaken in including it (since all of the duties recognized by strict libertarians concern *inter*personal matters—specifically, limitations on harm to others). But from a quite different direction one might challenge not the content of category (1), but the *priority* that Locke grants the duties of self-preservation over our duties to preserve others (which bind us, remember, only when our "own preservation comes not in competition"). If the fundamental law requires us to preserve mankind in general, shouldn't it require scrupulous neutrality between our own preservation and the preservation of others, all of us being equally persons and equally God's property? Locke even suggests that the reasoning supporting the duties in categories (1) and (2) (with [3] and [4]) is the same; for after affirming our duty to preserve ourselves, he says "so by the like reason" we should preserve others. How, then, can self-preservation have the priority that Locke also suggests?

I will argue (again in 6.4) that there are in fact good rule-consequentialist reasons for this priority of self-preservation over the *positive* preservation of others (although perhaps not over the *negative* preservation required in categories [3] and [4]). Here I wish only to briefly address the first, libertarian worry about the duties in category (1); for many besides libertarians find Locke's apparent absolute moral ban on suicide at least counterintuitive (and possibly abhorrent).[118] As a first observation, it seems clear that Locke cannot consistently allow that killing of others is sometimes permissible while at the same time insisting on an *absolute* prohibition

---

other hand, goes just as far wrong in the opposite direction by (apparently) asserting that morality for Locke is "primarily a set of positive duties to others" (*Discourse*, 102).

[117] Macpherson, *Possessive Individualism*, chapter 5. Others with different motives who find this same spirit in Locke include Strauss and Cox (whose views I discuss below).

[118] On these issues, see Windstrup, "Locke on Suicide."

on suicide. If one may justifiably kill a man who has abandoned reason (or who has because of disease gone out of control), and who stands to humankind as no more than a "beast of prey" and a "noxious creature" (II, 16), then one who is thus degraded may surely (in a lucid moment perhaps) justifiably kill himself.[119] But it also seems reasonable to insist, on Lockean grounds, that the suicide prohibition be relaxed ever further. If the natural law concerns preservation, then it may seem that no very strict prohibition could sensibly be imposed on killings that merely precede the inevitable death of the victim by a short period, while accomplishing some good by sparing the victim further pain and suffering (as in "mercy killings" of others or "mercy suicide" in one's own case).[120] Admittedly, this in some sense clashes with Locke's insistence that people are "made to last during [God's], not one another's pleasure" (II, 6); but the "clash" is not very violent.

Further there seem to be good rule-consequentialist grounds for supposing that the duty to preserve oneself should not be as *strict* as at least the duty to preserve others *negatively* (i.e., killing oneself should not be seen as "as wrong as" killing another).[121] For killing others both causes fear and a loosening of social bonds (which is detrimental to society's, and hence humankind's, preservation), and tends to beget more killing (in retaliation or as a result of the killer's own relaxed internal bars on killing). Killing oneself, by contrast, as a rule has none of these consequences ("copy-cat" sui-

[119] As is well known, Locke says of the degraded warmaker who is justly made a slave (because he has forfeited all of his rights) that "whenever he finds the hardship of his slavery outweighs the value of his life, it is in his power by resisting the will of his master, to draw on himself the death he desires" (II, 23). This appears to be a legitimation of suicide in at least this limited class of cases (see Windstrup, "Locke on Suicide," 172–73). Glenn argues that the slave's death in this case would not really be an instance of suicide, for the slave no longer has power over his own life ("Inalienable Rights," 84–85). But this seems to miss the relevant point, which is that the preservation of mankind (the point of natural law prohibitions) is no more or less affected by the self-inflicted death of the slave than by his master's punishing him with death (regardless of whether or not we call the self-inflicted death "suicide"). A better Lockean argument would be that since the slave is no longer a person (a moral being), moral bans on suicide simply do not apply to him. I argue below (in 4.3), however, that slaves should probably *not* be characterized by Locke as not at all under the moral law, rendering such arguments unpersuasive.

[120] Schwarzenbach claims that Locke *does* allow suicide in cases of unbearable suffering ("Locke's Two Conceptions," 144–45). While I agree that Locke *should* allow this, I can find no textual warrant for claiming that he *does* allow it. Locke's *absolute* ban on suicide seems to me a rationally unmotivated aspect of his prephilosophical theological convictions.

[121] This, of course, in no way conflicts with my earlier claim that there are good rule-consequentialist reasons for the priority of self-preservation over the positive preservation of others.

cide and group suicide clearly being mere exceptions to this rule).
And given that in most persons the inclination to kill themselves
is from the start rather weaker than the inclination to kill others,
one might again expect (contrary to Locke's pronouncements) that
the duties in category (1) would be less stringent than those, say,
in category (3). The best way to understand a Lockean duty of self-
preservation, I think, is as a duty only not to take or endanger
one's life frivolously or arbitrarily. One may lawfully give up or
risk one's life to better preserve life (as in risking dangerous surgery, fighting in a just war, or ending a depraved existence) or to
avoid unbearable and permanent pain. Indeed, one may do so
wherever "some nobler use than . . . bare preservation calls for it"
(II, 6).[122]

It is important to note that II, 6 is not the only passage in which
Locke describes the content of the law of nature. In several places
in the *Essays on the Law of Nature*, Locke produces quite different-
looking accounts of natural law's requirements. In essay 4, for instance, where he suggests that we can infer "a definite rule of our
duty from man's constitution," Locke mentions three duties in
particular:

(a) To praise, honor, and glorify God
(b) To "procure and preserve a life in society with other
     men"
(c) To preserve oneself (ELN, 157–59)

Anyone familiar with Aquinas, of course, will recognize this account of the content of natural law. But earlier, in essay 2, Locke
offers yet another (more specific) list of some of the "precepts of
the law of nature":

(d) "Respect and love for the deity"
(e) "Obedience to superiors"
(f) "Fidelity in keeping promises"
(g) Veracity (what Locke calls "fidelity in . . . telling the
     truth")
(h) "Mildness and purity of character"
(i) "A friendly disposition" (ELN, 129)

In order to square these accounts of the content of the law of
nature with our original categories of duty, we must recall first
that in the *Second Treatise* Locke is centrally concerned only with

[122] See Windstrup, "Locke on Suicide," 177; Grant, *Liberalism*, 131–32.

that aspect of natural law that deals with the actions of people toward others and themselves. He thus stresses those rules derivable from the fundamental law (the preservation of mankind) through a consideration only of the *natural* consequences of our actions. But our actions also have, as it were, *supernatural* consequences, for our relation to God bears centrally on the preservation and well-being of humankind and our ultimate happiness.[123] The duties specified in (a) and (d) (our purely religious duties), then, are also derivable from the fundamental law as a second "branch" of natural law.[124] But they are not central to the project of political philosophy (except perhaps as a limit on possible uses of political power[125]). These duties are the private concerns of each individual.

The rather odd "duties" in (h) and (i) (mildness, purity, friendliness) seem more like virtues in the strict sense—that is, desirable dispositions or traits of character, rather than moral requirements on action of the sort normally emphasized by Locke (particularly in the *Treatises*).[126] Elsewhere in the *Essays*, Locke mentions others—piety, merciful feeling, chastity (ELN, 141). There is, as far as I can see, no reason why, from the fundamental law of nature, we could not also derive another "branch" of natural law concerned with "good character" rather than "right action." For the possession of certain traits of character is certainly more conducive to humankind's preservation than the possession of others. But again, these are not central to the Lockean program in *political* philosophy,[127] and so are not discussed in the *Treatises*.

The remaining duties in our lists—(b), (c), (e), (f), and (g)—all

[123] "The highest obligation that lies upon mankind" is "doing those things in this life which are necessary to the obtaining of God's favor, and are prescibed by God to that end" (L, 151).

[124] See Tully, *Discourse*, 175.

[125] Ashcraft, *Revolutionary Politics*, 494, 497.

[126] Baldwin, "Toleration," 43. Of course, Locke discusses the virtues extensively in the *Education*, but they are not there explicitly presented as derived precepts of natural law. The virtues most stressed in Locke's educational writings are self-denial, civility, liberality, justice, courage, hardiness, humanity, industry, avoidance of waste, and truthfulness (see Tarcov, *Locke's Education*, especially 182). We will later see applications of this account of the virtues to Locke's theory of rights (primarily in chapters 5 and 6, with respect to the virtues of liberality, justice, and avoidance of waste).

[127] Tarcov, " 'Non-Lockean' Locke," 136; and *Locke's Education*, 3. Exactly how such virtues are to interact with the realm of requirements and prohibitions (and the "robust zone of indifference" it leaves us) is not, I suspect, a question to which Locke gave any real thought. On bringing together different types of value, see Nagel, "Fragmentation of Value."

seem to square reasonably well with those original categories of duty Locke set out in II, 6. Duty (c) (self-preservation), of course, is simply equivalent to category (1). Duty (e) (obedience to superiors) is, at least by the time Locke wrote the *Treatises*, simply the duty to keep one's promises (duty [f]), since only consent can give one person "superiority" of this sort over another.[128] Duties (f) and (g) (fidelity and veracity) can easily be subsumed under several of our original categories. For promise-breaking and lying not only do quite obvious *private* harm to the objects of the deception (harming them, at the very least, in their "liberty"), they also do palpable *public* harm, by undermining the fabric of trust essential to the stability of society (thus doing injury not only to the immediate victim, but also to both the victimizer and the rest of society). Although it is a position more famously associated with Hume, Locke defends throughout his writings the view that the fulfillment of pacts and agreements is absolutely central to the preservation of society and civilized life. "Every community among men falls to the ground" without the "faithful fulfillment of contracts" (ELN, 119); indeed, the obligation to keep promises is so important that it even binds God (I, 6; II, 195).[129] While Locke does not argue so prominently for the duty of veracity, truth-telling is for him just another kind of fidelity (notice the way in which "truth and keeping of faith" are referred to together by Locke in II, 14 and elsewhere[130]). And we know that for Locke "justice and truth are the common ties of society" (E, 1.2.2), and lying is a serious vice.[131] Many others have since joined Locke in making the case for veracity as an essential prop of society.[132]

[128] This claim, of course, requires further clarification. The "right of creation" by which God is owed our obedience is not properly a part of natural law (as we saw in 1.2). The duties of obedience owed by children and slaves are not owed by men in the full sense (i.e., moral agents), so their status under natural law is unclear (and discussed in subsequent chapters). All other duties of obedience are consensual.

[129] This is a bit of theoretically unsound enthusiasm on Locke's part. More direct evidence of the importance of fidelity in Locke's moral theory (and of its necessity in supporting society) can be found in the main arguments of "Morality" (see Grant, *Liberalism*, 134n). On the centrality of keeping agreements in Whig natural law theory of the period, see Ashcraft, *Revolutionary Politics*, 190.

[130] "Faith and truth, especially in all occasions of attesting it upon the solemn appeal to heaven by an oath, is the great bond of society" (*Some Considerations of the Consequences of the Lowering of Interest and Raising the Value of Money*, 6).

[131] *Education*, 131: lying ranks one "with the most contemptible part of mankind."

[132] Kant (in his essay "On a Supposed Right to Tell Lies from Benevolent Motives") makes such a case. More recently, it has been argued by Fried, *Right and Wrong*, 67–68; and Bok, *Lying*, 28.

This leaves only duty (b) unaccounted for—the duty "to procure and preserve a life in society." It is in one way the least clear of the duties Locke lists (although it is far from unfamiliar in natural law writings). For it is more than any other (except the duty of self-preservation) ambiguous in its status as a *prescriptive*, rather than a *descriptive*, law of nature. On the one hand, it is easy to see how a duty in this area could be derived from the fundamental law of nature. We need society with others to be comfortably preserved; only in society are our rational capacities best used and fully developed.[133] On the other hand, when Locke elsewhere speaks of the "obligation" to enter society, he is speaking not the language of *moral* obligation, but the language of psychological *compulsion* (of being "obliged"). God made us social creatures, and put us "under a necessity to have fellowship with those" of our kind (E, 3.1.1); we are "under strong obligations of necessity, convenience, and inclination" to drive us into society (II, 77).[134]

If we are naturally driven into society, so that society is a virtually inescapable feature of human life (indeed, the social character of even Locke's state of nature is almost universally conceded[135]), it makes sense to suppose that the primary moral obligation with regard to society is not so much to enter or procure it, but to preserve it. And the preservation of society, of course, is best accomplished precisely by doing the other duties defined by natural law. So, in a sense, the duty "to procure and preserve society" is not so much an independent duty of natural law for Locke, as a restatement of the duties we have previously discussed.

The one misunderstanding against which it is important to guard is the supposition that by "society," Locke here means *political* society. While there is also a sense in which we are "driven" into political society by the "ill condition" of the state of nature (II, 127) and "the pravity of mankind" (L, 152), any obligation to enter society can only be an obligation to enter society in the informal,

[133] Tully, *Discourse*, 48–49. See Ashcraft, *Revolutionary Politics*, 225, on the related views of Codrington.
[134] "We are born with dispositions to and desires of society; we are by nature fitted for it" (Fox Bourne, *Life*, 1:396); we have a "love and want of society" (II, 101) and are "urged to enter society by a certain propensity of nature" (ELN, 157). See Tarcov, " 'Non-Lockean' Locke," 136; Gough, *Political Philosophy*, 26; Tully, *Discourse*, 48.
[135] Taylor's charge that Locke was an "atomist" seems wrong for the reasons stated above ("Atomism," 40–41). We can also see that in one sense Locke *accepted* Taylor's obligation "to belong to or sustain society" (40). He only denied (rightly, in my view) the obligation to belong to *political* society (see below). I return to these issues in 2.5.

apolitical sense—the society of mankind (II, 128). If we had a moral duty to enter political society, of course, there would be no necessity of securing the consent of every member of the commonwealth (II, 96), since we can lawfully compel people to do their duty.[136] We *"may"* join political society (II, 95; my emphasis) (and we may quit it [II, 121], at least if we are not express consenters); we are not *obligated* to do so.[137] While creating a political society (of a certain sort) may be the act that would best preserve (part of) humankind, we should remember that it is the *rules* for preserving mankind (which allow us *liberty* in our choice of polities), not the usefulness of specific acts with which the law of nature is concerned.

The accounts of the content of natural law given by Locke in the *Essays*, then, are broadly consistent with that which we have seen in the *Second Treatise*.[138] While Locke never produced anything like a comprehensive list of moral duties, we can obtain from the sketch in II, 6 a good sense of how he wished to complete step (5) of the demonstration of morality. I turn now to the moral rights defined by this same law of nature.

[136] Alternatively, Locke may mean that while we are obligated to enter *some* political society, we are not obligated to enter any *particular* one, but only the civil society of our choice. If so, our choice to enter remains free, and our consent remains necessary to our leaving the state of nature. The language of the *Second Treatise*, however, seems to me to discourage this reading, especially (but by no means only) when Locke emphasizes the "freedom" and "liberty" of those who *remain* in the state of nature (while others are making a commonwealth) (e.g., II, 95, 97).

[137] Strauss, *Natural Right*, 221n; Lemos, *Hobbes and Locke*, 93–96. By contrast, see Pangle's view that the key rule of natural law in Locke requires joining or setting up a government with a monopoly on coercion (*Republicanism*, 245).

[138] Locke provides at least one other "list" of some of the precepts of natural law in the *Essays*; it includes duties concerning "thefts, debaucheries, and slanders," "religion, charity, fidelity," and others (ELN, 193–97). All those duties, we can now see, are consistent with the original categories of duty with which we began.

T W O

LOCKE AND NATURAL RIGHTS

2.1. The Place of Rights in Locke's Theory

In 1953 Leo Strauss wrote that in Locke's moral and political philosophy, the "emphasis" is on natural rights, not on "natural duties or obligations." These rights are "the foundation of the law of
nature."[1] Richard Cox followed Strauss' lead: "the 'law' of nature
turns out to be first and foremost concerned with the 'right' of self-
preservation, and only secondarily or derivatively with 'duty' to
others or to a transcendent order. . . . According to Locke, rights
are by nature absolutely superior to duties."[2] The idea that in
Locke rights are the "basic" or "primary" moral category (although not always expressed in so Hobbesian a fashion) is a common one.[3] Many other scholars, however, have advanced precisely the opposite view of Locke's moral theory. To David
Gauthier, "Law and duty, not right, is the foundation of Locke's
ethics."[4] And James Tully (apparently following John Dunn)
claims, "The law of nature is . . . the foundation of Locke's . . .
natural rights"; "the priority of natural law" shows that Locke uti-
lized only "a limited rights theory."[5] Again, it is easy to find examples of this "duty-based" reading of Locke's moral philosophy.[6]
  Any body of work that inspires such diametrically opposed in-

---

[1] Strauss, *Natural Right*, 248, 227.
[2] Cox, *Locke on War and Peace*, 84–85, 169. See also 151, 153, 163, 168, 189.
[3] Taylor writes that "the paradigm of primacy-of-right theories is plainly that of
Locke" ("Atomism," 40); and Raz speaks of "the Lockian tradition of regarding
rights as the foundation of political morality or even of morality generally" ("Right-
Based Moralities," 182). See also Hacker, *Political Theory*, 268. It is common to characterize the "modern theory" of natural law (to which Locke is taken to subscribe)
as not a theory of law at all, but a theory of rights (e.g., D'Entreves, *Natural Law*,
59).
[4] "Why Ought One Obey God?" 432.
[5] *Discourse*, 63, 131.
[6] See, for instance, Snyder, "Locke on Natural Law," 731; Ingram, "Natural
Rights," 5; Macpherson, "Natural Rights," 228–29; Polin, "Justice," 270; Ryan,
"Utility and Ownership," 179–80; Kendall, *Majority-Rule*, 68.

terpretations can be justly accused of being less clear than it ought to be. Against such a charge Locke has no defense. But neither of the opposed interpretations, I think, adequately captures the true place of natural rights in Locke's theory. Strauss and Cox miss the target altogether; but Gauthier and Tully also err (although far less so) in overemphasizing what Strauss seemed to completely ignore. I will argue for a view of Locke on which his moral theory is *neither* right-based *nor* duty-based.[7] Indeed, unless I can show that rights in Locke are more than mere secondary reflections of duties, I can hardly justify the extensive discussion of Locke's theory of rights that follows.

It is relatively easy to show that rights cannot have for Locke the kind of priority that is ascribed to them by Strauss. In the first place, if we look not at the *Treatises* but at other works in which Locke discusses morality (as we did in chapter 1), virtually all of his derivations and observations seem to concern law and duty, with hardly any mention of rights. This would make little sense if natural duties were really derivative from a foundation of natural rights. Even within the *Treatises*, however, there is little textual support for the priority of rights. Rights and duties seem to be roughly coextensive. Indeed, the derivations Locke stresses seem mostly to proceed from duties to rights, not from rights to duties (as when parental rights are said to arise "from that duty which is incumbent on them to take care of their offspring" [II, 58]). And the right of self-preservation that Strauss and Cox allege to be foundational corresponds (as we have already seen) to one of Locke's basic categories of duty, derived directly from the fundamental law of nature.[8]

[7] That is, for Locke neither right nor duty is defined in terms of the other, derived from the other, or more central to the spirit of Locke's project than the other. See Waldron, *Private Property*, 64–65, for these ways of characterizing right- and duty-based theories. Examples of duty-based theories are familiar; a good contemporary example of a right-based moral theory is that of Alan Gewirth. For more on these distinctions, see Dworkin, *Taking Rights Seriously*, 171–72; Raz, "Right-Based Moralities"; Mackie, "Can There Be a Right-Based Moral Theory?"; Louden, "Rights Infatuation."

[8] See Dunn, *Political Thought*, 160. The only sense I can make of asserting the conceptual priority of rights over duties in Locke derives from the priority of God's rights over us to our duties to obey His commands. Right is, in this minimal sense, conceptually prior to duty, since the idea of God's rightful dominion is the foundational notion in Locke's ethics. But as far as the rights and duties of *mortals* is concerned, the former have no obvious priority—logical, conceptual, psychological, or historical—over the latter. Shapiro takes right to be prior to law and duty in Locke precisely because "God's natural right is . . . basic" (*Evolution of Rights*, 107, 100–101). But this seems to lead him to assert both the priority of right for human-

These arguments against the priority of rights in Locke suggest immediately that perhaps duties have the kind of priority that Strauss tries to give to rights. This second position is rather harder to argue against, and my argument against it can be clearly stated only after a more specific examination of the kinds of rights at work in Locke's texts. But it is worth remembering as we proceed that the same style of argument that is often used by Locke to derive duties, sometimes has not duties but rights as its conclusion (e.g., I, 86). And we should also remember how completely unsurprised we would be to hear someone describe the *Second Treatise* as a book about persons' rights.[9]

Locke never gives us anything like a definition of a right in his works. Perhaps the closest he comes to one is in his claim that (natural) "right is grounded in the fact that we have the free use of a thing" (ELN, 111).[10] But careful attention to the ways in which Locke uses the concept of right in his arguments allows some safe assumptions about his position. We can distinguish (although Locke himself does not) four kinds of rights at work in the *Treatises*.[11] There is first (and least important) what is commonly referred to as a "liberty" or "liberty right" (following Hohfeld[12]).

kind (negative libertarianism) and that Locke's position opens the door for secular libertarianism. The priority of *God's* right, however, speaks not at all about the priority of our right; and the removal of God only points us toward libertarianism *if* right is prior for us, and *if* God's law is not replaced with a suitable secular substitute (such as the moral law of Kant).

[9] See, for example, Tarcov, " 'Non-Lockean' Locke," 131. Locke certainly emphasizes right-talk over duty-talk in many places, both in the *Treatises* and, for example, in *Education*, 185–86. Tarcov speculates that Locke's emphasis on rights over duties stems from his recognition that people will act with less resentment on what is characterized as a right than on what is characterized as a duty (*Locke's Education*, 114).

[10] In this passage Locke contrasts right with law, which "enjoins or forbids the doing of a thing." The contrast, of course, is a familiar one, as in Hobbes: "right consists in liberty to do or forbear, whereas law determines and binds to one of them" (*Leviathan*, chapter 14, paragraph 3).

[11] Locke's use of various synonyms for right—power, title, privilege, claim, liberty—does not, unfortunately, signal any substantive distinctions, as far as I can tell.

[12] Because of the legal origin of rights-talk, Hohfeld's analysis is an appropriate place to start talking about *moral* rights, despite the fact that Hohfeld discusses only the various types of *legal* rights (or "senses" the word "right" has in the law). See his *Fundamental Legal Conceptions as Applied to Judicial Reasoning*, 35–64. (Helpful discussions of different kinds of rights and of Hohfeld's distinctions can be found in, e.g., Brandt, *Ethical Theory*, 434–41; and Becker, *Property Rights*, 11–14.) The four legal relations Hohfeld distinguishes—liberty (or privilege), (claim) right (or right in the "strict sense"), power, and immunity—are usefully employed in classifying *moral* relations as well. I think we can clearly find the first three in the *Treatises* as types of *moral* rights, while Locke's insistence on the imprescriptibility of natural

This is a right only in the limited sense that one has a "right" to do what it is morally permissible to do (what is "alright"); a liberty right is the mere absence of an obligation to refrain.[13] Such rights are not protected by correlative duties on the part of others to respect or allow performance of the right, and hence are "competitive" with the liberty rights of others. Liberty rights exist where "the law of nature is silent." It is this kind of right that Locke must have in mind when he speaks of the right we have to appropriate by our labor some particular unowned good (e.g., II, 37). For he never intends to argue that others are bound to *allow* me to appropriate any particular good, that they may not labor on and appropriate it first. The duties of others are only to obey the law of nature in attempts to appropriate (by, e.g., not using violence, leaving enough and as good for others, etc.) and to respect others' property once it has been established by labor.

Liberty rights are, of course, familiar to readers of Hobbes, where they are the central moral concept in terms of which all others are defined. In Locke, liberty rights have a much more limited role, being relevant primarily in unprotected competitive contexts, of which (as we will see) there are few.[14] The central concept of right employed by Locke in the *Treatises* is clearly that of a claim right, a kind of protected liberty[15] (to which I will return momentarily).

---

rights might be taken to signal a moral immunity (of a sort). The basic distinction between liberties and claim rights, of course, was at work in many natural rights theories before Locke, but the first really precise formulation came rather later, in Bentham, *Pannomial Fragments*, chapter 3, section 2. On Bentham's contribution, see Hart, *Essays on Bentham*, chapter 7.

[13] More precisely: X has a liberty right to do A ≡ X has no obligation not to do A.

[14] See Brandt, *Ethical Theory*, 442–43. For Locke, "nature must be altogether negated before one can claim for himself absolute liberty" (ELN, 123) of the sort allowed by Hobbes. Locke's state of nature, although "a state of liberty, yet it is not a state of license" (II, 6); Lockean liberties are both limited by and (largely) protected by natural law. Liberty rights will play an essential role in my analysis of the natural executive right (the right to punish) (see 3.5). Strauss' apparent belief that Locke recognized only Hobbesian liberty rights (*Natural Right*, 226–29) is, in the face of the textual evidence, almost incomprehensible. Given Strauss' belief that duty in Locke is secondary to and derivative from right, it may seem even more odd that the rights he identifies are mere liberties—given that liberty is often defined as the area where law is silent (which seems to give law priority). But if one begins (as in Hobbes) with *absolute* liberty, unbounded by duty, then one can coherently define obligation in terms of voluntary transfer or renunciation of right.

[15] A protected liberty is a liberty right that others have a duty (to someone) to allow the exercise of. A claim right is a protected liberty where others' duties are owed to the holder of the liberty (as opposed to some third party), so that the rightholder (and not some third party) has a claim against the duty-bound parties.

A slightly more obscure type of right we can find in Locke is what we may call a moral power. A power is a "higher order" right—a moral ability to change or impose other people's (claim) rights or duties.[16] In exercising my powers, I alter the moral situation of others; they are "liable" or "subject" to these powers. The general right each person has (in Locke) to take property, for instance, is best understood as a moral power.[17] By taking previously unowned property and establishing exclusive rights in it, we impose on others new duties to respect our claims and thus limit their rights of free action. We must be careful here to distinguish the power to take property (in general) from the liberty we have to take some particular good as our own. We are only empowered to take some things as our own, not any specific thing. But we are as a result at liberty to take any particular thing (as long as it is unowned, not more than our share, etc.), as is each other person. It is in this sense that each individual is born with (or "to") a right to property (and in this sense that, e.g., the French Declaration's claim of a natural and imprescriptible right of property is best read[18]). We are born not with a right to any specific goods, but with a power to make property in specific goods (a right not to be excluded from our share).[19]

The third and central category of rights in Locke's moral theory is (what we have called) claim rights, rights that (unlike liberty rights, but like powers) *do* correlate with the duties of others.[20] A

[16] Here again I follow Hohfeld's analysis of legal powers. Such rights are "higher order" in the sense captured by Hart's distinction between the primary (requiring) and secondary (enabling) rules of a legal system (*Concept of Law*, chapter 5). Den Hartogh also has recognized Locke's use of the idea of a moral power ("Tully's Locke," 665–66).

[17] The right in question (to which we will return in chapter 5) is Tully's "inclusive" property right—the right to take and use one's fair share of the commons. Tully takes this right to be a simple claim right (*Discourse*, 61). I think it is better viewed as a power, for the reasons stated below.

[18] "The final end of every political institution is the preservation of the natural and imprescriptible rights of man. These rights are those of liberty, property, security and resistance to oppression" (*Declaration of the Rights of Man and the Citizen*, article 2).

[19] Moral powers, like legal ones, can be either perfect (requiring no one else's participation) or imperfect (requiring the willing cooperation of others). The power to make property is perfect (as is the legal power to make a will, for instance). The power to make contracts is imperfect (like the legal power of a priest to marry people).

[20] On right-duty correlation, see Ross, *Right and the Good*, 48–56; and Lyons, "Correlativity of Rights and Duties." In thus reading Locke, I agree with, for example, Tarcov, " 'Non-Lockean' Locke," 132; Lemos, *Hobbes and Locke*, 75; and Scott-Craig, "John Locke and Natural Right," 42. Shapiro denies that Locke thought in terms of correlative rights and duties (*Evolution of Rights*, 105), although

doctrine of duty-right correlation is clearly implied in most of the discussions of duties and rights in the *Treatises* (and is strongly suggested in one passage in the *Essay*[21]), although Locke never stated such a doctrine explicitly. He did, of course, know and admire the work of Pufendorf, who *had* explicitly stated it.[22] And the impression created by Locke's discussions is surely that for every duty there is a (logically) correlative right to the performance of that duty, held by another (or others); and that for every right (excluding liberties, which I shall hereafter ignore), there is a correlative duty on all others to allow the exercise of the right.[23] Perhaps the best illustrations of Locke's commitment to this view are his treatments of the rights and duties of charity (I, 42), the rights and duties concerned with the care of children (I, 88–89), and the rights and duties associated with our "natural equality" (II, 4–6).

Within the class of claim rights, however, we can distinguish two types (our third and fourth kinds of rights in Locke). The first type we may call "optional claim rights."[24] This type covers most of the familiar Lockean freedoms, those rights whose exercise is

---

he seems to offer no defense of this position. Finnis similarly claims that Locke means by "right" primarily "liberty" or "power," *not* "claim right" (*Natural Law*, 228); but the passages he cites as support merely use the *words* "liberty" and "power," uses that in no way correspond to the Hohfeldian categories. Locke much more often than not clearly means "claim right" when he uses words like "power," "privilege," and "liberty," as the contexts of the uses noted by Finnis show decisively.

[21] "Sometimes the foundation of considering things, with reference to one another, is some act whereby any one comes by a moral right, power, or obligation to do something. Thus, a general is one that hath power to command an army; and an army under a general is a collection of armed men, obliged to obey one man" (E, 2.28.3).

[22] "Not every natural faculty to do something is properly a right, but only that which concerns some moral effect on other men. . . . This faculty takes on the nature of a real right, at the moment when this moral effect is produced in the rest of mankind, that other men may not hinder him, or compete with him, against his will" (Pufendorf, *De Jure Naturae et Gentium Libri Octo*, 391 [3.5.3]).

[23] Locke's is thus a doctrine of two-way correlation, which implies, for instance, the absence of imperfect duties (a claim for which I argue in 6.4). I think, as a consequence, that Mendus is mistaken when she centrally relies on the claim that actions can be wrong in Locke even though they violate no rights (*Toleration*, 40–41). There are, of course, immediate problems with discovering the correlative rights for certain duties in Locke: for example, the duty to preserve yourself (who has a right that you do this?), or the duty of a parent to care for his child (how can the child have a *right* to care, if that child is not under the law of nature?). I discuss the first of these problem cases in 2.4 and the second in 4.3.

[24] What Golding calls "option rights" ("Towards a Theory," 546) and Feinberg calls "discretionary rights," defining them as follows: "I have a discretionary right in respect to X when I have an *open option* to X or not X correlated with the duties of others not to interfere with my choice" ("Voluntary Euthanasia," 105). On discretionary rights, see also Feinberg's *Social Philosophy*, 69–70.

CHAPTER TWO

protected by duties of noninterference on others, but whose exercise is optional for the rightholder. While I need not trade you the apples I gathered for your corn, should I decide to do so, others are bound to permit me to exercise my right to do this. In general, I am entitled to determine the course my life will take (within the bounds of natural law), without interference (beyond "competitive" interference) from others.

On the other hand, Locke also talks of rights that are held as a direct consequence of duties that the rightholder has. If I have a duty to do A, Locke believes, I must have a right to do A (which, in turn, correlates with others' duties to allow me to do my duty). This kind of right is, for Locke, a trivial consequence of possessing a duty; for it seems obvious that if something is my moral duty, I should be left free by others to perform it. We can call this a "mandatory claim right" (using Feinberg's term). Locke's commitment to this kind of right can be seen in the substantial overlap of rights and duties throughout the *Treatises*, but is probably clearest in his discussion of parental rights over children. As we have already seen, Locke derives parental rights directly from parents' duty to care for their offspring (II, 58), and he proceeds by making it clear that parental rights might just as well be called duties (II, 67, 69); all parents have a duty to "preserve what they have begotten" (I, 88; II, 56), and, as a trivial consequence of this duty, a right to care for and control their children, held against the world at large (i.e., a right to be allowed to do their duty). But the overlap of rights and duties is not limited to these isolated instances. Indeed, Locke clearly means to cover the whole of natural law; for the natural rights Locke specifies in II, 11 (the right of self-preservation and the right of preserving all mankind [in this case, all others]) are simply rights to do precisely what (as we have seen) Locke several paragraphs earlier says we have a duty to do (II, 6). No explanation of the inference from duty to right even seems necessary to Locke. We can conclude, then, that for Locke "X has a duty to do A" entails "X has a (mandatory) right to do A" (and also "Some other person or persons has a right that X do A");[25] similarly, "X

[25] This claim, for all its intuitive plausibility, is, I believe, false. It seems true that a *liberty* right to do A is a trivial consequence of a duty to do A, since what is required must be permissible. (Here Hart's discussion of unilateral and bilateral liberties is useful [*Essays on Bentham*, 166–67].) A *claim* right to do A, however, seems not to be even a nontrivial consequence. Anywhere that duties can be competitive we will find counterexamples to Locke's (implied) position. If you and I each promise our spouses to buy a particular (one-of-a-kind) lamp we have each seen, each of us has an obligation to buy the lamp (and is at liberty to do so). But

74

has a (mandatory *or* optional) right to do A" entails "All others have a duty not to interfere with X's doing A."

With this understanding in hand of the kinds of rights Locke recognizes (or is committed to recognizing), we can return to our problem of the relative priority of rights and duties in Locke's theory. The temptation to see moral duties as foundational and rights as secondary or derivative arises naturally from several sources. First, Locke's derivation of (mandatory) rights directly from the possession of duties seems to suggest that rights are simply *means* to the performance of our duties. The point of a right is, on this view, simply to secure the freedom necessary to pursue our duty to preserve mankind.[26] Second, one may think of rights as derivative or secondary because of the way that natural duties limit the *extent* of our rights. We are free, after all, only "within the bounds of the law of nature" (II, 4), and a *limiting* role seems to give priority; rights are defined negatively, as what is compatible with duty.[27]

---

neither of us has as a consequence a claim right to the lamp or a right that the other permit us to buy the lamp. Similarly, if each of us has (as Locke believes) a duty of self-preservation, and there is food enough only to feed one of us, neither of us has a right that the food not be taken and eaten by the other. Locke may not have considered such cases, perhaps believing that duties cannot be competitive in this way ("virtuous actions do not clash . . . : they kindle and cherish one another. . . . The duties of life are not at variance with one another" [ELN, 213]). But even Locke allows for the possibility of conflicting rights and duties (e.g., in II, 183, discussed above in 1.4). Indeed, they seem likely to be relatively common where promissory duties are at issue. And in the absence of a decisive factor for settling conflicts (say, the innocence or greater need of one party), we will have competitive, "first-come-first-served" situations. Stell argues that duties cannot even imply *liberty* rights, because the idea of a "mandatory liberty" is too paradoxical to allow ("Dueling," 9). But this seems to misunderstand the notion of liberty (i.e., mere moral permissibility, not moral freedom of some fuller sort) at work in the idea of a liberty right. See Feinberg's response to Stell ("Voluntary Euthanasia," 107).

[26] Tully and Ashcraft, I think, see duties as foundational and rights as derivative precisely because they hold this view of Lockean rights. "The priority of natural law renders all rights as means to this end" (i.e., the end of "supporting and comforting" humankind); "The law of nature is . . . the foundation of Locke's three natural rights. . . . Men have natural rights *because* they have natural duties" (*Discourse*, 131, 63). See also Ashcraft, *Locke's Two Treatises*, 109, 126, 135, 138–39. Others who seem to share this view include Polin ("Justice," 270) and Kendall (*Majority-Rule*, 68).

[27] This seems to be Dunn's view: "What defines human life is a set of duties and the right to promote happiness in any way compatible with these duties. It is a mistake to see man's right to promote his happiness, wide though it may be, as having a priority over his duty. Indeed the scope of this right is defined by the limits of its compatibility with 'our main duty which is in sincerity to do our duties in our calling as far as the frailty of our bodies or minds will allow us' " (*Political Thought*, 218). Dunn has more recently suggested as well the view ascribed above to Tully and Ashcraft ("What Is Living?" 16, 20).

But neither of these reasons for regarding rights as secondary in Locke can survive careful scrutiny. The rights we have that derive from our own duties (our *mandatory* rights) are only one kind of right each (mature, noncriminal) person possesses. We also have other rights that are the logical correlates of the duties of others, rights that create moral space for our own activities, free from the interference of others. Our mandatory rights *are* mere means to the end of doing our duty. Our optional rights, however, are precisely rights to act freely when we are *not* engaged in doing our duty; indeed, this is what distinguishes them from mandatory rights. We have no right to act contrary to duty; but between our required performances and the boundaries set by natural law's prohibitions there is ample space for free activity that is not simply a means to doing our duty. This "robust zone of indifference" that we have seen Locke embraces (1.4) is a zone of protected liberty that others are duty-bound to respect. If our optional rights are in this way the correlates of others' duties (and not merely consequences of our *own* duties, as are our mandatory rights), it seems to make no clear sense to argue that duties are somehow prior to rights. They are conceptually connected aspects of the very same moral relationship, neither of which has any obvious priority.[28]

Similarly, while it is correct to claim that our optional rights are limited by the demands of duty, the very duties that limit us are correlated with the rights of others. It is, then, as much (others') rights that limit our rights as (our own) duties, "breach of laws being mostly the prejudice and diminution of another man's rights."[29] Nothing here suggests the priority of duty or secondary status for rights. The precepts of the law of nature define duties and rights in the same logical breath, not *first* duties and *then*, as a necessary means to performing them, rights (and, finally, the correlative duties on others to allow us to do our duty).[30]

[28] Interestingly, one defender of the priority of duty in Locke inadvertently makes quite clear why the view *must* be wrong. Ashcraft contends that all Lockean natural rights are "derivative from obligations that individuals owe to God that they *cannot* renounce" (*Revolutionary Politics*, 494, 499). But if individuals cannot renounce these obligations, they cannot renounce (transfer, dispose of) the mandatory rights to perform those obligations. If *all* Lockean rights are mandatory in this way, *no* rights can be transferred or renounced, rendering morally impossible all contracts and agreements, including that which creates civil society. Locke's position requires the optionality of (some) natural rights.

[29] "On the Difference Between Civil and Ecclesiastical Power," 113.

[30] It is, of course, true that we can lose our rights (by forfeiture) in a way we cannot lose our duties (although *why* we cannot do so in Locke is not altogether clear). But when we thus lose our rights, others lose duties (toward us). It makes

The point I wish to stress here is only that natural law is for Locke as much a *protective* order as it is a *restrictive* one. Persons' natural condition is "a state of perfect freedom to order their actions, and dispose of their possessions, and persons as they think fit" (II, 4); I have "a liberty to follow my own will in all things, where the rule prescribes not" (II, 22). The optionality of action (and the moral protection for whatever choices we make) within the wide sphere of the permissible is clearly implied in Locke's claims. Dunn has argued that the freedom Locke ascribes to us is only what is necessary for us to do God's bidding (to pursue "the calling").[31] But while this may be one way of characterizing what Locke has in mind, it is, I think, a misleading way. Our "uncontrollable liberty, to dispose of . . . person or possessions" (II, 6) (as always, within the bounds of natural law) is in part a moral freedom to pursue our own life plan, independent of the call of duty. We have not only the rights to preserve ourself and others (rights to do our duty), but rights not to be harmed or interfered with (our optional rights) even when we are *not* doing our duty, but only pursuing our own innocent ends. Indeed, using our abilities to provide for ourselves the conveniences of life is precisely part of what God intends for us, so we must each be left free to pursue those projects that we choose.[32] Each person has naturally "a right of freedom to his person . . . , the free disposal of it lies in himself" (II, 190); each has "the right of innocent delights" (II, 128). Wherever others are not "prejudiced," "every man may consider what suits his own convenience, and follow what course he likes best" (L, 146, 136).[33] The law of nature is consistently described by Locke as a boundary to our free pursuits, not as that which alone gives these pursuits their point or only legitimate end (see, e.g., the clear statement of this position in II, 59).[34]

---

no better sense, then, to say that possession of rights is conditional on the performance of our duties, than to say that possession of duties is conditional on others' respecting our rights.

[31] *Political Thought*, 121, 245, 252, 264.

[32] So pursuit of our own innocent projects counts as an "indirect form of ethical behavior" (Ashcraft, *Locke's Two Treatises*, 235–36).

[33] See 4.5 below. Andrew argues that liberals, Locke included, are committed to "the right to do wrong" (*Shylock's Rights*, 12–13, 120, 131–32, 194). But Locke's optional rights are only rights to do what is *not best*, not rights to do what is *wrong*. Most of us believe, with Locke, that doing what is not best is often permissible, and that it would be confused to equate morally suboptimal behavior with wrongful behavior (as Andrew appears to).

[34] Even where Locke describes the law as "not so much the limitation as the direction of a free and intelligent agent to his proper interest," he goes on to characterize the law as a boundary: freedom is "a liberty to dispose, and order, as he lists,

It is important to the force of my claims here, I think, to fully understand how the moral freedom determined by our optional rights is related to the fundamental law of preserving mankind. For in one sense, it is surely true that the "point" of our freedom is the best preservation of mankind. Freedom is "the fence to our preservation" (II, 17). Mankind is best preserved when the laws of nature are obeyed; and this implies that the freedom that is left to us and protected by the law of nature is also best for the preservation of man. But to say that mankind is best preserved when left a large sphere of (protected) liberty (analogous, say, to Mill's claim that humankind is happiest in such conditions), is rather different than to say that this moral freedom is only a freedom to do what the preservation of man requires. To confuse the two claims is to confuse what we may legitimately pursue with our freedom (its particular objects) with what ultimately justifies our freedom. These can be (and are, I think, in Locke) quite different matters. Mankind is best preserved when it is left a large area of freedom (within the boundaries set by the direct requirements of preserving self and others), *regardless* of what (innocent) ends we choose to use our freedom to pursue. By analogy, Mill argues (in *On Liberty*) that leaving humankind a large realm of liberty will best promote our happiness (or our "permanent interests"). But this does not require him to argue that each person can only legitimately use personal liberty to do what best promote's humankind's happiness (or even personal happiness). The justification of our freedom is general utility, but its legitimate employments range far beyond the pursuit of this end.

In Locke, then, the mandatory rights are rights to do what is intimately concerned with the preservation of self and others, as required by our natural duties. These duties set the limits on and protect our freedom to do what we choose in those areas *not* intimately concerned with preservation (the sphere of our optional rights of "innocent delights"). Many interpretations of Locke—libertarian, Straussian, Marxist—have stressed (for various reasons) the latter realm of optional rights, arguing for the priority of rights in Locke, and painting a picture of the Lockean person as right-

his person, actions, possessions, and his whole property, within the allowance of those laws under which he is" (II, 57). The importance of optionality to Locke's views is revealed in his frequent use of the words "uncontrolled" or "uncontrollable" to describe the liberty of persons (e.g., II, 6; II, 87; Fox Bourne, *Life*, 1:178). Tarcov nicely characterizes the realm of choice provided by Locke's moral theory (*Locke's Education*, 7). See also his critique of Dunn's views on "the calling" (127, 136–37); and Medina, *Social Contract Theories*, 35–36.

holder without responsibilities, free to pursue unlimited accumulation of material goods and other private aims without regard for others.[35] We have seen (and will see in subsequent portions of this work) how mistaken this view is. Other interpreters have reacted with justifiable vigor to these bare and misleading caricatures of Locke, emphasizing the former realm of mandatory rights and the justification of all rights in terms of the fundamental law of nature (through stressing Locke's theology). But this emphasis has been, I think, if not equally, at least also one-sided. We will find the place of rights in Locke's theory between these extremes, in a form of "pluralism" that acknowledges neither right nor duty as primary, basic, or fundamental.[36]

2.2. Equal Rights and Special Rights

Nowhere in his writings does Locke present a complete or systematic accounting of our moral rights. Just as with the duties defined by natural law, Locke contents himself with mentioning some broad categories of rights (e.g., in II, 128 and II, 190). I will again try to gather together (in this section and the next) the bits and pieces of text in which Locke discusses rights in order to display the overall structure of his theory of rights.

At times Locke seems less interested in telling us *what* rights we have than in arguing that *whatever* rights we have, we all possess them equally. His polemic against Filmer, of course, requires this emphasis, as one of his central concerns is to deny Filmer's view that political authority is natural—that is, that it consists of rights of dominion that some persons naturally possess over others (hence, a natural *inequality* of rights).[37] Nonetheless, it is initially difficult to understand Locke's claims about the equality of rights

[35] Some of Locke's overzealous affirmations of our natural freedom (noted above) encourage such misinterpretations, as when Locke (incorrectly, on his own terms) claims that man is "absolute lord of his own person and possessions" (II, 123).

[36] The kind of "pluralism" I have in mind here is discussed in 2.4 and amounts to little more than the view that *no* single kind of moral consideration or value is primary (all others being derivative from it). See the arguments for pluralism (which is, in my view, the correct stance) in Raz, "Right-Based Moralities"; and Miller, "Rights and Reality." A pluralistic reading of Locke is briefly hinted at in Scott-Craig, "John Locke and Natural Right," 46.

[37] Filmer, *Patriarcha*, I, 1–4; III, 14. On this issue, of course, Hobbes and Locke are allies, marking the oddness of traditional readings of Locke that took him to be attacking Hobbes (as in, e.g., Sabine, *History of Political Theory*, 524). On the significance of Locke's claims of natural equality within the *political* climate of his day (and the association with anarchy and "rabble-rousing"), see Ashcraft, *Revolutionary Politics*, 161.

in the face of apparent inequalities of right in everyday life (and in illustrations of these supplied by Locke himself). When Locke's point in these claims is clearer, so will be the structure of his theory of rights.

Readers of the *Treatises* first encounter a defense of the equality of rights in I, 41 (where Locke is chiefly concerned with rights in external goods—i.e., property rights in the narrow sense):

> It is more reasonable to think, that God who bid mankind increase and multiply, should rather himself give them all a right, to make use of the food and rayment, and other conveniences of life . . . than to make them depend upon the will of a man for their subsistence, who should have power to destroy them all when he pleased.

Here Locke argues for equality of ("inclusive" property) rights by rule-consequentialist reasoning from the fundamental principle of God's will. Mankind will be best preserved if these rights are held equally, instead of an unequal distribution that makes one person dependent on another. But Locke offers another (more general) argument for equality of rights, one that is more central in the texts and does not in this way depend on God's will in its first premise. This style of argument is hinted at in I, 41, where Locke claims that no man is any "better than other men," but it is not stated fully until I, 67:

> [It] is very evident [that] man has a natural freedom . . . , since all that share in the same common nature, faculties and powers, are in nature equal, and ought to partake in the same common rights and priviledges, till the manifest appointment of God . . . can be produced to show any particular person's supremacy, or a man's own consent subjects him to a superior.

The same argument is repeated prominently at the start of the *Second Treatise*, where Locke claims that the natural condition of man is

> A state also of equality, wherein all the power and jurisdiction is reciprocal, no one having more than another: there being nothing more evident, than that creatures of the same species and rank promiscuously born to all the same advantages of nature, and the use of the same faculties, should also be equal one amongst another without subordination or subjection,

unless the Lord and Master of them all, should by any manifest declaration of his will set one above another. (II, 4)

We have seen already (1.3) one ambitious use by Locke of the "fact" of natural equality—his derivation (using Hooker's argument) of substantive duties not to harm (and to help) others. Here Locke's goals are more modest. Whatever rights we have, we must have equally, unless God has clearly granted exceptional rights to one person or another or we have by our own consent created for another greater right than that individual initially had. This *moral* equality, for Locke, follows simply (indeed, without explanation) from natural equality of "faculties and powers" (which here refers to *physical*, not moral, powers).

This style of argument is by now familiar.[38] It begins by justifying a presumption of moral equality and challenges nonegalitarians to advance a reason justifying some claim of inequality in rights.[39] Consent would justify inequality, but this could not explain *natural*, moral inequality (consent can create only "artificial" inequality, in Hume's sense of that word). God's appointment would also do the job, but there is (at least in interesting contemporary cases) no evidence of any such appointment. And physical inequalities that might be taken to ground moral inequality do not, Locke seems to say, exist. We must, then, assume a natural equality of rights (and duties).

Now Locke is not so silly as to believe that people do not have all sorts of physical inequalities (in intelligence, strength, beauty, etc.). But not just any kind of physical (or mental) inequality will ground an inequality in rights. It seems that the only kinds of inequalities relevant to differences in rights are those inequalities that bear on our ability to exercise or enjoy those rights and what they protect.[40] Since natural rights are protections for freedom to preserve oneself (and others) and to formulate and pursue projects and a plan of life, only those traits that determine one's capacities in these areas will be relevant to the justification of rights. We know that all persons desire their own preservation and happiness. These are universal "innate practical principles" (of the sort Locke's position allows: E, 1.2.3; I, 86), which seem to follow from mere human corporeality and consciousness. Similarly, all persons

[38] One well-known contemporary argument that approximates the one we find in Locke is that in Wasserstrom, "Rights, Human Rights," especially 51–52, 54–55.

[39] On the presumption of equality, see, for example, Feinberg, *Social Philosophy*, 99–102; and Becker, *Reciprocity*, 60–61.

[40] Wasserstrom, "Rights, Human Rights," 54–55.

are rational, by definition, for the concept of a person that is at issue in moral argument (as we saw in 1.2) is that of a "corporeal, rational being." In these respects, all persons are equal. No person is any better than another at *being a person*. And since the desires for preservation and happiness and the rational capacity for planning a life and living freely within the law (II, 57) seem to be precisely those traits relevant to exercising and enjoying rights, all persons are equal as well in their possession of whatever moral rights there are.

Locke's argument can supply ready answers to at least many of the objections that spring to mind in reaction to the egalitarian position. The familiar complaint that there are simply *no* respects in which "all men are equal"[41] is avoided by foregoing use of the natural concept of man. Those human beings who are not rational and purposive are simply not persons in the relevant sense, and do not possess the equality of rights that persons enjoy. To the further objection that while all "persons" may be rational, they are certainly not all *equally* rational (and so, perhaps, should not enjoy equal rights), Locke can respond that it is only some minimum threshold of rationality that must be reached for one to be capable of exercising and enjoying rights (the trait relevant to possession of rights).[42] To be an (equal) rightholder (i.e., a person), an individual must have an "understanding of his own to direct his will" and "regulate his actions" (II, 58). The individual can then rationally pursue personal good and the good of others, with knowledge of the law of nature and the boundaries to action it establishes.

With this threshold of rationality, Locke argues, come self-consciousness and purposiveness:

Person . . . is a forensic term, appropriating actions and their merit; and so belongs only to intelligent agents, capable of a law, and happiness, and misery (E, 2.27.26); we must consider what *person* stands for;—which, I think, is a thinking intelligent being, that has reason and reflection, and can consider itself as itself, the same thinking being in different times and places (E, 2.27.11); It is by the consciousness it has of its present thoughts and actions, that it is *self to itself* now, and so will be the same self, as far as the same consciousness can extend

[41] On this skeptical stance, again see Feinberg, *Social Philosophy*, 88–94; see also Williams, "Idea of Equality;" and Vlastos, "Justice and Equality."
[42] See Gewirth, *Reason and Morality*, 122–23.

to actions past or to come (E, 2.27.10); All of which is founded
in a concern for happiness, the unavoidable concomitant of
consciousness; that which is conscious of pleasure and pain,
desiring that that self that is conscious should be happy. (E,
2.27.26)[43]

All persons, then, are not only rational (which implies self-control
of an acceptable degree and the ability to follow laws); they are
self-aware pursuers of ends, so that it matters to each person both
how things turn out and by what means they are brought about
(persons are capable of happiness and deliberation). Persons can
reflect on and evaluate the ends they pursue and the means they
adopt.[44] It is in this combination of traits that our basic natural
equality consists. Unlike a mere thing, a person has a will (the
capacity for acting on reasons, on the rational recognition of what
ought to be[45]) and a unique point of view from which to view the
world and enter it purposely. Each individual "has shoes" into
which each of us can put ourselves.[46] (Comparison with a more
Kantian position on personhood [and on the foundation of moral
equality] is again, I think, unavoidable.) This secular side of
Locke's argument for moral equality sits perfectly comfortably
with religious respect for God's creations and God's desire that
they be effectively preserved.[47] The secular and religious argu-

[43] For one interesting interpretation of what Locke here means by "forensic," see
Alston and Bennett, "Locke on People and Substances," 43–46.
[44] Compare here Nozick's basic moral characteristic of being a "value-seeking I"
(1.3, note 73). Persons are moral agents (see Buchanan's brief discussion of the
main elements of moral agency in "What's So Special about Rights?" 76). A person
for Locke is a "rational, intelligent, concerned, rule-following being who acts in the
world and who is conscious of those actions as his" (Yolton, *Locke*, 31); persons act
intentionally, out of deliberation over the right and the good (ibid., 29, 38; see also
Yolton and Yolton, "Introduction," 17). See Lomasky's remarks on "project pursuers" (throughout *Persons, Rights*) and Becker's comments on the importance of
purposiveness and self-consciousness to rational agency (*Reciprocity*, 66–70).
[45] Locke's stated definition of will, of course, is less Kantian than the one I suggest here (see E, 2.21.5). But Locke's persons also have wills in this stronger sense
(see II, 57–58). See Riley's defense of the reading of Locke's conception of will as
(a la Kant) the capacity to act on one's conception of law (*Will and Political Legitimacy*, 81) and Rapaczynski's similar arguments (*Nature and Politics*, 161–62).
[46] This is a point well made by Feinberg in concluding his discussion of "grounds
for equality": "The real point of the maxim that all men are equal may be simply
that all men equally have a point of view of their own, a unique angle from which
they view the world. They are all equally centers of experience, foci of subjectivity.
This implies that they are all capable of being viewed by others imaginatively from
their own point of view. They 'have shoes' into which we can always try to put
ourselves; this is not true of mere things" (*Social Philosophy*, 93–94). See also Williams, "Idea of Equality," on "the human point of view" (esp. 236–38).
[47] I intend to suggest here that Locke's concept of personhood is sufficiently rich

ments (as I have already claimed) are bound together throughout the *Treatises*.

If this natural equality of persons establishes a natural equality of rights, however, how are we to explain all of those *unequal* rights persons can possess in the state of nature (rights that seem *not* to be founded on either consent or God's special appointment)—for instance, the property rights of those who labor, the parental rights of those who procreate, or the charity rights of those in need? It is best, I think, to read Locke as arguing that all persons are moral equals (possessing the same rights and duties) when considered *independent* of any special relationships or transactions into which they may have entered.[48] The moral position that persons assume on attaining maturity approximates this state of equality;[49] but in its pure form it is just the logically "prerelational" state of persons. We acquire greater or lesser rights than others by things we do and special positions we enter. These activities may result in greater or lesser merit for some; they may make one person "better than another." But moral equality is not based in merit. It is grounded in some more basic notion of human worth, established not by what we have done or what has happened to us but by what we essentially *are*.[50] All persons must respect "the dignity and excellency of a rational creature" (*Education*, 31).

---

and similar to a Kantian (if not Kant's) position, that it can ground the kinds of arguments suggested in 1.3 and motivate "respect for persons." Waldron's claim that rights in Locke represent "the respect owed by ourselves and others to our nature and status as creatures of God," and that without God Locke would be left with "Hobbism" (*Nonsense upon Stilts*, 13–14) thus seems to me mistaken, as does his claim that one cannot state Locke's argument for the juridical equality of persons in secular terms (*Private Property*, 142). See also Gauthier's similar claim that "Locke minus God equals Hobbes" ("Why Ought One Obey God?" 427) and Herzog's assertion that there are in Locke no secular justifications for the wrongness of violating rights (*Without Foundations*, 109). Respect is owed other persons in Locke because they are our *equals*—not simply as equally God's creatures (which, after all, the lower animals are as well), but as equally purposive and rational and so with as much claim as we ourselves could have to freedom and happiness.

[48] The equal rights Locke defends are thus not rights that necessarily *stay* equal in all contexts, as Macpherson seems to assume in charging Locke with a contradiction on this point ("Natural Rights," 234).

[49] It only approximates a state of equality, of course, because on attaining maturity persons may have differential rights not grounded on anything they have *done*—for instance, they may inherit property at maturity or owe special duties (and hence have diminished rights) to their parents (if the parents still survive and have not, say, abandoned their child).

[50] For an elegant statement of the difference between merit and worth, and of the importance of this distinction to an argument for equal rights, see Vlastos, "Justice and Equality," especially part 2. See also Becker, "Individual Rights," 204, 209.

The distinction I am suggesting is at work in Locke, of course, is just Hart's well-known distinction between *general* and *special* rights. Our general rights "are rights which all men capable of choice have in the absence of those special conditions which give rise to special rights," while our special rights are those that "arise out of special transactions between individuals or out of some personal relationship in which they stand to each other."[51] It is equality of *general* rights that for Locke follows from natural (nonmoral) equality. And just as in Hart our general rights are simply specific instantiations of the overarching natural and "equal rights of all men to be free," Locke calls the sum of our naturally equal (general) rights our *"natural freedom."*[52] We all have (in the logical, prerelational sense) an equal right to freedom from harm and interference by others, provided only that our actions stay within the bounds of natural law. We are morally free (enjoy a protected liberty) to do our duty and to pursue our own nonobligatory plans and projects. We are born "with a title to perfect freedom" (II, 87).

The natural freedom each enjoys can thus be characterized either as a set of many specific rights or as one grand, composite right (like Hart's "right to be free"). The composite right is what Locke calls "the right of freedom to his person" (II, 190) and what I will hereafter refer to as the *right of self-government*. It includes the right to do our duty (our equal mandatory rights), the right to pursue our nonobligatory ends (our equal optional rights), and the powers to make special rights (e.g., in property or by contract) that are important to our freedom of action. In discussing the transfer of rights required for effective civil government, Locke divides the right of self-government into the right of "innocent delights" and the right "to preserve himself and others" (II, 128), to emphasize its composition from optional and mandatory elements.[53] Each

---

[51] Hart, "Are There Any Natural Rights?" 188, 183. Waldron, like Hart, correctly observes that special rights can arise from both voluntary and nonvoluntary relationships, but notes additionally that they can arise as well from "transactions" that do not involve *choice* at all—as in the right to reparation for damage done in an accident (*Private Property*, 112–13).

[52] See Pangle, *Republicanism*, 263. For a discussion of the related Thomist conception of natural freedom, see Skinner, *Foundations*, 2:155–56. Filmer's attack on claims of natural freedom is in *Patriarcha*, I, 1.

[53] Dunn argues (*Political Thought*, 223–25) that even innocent delights are permissible only because of their necessary role in rejuvenating us for laboring and doing our duty. And Locke does say such things, for example, in his letters on "recreation" to Grenville. Those same letters, however, strongly emphasize the *optionality* of rights, and are, indeed, a source for my argument that Locke defended a "robust zone of indifference" (1.4). (How seriously we should take these letters is unclear, however, if Ashcraft is correct in his conclusion that they were written to someone

person is "born to" the "full state of equality" (II, 55) that consists in possession of the right of self-government (natural freedom); each receives this birthright upon (if ever) reaching the maturity necessary for personhood.

Beyond this background of general and equal rights are all sorts of special rights generated by special relationships in which we stand or by "acts purely personal" (I, 98) that we perform.[54] Locke explains in the *Essays* the difference between those precepts of the law of nature "which are absolute and . . . binding on all men in the world equally" (those which define general rights) and "those decrees of nature which are concerned with the various conditions of men and the relations between them" (those which define special rights) (ELN, 197). And Locke mentions some of the special rights (powers) at the start of the *Second Treatise* (II, 2), including those grounded in consent (political power, conjugal rights, and rights of masters over servants), those grounded in forfeiture (despotical rights), and those grounded in natural relationships (parental rights).[55] Other special rights are discussed throughout the *Treatises* and are distinguished from the background of natural freedom (general rights) with which each person "starts":

> Though I have said . . . that all men are by nature equal, I cannot be supposed to understand all sorts of equality: Age or virtue may give men a just precedency: Excellence of parts and merit may place others above the common level: Birth may subject some, and alliance or benefits others, to pay an observance to those to whom nature, gratitude, or other respects may have made it due; and yet all this consists with the equality which all men are in . . . , being that equal right that every man hath to his natural freedom. (II, 54)

Here Locke lumps together sources of special rights some may have (such as procreation, benefaction, or compact) with good rea-

---

Locke knew to be "spying" on him. See *Revolutionary Politics*, 135–36.) Elsewhere, when Locke contrasts "innocent diversions and delights" with "vicious delights," innocent delights are *not* justified by their necessity for labor, but by their connection with happiness (only *part* of which is connected with "doing good"). See "Thus, I Think," 164–65.

[54] In an extended sense, of course, all rights derive from acts that have been performed: most of our special rights from our own acts, some from the acts of others (e.g., criminal acts, acts of procreation, gifts, etc.), and our general rights from acts of God—the "grants and gifts" from God that Locke refers to in the *First Treatise* (e.g., I, 6, 63, 116).

[55] While Locke refers to nature as giving parental rights (II, 173), the true ground of these rights is not so clear (see 4.3).

sons for showing others appropriate signs of respect (such as their age or virtue[56]). But both are described against the background of our general right to freedom. The most important of the special rights in Locke will be the subject of chapters 3 to 6 of this study. Here, however, I want to attempt the preliminary task of locating these special rights within the general structure of Locke's theory of rights.

2.3. The Structure of Locke's Theory of Rights

We can fruitfully organize the rights Locke recognizes into three groups, as follows:

I. *General Rights*—the right(s) of self-government

II. *Nonconsensual Special Rights*—(exclusive, original) property rights, charity rights, the natural executive right, despotical rights, parental rights, filial rights, rights to reciprocation

III. *Consensual Special Rights*—All consensual, promissory, and fiduciary rights, including political rights, conjugal rights, economic rights, civil rights

While all of these rights will be discussed in subsequent chapters, a few preliminary remarks on this organization are in order.

I. *General Rights*: As we have seen, this "group" of rights includes our mandatory rights, some optional claim rights, and the moral powers to make special rights (e.g., our right to make contracts and our inclusive, common right to make exclusive property rights).

II. *Nonconsensual Special Rights*: This group consists of those special rights that derive from relationships *not* based in promises or consent. The grounds of the rights at issue here are, for instance, labor, need, forfeiture, procreation, benefaction—all the bases of nonconsensual moral relationships.[57] Several of my classifications in this group require comment. As we will see (in chapter 3), the executive right (II, 7–13) can be viewed either as a general right all

---

[56] Age, virtue, or goodness give one "a kind of natural authority" (II, 94). But Locke makes it clear that this is not a *right* to rule in itself. It is only our "tacit consent" to such "natural authority" that gives it any status it may have in terms of rights.

[57] As in Hart's fourth class of special rights ("Are There Any Natural Rights?" 186–87). Waldron rightly observes that these special rights can be either *in personam* (as in the rights of children against their parents) or *in rem* (as in the exclusive property rights established by labor) (*Private Property*, 108–9).

persons possess at all times as agents of God, or as the special right persons come to have on specific occasions of criminal (i.e., morally wrong) conduct by others. I choose the latter characterization both for its own appeal and because despotical rights (the rights of lords over slaves [II, 172]), which cannot reasonably be characterized as general rights,[58] seem to be simply the logical "endpoint" of executive rights. Parental rights (II, 58, 68, 170) may (as we will see in chapter 5) turn out to be (at least in part) just special rights of reciprocation (rights to a return of benefits, to a display of "gratitude" [II, 70]). Indeed, I have argued elsewhere that even *political* rights in Locke (the rights of governors over subjects[59]) perhaps may also be best understood as nonconsensual rights of reciprocation.[60] Finally, charity rights (I, 42) should be mentioned as an odd case, being the only special rights Locke recognizes that need not arise from anyone's voluntary acts. Need (the ground of these rights) may result simply from what *happens* to people, as opposed to what they or others *do*.

III. *Consensual Special Rights*: This last group includes the rights arising from voluntary transactions between persons. Locke argues that all conjugal rights (II, 78) belong in this class, as do political rights and (what I will call) civil rights (i.e., the rights granted to citizens by civil law—what Locke sometimes calls "the rights of the subject" [II, 136]). By economic rights, I mean rights to goods (*excluding* original appropriations of exclusive property, but *including* property acquired as payment, or by trade, sale, etc.[61]), rights to services (as the rights of masters over servants [II, 85], employers over employees), and so on.

All of the rights considered above are for Locke *moral* rights, for they all derive from the precepts of natural law. They do not derive their force from any legal or institutional recognition (so they are

---

[58] In one sense, of course, all special rights can be characterized as general, for example, as the general right to enjoy specific rights on particular occasions. So our despotical rights can be the "general" right of dominion we possess over those who happen to forfeit to us all their rights; our parental rights are our "general" rights of control (etc.) over any children we happen to have; our right of reciprocation is our "general" right to a return of any benefits we may happen to confer on others, and so on. The division I have suggested is, I think, both truer to Locke's intentions and more illuminating than trying to treat *all* rights as general in this way.

[59] What Locke calls political power (e.g., II, 6, 65, 171), the "rights of government" (II, 111), or the "right to obedience from their subjects" (I, 105).

[60] *Moral Principles and Political Obligations*, chapter 4.

[61] Gifts of property, of course, might be taken to fall in my class II, as might property rights acquired by inheritance (which I discuss in 4.4), since neither seems to require the consent of the recipient. But I take accepting a gift or bequest as both consensual and a necessary condition for the transfer of right in both cases.

not merely conventional or positive "moral" rights either). Even the civil rights we have as subjects in a political society derive from natural law, although the content of the rights (if not the binding force) may be specified by civil law. In Locke's early (1667) *An Essay Concerning Toleration*, he writes that while it is God's law that "forbids the vice, . . . the law of man often makes the measure of it"(ECT, 182–83). And elsewhere he says that "the rule and obligation is antecedent to human laws, though the matter about which the rule is, may be consequent to them."[62] Because the agreement that creates a commonwealth is morally binding, those rights granted subjects under civil law have the moral force of contractual rights under natural law, in spite of the fact that the *content* of civil rights may vary from society to society. Locke, firmly grounded in the natural law tradition, never talks, for instance, of "legal rights" without referring to the source of their moral backing. There are no legal or political rights in the "positivist" sense— institutional rights defined in terms of what the civil law guarantees protection to, independent of any moral evaluation of the laws or legal system. The only "real" rights are defined by natural law.

Are all rights in Locke, then, *natural rights*? This question would be easier to answer if the concept of "natural right" were clearer. To some, natural rights are those rights that all persons have qua persons, independent of their voluntary actions and special relationships.[63] Others reserve the term "human rights" for these rights or make "natural rights" and "human rights" synonymous.[64] On this perfectly intelligible conception of natural right, only our *general* moral rights are natural rights; we here contrast what is "natural" with what is "created." Of course it also makes perfectly good sense to identify as natural rights larger classes of our moral rights,[65] depending on the meaning one gives to the

[62] "Obligation of Penal Laws," 114. See also ELN, 189.
[63] Hart, "Are There Any Natural Rights?" 175; Wasserstrom, "Rights, Human Rights," 49–50.
[64] Claims of synonymy can be found, for example, in Wasserstrom, "Rights, Human Rights," 47n; and Finnis, *Natural Law*, 198. Just as common is the claim that human rights are those natural rights possessed by all and only human beings (as in Becker, *Property Rights*, 16). As we have seen (and will see further below), however, natural rights in Locke should not be understood as those rights possessed by all human beings; for there *are* no rights that all humans necessarily possess. Rights in Locke are possessed by *persons* (i.e., "men" in the *moral*, not the biological sense), not by human beings qua humans.
[65] For alternative definitions of natural right, see, for example, Plamenatz, *Consent, Freedom*, 84; Christman, "Can Ownership Be Justified?" 157–58; Lemos, "Con-

term "natural" (what one *contrasts* it with), producing a range of possible accounts such as this:

(1) *Natural versus "Created"*: Our natural rights are those rights we have that are not created by human action—that is, our general rights (plus charity rights?).

(2) *Natural versus "Interactional"*: Our natural rights are those not requiring interaction with others for their creation (our "atomic" rights—i.e., our general rights, property rights [perhaps charity rights and executive rights?]).

(3) *Natural versus "Conventional" (or "Artificial")*: Our natural rights are those requiring no conventions (here distinguished from deliberate agreements) for their binding force or content—that is, our general rights and some or all of our special rights (depending on which we take to involve conventional elements, with property and promissory rights as the best candidates for exclusion [a la Hume]).

(4) *Natural versus "Transactional"*: Our natural rights are those not requiring for their creation any deliberate transaction between persons—that is, our general and nonconsensual special rights.

(5) *Natural versus "Civil"*: Our natural rights are all those we could (logically) have prior to the creation of civil society—that is, all but our political and civil rights.

(6) *Natural versus "Institutional" (or "Nonmoral")*: Our natural rights are all those whose binding force is moral—that is, *all* of Locke's rights.

Which of these classes of rights we identify as natural rights seems very much a matter of the contrast we happen to wish to emphasize. And, of course, we can define natural rights in terms of several of these classes together. For instance, the account I will use in this work utilizes elements of classes 3, 5, and 6. I will count as a natural right any right that could be possessed independent of (logically prior to) civil society, whose binding force is nonconventional.[66] Rights are natural that have natural grounds and

cept of Natural Right"; Benn and Peters, *Social Principles*, 95–100; Sumner, "Rights Denaturalized," 22.

[66] Accounts of "natural right" that approximate the one I articulate here include Raphael, *Problems of Political Philosophy*, 103–6; Gibbard, "Natural Property Rights," 237; Lemos, "Locke's Theory of Property," 226–27.

could be possessed in the state of nature. A natural right could have conventional *elements* (i.e., determining its specific content, since conventions can arise in the state of nature), but could not have conventional *grounds*. Since Locke recognizes *no* conventional moral grounds of rights, I will count as natural rights in Locke those rights whose binding force derives from natural law and that are (logically, not historically) prepolitical (i.e., the intersection of classes 5 and 6).

Locke's own use of the term "natural right" is infrequent, and his intentions when he does use it are not altogether clear. The (few) uses in the *Second Treatise* (e.g., II, 1, 76, 82, 115) give us no guidance in formulating a view of Locke's intended meaning.[67] In I, 88, however, he usefully contrasts natural rights with "positive" rights, apparently meaning by "positive" rights those derived from consent. This strongly suggests our class 4 as Lockean natural rights.[68] However, three paragraphs later (I, 91) the contrast is between natural and "municipal" rights, suggesting our class 5 or 6. Of course, since the rights in class 4 are a proper subset of those in class 6, there is no real inconsistency. We could simply ascribe to Locke class 4 sympathies. Locke does, however, later seem to equate "positive" with "municipal," "civil," and "institutional" (e.g., I, 123, 126, 140; II, 12). So it seems plausible to maintain in the end that it is only *some* consensual rights (i.e., those granted by civil governments whose authority derives from consent) that Locke really wishes to regard as non-natural. A best guess from the textual evidence, then, seems to point to the intersection of our classes 5 and 6 as the class of Lockean natural rights. But another

[67] Locke also occasionally uses terms like "right of nature" (e.g., II, 65, 85) or "native right" (e.g., II, 176, 194, 220). Locke's use of "natural right" is actually more frequent in the *First Treatise* (e.g., I, 6, 11, 17, 50, 69, 88–89, 91, 98, 111, 126, 142, 147), but, as I argue below, Locke's uses of the term are seldom helpful in determining what meaning he gave it.

[68] It has been common since Locke, of course, to in this way characterize the class of natural rights as excluding contractual or consensual rights, since rights that are created by our voluntary transactions seem not to be appropriately "natural." See, for example, Ross, *Right and the Good*, 55–56; and Becker, *Property Rights*, 16. Indeed, Steiner takes it to be *trivially* true that natural rights are noncontractual ("Natural Right," 41). Similarly, it is common to read Locke as excluding consensual rights from the class of natural rights (see, e.g., Ashcraft, *Locke's Two Treatises*, 138–39; and Lemos, *Hobbes and Locke*, 75–76, 164). But there is no very good reason for thinking that the "natural" in someone's use of "natural right" must be understood as meaning "not arising from human actions" rather than "logically prepolitical" (i.e., possessable in our natural condition). And I argue below that there is in fact good reason to believe that if Locke had anything clearly in mind at all, he probably had in mind the latter meaning of "natural," not the former, when he used the term "natural right."

reason for accepting some consensual rights as natural in Locke (contrary to his apparent suggestion in I, 88), is that it is hard to believe he wishes to count as natural (e.g.) the right to inherit, but not promissory or consensual rights in the state of nature—especially when he says that "keeping of faith belongs to men as men, and not as members of society" (II, 14), and that promises and oaths are such basic grounds of obligation as to even "hold the Almighty" (II, 195). In any event, however prominently we employ the concept of natural right in explicating Locke's moral and political philosophy (and however accurate it may be to describe Locke as a natural rights theorist), Locke himself never really seemed particularly concerned with presenting or using any very precise notion of "natural right" in his work.

As we saw earlier, Locke also offers no definition of "right" generally, nor does he ever say clearly what a right is. We know that rights are "freedoms" of a sort, and that the central rights in Locke are the logical correlates of others' duties (and so are *protected* freedoms). We also know that Locke characterizes all rights (and not just rights in external goods) as property, that is, what is properly our own (e.g., II, 123, 173). This suggests the idea of a right as a kind of moral control or sovereignty over a particular area of our lives, defining a moral space within which we are free to operate. On balance, the account of rights which probably best fits the ways in which Locke talks about rights will utilize at its roots notions of "claim" and "entitlement"[69]: "all rights seem to merge *entitlements to* do, have, omit, or be something with *claims against* others to act or refrain from acting in certain ways. . . . We can say that all claim-rights necessarily involve both, though in individual cases the one element or the other may be in sharper focus."[70] By thus suggesting the importance of the idea of a right as a "freedom" or "claim" in Locke's theory, I do not intend to argue (as

[69] In *Education*, 111, Locke virtually equates rights with "claims" and "titles." See Tully's analysis of Lockean rights (and of rights in Suarez before Locke) as claims (*Discourse*, 67); and Becker's definition of right (*Property Rights*, 8).

[70] Feinberg, "Nature and Value of Rights," 91. Feinberg actually prefers the account of rights as "valid claims" (in which many, such as Wasserstrom, agree with him). He offers the idea of rights as conjunctions of claims and entitlements in response to McCloskey's insistence that rights are essentially *entitlements*, not claims at all (in "Rights"). Others who share this view of rights as entitlements include Nozick, Shapiro (*Evolution of Rights*, 14), and Finch ("Alternative"). Among those who follow Feinberg in the "conjunction" thesis are Young ("Dispensing with Moral Rights," 64) and Bandman ("Do Children Have Natural Rights?" 236–37).

many have done[71]) that Locke subscribes to (or is a precursor of) what is commonly referred to as the "choice theory" of rights (or the "will theory"). Choice theories claim that the point of rights is to protect the control or autonomy of the individual within an area of life; rightholders are those who may choose how they and others are to act. By contrast, the "benefit theory" of rights (or "interest theory") claims that the purpose of rights is to confer on individuals certain benefits (or to promote their interests); rightholders are the beneficiaries (or direct, intended beneficiaries; or justifiable beneficiaries) of others' duties.[72]

It is natural for benefit theories to accompany views on which moral duties are seen as basic or fundamental, with rights as derivative notions (concerning the beneficiaries of the duties); and on the opposed view, in which rights have priority, it is equally natural to embrace a choice theory of rights. I have tried to argue, of course, that Locke occupies neither extreme in this controversy, so we would expect him to unqualifiedly endorse neither a benefit nor a choice theory of rights. In fact (for reasons I will elaborate on in the next section), I think Locke is best thought of as holding that both choice and benefit are central to the idea of right. Thinking of rights as claims, I concede, does incline one toward a choice theory (since the claim is seen as somehow basic, "pulling" duties to the source of the claim). But (as we will see) the natural law roots of Locke's theory of rights makes it complex in ways that cannot be captured simply by taking rights as claims.

I would like to conclude this section by briefly commenting on some further properties of rights in Locke that are important to his arguments. Of the most important remaining properties of rights, two kinds come immediately to mind—the properties of rights with regard to loss and transfer of those rights, and the "weight" of rights in comparison with other kinds of considerations that bear on action. The status of Lockean rights in connection with loss and transfer I will deal with in chapter 3. As to the relative weight of rights, it is easy enough to assume that for Locke rights

[71] See, for instance, Finnis, *Natural Law*, 208; and Shapiro, *Evolution of Rights*, 105.
[72] The choice theory is most familiar in contemporary literature on rights from papers by Hart (e.g., "Are There Any Natural Rights?" and "Bentham on Legal Rights"). See also the papers by Feinberg cited in this chapter and Wellman, "Upholding Legal Rights." The benefit theory is classically associated with Bentham, and is defended more recently in various forms in Lyons, "Rights, Claimants"; Raz, *The Morality of Freedom*; MacCormick, "Rights in Legislation"; and in several works by Waldron. For general discussions of the two theories, see Nickel, *Making Sense of Human Rights*, 19–23; and Waldron, *Private Property*, 79–99.

are *absolute* in weight[73]—that is, that there are no conditions under which they can be justifiably infringed or overridden by competing considerations. Rights would then be "trumps" or "side-constraints" in the strongest possible sense, final moral claims on action. It is probably fair to say that Locke treats rights as *virtually* absolute, but he cannot plausibly be read as making them *entirely* absolute. For we have already seen one passage (II, 183) in which Locke discusses a conflict of rights, arguing that one of the rights is justifiably overridden by the other (which entails, of course, that the overridden right is *not* absolute).[74] And there are good reasons to suppose that the value of preserving peace in society may sometimes override individual rights to reparation for wrongs done (II, 176, 230).[75] Rights can still be trumps with respect to ordinary matters of utility gain or loss;[76] but extraordinary social costs or conflicts with competing rights may sometimes justify infringement. Not only is this Locke's view; it is the most persuasive view to take of the moral weight of rights.[77]

[73] For instance, Brandt writes that "the only rights [Locke] recognized at all were absolute rights, ones that could not be overridden (he thought) in any circumstances" (*Ethical Theory*, 442); this seems to be Taylor's view of Locke as well ("Atomism," 40). Locke does occasionally speak of some rights as "absolute" (although it is not entirely clear what "absolute" means in context)—as when he claims that "speculative opinions and divine worship . . . have an absolute and universal right to toleration" (ECT, 175–76).

[74] Many have noticed either that Lockean rights can conflict or that Lockean rights are not absolute. See, for example, Vlastos, "Justice and Equality," 37–38; den Hartogh, "Tully's Locke," 660; Dunn, "Justice," 82; Ryan, "Locke and the Dictatorship," 244–46; Richards, "Inalienable Rights," 403–4; Lemos, "Locke's Theory of Property," 227; Glenn, "Inalienable Rights," 98–99. Machan thinks that natural rights theory must reject the possibility of conflicts of rights (*Individuals and Their Rights*, 63–64), apparently because he believes that the choice between conflicting rights will be left "entirely arbitrary" (ibid., 197). But, of course, if different natural rights can have different weights or importance (as we have seen they do, for instance, in Locke), resolution of conflicts need not be arbitrary. Steiner is the foremost defender of the still stronger (and, I think, even less defensible) view that conflicts of rights are not possible ("Natural Right," 42; "Structure of a Set," 768–69; "Slavery," 247).

[75] Considerations of the common good "limit and alter the obligation even of some of the laws of God" (ECT, 183). See Dunn's passing remarks along these lines (*Political Thought*, 179n; "Consent," 32n).

[76] This is really all Dworkin intends in calling rights "trumps," as seems clear in *Taking Rights Seriously*, xi, 191–92, and in "Rights as Trumps." On the significance of this "trumping power" of rights, see Buchanan, "What's So Special about Rights?" 63–64.

[77] Even Nozick, strongly committed to the absoluteness of rights in *Anarchy, State, and Utopia*, seems to have softened his stance (*Philosophical Explanations*, 479); and Fried, who asserts that "every violation of a right is wrong," nonetheless allows that "extreme cases" may change matters (*Right and Wrong*, 108, 9–13). See Plamenatz, *Consent, Freedom*, 85, for a rejection of the absoluteness of certain rights.

2.4. The Significance of Natural Rights

We have seen the central role that rights play in Locke's moral theory. I will try now to articulate a simple model for understanding the shifting conceptual framework that permitted the idea of a natural right to emerge in the reasonably strong form we find in Locke. I can here add little to the recent careful studies of Locke's natural right predecessors and the changing meanings of *ius* and *dominium* in their hands.[78] My aim will be only to describe in quite general terms the moral viewpoint (the view of moral relation-

---

For defenses of the absoluteness of certain rights, see, for example, Feinberg, *Social Philosophy*, 86–88; Finnis, *Natural Law*, 225; Lemos, "Concept of a Natural Right," 142; Gewirth, "Are There Any Absolute Rights?"; Machan, *Individuals and Their Rights*, 202. A good general discussion of conflicts of rights and strategies for dealing with them can be found in Waldron, "Rights in Conflict."

The analysis of Lockean rights just completed allows us to be a bit more precise as well about Lockean moral requirements with respect to their grounds and the rights with which they correlate. It is common in recent moral and political philosophy for a distinction to be drawn between obligations and duties. Obligations are those moral requirements that are generated by some voluntary performance or forbearance by the one obligated (such as making a promise or entering into a cooperative undertaking with others). Duties, by contrast, are those moral requirements that bind all persons, regardless of their special performances or transactions (see Brandt, "Concepts of Obligation and Duty"; Rawls, *Theory of Justice*, §§ 18–19; Simmons, *Moral Principles and Political Obligations*, 11–15). From the classification of Lockean rights we have presented, however, it is obvious that Locke must acknowledge a third kind of moral requirement, not neatly describable as either an obligation or a duty (as these are commonly defined). The general rights (our class I) are clearly those rights that correlate with duties; our equal rights depend on no special performances, so neither do the moral requirements they entail. Similarly, consensual special rights (our class III) clearly correlate with obligations, being generated by the same kinds of special transactions. But our second class of rights, the nonconsensual special rights, seems harder to place in terms of correlative moral requirements. The "duties" that correlate with these rights seem to be based in special, but not necessarily voluntary, relations. For instance, the child's duties that correlate with parental rights are not grounded in any voluntary performance by the child (and so are not "obligations"); but neither are they duties possessed by all persons qua persons, and so are not "duties" in this sense (since the death of or abandonment of the child by parents dissolves some of the child's duties and maturity appparently dissolves others). The same is true of the duties correlating with rights of reciprocation (and a similar plausible case can be made for all of the other rights in this class with their correlative duties). We must remember, then, that in discussing moral requirements in Locke (and indeed, in discussing moral requirements generally), we must add a third kind of moral requirement ("special, nonvoluntary" requirements) to the more familiar categories of duties ("general, nonvoluntary" requirements) and obligations ("special, voluntary" requirements) (see my "Obligations of Citizens," 74–82). Duties and obligations, as these are commonly defined, do not exhaust the realm of moral requirements.

[78] See especially, Tuck, *Natural Rights Theories*; and Tully, *Discourse*.

ships) into which fit the Lockean conceptions of the duties and
rights of persons.

It has until recently been almost obligatory to begin discussions
of natural rights theory with the observation that the concept of a
natural right is primarily a modern concept. One can point to the
concept's conspicuous absence in Greek and Roman thought and
to the many and prominent later theories of natural law that seem
to operate with no corresponding notion of natural right—for instance, the theory of Aquinas.[79] We now know, of course, that natural rights theories (at least in rudimentary form) were developed
rather earlier than this conventional wisdom suggested. Richard
Tuck argues, for instance, that as early as the twelfth century, and
certainly by the fourteenth, "it was possible to argue that to have
a right was to be the lord or 'dominus' of one's relevant moral
world, to possess 'dominium', that is to say, property."[80] In Jean
Gerson's work, Tuck shows, *ius* was already conceived of as an
ability (*facultas*) or power, and liberty as a kind of *dominium*.[81] Such
early rights theories were largely ignored during the Renaissance,
but were revived in the 1580s,[82] finally developing through the
work of Molina, Suarez, and Grotius into the form of natural rights
theory that most directly influenced Locke.

A great deal, then, went on both before Aquinas and between
Aquinas and Locke. But the natural law theories of Aquinas and
Locke stand out as high water marks in the shifting tides of theory,
making it interesting to ask this question: What in their respective
views of our moral position allows rights to play so much more
central a role in Locke than in Aquinas? Any adequate answer, of
course, must emphasize the role of God in moral relations, God
being at the center of the moral landscape for both philosophers. I
want to begin (following Feinberg[83]) by presenting two pictures of
our moral condition in the bluntest possible terms. I suggest neither that these were the respective views of Aquinas and Locke
nor that either picture was ever embraced by anyone in so unso-

[79] Aquinas does arrive at a conception of human equality (for instance, in his
discussions of slavery) that cries out for the development of a theory of natural
rights. But nothing in his texts suggests that he had in mind anything like the
modern concept of natural right. See Tuck, *Natural Rights Theories*, 18–20.

[80] Tuck, *Natural Rights Theories*, 3. Finnis locates the "watershed" in which *ius*
comes to have its modern meaning "somewhere between" Aquinas and Suarez
(*Natural Law*, 206–7).

[81] Tuck, *Natural Rights Theories*, 26–27.

[82] Ibid., 50.

[83] "Nature and Value of Rights," 82–83.

phisticated a form. Indeed, the differences between the pictures are largely a matter of emphasis. But this contrast in emphasis is helpful, I think, in understanding the moral fence Locke straddles.

(a) *The First Picture*: God occupies the center of this picture in the fullest possible sense. His creation of the universe and His plan for humankind allow Him to give binding law to us. Our moral duties are owed to God, as creator, moral lawgiver, and sovereign. Importantly, God stands at the center of all moral relations, as a kind of intermediary. Each of us has duties not to harm others, but these duties are owed to God. The benefits others receive as a consequence of our performance of our duties are in part the point of these duties. But other persons exert no direct "ethical pull" on us. Others are to be respected not so much for themselves, but for their status as God's property and parts of His plan. Our moral status is thus largely that of a tool, a cog, a part of some larger enterprise, and the appropriate virtues for such a being are obedience, humility, and industry. Another's property, of course, merits a kind of respect that is rather thin. When I break your shovel (even if it is quite a wonderful shovel), I wrong you, not the shovel. Similarly, breaches of our moral duties to treat others well are in the first instance wrongs done to God, and only derivatively wrongs done to others. This sort of "moral occasionalism" permits me to argue that "to God only have I sinned" even when I have harmed other persons.[84]

Where do rights enter this picture? God has rights of a sort, of course, over His property, although it is in a way demeaning to God to conceive of these as rights, exactly—as if they were mere claims held against others. The more appropriate emphasis is on our duties of obedience and worship. And we can perhaps also have rights, as third party beneficiaries of duties owed to God (according to certain theories of rights[85]). These rights would, of course, belong to the class of "protected liberties," for the moral freedom to act would be protected by others' duties owed to God. But there is in this picture no room for claim rights of the sort we have discussed, involving pressable (and waivable) claims against those bound by the corresponding duties. Against whom could

---

[84] Ibid. For the related conception of a *sovereign* monopoly on rights, see the *Vindiciae Contra Tyrannos*.

[85] Because other persons are the direct, intended beneficiaries of our duties owed to God, others would appear to count as rightholders in this picture, provided we subscribe to a view (following Bentham) like Lyons' "Qualified Beneficiary Theory" of rights ("Rights, Claimants," 63–64). See Hart's reply in *Essays on Bentham*, especially 187–88.

such claims be pressed? Presumably it would be both unwise and conceptually odd to press claims against the God to whom others' duties are due.[86] For several reasons, then, in this first picture right-talk is naturally suppressed.

(b) *The Second Picture*: God is still central in this picture, although He is not at the center of all moral relations in the same way.[87] While God is still creator, planner, and lawgiver, the ends promoted by God's law are now seen as "detachable," so that the law is now more *for* us and less *over* us. The law's facilitation of humans' own ends is in this picture as prominent as its facilitation of God's ends.[88] Our fellow persons are not now seen just as God's creatures but as our equals in other ways; their rationality, purposiveness, and manifest similarities to ourselves require that they be taken seriously in themselves. Moral relations hold directly between persons as well as between persons and God, as others exert a "pull" on us. Breaking God's law can involve wronging others directly, so that we have duties that are *owed* to others, not just duties *with respect* to others (the other is not just the "occasion" of the wrong, but the one actually wronged). The deeper equality this signals both requires a different order of respect and makes different virtues appropriate for us. Self-assertion can now be based on a conception of one's independent worth, on the dignity of being "one's own person " (which brings with it, of course, new stances with regard to consent, obligation, obedience, and resistance).

In this second picture, rights naturally move into sharper focus, along with making and pressing claims concerning one's *due*. "Duty," of course, had to do precisely with what was "due" another, typically by virtue of superior status.[89] The claim of status "pulls" duties to it. In the first picture, God's is the relevant moral

---

[86] As Locke writes, "if God afford [men] a temporary mortal life, it is his gift; they owe it to his bounty; they could not claim it as their right, nor does he injure them when he takes it from them" (R, 5 [6]). I return later (2.5) to the more general question of whether or not the activity of "claiming" or "demanding" could intelligibly go on in the absence of rights. In this context (where God would be the party against whom claims would have to be pressed), it seems clear that these activities lose their force.

[87] "In the great [natural law] treatises of the seventeenth and eighteenth centuries . . . God is increasingly withdrawn from immediate contact with men" (D'Entreves, *Natural Law*, 55).

[88] We must now think of the law "as rules placed at the disposal of individuals and regulating the extent to which *they* may demand certain behavior from others" (Hart, "Are There Any Natural Rights?" 182).

[89] See Feinberg's discussion of "duties of status" in "Duties, Rights, and Claims," 140–41.

status to which our duties are pulled, but the "rights" of one who is omnipotent need no special emphasis. In the second picture, every person enjoys a status that is also the ground of a "due"; but emphasis on our rights is not at all pointless. Duty's primacy in the first picture stems from the gross inequality of the parties concerned (God and humankind). Once the relevant parties are conceived of as equals, rights take a more prominent place.

The two pictures just described, while no better than caricatures of any philosopher's actual views, do capture, I think, a shift in thinking about moral relations that was still taking place when Locke wrote. This shift corresponded, of course, to more obvious changes in economic and social organization and to changes in more inclusive theological and political theories (on which I shall not comment here). My intention in presenting these pictures is only to try to better locate the character of Locke's theory of rights. By contrast with the conceptual scheme for Aquinas' natural law theory, which inclines toward the first picture, Locke's moral-conceptual framework seems to be an attempt to embrace both pictures at once. It is hardly surprising that Locke, who lived "in a 'transitional' society,"[90] should employ a conceptual scheme which is also transitional. Locke works with both pictures, or, better, with a kind of synthesis of the two, emphasizing the chief characteristics now of one and now of the other (as his rhetorical, political, and theoretical concerns dictate), trying always to leave room for both. Locke stands near a crossroads. On the one hand, he emphasizes God's rights—His right of creation, His right to our obedience to His law (E, 2.28.8). But Locke also stresses our rights, for reason and its law is what "God hath given to be the rule *betwixt man and man*" (II, 172; my emphasis; see also II, 181). Strong elements of both pictures are thus prominently displayed in Locke's work.[91]

Is it theoretically coherent for Locke to work within both pictures at once? It is easy to see why one might think not, and why this judgment might lead one to dismiss those aspects of Locke's work that emphasize one or the other picture. If we focus on the centrality of rights in Locke, the person-to-person character of moral relations, and the secular arguments he offers, we can plainly see where Hobbesian and libertarian readings of Locke find

[90] Dunn, *Political Thought*, 212. See also Macpherson, *Possessive Individualism*, 220, 248, 269–70; and Wood, *Politics*, 15.
[91] Dunn notes this "dual structure" of moral relations in Locke, although only in passing (*Political Thought*, 108n).

their support, and whence come their claims for the priority of right. And it is just as easy to focus on those aspects of Locke more amenable to the first picture—the centrality of God, His rights over us, and the theological foundational arguments—and offer as a consequence a reading of Locke that bends too far in its avoidance of his more individualistic moments. Much of the recent history of Locke scholarship revolves around turning a blind eye to one or the other aspect of Locke's thought.

But we save Locke from no very terrible fate when we insist that he work entirely within one picture or the other. For there is no obvious incoherence involved in combining the two views. It is perfectly intelligible for our moral duties to be owed both to God and to other people, and for both God and people to be holders of correlative moral rights. We owe God obedience to His law because He is our creator and rightly superior lawmaker. We owe duties to others because of our natural equality as rational, purposive beings. There is only a kind of "moral overdetermination" in this view, but no conceptual incoherence. The grounds of the rights and duties are different in the two cases, with only their content being the same. To see that this amounts to no incoherence in other kinds of cases, consider: if I promise the concerned best friend of my invalid mother that I will care for my mother, I may have an obligation to do so that is owed to both my mother (because of my moral debt to my parents) and her friend (because of my promise). Both hold rights against me. (Note that my mother's right is *not* merely the right of a third party beneficiary, but a claim right based on [say] benefits she gave to me in the past.) The *content* of the obligations owed to each will be the same, but the *grounds* will be different. Either source of obligation would, as in Locke's moral theory, be sufficient for the moral relation. Such overdetermination is a common feature of Locke's moral and political philosophy.

·But Locke seems sensitive to the need to pull his disparate lines of thought together. His emphasis on God's ownership of and interest in humankind as a whole points to the importance of the common good and to the collectivist, communitarian aspects of Locke's thought (the irresistible teleological pull of natural law theory). His emphasis on the natural equality, freedom, and purposiveness of persons points to the sanctity of each person's life and plans and to the individualist, libertarian aspects of his thought. But his Kantian and rule-consequentialist arguments constitute a way of pulling the two lines together in what really amounts to a pluralist moral theory. The teleological and deontological aspects of Locke's thought sit coherently together. Locke recognizes both collective and individual goods, acknowledging that rights (and individual goods generally) are not all there is to morality.

The "overdetermination" and pluralism in Locke's moral-conceptual scheme can be seen nowhere more clearly than in his theory of property (to which I will only gesture here, reserving more careful consideration for chapter 5). It is easy to find support in Locke for a negative libertarian, accumulative conception of property in external goods; or we can stress instead, against such views, the social character of property in Locke, God's command that we labor, and so on. But to suppose that one or the other of these views must miss completely Locke's point is to ignore the ways in which Locke blends these views together. God commands us to labor; industry is our duty and "calling." We have as well our own private plans and our own (albeit limited) sovereignty. But when we pursue our own plans, our industry in fact does God's will as well. The "two lines" must be seen to move forward together as one line in Locke, however tempting it may be to generalize one aspect of Locke's position and pass it off as his real view about rights (property).

Similarly, Locke's view of the property we possess in ourselves illustrates the balancing, pluralistic approach Locke employs. On the one hand, as we have seen, each person is God's creation, His property, with whom God can do as He pleases. On the other, of course, Locke wishes to stress that "every man has a property in his own person. This nobody has any right to but himself" (II, 27). It is at least partly on the basis of this property in ourselves that exclusive rights in external goods are said to be possible. The first position, viewed in isolation, seems to leave inadequate room for our own plans and ends. But the second, by (apparently) giving us absolute sovereignty in the personal realm, might seem to leave too much room for, example, voluntary suicide, self-enslavement, or submission to arbitrary government. If I can do as I wish with myself, one thing I can do is give myself away.[92] Locke is clearly attracted by elements of both positions but the whole of neither, and he works, as it were, from both ends to the middle—our personal sovereignty is important but limited; and, for that reason, the power over another that we can rightfully exercise is also lim-

[92] As Tuck shows, it was on this kind of reasoning that most early natural rights theories based their defenses of slavery and absolutism (*Natural Rights Theories*, 49–57).

ited. If we think of our property in ourselves as a kind of trust from God (as I argue in chapter 5 that Locke did), it is easy to see the nature of this limit. For trusts typically allow discretion within terms, providing both freedom and duty (although in this case, the trustee and the beneficiary with whose interests the trustee is concerned are precisely the same person).[93]

The point is this: Locke's arguments proceed from many different starting points (both secular and theological), and his main burden is often that of rendering disparate lines of thought compatible, by compromise or by (coherent) overdetermination. From the resulting Lockean morass, it is tempting to pull single threads and pass them off as Locke's argument, particularly when Locke's philosophical or political purposes require him to give special emphasis to one line or another. But to do so is to ignore the complexity of Locke's work. Locke is not Hobbes in disguise, or an "entitlement theorist"; neither is he the champion of majority rule, a simple throwback to traditional natural law theory, or an ardent defender of the commons. Rights in Locke are neither the mere shadows of duties under the law, nor property over which we have absolute control. If we must identify Locke's "true stance," I have tried to argue, it is almost certainly on some middle ground between these extremes.[94] The remainder of this work will, I hope, lend further support to this thesis.

2.5. Natural Right Skepticism

In subsequent chapters I will proceed as if assertions of natural right at least make sense, assessing the plausibility of claims for particular rights from inside the natural rights camp. Since I offer only hints and sketches of what the foundations of a defensible

[93] The nature of this "compromise" can also be seen in the objects of our duties for Locke. A secular, libertarian emphasis on absolute personal sovereignty leads naturally not only to a rejection of paternalism, but also to a rejection of self-regarding duties (i.e., duties to do what is best for oneself—e.g., self-preservation, moderation, self-improvement or perfection, and so on). For it is hard to see to whom such duties could be owed. The Kantian answer, of course, is that such duties are owed to *oneself*, or rather, to the rational nature in oneself, which demands the same respect as the rational nature in others. This position permits a secular ground for self-regarding duties. Locke, in accepting self-regarding duties (1.5), often seems sympathetic to these Kantian points; but at least as often he seems to have in mind that self-regarding duties are owed directly to God (as are our purely religious duties). On this question again Locke is working within both pictures at once.

[94] See Rapaczynski, *Nature and Politics*, 202.

natural rights theory would look like, the reader is owed at least an effort to show that natural right talk is not utterly confused or incoherent. For that reason, I will in this section provide brief responses (or at least indications of appropriate strategies of response) to the most familiar and potent forms of natural right skepticism (although I make no effort here to deal with forms of general *moral* skepticism, such as relativism or strong noncognitivism). Those who find this approach inadequate can, of course, read the rest of this work primarily as a commentary on Locke. But there are, I think, reasons to reconsider the longstanding (and recently much amplified) prejudices within philosophy against theories that refer to a "natural law" or to "natural rights."

Natural law theory has been rejected by many, of course, because they reject the theological commitments that seem necessary to make natural law a "real law"; unless natural law is laid down by God, the argument goes, it cannot be a real law at all, and so cannot define real duties or rights. But this view is doubly mistaken. For, in the first place, it assumes that the concept of "law" possesses a simplicity and clarity that it in fact lacks. Not only authoritative commands, but a wide range of patterns, practices, rules, and principles are properly called laws, whether imposed by others, by self, by reason, or by nature. It is thus not necessarily confused to call valid principles about duties and rights "laws," even if these principles are not taken to be the commands of God (or the law of the land). And, in the second place, many theorists we identify as natural law theorists have in fact not made the theological commitments in question.

Indeed, the "common core" of natural law doctrine seems to amount to little more than this: that there are universally binding ("objectively valid") moral rules, knowable by use of our natural faculties, which may be appealed to to evaluate and criticize "human institutions, rules, and actions."[95] Natural law theory, in this sense, implies some form of value objectivism—a position that is controversial enough, of course, but one that is still well within the mainstream of active theoretical debate. Secular natural law theory, then, is a perfectly intelligible enterprise,[96] and one that can be pursued not only by Aristotelians, but by Kantians, by some kinds of utilitarians, and by other value objectivists. And if the rules or principles of such a natural law theory specify duties

[95] Frankena, "On Defining," 209; Oppenheim, "Metaphysics," 241.
[96] Contrary to the claims of many (e.g., Ryan, "Utility and Ownership," 180).

owed to others (such that these others are wronged by noncompliance), those rules define natural rights as well as natural duties (natural rights being simply the logical correlates of such duties). Locke's natural law theory, as we have seen, is based in a commitment to God's role as lawgiver and creator. But a defense of natural rights theory (and even of a Lockean theory) can proceed (as many of Locke's own arguments for natural rights *do* proceed) independent of such commitments. With this in mind, I proceed now to discuss in more detail some familiar sources of natural right skepticism.[97]

(a) *The "naturalness" of rights*: According to some skeptics, calling a right "natural" requires committing oneself to metaphysical or epistemological positions that are hopelessly backward or confused.[98] Charles Taylor, for instance, associates natural rights with the idea of "an extensionless subject, epistemologically a *tabula rasa*."[99] It is hard to assess the complaint at this level of generality, particularly given how "ambiguous and equivocal" the word "natural" is in such contexts (as Hume reminded us[100]). We have seen (in 2.3) some of the many attributes to which "natural" may be contrasted in calling rights "natural." The only salient meaning "natural" seems to have for Locke in connection with rights (as we also saw in 2.3) is "nonconventional" or "logically nonpolitical." If this is what a natural right is, the defender of natural rights is not obviously committed to any more than the existence of objective (not essentially conventional) moral rules defining rights (although the *content* of these rights might be conventionally determined). The standard (but not only) epistemological and metaphysical positions accompanying these views are admittedly *realist* in character (although what counts as moral realism is almost as controversial as whether moral realism is defensible).[101] But since

[97] For a critique of other and related sources of natural right skepticism, see Raphael, *Problems of Political Philosophy*, 105–6.

[98] MacDonald's well-known discussion of natural rights prominently advances this kind of charge ("Natural Rights"). Feinberg discusses "human rights" instead of "natural rights" precisely to avoid such problems (*Social Philosophy*, 85).

[99] "Atomism," 60.

[100] *A Treatise of Human Nature*, 3.1.2.

[101] Sumner is right, I think, in seeing realism as central to most natural rights theories ("Rights Denaturalized," 22, 26). His critique of natural rights theories is flawed, however, by his use against them of their alleged commitment to a view of rights as "morally basic" (22–25). Since Locke's theory, as we have seen, is a "mixed theory" (in Sumner's terminology) in which rights are *not* basic (as are many other natural right theories, both classical and contemporary), those central aspects of Sumner's argument that turn on this attribution will hold only against a limited class of natural rights theories (and not against these theories as such). Lou-

moral realism and objectivism are clearly still live issues in moral philosophy,[102] neither of these commitments for the natural rights theorist is obviously damning. The defender of natural rights need not embrace intuitionism, "odd properties," or any other "hopeless" positions.

Locke, of course, also uses "natural" (in connection with the natural law that defines natural rights) to mean that the thing in question can be "perceived by use of our natural faculties" and that it is "in accordance with man's nature" (1.1, especially note 3). The first of these meanings is already implicit in the commitments noted above, but the second is the basis for some of the most familiar criticisms of natural rights theories.[103] Natural rights must be derived from or somehow turn on facts about human nature, the argument goes. But (1) one cannot simply read off moral facts from natural facts in this way;[104] (2) there *is* no fixed "human nature" to appeal to in such arguments; and (3) any moral theory derived in this way would be either too abstract or too inflexible to be relevant to the many different social and economic contexts to which moral concepts ought to be applicable.

We have seen, however, that (1) Locke makes no real effort to simply "read off" his natural morality from facts about human nature (1.4) (nor does the related Kantian position we outlined). His argument concerns not what is "natural" for humankind in this simple sense, but rather what is *rational*. To the extent that his derivation of natural rights relies upon facts about human nature, it relies only upon relatively uncontroversial and extremely general claims (about, e.g., rationality, desire for self-preservation, moderate sociableness, etc.). Further, (2) possession of rights for Locke

---

den's critique ("Rights Infatuation") is another (identically flawed) entry in the growing (and, in my view, misguided) literature that attacks natural rights theories as if they all take rights to be morally basic or primary (and are feebly and unsuccessfully trying to derive duties, virtues, and all other moral categories from rights).

[102] See the essays in Copp and Zimmerman, *Morality, Reason and Truth*; Sayre-McCord, *Essays on Moral Realism*; and Gillespie, *Moral Realism*.

[103] See, for example, MacDonald, "Natural Rights," 27–31; Sumner, "Rights Denaturalized," 38–39; Ingram, "Natural Rights," 6–12; Olafson, "Essence and Concept," 235–37; Freeden, "Human Rights and Welfare," 500. Waldron discusses and replies to some similar criticisms (leveled by Hegel and Marx) in *Nonsense upon Stilts*, 166–74.

[104] The problem here is not just that of deriving "ought" from "is," although Machan, for one, takes worries about the naturalistic fallacy to be the primary source of natural right skepticism (*Individuals and Their Rights*, 183–86). I do not here address these worries, since I aim only at defending natural rights theory from charges that it is a nonstarter, and legitimate philosophical debate about the coherence of ethical naturalism has clearly not yielded a decisive verdict on the subject.

(and on the Kantian reconstruction as well) turns not on the possession of "essentially" *human* traits, but on the capacity for *moral agency*, which is not logically tied to a particular conception of human nature. Finally, (3) the view that the "eternal, immutable" character of natural law (and rights) makes it obviously unacceptable given the widely different kinds of people and societies to which it is supposed to apply, ignores several points. First, of course, it ignores the extent to which Locke's reasoning is based on what may reasonably be perceived as elemental, enduring features of the human condition that do in fact unite cultures and economies that are otherwise quite diverse.[105] But second, it ignores Locke's view that the *content* of natural law and rights may be, at least in part, determined by specific human rules, conventions, and ways of life (2.3). Morality sanctions rules that are "suited to the interest and welfare" of particular societies, however much this may seem "to limit and alter the obligation even of some of the laws of God, and change the nature of vice and virtue" (ECT, 183). Similarly, Kantian arguments that require respect and forbid using others as means can acknowledge that what *counts* as respecting and using others may vary in certain regards (with varying customs and expectations) from place to place and time to time.[106]

(b) *Rights as products of (eliminable) class conflict*: The above critique of natural rights for their (supposedly) "static" character naturally leads one to the fuller Marxist assault on liberal rights theory. (I here treat Marx's arguments as applying only to *rights*, leaving aside his occasional suggestions that *all morality*, and not just bourgeois morality, being a product of class conflict, is ultimately dispensable.) The outlines of the argument are familiar. The "rights of man," according to Marx,[107] are really only the rights of the bourgeoisie, the interests of the ruling class, selfishly and deceptively portrayed as eternal law. There is nothing natural about natural rights. Rights presuppose the egoism and alienation of humankind, are necessitated by the conflict between people that is "natural" only to certain stages of socioeconomic history. When class conflict is overcome, so will be the need for rights. Natural rights are a tool for class domination, designed (albeit perhaps unconsciously) to preserve the status quo in the unequal division of

---

[105] Waldron, *Nonsense upon Stilts*, 169–74.

[106] See, for instance, Lomasky, *Persons, Rights*, chapters 4–5.

[107] I draw for this (truncated) account primarily on Marx's *On the Jewish Question, Critique of the Gotha Program*, and *The Communist Manifesto*.

power and property, to allow those who have most to keep it, un-fettered by the desires and needs of others.[108]

The soundest Lockean response to Marx would, I think, attack his apparent reduction of all conflict to class conflict. Supposing that rights only have a point where interpersonal conflict is possi-ble, it is a mistake to think that *any* form of economic life could eliminate this point, even a form in which scarcity is not a problem (as Marx, not very convincingly, supposes will be the case in the last stage of communism). This is not to argue that egoism and social irresponsibility are ineliminable features of human life, but only that the need for certain kinds of security may well be. "The sorts of interpersonal conflicts which rights-principles are or can be invoked to cope with do not presuppose egoism or class con-flict, but merely conflicting preferences and the need to coordinate social activity in an efficient way."[109]

(c) The institutional character of rights: Bentham's skepticism about natural rights, while admittedly sharing certain superficial features with that of Marx,[110] attacks rights theories from a quite different direction. Again, the arguments are well known.[111] One promi-nent part of Bentham's attack is his charge that natural rights the-ories are dangerous or "mischievous." They encourage anarchy, subversion of government, chaos, and license; when used in polit-ical argument, they either cause great controversy or merely serve as an excuse to substitute wickedness and caprice for argument.[112] This portion of the attack, however, is either not a *philosophical* concern (since the uses bad people make of a true theory do not reflect on the theory's merits[113]) or rests importantly on the sound-ness of Bentham's *other* arguments (if natural right talk is simple nonsense or eliminable without loss, for instance, then its mischie-vousness *is* a good reason for doing away with it). Bentham is also

---

[108] Waldron argues that Marx is not really hostile to rights as such, but only to the "atomistic rights of man" (*Nonsense upon Stilts*, 129–36). For an opposed inter-pretation, on which Marx rejects all rights as products of class conflict, see Bu-chanan, *Marx and Justice*, especially 50–85.

[109] Buchanan, "What's So Special about Rights?" 62. The full presentation of the argument is in *Marx and Justice*. For a defense of rights against the charge that they are essentially egoistic, see Waldron, *Nonsense upon Stilts*, 190–209.

[110] Waldron, *Nonsense upon Stilts*, 3.

[111] Here I draw primarily upon Bentham's *Anarchical Fallacies*, *Pannomial Frag-ments*, and *Of Laws in General*.

[112] See, for example, Harrison, *Bentham*, 77–79; Waldron, *Nonsense upon Stilts*, 40–44; Hart, "Natural Rights," 82–83, and "Utilitarianism," 186. I draw on these same works below.

[113] Plamenatz, *Consent, Freedom*, 99–100.

frequently credited with the view that rights, being wholly derivable from duties, are eliminable and hence superfluous moral concepts. I address this claim in (e) below.

The centerpiece of Bentham's attack on natural rights, however,
is the charge that they (like natural laws) are fictitious entities and
talk about them is so much nonsense. This is, in part, a positivistic
insistence that if rights-claims cannot be tied to something concrete and thus made verifiable, they are not defensible. Laws and
sanctions, for instance, are real, concrete entities; but they require
legislators, enforcement mechanisms, and complex institutions.
Lacking this grounding, *natural* rights are nonsense (although, of
course, natural law theorists typically thought they *could* tie the
rights they defended to a real [albeit divine] lawgiver and real
sanctions). More precisely, all rights are fictions for Bentham, including legal rights. But legal rights can be subjected to an analysis
that ends in real entities (since laws are real, and the primary fictions—legal duties—can be analyzed in terms of law; and the secondary fictions—legal rights—can be analyzed in terms of duty).
The analysis of natural rights ends only in natural law, which is
also a fiction, having no real effect on the world.[114] The only "real"
(i.e., grounded) rights, then, are legal rights.

Bentham's position cannot really be quite so simple as this,
however. For, in the first place, Bentham allows that the duties
defined by a society's conventional morality (and enforced by social sanctions) are not nonsensical. Since he allows moral duties of
this sort, he is committed to allowing conventional moral rights as
well.[115] Rights, then, require not so much formal institutional definition as concrete social recognition. But second, and more important, Bentham also seems to accept *nonconventional* moral duties—those grounded in the principle of utility—which are not
analyzable in terms of sanctions or even concrete social recognition. It is thus not clear why Bentham is not also obliged to recognize moral rights that are based not in actual social institutions
or practices but in a conception of *justifiable* or *ideal* practices (a la
Mill).[116] And this, of course, is perilously close to what natural
rights theorists have wanted.[117]

[114] Harrison, *Bentham*, 80–86.

[115] Hart, *Essays on Bentham*, 84–85; Sumner, "Rights Denaturalized," 28–29.

[116] Hart, *Essays on Bentham*, 85–90; Waldron, *Nonsense upon Stilts*, 37–38.

[117] Because the "need for security" is a need that is present in all societies, on
Mill's view, the utilitarian derivation of rights he offers in chapter 5 of *Utilitarianism*
is virtually a defense of *natural* rights. See Oppenheim, "Metaphysics," 245.

The real question for Bentham seems to be just this: how can we defend the existence of moral rules (defining rights) independent of their concrete grounding in some form of social recognition? Bentham, for the most part, seems to simply assume that this is impossible. Moral rules would, for him, have to be like legal rules in order to be respectable entities; because they manifestly are not like this, they are discarded.[118] But this, of course, simply begs the question at issue, and can in no way be regarded as a refutation of natural rights theory. It is precisely because natural rights concern what *ought* to be the case, how people *should* be treated, that attempts to portray them as confused or silly accounts of what societies in fact recognize must themselves be admitted to be confused.[119]

(d) The social character of rights: The way of characterizing Bentham's concerns that I presented above suggests different (and more Hegelian or Aristotelian) approaches to the charge that traditionally recognized natural rights are flawed by virtue of their distance from concrete social recognition. In a way, it is Bentham's position as liberal reformer, embracing a critical moral standard (the principle of utility) that is *not* "socially instantiated," that ultimately undermines his own attack on natural rights. Conservative theorists, who acknowledge no such critical moral standards, avoid Bentham's difficulty (although their conservatism can, of course, still involve defending precisely those practices and institutions that have often been thought to be justified by appeals to natural rights[120]). T. H. Green, for instance, allows that persons have "natural rights" in a sense, but only as members of some (not necessarily political) community. His conservatism flows naturally from the view that a kind of shared social consciousness and mu-

---

[118] This same style of argument, in a more sophisticated form, is still being used against natural rights theories. See Sumner, "Rights Denaturalized," 30–33.

[119] Harrison, *Bentham*, 99–104. In light of the recent popularity of Alasdair MacIntyre's *After Virtue*, it is worth mentioning here that a significant part of MacIntyre's attack on natural rights has very much the sound of Bentham's critique. Like Bentham, MacIntyre dismisses natural rights as "fictions" (*After Virtue*, 67). He argues as well that rights require "the existence of particular types of social institution or practice," that without these institutions, making claims will not be an "intelligible" activity that will have any social effect (although their different metaphors reveal one difference in their views—where Bentham compares natural rights to counterfeit currency, MacIntyre compares them to checks in a society lacking the institution of money [ibid., 65]). In part, MacIntyre's case here begs the same questions as did Bentham's; but it rests as well on a different kind of foundation (to which I turn now).

[120] As in what Rorty calls "postmodernist bourgeois liberalism" ("Postmodernist").

CHAPTER TWO

tual recognition of right are necessary for the generation of rights (although a political association; with a legal system, is not).[121] Related positions have recently reemerged in the writings of many contemporary communitarian critics of liberalism (and of the concepts liberalism employs), such as MacIntyre, Taylor, and Sandel.[122] As suggested above, in some cases these views seem to rest on little more than straightforwardly question-begging assumptions: for example, that it makes no sense to talk of rights independent of the social effects of positive recognition of those rights.[123] But clearly many (especially recent) arguments on these lines cut rather deeper.

In one sense these arguments revive the critique from "human nature" we considered in (a) above. There is no "nature of man," the arguments go, independent of all aspects of social determination. "To be a man is to fill a set of roles each of which has its own point and purpose: member of a family, citizen, soldier, philosopher, servant of God."[124] The person (self, man) is not somehow *prior* to these essentially social roles; we are (in part) *constituted* by our playing these roles. It is only "as members of this family or community or nation or people, as bearers of this history, as sons and daughters of that revolution, as citizens of this republic" that we can understand the persons we are.[125] We are selves partly "encumbered" by the aims, beliefs, conceptions of the good that are given in the relations we have with others in society. Such

[121] *Lectures on the Principles of Political Obligation*, paragraphs 138–41. See also the similar views of Bosanquet (*The Philosophical Theory of the State*) and Laski (*A Grammar of Politics*). I confess that at times Green seems to me to be advancing a position that Locke could easily accept, although the general thrust of Green's argument is clearly quite different—for him, a Lockean right is only a "right potentially, which becomes actual through the recognition . . . by a society, and through the power which society in consequence secures to the individual" (paragraph 151). Plamenatz agrees with Green that there are only rights in societies, but he forcefully denies Green's claim that these rights depend for their validity on social recognition (*Consent, Freedom*, 86–87, 90–97). See also Ross' well-known critique of Green's view (*Right and the Good*, 50–52).
[122] For selections from their work and from that of other recent critics of liberalism, see Sandel, *Liberalism and Its Critics*. Traditional conservatives—for example, Burke and more recently, Oakeshott—defend similar criticisms in rather different ways.
[123] Benn and Peters, *Social Principles*, 97. See also Anscombe, "On the Source," 13–14; and Bandman, "Do Children Have Natural Rights?" 244.
[124] MacIntyre, *After Virtue*, 56. Elsewhere MacIntyre writes: "The rational justification of my political duties, obligations and loyalties is that, were I to divest myself of them by ignoring or flouting them, I should be divesting myself of a part of myself, I should be losing a crucial part of my identity" ("Philosophy and Politics," 158).
[125] Sandel, *Liberalism and the Limits*, 179.

110

claims seem to bind the otherwise different contemporary criticisms of natural rights together.[126]

But are these claims a problem for the natural rights theorist? Locke, after all, acknowledges the indispensability of the family and society in helping the individual to develop and mature.[127] As we have seen, Locke's persons are naturally "driven" into society and will clearly be "partly constituted" by their social relations; indeed, it is hard to see just who would want to deny this view of humankind.[128] But Lockean persons still seem able to be bearers of natural rights. Is the problem that (a la Sandel) accepting this, Locke can no longer defend the priority of the right over the good, since he can no longer appeal to an individual who is a bearer of rights without being equally a bearer of "goods"? We cannot derive rights first from the "real" person, then worry about the good later, as if the good were an object of perfectly free choice for conceptually prior rightbearers. Our selves are constituted in part by ends and aims we have *not* chosen.

But, in the first place, this can all be accepted *without* denying that individuals still feel free and must be left free to question, revise, and possibly reject the communal or familial values they inherit.[129] Indeed, to the extent that rights are *not* allowed to protect such freedom, the possibility of true personal commitment to the values favored by communitarians may be replaced by a kind of mindless "herd solidarity."[130] Second, rights need not have ab-

[126] "Our identity is always partly defined in conversation with others or through the common understanding which underlies the practices of our society" (Taylor, "Atomism," 60). The "moral self" is not "the embodiment of rationality," but "a network of beliefs, desires, and emotions" tied to "other members of some relevant community" (Rorty, "Postmodernist," 585–86). As Walzer notes, however, communitarian attacks on liberalism are often an uneasy mixture of claims such as these *and* claims that the people we have become are in fact individuals cut loose from ties, commitments, and shared ends ("Communitarian Critique," 7–11).

[127] See, for example, Tully, *Discourse*, 11, 24, 49; Arnhart, *Political Questions*, 231; Kendall, *Majority-Rule*, 73–74; Parry, *John Locke*, 44; Rapaczynski, *Nature and Politics*, 163n; Yolton, *Locke*, 56–57; Ashcraft, *Locke's Two Treatises*, 107, 111; Shoeman, "Social Theory of Rights."

[128] Walzer, "Communitarian Critique," 20–21; Pettit and Kukathas, *Rawls*, 117.

[129] See the forceful defense of this point in Kymlicka, "Liberalism and Communitarianism," 189–95.

[130] Buchanan, "Assessing the Communitarian" 871–72. "The communitarian begs the question against liberalism if she simply assumes that individual rights will not be needed to make community compatible with commitment—genuine commitment, as distinct from unreflective, herd solidarity. While it might so happen that a community that did not exist within a liberal framework of individual rights managed to achieve self-criticism and progress or was blessed at the outset with a stable set of humane values, this would be sheer good fortune" (872).

solute priority for the natural rights theorist (as we have seen they do not have for Locke); this claim of absolute priority is in no way a necessary feature of the position. Natural rights in Locke are absolute neither with respect to other rights nor with respect to considerations of social good, and this seems a view liberals should accept.[131] Most important, however, what priority rights *do* have can be based (as it is in Locke) not on some intrinsic conceptual or psychological priority, but on the permanent possibility of conflict caused (in part) by the diversity of sources of "the good" to which communitarians appeal. In pursuing both the good for humankind and the various goods for particular human beings, communities, and societies, the necessary limitation and coordination of our activities are expressed morally in the natural rights we possess, derivable from certain features of the admittedly more complex self and the enduring aspects of its many possible social embodiments.[132] These natural rights do not destroy the possibility of genuine community among persons; rather, they can facilitate and protect community, not only in hopelessly pluralistic, but in strongly homogeneous societies.[133]

Perhaps the problem is that society is necessary even for the possession of those minimal human capacities on which natural rights are allegedly based, such as rationality or the capacity for choice or valuing. Taylor argues, for instance, that people "can only develop their characteristically human capacities in society. . . . living in society is a necessary condition of the development of rationality . . . or of becoming a moral agent."[134] Indeed, the bearer of the liberal rights Locke champions could exist only in a

[131] Ibid., 881.

[132] This may be part of what Amy Gutmann has in mind in "Communitarian Critics," 310–11.

[133] It remains a fact, of course, that most existing societies *are* sufficiently pluralistic as to require their current focus on rights and justice (Walzer, "Communitarian Critique," 9). But rights are extremely valuable even where there is unanimity about pursuit of a common good; for even there will exist the permanent possibility of conflict over strategies and concrete instantiations, which rights can diminish or resolve (Buchanan, "Assessing the Communitarian," 877). Buchanan has persuasively argued for viewing the liberal rights theorist as a kind of cautious or pessimistic communitarian (ibid., 860), one who wants to encourage genuine commitment, not social fragmentation (867–71), and to protect community by the enforcement of individual rights to form new communities and to depart from existing ones (862–63), but who lacks the communitarian's optimism that these freedoms will be likely to be respected without acknowledgment of individual rights to them.

[134] "Atomism," 42.

particular form of political society.[135] If this is true, however, it seems there could be no *natural* rights in our sense (i.e., rights that could be possessed in the state of nature), for only in certain kinds of societies could the capacities on which those rights are based develop. Natural rights presuppose the self-sufficiency of the moral agent (the view Taylor calls "atomism"[136]).

Taylor's argument rests in the end, I think, either on a confusion or on mere assertion (and in the latter case, on an assertion that is not independently plausible). For he must maintain that it is not even *possible* that moral agency (of the minimal sort claimed by liberals to be sufficient for natural rightholding) could develop outside of political society. If this were possible, there could be natural rights. It is, as we have seen, open to the natural rights theorist to maintain that our natural condition is typically *social*, involving significant relations with family and others, and even that only in this social natural condition can we become rightholders. What may seem to undermine the natural rights position (and perhaps what bothers Taylor) is that the state of nature (e.g., when it is particularly poor or primitive or asocial) might well *not* in this way provide the necessary conditions for the development of moral agency. Indeed, particularly bad sorts of societies might also be so oppressive that their members (or, at least, significant numbers of them) never develop the capacities on which rights depend. What becomes of the supposed natural rights of people in these conditions below the "threshold" of sociability necessary for moral agency?

The answer, of course, is that where people cannot (or simply do not) develop the capacities necessary for rightholding, they do not *have* natural rights (in the same way that the insane, idiots, and [perhaps] young children seem to have no rights in Locke). Those who are not persons (moral agents) are not under the moral law. The natural rights theorist (and certainly Locke) is not committed to asserting that all humans in all places at all times have rights, but only to the claim that all persons naturally acquire certain rights along with their personhood. But being a person or moral agent does not, in the way Taylor suggests, presuppose any particular conventions, rules, laws, or practices. Many different kinds

---

[135] Ibid., 58–60.

[136] Ibid., 41. See Scott-Craig's similar claims about Locke's "atomism" and his assertion that "only in the construction of, and by participation in, the constitutional state are . . . rights perfected, fully naturalized, fully actualized" ("John Locke and Natural Right," 33–34).

CHAPTER TWO

of arrangements, both political and nonpolitical, can clearly suffice for the development of those minimal capacities necessary for Lockean agency or personhood.[137] Families in isolation can provide conditions adequate for this, as can virtually all kinds of societies (although neither will necessarily do this). It may well be true that certain kinds of societies and, perhaps even more so, certain kinds of political societies will best facilitate the growth of moral agency, true autonomy, and healthy independence (so that we ought, as a consequence, to promote such societies). But this observation is a non sequitur as far as any argument (Lockean or Kantian) for the possibility of natural rights is concerned.[138]

What about societies above the "threshold" for promoting agency that nonetheless do not recognize natural rights, such as the ancient Greek or Roman societies? "It would of course be a little odd," MacIntyre writes, "that there should be such rights attaching to human beings simply qua human beings in light of the fact . . . that there is no expression in any ancient or medieval language correctly translated by our expression 'a right' until near the close of the middle ages."[139] This is not, of course, proof "that there are no natural or human rights," but it should raise suspicions. And MacIntyre tells a story to support these doubts. We moderns have "very largely, if not entirely—lost our comprehension, both theoretical and practical, of morality."[140] The rules of morality we embrace have been cut loose from their original grounding in a conception of what is "teleologically appropriate for a human being" and in the commands of God.[141] Deprived of these foundations for our moral beliefs, desperate invention was required to anchor us again. One important part of this self-deceptive project was the invention of "the modern individual," the ra-

[137] Pettit and Kukathas, *Rawls*, 108–9.
[138] This observation is also, contra Taylor, irrelevant to the natural rights theorist's view that each person is morally free to choose which political society to join or support (or whether to enter or support one at all). For our obligations toward our children (and our limited obligations to others) are only to provide the conditions necessary for their development of personhood, *not* to provide those conditions in any one, particular, specifiable way (e.g., by joining a certain kind of polity that *best* fosters these conditions).
[139] *After Virtue*, 66–67.
[140] Ibid., 2.
[141] Ibid., 57–60. It is not clear if MacIntyre intends to attack Locke on these grounds (since Locke is barely mentioned in *After Virtue*). Locke had not, after all, broken from these "original groundings," but, as I have argued, merely added to them. The characterization of Locke in MacIntyre's other work, however, seems to suggest that Locke should come in for the same kind of assault (see *Short History*, 157–60).

114

tional, autonomous bearer of the natural rights of man, rights attaching to this individual "as such." This "individual" was "a new social and cultural artefact."[142]

But it is possible to tell other kinds of stories in which "the modern individual," the person who bears natural rights, is not so much invented as discovered.[143] We have seen (in 2.3) how on certain theological views, rights-talk, and the perception of natural equality on which it rests, is naturally suppressed. It is even more plain that rigid social classes and hierarchies of certain sorts, as well as the economic forms of life that shaped and accompanied them, greatly reduced the visibility of equality, and consequently also prevented the perception of shared natural rights. In addition to these factors, simple ruling-class self-interest (and self-deception from other sources) contributed to the failure to take seriously the moral conclusions which followed from feeble recognitions of natural equality.[144] It would, then, be far from surprising, and certainly not unintelligible, if persons in other cultures and times possessed the natural rights of which Lockeans write, without any general social recognition that this was the case.[145] The Greek's "barbarian" slave, ignorant of the language and culture of his captors, could no more be perceived as his equal than the Greek's wife, hidden by different but equally impenetrable blinders. But that they were (often) his equals in the ways Locke suggests is hard to deny. The "moral moorings" of past philosophies can be portrayed as shallow and self-deceptive too.[146]

[142] MacIntyre, *Whose Justice? Which Rationality?* 339.

[143] Indeed, even the language of "discovery" seems too strong here, given that in many cultures that employed no explicit concept of rights, some such concept clearly operated "just below the surface" of moral discourse, not being fully articulated until the rights in question became more important socially (see Golding, "Primacy of Welfare Rights," 125).

[144] This seems the best Lockean response as well to Young's claim that "it ought to be deeply disturbing that our talent for moral epistemology should apparently have developed so rapidly in recent human history thereby enabling us to detect so many previously unrecognized rights" ("Dispensing with Moral Rights," 70). It is not any "talents" that moderns have miraculously acquired, but the removal of certain personal, social, economic, and religious blinders, which accounts for the "discovery" of natural rights.

[145] Plamenatz, *Consent, Freedom*, 91.

[146] It is, I think, often tempting to allow historical and social explorations, which sometimes show us how moral concepts come into use and become firmly entrenched, to deflect our attention from the project of determining whether moral judgments using those concepts are justified or valid. That the two are *distinct* projects seems undeniable. To maintain the contrary would be like arguing that because the church is responsible for our views of God, there is no independent question of the meaningfulness, truth, or justifiability of religious propositions. This is

MacIntyre asserts, however, that "the truth is plain: there are no [natural] rights." We have a good reason to assert this, which is "of precisely the same type as the best reason which we possess for asserting that there are no witches and the best reason which we possess for asserting that there are no unicorns: every attempt to give good reasons for believing that there *are* such rights has failed."[147] Now, first, nothing is plainer than that what will be counted as success in an attempt to give "good reasons" here is every bit as controversial as whether or not there are natural rights. But second, our reasons for asserting that there are no witches or unicorns are not at all the same as the reasons we might have for doubting the existence of natural rights. Belief in witches and unicorns conflicts in a straightforward way with belief in firmly entrenched and well-supported physical theory and biological evidence. A belief in the former requires a decision to abandon the latter, which is at best difficult and at worst irrational. No such choice is forced by a belief in natural rights.[148] That such rights are not "out there" to be discovered is a problem only for one who does not understand, or willfully ignores, the functions of moral judgments. Whether the existence of natural rights has been, or can be, proven, is a reasonable ground for controversy. MacIntyre is surely right that we must look to the actual arguments for natural rights and judge their success, rather than simply deciding in advance that such arguments could not succeed or could not fail to succeed.[149] But belief in natural rights is neither obviously irrational nor clearly wishful in the way many skeptics suggest.

(e) Natural rights as eliminable: Whether or not natural rights are mischievous fictions or desperate and self-deceptive inventions, it is sometimes argued, they are at least *eliminable* from our moral repertoire as superfluous dead weight. Right-talk does no new work that cannot be done equally well by more basic (and respectable) talk of duties. Since all statements about rights are translatable without loss into statements about their correlative duties, we can dispense with talk of natural rights altogether.[150]

---

not, of course, to argue that explanations of how our moral language comes into use or of its role in our lives is not relevant to the latter kind of question, but only that the first project cannot be a simple substitute for the second.

[147] *After Virtue*, 67.

[148] See Gutmann, "Communitarian Critics," 314–15.

[149] Kymlicka, "Liberalism and Communitarianism," 202–3.

[150] Tuck attributes this argument to Pufendorf and Bentham (*Natural Rights Theories*, 1), although I confess to being unable to find exactly these claims in either (for suggestions that Bentham, at least, had nothing so simple as this in mind, see Har-

It is worth making at least two points in response to such arguments. First, they obviously require a strong defense of the claim that duty is a more basic or indispensable concept than right; for otherwise, the same style of argument is available for the elimination of duties from our moral vocabulary. Locke, for instance (or so I have argued), treats neither concept as more basic than the other. It is sometimes thought sufficient to prove that duty is more basic, that rights always have correlative duties (in terms of which they can be analyzed), but that some duties (imperfect duties) do not correlate with any rights (and so cannot be analyzed in terms of correlative rights). But this defense depends, first, on there being imperfect moral duties (which, I will claim, Locke does not acknowledge); and, second, on it being the case that the meaning of "duty" remains perfectly constant between the cases in which duties do and do not correlate with rights of others (which it by no means obviously does).

The second point that needs making is how controversial it is to claim that there *is* any simple translation available of the sort this argument requires. Those who reject simple versions of the benefit theory of rights (as, I have claimed, Locke would) will be hard pressed to find an alternative theory that will also make rights look eliminable without loss. It is worth emphasizing that being committed to the logical correlativity of rights and duties in no way commits one to the view that the meaning of "right" can be fully captured in statements about correlative duties. Logical correlativity involves no more than the availability of valid inferences from propositions concerning the existence of a right to propositions concerning the existence of a duty.[151] Even the stronger thesis of *conceptual* correlativity[152] does not entail simple translatability. For rights to be correlated with duties is not necessarily for rights to be *"mere* correlates" or "shadows" of those duties.[153]

And what is in any event undeniable is that right-talk *does* add

---

rison, *Bentham*, 94–95). Hart finds this style of argument in Ihering (*Essays on Bentham*, 181–82) and Lemos tries to use it against Locke (*Hobbes and Locke*, 168–69). It is, in any event, a natural move for anyone who holds that to have a right is simply to be the intended beneficiary of a duty or for any others who believe in simple translatability—for example, Brandt, *Ethical Theory*, 441; or Benn and Peters, *Social Principles*, 89.

[151] As Louden correctly observes, the argument from correlativity to eliminability is a "red herring" ("Rights Infatuation," 92). One pursuit of this red herring is in Arnold, "Analyses of Rights," 78–79, 82–83.

[152] Lyons, "Correlativity of Rights and Duties," 47.

[153] The first phrase is Shapiro's (*Evolution of Rights*, 105; my emphasis); the second is how Warrender describes rights in Hobbes (*Political Philosophy of Hobbes*, 19).

considerably to our moral world, beyond what duty-talk brings with it. There is no "adequate replacement" for rights.[154] As we have seen (in 2.4),[155] rights bring with them the ideas of something being *owed* to another person and of persons being *wronged* (as opposed to the idea merely of wrong being done with respect to another). Duty, by contrast, lays its emphasis on what "must be done," not on what is owed to another. We cannot capture in the language of duty several of the distinctive features of right-talk or the concepts with which rights are inextricably bound up. I emphasize here just three (already familiar) features of rights that illustrate their ineliminable character.

(1) Rights are inseparably connected with a distinctive sort of respect for persons, a kind of respect that is not possible in the absence of rights (as I argued in 2.4). In Feinberg's words, "To respect a person then, or to think of him as possessed of human dignity, simply *is* to think of him as a potential maker of claims"; "respect for persons . . . may simply be respect for their rights."[156] Rights are grounds for *self*-respect; rightholders are *entitled* to things and have a kind of personal sovereignty, rather than being entirely dependent on others' personal decisions about whether or not to do their duty. This ground of self-respect is intimately connected with respect for other, similarly endowed beings. And without the conception of moral agents as bearers of natural rights, this sort of respect for persons would not be possible.[157] The point here is not that rights justify conduct that would not otherwise be justifiable, but rather that they change the way we look at persons; the bearer of rights can think of self and others quite differently than can the bearer of (only) duties.[158]

---

[154] Brandt, "Concept of Moral Right," 30. See Louden's convincing argument that attempted reductions of rights all fail ("Rights Infatuation," 94–95). Brandt seems to share this view, allowing that rights are part of "an optimal conceptual scheme for morality" (45). Even some of those who think Feinberg's claims (see below) are mistaken, nonetheless accept that rights are valuable (not eliminable without loss). See, for example, Nelson, "On the Alleged Importance of Moral Rights," 155.

[155] And as Feinberg has emphasized in his much-discussed paper, "The Nature and Value of Rights."

[156] Ibid., 87. See also Hill, "Servility and Self Respect," 119.

[157] See Buchanan, "What's So Special about Rights?" 75–77; Melden, *Rights and Persons*, 23–26; and Bandman, "Do Children Have Natural Rights?" 236. This may also be part of what Shoeman has in mind in asserting that "a theory of rights . . . serves to describe a moral picture of what it is to be a person" ("Social Theory of Rights," 130).

[158] As even some critics of rights theories acknowledge: for example, Louden, "Rights Infatuation," 93; Nelson, "On the Alleged Importance of Moral Rights," 155.

(2) It is often (and, I think, correctly) claimed that rights are indispensable for such activities as claiming, demanding, or insisting on actions or outcomes.[159] Natural rights, of course, would be necessary for these activities to be available to persons generally (and not just to citizens within legally defined channels). Attacks on this position have come from two main directions. On the one hand, it is argued that we can perfectly well make sense of claiming or demanding in a world without rights. Duties can do the job as well as rights. Where the rules impose duties on others, and where I am harmed (or not benefited) as a result of another's breach of duty, it makes good sense for me to complain and demand satisfaction. Rights are not needed to justify or make intelligible "claiming."[160] Second, it is argued that tying rights in this way to claiming or demanding shows that right-talk is objectionably contentious or strident. This is either a reason for rejecting rights as unnecessary (and, indeed, as "mischievous") or a reason for seeking a different way of talking about rights.[161]

To the first attack it seems adequate to reply that without rights the best one can do is to "invoke enforceable prohibitions"—I can call on others to do their duty or on the law (or society) to enforce others' legally (or morally) prescribed duties. But if these performances are not *owed to me,* my position is not interestingly different than that of an uninvolved bystander (in spite of the harm I suffer or benefit I am denied by the breach of duty). I can demand compliance with the rules as an outraged member of the rule-governed community. But I cannot *claim* compliance as due *me.* It is *this* kind of claiming that makes sense only in a world with rights. As *rightholder* (but *not* otherwise), when some decide it is best *not* to require others to do their duty, and when their breach of duty also harms me, I have something left to say. To the second attack it is

[159] Feinberg, "Nature and Value of Rights" (and other works); Hart, "Are There Any Natural Rights?"; Wasserstrom, "Rights, Human Rights"; Brandt, "Concept of a Moral Right"; Lyons, "Human Rights"; Becker, "Individual Rights"; and many others.
[160] Buchanan, "What's So Special about Rights?" 71–75; Nelson, "On the Alleged Importance of Moral Rights," 149–54; Young, "Dispensing with Moral Rights," 67–71; Arnold, "Analyses of Rights."
[161] The first line is taken by Young ("Dispensing with Moral Rights," 68); the second is taken by Waldron (*Nonsense upon Stilts,* 196–97, 200). See also Narveson, "Commentary," 158; and Andrew's claims that right-talk is not only confused and contradictory, but isolating, friendless, and contentious (*Shylock's Rights,* 15–21, 35–36, 78, 127, 169–70, 174–75, 192, 197–99). Walzer comments on and effectively criticizes Weil's similar view of right-talk as "shrill nagging of claims and counter claims" (*Just and Unjust Wars,* 134n).

sufficient to respond that being entitled to press claims (by virtue of possessing rights) is not the same as being entitled to be contentious, adversarial, egoistic, or strident. There is no need for claiming to be an obnoxious activity. We may make claims on behalf of others and recognize that there are sometimes good reasons *not* to press claims we have. Indeed, Locke insists that children should be taught *not* to insist on their rights in a rigid way that produces conflict (*Education*, 109).[162] The idea is only that rights give us claims that can be pressed forcefully where necessary. It is not at all obvious that this is a mischievous or undesirable feature of rights. But it is certainly a feature that cannot be captured with alternative moral concepts.

(3) A final feature of rights (discussed earlier, in 2.1) that would be eliminated in a world of (only) duties, is the realm of optionality and discretion they bring to our moral lives.[163] Morality is more flexible when individuals have (limited) sovereignty over a portion of their moral worlds. Rightholders need not always exercise their (nonmandatory) rights; they may waive them or invoke them as the situation requires. This allows both the full consideration of other morally relevant aspects of our situation (beyond our rights) and the possibility of justified departures from the morally optimal (a point we have seen stressed by Locke [above in 1.4]).[164] A world of duties (including even imperfect duties) cannot account for these useful and prominent features of our moral landscape.

There are no doubt other sources of natural right skepticism than those I have tried to deal with here. But perhaps I have said enough to allay the doubts of some, or at least to make interesting the ventures into natural rights theory that follow. I turn in chapter 3 to the first of the central special rights at work in Locke (and in the Lockean theory of rights): the natural executive right, the right of all to punish.

[162] See Tarcov, *Locke's Education*, 140, 150.

[163] Among those who have stressed this feature are Hart, "Are There Any Natural Rights?" 180–81; Buchanan, "What's So Special about Rights?" 79–80; Nelson, "On the Alleged Importance of Moral Rights," 155; Benditt, *Rights*, 45–50.

[164] Thus undercutting the moral necessity of "calculation" (see Finnis, *Natural Law*, 221). Here, of course, we are speaking of the level of rights and duties. At the level of "all things considered" judgments, a different kind of flexibility is available (even in a world without rights).

T H R E E

THE RIGHT TO PUNISH

3.1. A Natural Executive Right

Most philosophical discussions of punishment focus in one way or another on the question "When is punishment just?" Even a brief glance at these discussions, however, reveals the many different ways in which that question may be understood (as Hart, for example, made clear long ago[1]). We might, for instance, take it to be a question about the kind or amount of punishment that is just in response to various offenses, or a question about who can be justly punished, or a question about when (if) punishment is the proper response to crime or wrongdoing. The array of possible answers to these three versions of the question, and observations about the ways in which these answers must be related to one another, are well displayed in contemporary philosophical literature on punishment. There is, however, a fourth way of understanding the question "When is punishment just?" that is not so often touched on in the literature on punishment, because it places the question more squarely within the province of political philosophy. This interpretation of the question makes it a question about authority and the "right to punish." What makes it just for one particular person or group (the legal authorities of our country of residence, for instance) to punish us, as opposed to some other person or group (private citizens, television talk-show hosts, the officials of some other government)?

Now the territory covered in answering these questions is hardly virgin. It has been popular ground for political philosophers for as long as there have been political philosophers. What is distinctive about this fourth interpretation of the question "When is punishment just?" is not its novelty, but rather the fact that the kinds of answers often given to the other three interpretations of the question seem quite feeble when offered as answers

[1] Hart, "Prolegomenon to the Principles of Punishment."

121

to this version of it. While one may be convinced that the practice of punishment is justified by its social utility (or the deterrent value of punishment), it is much harder to believe that just *anyone* may rightfully punish (and so deter) others, or that the person or group that may rightfully punish another individual is that person or group whose doing the punishing would maximize total happiness (or most effectively deter crime). This latter position might entail that citizens of country A could be justly punished for their ordinary crimes by the government of country B, provided only that this arrangement would be maximally useful. And again, while one might be convinced that only those who deserve punishment may be justly punished, and only then to the extent deserved, it is much harder to believe that just anyone may rightfully punish those citizens who deserve it, or that those who most deserve to do the punishing are the ones entitled to do so. Neither one's general level of virtue nor one's peculiar talents in the area of punishing (e.g., special aptitude for being a judge, jailer, or executioner) are normally taken to establish any special claim to be the one who punishes others.

When we ask what makes it just for one particular person or group, rather than another, to punish some person, the answer that seems most natural concerns neither utility nor desert. It is not that our governments deserve to punish us, or that their doing so maximizes happiness; it is rather that they have authority or the right to do so. Locke puts the point thus:

> To justify bringing such evil [i.e., punishment] on any man two things are requisite. First, that he who does it has commission and power to do so. Secondly, that it be directly useful for the procuring of some greater good. . . . Usefulness, when present, being but one of those conditions, cannot give the other, which is a commission to punish.[2]

The natural answer to our question makes central reference to authorization and rights, and it has been the natural rights tradition in political philosophy that has emphasized this point most forcefully. According to that tradition, one person (A) may justly punish another (B) only if either (1) A has a natural right to punish the crimes (wrongs) of B, or (2) B has alienated to A or created for A by forfeiture a right to punish B for B's crimes (wrongs). This po-

---

[2] *A Second Letter Concerning Toleration*, 112. Locke seems to have the same point in mind when he distinguishes between the justifications of punishment on the separable grounds that "it is effectual" and "it is just" (King, *Life*, 1:113).

sition cannot adequately be characterized as either purely utilitarian or purely retributivist.[3]

It will not be my purpose here to evaluate the entire natural rights position on punishment, or to explore its relations to other views (for instance, whether it is consistent with or even reducible to[4] retributivist or deterrence views). I wish to concentrate instead on the natural rights tradition's claims about who may justly mete out punishment, the tradition's answer to my fourth version of the question of just punishment. And, even more specifically, I will pay special attention to one aspect of those claims, a position shared by classical natural rights theorists (such as Grotius and Locke) and contemporary ones (such as Nozick and Rothbard). All persons in a state of nature, these authors claim, have a moral right to punish (moral) wrongdoers. This "natural executive right," of course, plays a very central role in Locke's account of how a government can come to have the right to punish its citizens (as it must in any Lockean account of these matters). But any theory of punishment must either accommodate or reject this right.

The motivation for defending the natural executive right seems reasonably clear. Locke (and other philosophers in the natural rights tradition) wanted to claim that all political authority (or "power") is artificial, and so must be explained in terms of more basic, natural forms of authority. Governments have rights to limit our liberty, for instance, only insofar as they have been granted those rights by us; we, however, possess these rights naturally (or, rather, are "born to" a basic set of moral rights). Governmental rights, then, are simply composed of the natural rights of those who become citizens,[5] transferred to government by some volun-

---

[3] By which I do *not* mean to claim that, for example, utilitarians do not have alternative accounts of authority and rights to punish. For an elegant statement of the sort of position I have in mind here, and an explanation of how it lies between classical utilitarianism and classical retributivism, see Ross, *Right and the Good*, 56–61.

[4] Honderich, *Punishment*, 158–62. I do not believe that rights theories of punishment collapse (as Honderich argues) into retributivism. I trust my argument below (3.5) will show why this need not happen, since fairness, not desert, is the central notion at work. Honderich now classes rights theories as "rights retributivism," one form of the "new retributivism," with another being "restorative retributivism" ("Punishment, the New Retributivism"). The theory I outline below utilizes both "rights" and "restorative" elements. For some current examples of rights theories of punishment, see Goldman, "Paradox of Punishment"; Hurka, "Rights and Capital Punishment"; Haksar, "Excuses and Voluntary Conduct"; Quinn, "Right to Threaten."

[5] See Macpherson, *Possessive Individualism*, 218. Grotius' defense of this view

---

tary undertaking (e.g., contract, consent, or the granting of a trust). This transfer of rights may go unobserved by some (as when consent is "tacit" only), but it must take place if government is to have any *de jure* power. However beneficial and fair the practices and policies a government enforces, it has no right or authority to enforce them against an uncommitted "independent."[6]

The same story can be told about a government's right to punish criminals. This right, like all governmental rights, must be composed of the redistributed natural rights of citizens, rights that the citizens must therefore have been capable of possessing in a nonpolitical state of nature. It is hard to deny that governments do, at least sometimes, have (or are capable of having) the *de jure* authority or right to punish criminals. But if they do, the argument continues, persons in a state of nature must also, at least sometimes, have the right to punish wrongdoers. From what other source could a government have obtained its right?

Locke was surely correct when he guessed that this would seem "a very strange doctrine to some men" (II, 9). Critics in Locke's own day were uncomfortable with the idea of a natural right to punish, and contemporary philosophers have been quite solidly against it. We naturally tend to think of the right to punish as something denied private persons and possessed only by special authorities within a carefully defined institutional framework. The "private application of force," at least in matters of punishment, seems both institutionally and morally indefensible.[7] But these views are mistaken, according to the natural rights theorist; they are true only of private punishment in *civil* society, where government must have a "monopoly on force."[8] Perhaps the view that *all* private punishment is indefensible arises solely from the fact of our constant exposure to institutionalized forms of punishment. But however that may be, the institutional authority can be explained only by conceding the existence of a natural executive

---

was, of course, extremely influential within the tradition. See Tuck's discussion of Grotius (*Natural Rights Theories*, especially 62–63).

[6] Hodson, *Ethics of Legal Coercion*, 117.

[7] Grotius, *De Jure Praedae Commentarius*, 8 (question 7, article 1), 89. Grotius' purpose here is to explore the general justifications for the private use of force (i.e., in his terms, what "causes justly give rise to private wars"). In discussing "the fourth cause" of just private war, namely wrongdoing, Grotius is led to a defense of the natural executive right. Parallel, but less complete, discussions of these matters occur in *De Jure Belli ac Pacis Libri Tres*, II, xx.

[8] Note Locke's claim: "For all force (as has often been said) belongs only to the magistrate, nor ought any private persons at any time to use force unless it be in self-defense against unjust violence" (L, 132).

right. And further, when we really set our minds to the task, the idea of a nonpolitical or prepolitical right to punish seems less and less counterintuitive. For the early natural rights theorist, it was not at all implausible to point to the prepolitical authority to punish wrongdoers possessed by God and by the fathers of families. And there are ample scriptural grounds for concluding that God intended all persons to have such authority, as the earthly executors of His law.[9] But even if we insist on a secular foundation for natural rights theory,

> Is the general right to punish so counterintuitive? If some great wrong were committed in another country which refuses to punish it (perhaps the government is in league with, or is itself, the wrongdoer), wouldn't it be all right for you to punish the wrongdoer, to inflict some harm on him for his act?[10]

Is Locke's "very strange doctrine" defensible after all? My motivation for exploring the doctrine further is primarily, of course, a desire to explore and evaluate the resources available to the Lockean theory of rights (combined with my dissatisfaction with alternative accounts of the origin of a just government's right to punish). And it is important to see from the start that, properly understood, the idea of a natural right to punish can have a strong intuitive appeal; it can seem hard to deny that free and equal persons would have a right (or be morally at liberty) to punish in at least certain kinds of states of nature[11] (remembering now that persons can be in the state of nature not only *before* the institution of government, but also after its collapse or during the rule of a despotical government). Imagine that, for whatever reason, your society "dissolved" into disorder and chaos. Once again in your nat-

[9] Grotius, for instance, cites Judges 15 (Samson's punishment of the Philistines) and Genesis 9.6 ("Whoso sheddeth man's blood, by man shall his blood be shed") as supporting a natural executive right (*De Jure Praedae Commentarius*, 90). Locke follows Grotius in citing Genesis 9.6 (along with Genesis 4.14) for support (II,11). Neither author cites those passages that seem to support the view that only God has the right to punish: Romans 12.19 ("Vengeance is mine, I will repay, says the Lord") or Genesis 4.15 ("If anyone slays Cain, vengeance shall be taken on him sevenfold"). See Pangle, *Republicanism*, 303.

[10] Nozick, *Anarchy*, 137. The "wouldn't it be all right" formulation here suggests a liberty to punish, rather than a full claim right to do so. As we will see, however, Locke disagrees with Nozick about the rights of citizens in political societies to punish alien citizens. Locke's claims (and mine) concern only the rights of those in certain kinds of state of nature relations (see below).

[11] Some take such a denial to be "implausible on its face" (Sayward, "Anarchism," 110).

ural state, unprotected by the rule of law, you witness a man brutally robbing and murdering a defenseless victim. If it were within your power to do so, would you not feel justified in seeing to it that the murderer suffered for his crime? Would there be anything morally objectionable in your inflicting on him some harm, either to save others from his atrocities or (supposing you somehow know that he will commit no more) simply as a response to *what he did*? Would not anyone in that state of nature have a right to *punish* him for his (moral) crime? If you are in any way tempted to answer "yes," there are obvious reasons to think more about the executive right. But even if your inclination is to say "no," theoretical considerations may persuade you to excise this belief from your set of "considered judgments" about morality. And if you eventually accept the idea that there is such a right, as we will see, you will be hard pressed to reject the natural rights tradition's account of the origin of the state's right to punish.

Now I would not want to appear to be resting much weight on (as yet) undefended intuitions. They are, at best, only a very provisional starting point. If there are sound theoretical grounds for rejecting the idea of a natural right to punish, then we must, of course, discount intuitions to the contrary. And contemporary philosophers have certainly argued that there are such theoretical grounds. Their criticisms of the natural right to punish can, I think, fairly be reduced to three main claims: (1) The very idea of a natural right to punish involves a fundamental confusion, or even incoherence; (2) One cannot, in any event, give a satisfactory account of the origin and nature of the natural right to punish; and (3) If we begin with a private right of punishment, we can give no persuasive account of how a just government can come to have an exclusive moral right to punish wrongdoers.

In addition, it may seem that even those who share my intuitions in the case just described will probably also have intuitions about punishment that Locke and the natural rights tradition would seem to want to reject—for instance, that private citizens even in a just state would be justified in punishing a criminal whose cleverness made legal punishment impossible, or that private citizens in one country might justifiably punish a criminal in another, if both governments refuse to punish the wrongdoer.

I will try to argue here that none of the objections mentioned above is convincing and that there is good reason to take seriously the idea of a natural right to punish. I begin this task by examining the case for a natural executive right as it was presented by its most famous advocate.[12]

3.2. Locke's Case

In chapter 2 of the *Second Treatise*, Locke argues that in the state of nature all persons enjoy an equal right to punish violators of the law of nature, that is, those who "invade" the rights of others:[13] "The execution of the law of nature is in that state [i.e., the state of nature], put into every man's hands, whereby everyone has a right to punish the transgressors of that law to such a degree, as may hinder its violation" (II, 7).

While the exercise of this right in a state of nature is necessary to give force to natural law, it is also a great inconvenience. Because people will tend to be partial toward themselves and their friends, they will not always properly use this right to punish. They may punish excessively (or where there is no guilt at all), which will prompt a similar response from the ones punished, and "confusion and disorder" (or a state of war) will follow (II, 13). What is needed, of course, is a common judge standing over them all, and authorized to decide the proper remedy for conflicts between them.[14] If each surrenders the right to punish to such a judge, each will profit from the greater security and consistency of decision that will result. This, as we have seen, is one of Locke's main arguments for the desirability of civil society, his main response to the anarchist. Life under government is preferable to life in a state of nature at least largely because of the improved procedures for the rightful punishment of criminals. Indeed, the transfer of the executive right from citizen to common judge (i.e., the state) is so important to Locke's justification of civil society that he at times seems to define political society in terms of this transfer having occurred (II, 19, 91). The citizens' executive rights, once entrusted to government, become the executive power of the state.

Locke's defense of a natural executive right, then, lies at the very heart of his political philosophy.[15] For this reason, if no other,

---

[12] For a concise recent summary of Locke's views on punishment, see Tully, "Political Freedom," 517–18.

[13] Locke calls this right the "executive power of the law of nature" (II, 89).

[14] This view—for example, that the partiality of each in judging for self is what makes government necessary—was already present in Locke's early *Two Tracts*. See *First Tract*, 137–38.

[15] Ashcraft characterizes Locke's defense of the executive right (and of the possibility of others assisting in enforcing natural law) as "the whole point of the *Sec-*

we should be careful to understand his claims. First, Locke is not claiming that we in a state of nature have an unlimited right to treat a criminal however we please. While "every man in the state of nature has a power to kill a murderer" (II, 11), "lesser breaches" of the law of nature must be punished less severely (II, 12). The executive right is a right "only to retribute to him, so far as calm reason and conscience dictates, what is proportionate to his transgression, which is so much as may serve for reparation and restraint" (II, 8). Locke seems unconcerned about having here identified the limits to rightful punishment at once in both retributivist terms ("retribute" what is "proportionate" to the crime) and consequentialist terms (what is sufficient for "restraint"). During the remainder of the chapter, Locke talks almost exclusively like a consequentialist; but later in the text, retributivist language seems to dominate.[16] Similarly, while we have seen Locke's claim (in the *Second Letter*) that punishment, to be justified, must "be directly useful for the procuring some greater good," in other portions of the same work he talks like a pure retributivist.[17] As we have noted earlier, of course, Locke's rule-consequentialism allows him to blend deontological and consequentialist notions in his theory with reasonable ease. It may be, of course, that Locke is simply (and not very carefully) following the lead of Grotius, who maintained that while punishment should "fit the crime" as far as possible, punishment that accomplishes no substantial good end (in terms of future consequences) should be avoided as unjust.[18] But we should notice that when Locke employs the right to punish in the arguments of the *Treatises*, he does so as if it is a right to punish *all* wrongdoing, *not* as if it is a right to punish only when punishment can be shown to be directly useful.

Second, we should be sure that we remember what Locke

---

ond Treatise," since it is this position that legitimizes popular resistance against the king (*Revolutionary Politics*, 332). I would put the point slightly differently. Locke cannot give up his defense of the natural executive right without surrendering as well the right of the people to punish a deposed king.

[16] As in his talk of crimes "which deserve death" (for example, II, 23). See also II, 11 and II, 87: "Man . . . hath by nature a power . . . to judge of, and punish the breaches of [the law of nature] . . . as he is persuaded the offense deserves." These passages are hard to square with Farrell's claim that Locke "neither suggests nor needs" the idea that punishment should be proportionate to desert ("Punishment Without the State," 452). Farrell's Locke seems to be a pure consequentialist, contrary to my earlier suggestions concerning Locke's apparent willingness to argue from both deontological and consequentialist viewpoints.

[17] For example, *Second Letter Concerning Toleration*, 71, 105.

[18] *De Jure Praedae Commentarius*, 93–104; *De Jure Belli ac Pacis*, II, xx.

means by saying that each person possesses the executive right in a *state of nature*. The state of nature is that state in which prepolitical persons existed; but it is also the state into which each of us is born today, and in which we remain until we consent to join some commonwealth; it is the state to which we return when our political society dissolves (as in times of civil war), and (perhaps also) when our political leaders overstep the bounds of their rightful authority (i.e., cases of tyranny); it is the state in which all political rulers stand with respect to one another, and in which all citizens of one state stand with respect to citizens of another state.[19]

Third, Locke's position is not really that *all* persons in the state of nature with respect to others have the natural right to punish those others for their crimes. Children (i.e., those below the "age of reason") do not possess this executive right in spite of being in the state of nature with respect to all persons (and presumably the same is true of idiots, the insane, warmakers, and any other classes of "persons" who are not full rightholders in Locke's view). Perhaps more important, Locke believes that when we join together to form a political society we must be understood not only to be agreeing to allow a common judge to exercise our executive rights in conflicts between us. We must also be understood to entrust to government the right to punish transgressors of natural law who are *not* members of our commonwealth. That right, thus entrusted, becomes the state's *federative* power (II, 145–48). As members of a legitimate civil society, then, we have no right to punish anyone. Our natural right to punish certain persons (those who become our fellow citizens) is entrusted to government as its executive power, while the natural right to punish all other persons is similarly entrusted as the government's federative power.[20] In short, we have a natural right to punish those who breach natural law only after we reach the age of reason (and while we remain committed to the law of reason), and during those times when we are not members of some legitimate political society.

We have seen one reason why Locke was so eager to defend the natural right to punish: it is difficult to understand how an artificial body like a state could possess the moral authority to punish

[19] A person (A) is in the state of nature with respect to another (B) if and only if A has not voluntarily agreed to join (or is no longer a member of) a legitimate political community of which B is a member. For defense of and elaboration on this reading, see my "Locke's State of Nature," 449–55.
[20] Locke earlier calls these two powers "the power of making laws" and "the power of war and peace" (II, 88), although the first of these must also incorporate some of the *legislative* power.

unless it received this authority from persons who possessed it naturally.[21] But surely, it seems reasonable to respond, a government might receive the right to punish from citizens without it following that each person, prior to becoming a citizen, had a right to punish every wrongdoer. Locke's first reply to such concerns— that the state of nature is a state of equal rights, so that if anyone has a right to punish another, everyone must have that same right (II, 7)—will not suffice. For mightn't it be the case that we all equally possess a more *limited* right to punish, say, the right to punish criminals who victimize *us* (i.e., a right to punish held only by the victim of a crime, not all persons)? There would then be equal natural rights, but no general right to punish just any violator of natural law; and by entrusting these more limited rights to government, our governors would still receive the right to punish any who violate the rights of a citizen of the commonwealth.

Locke's response to this proposal has two parts. To the suggestion that the victim has special rights against the criminal, Locke agrees (as we will see). But the victim cannot hold the sole right to punish a wrongdoer, for the victim is not the only one who suffers from a crime. In a sense, Locke claims, humankind as a whole is the victim of every crime, every offense is "a trespass against the whole species" (II, 8). Those who violate the rights of others cast aside reason as a guide to their actions, making themselves a danger to all persons. Every person has a stake in protecting self and others from future attacks, so every person shares in the right to punish the criminal.

These claims may seem extravagant. In what way can a harmless petty thief (or even a local bully) be seen as a threat to all humankind? The idea that someone who commits any kind of wrong against another is therefore liable to do all manner of immoral things to people far and wide seems a bit far-fetched. On the other hand, if your neighbor (the victim of a violent assault, say) had sole right to punish a sadistic attacker, and chose to be lenient, you might well feel that the "public element" of the crime gave you a right to try to more effectively deter that criminal from future attacks. Much more needs to be said about Locke's claim

[21] There is, of course, a clear sense in which the state for Locke is perfectly "natural"—that is, there is every reason to suppose that persons (acting "naturally") will in fact create states where they do not exist (indeed, they will be "driven" into them) (see Seliger, *Liberal Politics*, 221–23). But the *moral authority* of states is for Locke created or artificial, not natural. Against Filmer, Locke argues that "governments must be left again to the old way of being made by contrivance and the consent of men" (I, 6).

that every crime is against all persons, and I will return to it later. It was, in fact, a popular argument in Locke's day (Grotius and many others used it), and it continues to find supporters today.[22]

No one (but the most eager disciple of Locke) would be persuaded by the considerations thus far advanced that there is a natural executive right, or that we can only explain a government's right to punish in terms of a transfer of the executive right. Locke's insistence that God must have intended each person to be executor of His law obviously requires further support. And there are, of course, other arguments in the *Second Treatise* designed to provide this support. While only one of these is prominent in the text, it might be reasonable to ascribe to him two others as well.

(1) Locke's language (in II, 7) might suggest the following view (although Locke nowhere in the *Treatises* explicitly states it): the ideas of duty and right (and, more generally, of morality) imply the existence of law. But there can only be a real law where there are sanctions attached to disobedience, where violations of the law are rightfully punished ("where the laws cannot be executed, it is all one as if there were no laws" [II, 219]). If, then, the law of nature is to be a genuine law (and the duties and rights it defines genuine), the law must rightly be backed up by physical force. Since it *is* a genuine law, binding even in our natural state, Locke supposes, someone in the state of nature must have the right to enforce natural law (and if someone has that right, everyone must have it, as we have seen). The internal sanction of the pains of conscience, which (sometimes) accompanies wrongdoing, is insufficient to constitute real enforcement of the law. While little of this is stated in the *Treatises*, Locke does (as we saw in 1.2) say such things in the *Essay*:

> What duty is, cannot be understood without a law; nor a law be known or supposed without a lawmaker, or without reward and punishment. . . . Since it would be utterly in vain to suppose a rule set to the free actions of men, without annexing to it some enforcement of good and evil to determine his will, we must, wherever we suppose a law, suppose also some reward or punishment annexed to that law. (E, 1.2.12, 2.28.6)

[22] For instance, J. Roger Lee argues that every crime "undercuts the rational expectation framework" among citizens in political society ("Arrest and Punishment of Criminals," 96). Presumably, this would hold true as well in some reasonably civilized, but nonpolitical, society in a state of nature.

The very idea of morality (and of law), Locke seems to be claiming, implies a natural executive right.[23]

(2) It is clear from the text that Locke believes there is a strong connection between the executive right and the right that we have to preserve ourselves (and others). The idea that a right to punish is somehow implied by our right to defend ourselves (or others) was neither new with Locke nor confined to philosophers in earlier centuries. Grotius, in the earliest systematic defense of a natural right to punish, argued in this way,[24] as do many of the most recent such defenses.[25] The idea they share, presumably, is that insofar as punishment can serve as a means for deterring future crime (both crime committed by the criminal punished and by others, suitably impressed by the example of that punishment), it is a way of defending ourselves against aggression by others. If we have a right to defend ourselves (and who would deny that?), then certainly we have a right to employ one means of self-defense, namely, punishment of criminals.

It might be natural to respond to the line of argument suggested above as we earlier responded to the claim that every crime threatens all persons. Surely it is not true that our right of self-defense could justify punishing just any violator of natural law (as the executive right allows), for some criminals seem to pose no real threat to our safety at all. Simple considerations of self-defense are insufficient to derive a general right to punish.

Locke seems sensitive to this worry, for his position is more complicated than the one just summarized. He in fact distinguishes between two separate aspects of our executive right. Two legitimate aims of punishment, remember, are "reparation and restraint"; these two aims define distinct rights. All persons have the natural right to punish transgressors of natural law for the purpose of restraining (deterring) criminals; this right, however, de-

[23] Strauss has written as if this is Locke's only (or at least central) defense of the executive right (*Natural Right*, 222). The text, of course, does not support such an extravagant claim (if, indeed, Strauss intended to make it). But there are also reasons, as we will see, to doubt that Locke had any such argument in mind.
[24] *De Jure Praedae Commentarius*, 91: "The causes for the infliction of punishment are natural, and derived from that precept which we have called the First Law." (The First Law is: "It shall be permissible to defend [one's own] life and to shun that which threatens to prove injurious" [369].)
[25] See, for example, Rothbard, *Ethics of Liberty*, 89 ("All rights of punishment derive from the victim's right of self-defense"); and Farrell, "Punishment Without the State," 443–44. Farrell's case is actually (like Locke's) the more complicated view that self-defense is justified by the same principle that justifies defense of other innocents, and hence punishment.

rives not from our right of self-defense, but from our right "of preserving all mankind." From the narrower right of self-defense (or
self-preservation) that each of us possesses, Locke thinks, we derive only a right to take reparation from a criminal, when we have
been victims:

> The damnified person has this power of appropriating to him-
> self the goods or services of the offender, by right of self-pres-
> ervation, as every man has a power to punish the crime, to
> prevent its being committed again, by the right he has of pre-
> serving all mankind. (II, 11)[26]

Locke is not, then, committed to holding that considerations of
self-defense justify my punishing just any criminal in a state of
nature; such considerations do not, strictly speaking for Locke,
justify punishment at all, but only the exacting of compensation.
Whether this claim is defensible or not, the important point for our
purposes is that the executive right *is* implied, according to Locke
(and, more plausibly, I think), by the more general right to preserve persons.

(3) We arrive finally at Locke's most prominently presented argument for the executive right. Unless there is a natural right to
punish, Locke maintains, the ruler (government) of a state could
never rightfully punish an alien who commits a crime in that state.
Since rulers clearly *can* rightfully punish alien criminals when they
break the laws of the countries they are visiting, there must be a
natural executive right (II, 9). Locke's thinking here runs as follows: aliens are not bound by the laws of the states they visit; they
have not consented to the authority of those states' governments.
Aliens remain in the state of nature with respect to those governments. If that is true, however, the government can only rightfully
punish aliens if it could rightfully punish them in the state of nature (i.e., if the citizens who gave the government its rights could
have punished them in the state of nature). Since most of us believe the government *can* legitimately punish in such cases, we
must accept the natural executive right as the only possible explanation of this fact. In punishing aliens, the state is merely doing
what its citizens would have been entitled to do, had they not left

---

[26] Note Locke's apparent claim that this second right cannot be transferred to
civil authorities, so that they might remit the requirement of compensation (II, 11).
Locke is, I think, better read here as saying that the transfer of this right is not to
be presumed to be part of any contract of government (than as saying that the right
literally *cannot* be transferred).

the state of nature by entrusting their executive rights to their government.[27]

3.3. Replies

We have now seen Locke's arguments for a natural right to punish. Let me examine them in turn:

(1) Take first Locke's apparent argument that we cannot understand the idea of duty (or moral ideas generally) without supposing a natural right to enforce the duty (by punishing offenders). The argument really proceeds in three stages:

(a) Moral duty implies the existence of law.

(b) True law requires the likely application of rightful sanctions for breach of the law.

(c) The only possible sanction for natural (moral) law that is likely to be applied at all times is punishment by other people. For this punishment to be rightful, people must have a right to punish wrongdoers.

Even granting Locke the truth of (a) and (b) (and, of course, many of Locke's contemporaries would have done so), the truth of (c), the crucial claim in the argument, still seems doubtful. Why is an appropriate sanction for natural law not the rightful sanction of divine punishment (or reward)? That God backs up natural law with sanctions "of infinite weight and duration" (E, 2.28.8) is surely sufficient for it to count as "true law"; indeed, this seems to be precisely what Locke had in mind in the passages from the *Essay* quoted earlier. There is no need for the sanctions of a general executive right in order to explain the possibility of moral duty

---

[27] This argument will not, of course, convince anarchists or any who doubt that the state *can* legitimately punish aliens. Let me add to the above explanation of Locke's case for the executive right a purely historical observation. In his notes to the argument just considered, Laslett comments that Locke's language announced "that his doctrine of punishment was, or was intended by him to be, a novelty" (Locke, *Two Treatises of Government*, 313n; on this point, see also Von Leyden, "Locke's Strange Doctrine"). Philosophers and political scientists have, by and large, accepted at least Locke's arguments for his "strange doctrine" as a novelty (see, for instance, Parry, *John Locke*, 58; an exception to this rule is Tuck, *Natural Rights Theories*, 62–63, 79). But it is worth noting that even Locke's last, central argument (concerning the punishment of aliens) was used previously by Grotius (*De Jure Praedae Commentarius*, 92). And, as the earlier portions of my discussion have suggested, much of the rest of Locke's position seems also to have been borrowed from Grotius. Locke's original contribution on this subject lay not so much in the formulation or defense of the executive right, but rather in his systematic presentation of its importance for political philosophy.

(and natural law), and Locke seems (rightly) not to insist that there is such a need in the *Treatises*.

What Locke does say in the *Second Treatise* is that "the law of nature would, as all other laws that concern men in this world, be in vain, if there were nobody that in the state of nature had a power to execute that law" (II, 7). While, as we have seen (1.2), Locke is not holding that the sanction of the law is what makes it obligatory, he does hold that the law has no point without sanctions (e.g., E, 2.28.6; ELN, 173). And God surely wants His law to have a point. But God's sanctions are not sufficient to compel widespread obedience, so the law of nature will not be effectively enforced in the state of nature. What we need is sanctions immediately applied in this life, not the next. Now Locke undoubtedly means all of this, but he cannot mean to conclude that there can be no "real" law of nature or true morality unless people enforce that law in the state of nature. For in the *Essay*, immediately after insisting that law requires sanctions, and that in the case of moral (divine) law the relevant sanctions are those applied by God, Locke comments that "the penalties that attend the breach of God's laws some, nay perhaps most men, seldom seriously reflect on: and amongst those that do, many, whilst they break the law, entertain thoughts of future reconciliation" (E, 2.28.12). This observation that God's sanctions are insufficient to compel obedience does not lead Locke to doubt that the law of nature is a true law; quite the contrary.

The ineffectiveness of God's sanctions does not seem to force us to choose between accepting the executive right or rejecting natural law, on Locke's view. What Locke is thinking, I believe, is that where a (good) law is not being obeyed by those bound to do so, those to whom the law applies have a duty (and right) to assist in its enforcement. The only apparent basis for such a claim in the case of natural law, however, would be that since natural law promotes the well-being of those to whom it applies, our general duty (and right) to help preserve mankind requires (and permits) that we enforce that law. This, of course, brings us to the second of Locke's arguments for the executive right, and forces the conclusion that the first argument we considered neither has any independent force (as a defense of the executive right) nor was intended by Locke to have any.

(2) I turn now to Locke's second argument for the executive right: that it is implied by our right (and duty) to preserve all mankind. This right, as we saw in 2.1, is for Locke a particularly "fun-

damental" right, a trivial (mandatory) consequence of the fundamental law of nature. So let us accept it for the moment. Does a
right to preserve mankind imply a natural executive right?

First, how are we to understand the idea of a right to preserve
mankind? Presumably, like the right of self-defense, this right
could be taken at least two ways. Construed narrowly, the right to
preserve others might be viewed as a right only to help defend
them when they are actually being attacked by others. More
broadly, the right to preserve others could be taken to include not
only the right to defend them, but also the right to protect them in
other ways, such as by creating a "deterrent climate" or by preemptive attacks against those whose presence endangers them.

It is difficult to see how the former of these versions of the right
to preserve mankind could naturally yield a right to punish, for
punishment of a criminal involves far more than defending someone against attack; punishment begins where defense leaves off.
Much more than the narrow right to preserve will be required to
derive a right to punish. What about the broader version of the
right? It would clearly justify more than simply punishment, since
preemptive attacks on the dangerous might well include harming
those who have not yet broken the natural (moral) law (in order to
prevent their doing so in the future). But Locke's remarks elsewhere suggest that he might well be comfortable with this sort of
consequence: people "have not only a right to get out of [tyranny],
but to *prevent* it" (II, 220; my emphasis). And while the broad version of our natural right to preserve mankind justifies more than
punishment, it appears also to justify punishment. It will explain
our right to harm in response to wrongdoing, since doing this will
help to preserve persons (by virtue of having, in many instances,
beneficial deterrent effects).

Here, then, we have a first, initially convincing Lockean argument for the natural executive right, although in Locke this argument is ultimately tied (as we saw in 1.5) to rule-consequentialist
reasoning about the content of God's will for humankind. Each
person is thus empowered by God to be an executor of His law.
This argument, of course, will not satisfy secular concerns about
the right to punish without independent derivation of the right to
preserve humankind (a derivation that may well be possible). But
whether presented in its religious or secular form, this argument
simply cannot account directly for all of what Locke wants in a
natural executive right. Locke seems most often to want to defend
a right to punish *any* wrongdoer, not a right to punish that is con-

ditional on the direct usefulness of particular acts of punishing. But it is manifestly false that punishment of wrongdoers will always be causally related to effective deterrence. Some punishment neither advances nor can be reasonably believed to advance the preservation of mankind. Only by further employment of rule-consequentialist reasoning (i.e., by arguing that punishment *tends* to deter crime) will a Lockean be able to draw from the right to preserve mankind a right to punish every breach of natural law. And the appeal of this style of reasoning is clearly limited.

(3) Now for Locke's third and most prominent argument: that we cannot explain the rightful punishment of aliens unless there is a natural executive right. What is striking about Locke's prominent presentation of this argument is his apparently total failure to see how badly it fits the overall position he defends in the *Second Treatise* (indeed, it looks as if Locke may have simply taken the argument from Grotius without seriously considering its implications). For there seems to be an extremely simple refutation of the argument available, one that can be found in Locke's own text. Locke is well known for his theory of tacit consent, according to which any person that has "any possession or enjoyment of any part of the dominions of any government" can be taken to have consented to the authority of that government, "whether this his possession be of land, to him and his heirs forever, or a lodging only for a week; or whether it be barely travelling freely on the highway; and in effect, it reaches as far as the very being of anyone within the territories of that government" (II, 119).

The implication of these passages is clear: aliens, merely by (freely) entering the territories of the state, can be taken to consent to its authority over them. These aliens, we might say, have authorized the state to punish them should they violate its laws. We can, then, explain the government's right to punish aliens entirely in terms of Locke's own account of the tacit agreement between government and alien.[28] No reference to a natural executive right seems necessary. The state's laws do "reach" (i.e., bind) aliens, for they are not in a state of nature with respect to the state once they enter its territories. They are "temporary members" of the commonwealth, like any resident or visitor who has not *expressly* consented to be a full member (II, 121–22).

Even more embarrassing for Locke is the following question: if

[28] This seems to be what Murphy has in mind ("Paradox," 267). Farrell also notes the availability of this argument to Locke ("Punishment Without the State," 451).

we can explain the state's right to punish aliens without reference to a natural executive right, can we not similarly explain its right to punish citizens? Instead of starting with the assumption that citizens have a right to punish everyone else, which they entrust to government, why not assume that citizens begin with only a right to control their own lives (as it were, they have a right only to "punish" themselves). Citizens then entrust a portion of this natural right of self-government to the state, authorizing government to punish them (i.e., control their lives) for violations of its laws. The net result of all citizens so authorizing government, of course, would be that the government had the right to punish all citizens. This is the conclusion that Locke wants to reach; but, contrary to Locke's suggestions, it seems possible to reach it without appealing to a natural executive right. We can explain the right of governments to punish both citizens and aliens, without having to suppose that any "natural man" ever had the right to punish another. And we can explain it in a way that is consistent with Locke's desire to show that all governmental rights are derived (by transfer in trust) from the citizens of the state.

This alteration in Locke's program seems even more desirable when we remember that if the government's right to punish is merely its citizens' executive rights, suitably transferred, the government's power to punish must be limited to cases where the law of nature has been transgressed. This, after all, was all that the natural executive right allowed. And while much of the behavior that a state will want to make criminal surely violates natural law, other clearly does not—for instance, violation of at least some tax laws, drug and "morals" laws, traffic and parking laws, and many other regulatory statutes hardly seems naturally immoral. How can we explain the government's right to punish in such areas? It is easy to reply that in addition to giving the state the right to punish violations of natural law, citizens also give up some further portion of their right to control their lives (justifying punishment in these additional areas). This seems to be what Locke has in mind (e.g., II, 128–30).[29] But surely, if we must appeal to transfers of our natural right of self-government to explain *parts* of the state's right to punish, it would be theoretically more elegant to explain *all* of its right to punish in these terms. We would also thus spare ourselves the effort of defending Locke's "strange doctrine"

[29] Contrary to Macpherson's apparent claim that Lockean government can do no more than enforce natural law (*Possessive Individualism*, 218).

of the executive right, telling Locke's story entirely in terms of citizens entrusting to government portions of their rights to govern themselves.[30]

What is wrong with this simpler, more elegant, revised Lockean account I have just outlined? Why did Locke not choose this course, with all of its apparent advantages? We might speculate about his reasons. First, Locke seems to have confusedly supposed that if all governmental rights come from the citizens, and the government has the right to punish everyone, then some citizen must have had the (entire) right to punish everyone. And if any citizen had it, everyone must have had it. He seems not to have considered that the government's right to punish might be composed, piecemeal, from the many and much more limited rights of citizens to "punish" themselves only. Second, there seems to be a serious problem, on our revised account, about capital punishment. No person, according to Locke, has the moral right to commit suicide (nor is this morally permissible) (see above, 1.5). How, then, could government come to have the right to punish us with death, if this right must have come from each citizen?[31] The natural executive right, of course, includes the right to punish *others* with death (where appropriate), not ourselves. It might thus be supposed to be transferred to government, justifying capital punishment, without Locke having to defend a right to commit suicide. I will say about this problem only that there are quite general difficulties in Locke about capital punishment, of which this is only one.[32] Perhaps the proper resolution of them, within a broadly Lockean framework, will require the abandonment of Locke's prohibition on suicide (which seems to me, on independent grounds, a good idea—see 1.5). Third, Locke may have been concerned about the revised account's apparent inability to ground a *federative* right of government. Insofar as the federative right includes a right to punish noncitizens, it is unclear how this could in any way be derived from citizens' rights over themselves only.

There is, I think, a final (and much more interesting) problem

---

[30] This seems to be roughly the solution proposed by Altham (as a remedy to problems in Nozick, not in Locke). Nobody has a right to punish others in a state of nature; the government's right arises from individual contracts ("Reflections on the State of Nature," 140–41).

[31] See Beccaria's related difficulties in deriving the state's right to punish crimes with death from the individual transfer of rights in a contract of government (*On Crimes and Punishments*, 45–52).

[32] On these problems, see Dunn, *Political Thought*, 126–27.

with the revised account proposed above, one of which Locke may well have been aware (as I argue in 3.5). The revised account can succeed only if there is no natural right to punish. My remarks thus far have suggested only that the revised account obviates the need to defend a natural executive right, but the point must be put more strongly. It is not just that a defense of our revised account saves us the trouble of proving Locke's "strange doctrine"; the revised account cannot be defended, if there is a right of all to punish. I will elaborate on this point more fully and explain the shortcomings of the (apparently superior) revised account below in 3.5.

3.4. The Coherence of Locke's Position

The problem is not, it may be claimed, merely that Locke's arguments for the natural executive right are weak. What he is arguing *for* is a position that makes no clear sense. This objection to Locke has taken a variety of forms. In its first (Benthamic) form, it is an objection we have touched on already (in 2.5); it challenges not specifically the intelligibility of claims that there is a natural executive right, but rather the intelligibility of any defense of any natural right. The concept of a right, it is claimed, is one of enormous complexity, presupposing an intricate system of institutional rules, for which there could be no analogue in a nonpolitical state of nature.

A related, but milder, form of natural right skepticism attacks only the idea of private natural rights. Green, remember, allowed that persons have natural rights, but only as members of some (not necessarily political) community. Green (following Hegel) specifically attacks the idea of a natural executive right as the incoherent notion of a purely private natural right, a "right of private vengeance." This would be a right neither "derived from society nor regulated by reference to social good." Since "all right is public," there can be no natural right to punish.[33] The stronger (Benthamic) form of skepticism and the milder skepticism of Green have this much in common: they both centrally employ the idea that the concept of a right severely limits the possible content of any theory of natural rights.

I have already attempted to reply to these versions of natural right skepticism (above in 2.5). I mention these forms of general

---

[33] Green, *Lectures on the Principles of Political Obligation*, section 178.

skepticism here only because they both point toward much more specific worries about a natural right to punish. Regardless of what limits the concept of a right may place on natural rights theory, the concept of punishment, at least, seems to centrally involve conventional or institutional rules by which it is administered, and some notion of a shared community response to wrongdoing (these claims, of course, are simple corollaries of the more general skepticisms I have associated with Bentham and Green). Even, then, if simple conceptual analysis could not dispose of natural rights theories generally, perhaps it can dispose of one particular natural right—the right of all to punish.

Several contemporary philosophical treatments of the natural right to punish have taken this route. Jeffrie Murphy has argued that

> The notion of a natural right to punish, in a sense of "punish" strong enough to count as an entrusted governmental right, is unintelligible. It is not simply that such punishing is inefficient; it is conceptually impossible.[34]

And, more recently, Gerald Postema has claimed that

> The right to punish . . . cannot rightly be said to exist prior to the establishment of an institutional arrangement for punishment. This is because punishment is conceptually linked to the notion of a public or community response to wrong-doing.[35]

These charges seem both serious and reasonable. How (if at all) can a defender of the natural executive right (and of the intuitions expressed in 3.1) reply? Let us start to answer this question by trying to understand exactly what it is about the natural right to punish that renders claims for its existence "unintelligible." Critics seem to emphasize the following points:

    (a)   The natural executive right would be a purely private right to punish; but punishment can only (logically) be

[34] "Paradox," 257.
[35] "Nozick on Liberty," 326. Similarly, David Hoekema maintains that "the right to punish must in this respect be like the right to vote, or the right to due process: it is a right which has no application—whose assertion does not even make sense—apart from the social institutions which confer it" ("Right to Punish," 240).

inflicted by an agent of a community, in a representation of the community's response to crime.[36]

(b) The natural executive right would be merely a right to inflict harm on others; punishment conceptually involves much more than this.[37]

(c) The natural executive right would be a right exercised by persons who had no *authority* to punish; punishment, to distinguish it from other applications of force, must be understood to involve both authoritative application of certain rules, and authoritative administration of sanctions.[38]

In evaluating these conceptual claims, we must try to remember the constant dangers faced in making them—the dangers of pretending that a concept is far sharper than it really is, and of losing sight, in the process of conceptual analysis, of what our interests in a thesis really are[39] (in this case, our interest in understanding what kind of response to wrongdoing is naturally defensible, and what changes from our natural condition are necessary to make rightful punishment by the state). The first kind of danger seems to wait for claim (a) above—the claim that infliction of harm cannot count as punishment unless it is a community response to wrongdoing. Perhaps most familiar cases of punishment satisfy this condition. But to refuse on conceptual grounds to count as "punish-

---

[36] Postema, "Nozick on Liberty," 326. Recall Green's arguments.

[37] Ibid., 325; Murphy, "Paradox," 261.

[38] Ibid., 261–64; Postema, "Nozick on Liberty," 325–26. I assume that this is part of what Hoekema has in mind as well. Postema also stresses the requirement that the right to punish be a full claim right (i.e., a right correlated with an obligation on others to refrain from interference). I comment on this matter below in 3.5. Both Murphy and Postema present layered arguments against the natural executive right. Both reject it on conceptual grounds; but both suggest that more is wrong as well. Murphy argues against the right on conceptual grounds, and also claims that it could not, in any event, be used by Locke within his theory in the way Locke intended. Postema maintains that the form of the right to which Nozick is committed cannot be made to do the work required of it by Nozick's theory. I address Murphy's complaints later in this section; I discuss the issues about which Postema is concerned in the next. We should remember that *neither* of these arguments concerning the internal consistency of the theories (of Locke and Nozick) in any way shows that there is not a natural executive right.

[39] A classic example in the literature on punishment was the "definitional stop" used in the debate about whether or not utilitarians were committed to the possible punishment of innocent persons. The conceptual argument—that it is not possible to (deliberately) *punish* an innocent person—lost sight of the fact that people were interested not in what to *call* what utilitarians were committed to doing to innocent persons, but in *what* they were committed to doing.

ments" the sanctions applied by God to people, or by parents to their children, or by teachers to their students, would seem very odd. Indeed, it is generally conceded that a community (or political-legal) response (and, I assume this means, a highly structured institutional framework) is not an essential aspect of punishment; only an "authoritative hierarchy" is really necessary for punishment.[40] This concession, however, just reduces claim (a) to a version of claim (c), which I will consider in a moment.[41]

What about the suggestion (b) that the right to punish must be much more complex than simply a right to inflict harm on others? This seems indisputably true, but no defender of a natural executive right would try to deny it. No one defends a right to inflict harm (simpliciter). Rights to inflict harm are rights to do so in some particular context or for some particular reason. Thus, you might have a natural right to inflict harm on others in self-defense, in order to insure that your rights are respected, to protect others, to promote the common good, and so on. The executive right is (and is thought by Locke and others to be) a right to inflict harm for (in response to, because of) wrongdoing.[42] As Locke's critics insist, no other kind of right to inflict harm (no matter how interesting in other respects) can count as a right to *punish*. Punishment essentially involves a set of rules (or, at least, a single rule—which includes, of course, some shared expectation of obedience), and the infliction of harm for the breach of a rule.[43] But the natural executive right can live up to these requirements. There is (or can be) a set of rules (and an expectation of obedience) in the state of nature, independent of any hierarchical structure. The rules of

[40] Murphy, "Paradox," 268; Hoekema, "Right to Punish," 239–40.
[41] Murphy argues as well that none of the kinds of punishment that can exist without government could be appealed to in an argument about the justification of civil punishment. This, of course, assumes that there is no right to punish of the sort Locke defends, which Murphy believes he has demonstrated.
[42] Farrell argues that "Locke's position is not that each of us has the right to punish wrongdoers simply because they are wrongdoers, but, rather, that each of us has the right to punish wrongdoers insofar as it is plausible to suppose that the innocent will be better off if wrongdoers are punished than if they are not" ("Punishment Without the State," 440). But Locke never seems to make the right to punish *conditional* on effective deterrence. Preserving humankind is part of the (rule-consequentialist) justification for punishment, but the right to punish is a right to punish wrongdoers simply because they have breached natural law (and regardless of whether or not *their* punishment will in that particular case help to preserve the innocent). Helping innocents in other ways may also be justified, but punishment is distinguished by its being a response to wrongdoing.
[43] More precisely, punishment is loss or harm inflicted on another for failure to observe applicable standards of behavior. This definition, of course, does *not* make impossible genuine punishing in the state of nature.

143

morality (natural law) can fill this role. And if Locke is right that a breach of these rules can justify inflicting harm (for wrongdoing), can there not be genuine punishment (and a true right to punish) in the state of nature?

We are thus pushed naturally to the third, but apparently most important, conceptual claim (c): that there can be no punishment without authority. There is no one in the state of nature with the authority to punish all others; much less could *everyone* have such authority. Its being permissible to harm another for wrongdoing is not the same as having the authority to punish that person. There could be, then, no natural right to punish.

What exactly is required to have the authority to punish? It seems to involve more than simply being at liberty in a certain way (having a right). Perhaps having the authority to punish involves having an *exclusive* right to do so. But could not both a father *and* a mother, say, have the right to punish their children, without this implying that they were not really punishing (in the strict sense) at all? Perhaps, then, having authority has something to do with having been authorized by some person or group to punish, as our legal authorities could be taken to have been authorized by the public. This also seems unpromising as a necessary condition for the infliction of harm counting as punishment, as the examples of God and parents again make clear. Neither God nor parents have been authorized by anyone to punish (perhaps God *has* authorized parents; but, in any event, someone has not been authorized). Yet what they do, even in the state of nature, seems properly to count as punishment. Locke, of course, would not have been troubled by this condition, for he supposed that each person *had* been authorized to enforce natural law—each person acts as an agent of God in enforcing His law.[44] This is one explanation of how a person gets the executive right in the first place. Locke's other arguments, considered earlier, are all designed to convince us that God must have had such an authorization in mind (i.e., the authorization is entailed by other propositions we know to be true).

We still have not seen how authority is essential to punishment. Murphy explains it the following way: punishment requires an "*authoritative* interpretation of law and infliction of harm." What sense can we make, though, of the claim that *everyone* is an authority on punishment? "Where everyone is said to be an authority, the concept of authority operates without sense," as cases of

---

[44] See the discussion of this point in Dunn, *Political Thought*, 127.

possible conflicting "authoritative" judgments show. And whatever gives a person authority, it cannot be "mere conscientiousness." Locke seems to be saying that each person has the authority
to punish as conscience dictates; but surely the "white racist's"
conscientiousness cannot give that person the authority to kill a
black man "who has committed the 'crime' of befriending a white
woman." In short,

> What Locke describes as a natural right to punish is not de-
> scriptive of punishment at all, for it describes a practice in
> which everyone, at all times, has authority to inflict harm for
> felt wrongs. This is not punishment but merely the exercise of
> vigilante force—something we are surely able to do but noth-
> ing we have a right to do.[45]

Now part of this complaint seems reasonable; but another part
seems quite unfair to Locke. Locke does not, of course, ever say
or imply that "conscientiousness gives authority." It is God and
criminals (by their actions) that give us the authority to punish
criminals. But even if Locke *were* claiming that conscientiousness
gives authority, it would seem beside the point to attack this claim
by pointing to cases where conscientious people (e.g., white rac-
ists) act wrongly in punishing. After all, judges in a legal system,
with the kind of authority that seems to satisfy us, also act
wrongly (from bias, confusion, ignorance, etc.). But this fact in no
way seems to limit their authority to make binding judgments. No
ground of authority rules out the possibility of mistake or wrongdoing. Obviously, holding authorities to higher standards than
mere conscientiousness is a good thing. This, however, is precisely part of Locke's point in arguing for the desirability of civil
society.

We must be careful to keep in mind two things that Locke is *not*
claiming about the natural executive right. He is not claiming that
as long as punishment is administered conscientiously it is morally
defensible. There are objective standards both for innocence and
guilt and for what constitutes a just punishment: "If he that
judges, judges amiss in his own, or any other case, he is answer-
able for it to the rest of mankind" (II, 13). Wrongful punishment,
even *conscientious* wrongful punishment, is itself a violation of natural law. Second, Locke is not claiming that a criminal may be
punished over and over again for a single crime, by each person

[45] Murphy, "Paradox," 262–64.

145

who holds the right to punish.[46] There is clearly meant to be a ceiling on just punishment—that is, that total amount (and kind) of punishment that is appropriate to the crime. What Locke *is* saying is that, subject to this limit, we in the state of nature have the moral right to try to enforce the law of nature, by meting out the punishment that is lawful. If we enforce the law wrongly, we ourselves are punishable. What no one has in the state of nature is the power to *declare* (i.e., make) a person guilty or innocent, or to *declare* a certain punishment just (appropriate, fitting). These are matters of objective (moral) fact (II, 12). Our natural right to punish, then, is only a right to punish properly; there is no right to make authoritative pronouncements or punish authoritatively (in the sense in which this involves the power to make declarations).

Now this fact seems to be part of what worries Murphy. In an established legal system one might argue that there is a sense in which somebody (or some body) has the power to declare a person (legally) guilty or innocent and declare a punishment (legally) just. There is nothing like this power that anyone could have in a state of nature. Locke's problem is not, as Murphy seems to suggest, that he is committed to maintaining that everyone in the state of nature has such a power, so that one could declare a person guilty while another (incoherently) declared that same person innocent. Locke admits that no one (in the state of nature) has such a power. The problem could not even really be the conflicts to which granting everyone this power would commit Locke. (It is possible to have a legal system in which there is more than one judge with the authority to punish, but no highest authority to resolve conflicts. Could there be no punishment in such a [far from ideal] system?) Locke's real problem must be simply that in a state of nature there can be no authoritative punishing.

Does this mean that there could be no such thing as punishing (properly so called) in a state of nature? I confess that I simply do not see why this should be our conclusion, why this element should be taken to be essential to punishment. But even if that *is* the proper conclusion, it is not really one that touches our central concerns in this matter. What should interest us are the questions of what, in the state of nature, we are morally entitled to do to others for their wrongdoing, and how this natural condition must be altered to make possible legitimate punishment in civil society. I think that Locke is right at least this far: that we are (or at least

[46] On this point, see Lyons, "Rights Against Humanity," 210.

can be) entitled in a state of nature to harm others for their wrong-doing and that this right must be laid aside in the creation of a legitimate political society. Whether or not we call our natural entitlement a right to *punish* is uninteresting.

Murphy, of course, is extremely careful to avoid the charge that his objections to Locke are "merely verbal." Even if we forget about what to *call* the infliction of harm in the state of nature, no "reasonable man could regard as justified a system in which harm could be inflicted at will by any person so long as that person merely *thought* that another was deserving." That would be equivalent to a system of vigilantism. Even, then, if the idea of a natural right to punish were not unintelligible, there surely *is* no such right. And further, if Locke claimed that all persons in the state of nature were "fully rational, all knowing, and all good," so that vigilantism didn't look so bad, Locke would be forced to admit that there was no reason to form a political society, after all.[47] Thus, the only move that would make Locke's vigilantism look at all palatable would both involve an implausible factual claim (that persons are fully rational, etc.) and undercut his main argument for the desirability of civil society.

The heart of this criticism of Locke is the (false) assumption that he was attempting to justify punishment (or "punishment") for felt wrongs. We have already seen that this was not his intention. The kind of vigilantism Locke thought jusified was not the brand familiar to us from Hollywood Westerns. We all know what is (usually) wrong with vigilantism in civil society; but what about vigilantism in the state of nature? We will condemn it insofar as we believe that it is bound to amount to mob violence, with harm inflicted in rash, passionate, ill-considered, unfair (etc.) ways. We will think of cases where innocents are vengefully lynched (as in *The Ox Bow Incident*), or where the guilty are lynched without being given a fair (dispassionate) hearing. But none of this is a necessary component of vigilantism, nor would Locke have approved of it. Revenge is for Locke a motive unworthy of a rational being (*Education*, 37). Vengeful vigilantism is a breach of moral law, itself a crime deserving punishment. What Locke argued for was a conception of our natural state in which each person (or that person banded together with others) was entitled to harm a criminal for wrongdoing, to the extent allowed by natural law. Whether a state in which such rights were generally recognized would be morally

[47] Murphy, "Paradox," 264, 266.

unthinkable, as Murphy's argument suggests, seems to me open to argument. Of course, if people merely use these rights as a feeble excuse for trying to enforce their own irrational prejudices, life will be solitary, poor, nasty, and the rest. But the same unbearable existence will be achieved by such people even without the recognition of the natural executive right. If, on the other hand, with Locke we assume that persons in the state of nature will at least often care about morality, take rights reasonably seriously, and are frequently prepared to appeal to "calm reason" in times of conflict, life will look less brutish. When people are prepared to act responsibly, Locke might say, we should take advantage of this to encourage them to do what is best—in this case, seeing to it that deserving wrongdoers suffer for their wrongs. It will not be the best possible arrangement (people not being fully rational, etc.), but it will be better than one in which criminals know that no one feels entitled to punish their crimes. Excesses in punishment will tend to be curbed both by the clarity and force of natural law, and by each person's desire to avoid being punished by others for excessive punishment.

Things could be still better, of course. The inevitable mistakes and passionate excesses could be avoided, and the times when calm reason and moral sensitivity are left entirely behind could be made less harmful. Hence, Locke's argument (against the anarchist) for the preferability of civil society. I think, then, that the critics have not succeeded in undermining the Lockean project. Locke neither describes a morally unthinkable system of natural punishment, nor in the process sacrifices his arguments for the preferability of political life. But it must be conceded that we have not yet examined any very satisfying account of the origin or force of the supposed natural right to punish, or of how a just government can come to have an *exclusive* moral right to punish wrongdoers.

3.5. Forfeiture and Punishment

Locke does not always talk of our natural right to punish as something derivable from our right to preserve mankind (itself a consequence of God's positive authorization). There is in Locke another line about the right to punish, one that he does not really distinguish from those we have considered thus far. Sometimes (particularly where he is concerned with war) Locke talks not as if the right to punish is a *general* right all persons have as agents of

God, but rather as if it is a *special* right that is created by the criminal, in committing a crime (indeed, I categorized the executive right as a special right in 2.3). By breaching the law of nature, a criminal *forfeits* certain natural rights, lowering moral barriers that previously existed against the infliction of harm. This leaves others with greater right to interfere in the criminal's life and makes legitimate the punishment they may impose. In violating another's natural rights, in other words, we lose some of our own. This seems, at first blush, a plausible story about how punishment might become (morally) lawful in a state of nature. What is, perhaps, especially attractive about this account is that it seems not to require any reference to God's authority, making it an explanation of a natural right to punish that would be consistent with even a purely secular theory of natural rights, and with the secular strain of Locke's own thought (as we will see).

Remarks about the forfeiture of rights are scattered throughout both of Locke's *Treatises*, but no careful formulation of the doctrine is ever given. In the *Second Treatise*, comments on forfeiture are most prominent in discussion of those cases where an individual forfeits *all* rights by some act that deserves death. Murderers, and those who unjustly put themselves into a state of war against others (by declaring a wrongful intention to take their lives), lose all of their rights. All moral barriers to harming them are lowered, making punishment even by death rightful. It is only thus that arbitrary, despotical power of one person over another is possible (Locke also, however, keeps the fundamental law of nature always in mind, for he observes that "even the guilty are to be spared, where it can prove no prejudice to the innocent" [II, 159]). In the *First Treatise*, Locke speaks of less complete and dramatic cases of the forfeiture of rights (as when a father forfeits his rights over his children [I, 100]). Presumably, the idea is that by performing acts contrary to natural law one forfeits that portion of one's own rights against others that will make an interference in one's own life, proportionate to one's interference with others, morally permissible.[48] The most serious offenses leave a criminal altogether rightless, like some lesser animal, which may be used or killed at will.

This kind of account of the forfeiture of natural rights seems very much like what some contemporary libertarians have had in

---

[48] Locke does not have in mind (as we saw in 3.2) that just *any* crime, no matter how small, results in a forfeiture of *all* rights. See Bayles and Henley, *Right Conduct*, 182; Green, *Lectures on the Principles of Political Obligation*, section 177; Goldman, "Paradox of Punishment," 44–45.

mind. Rothbard, for instance, writes that "the criminal, or invader, loses his own right to the extent that he deprived another man of his."[49] And Nozick puts it only slightly differently:

One might take a contract-like view of moral prohibitions and hold that those who themselves violate another's boundaries forfeit the right to have certain of their own boundaries respected. On this view, one is not morally prohibited from doing certain sorts of things to others who have already violated certain moral prohibitions (and gone unpunished for this). Certain wrongdoing gives others a *liberty* to cross certain boundaries (an absence of a duty not to do it); the details might be those of some retributive view.[50]

There is one (prominent) difference between the views of Rothbard and Nozick on forfeiture, however. Rothbard believes that the victim of a crime has a special right (not shared by others) to punish the criminal; Nozick regards the right to punish as shared by "all mankind." This disagreement in fact reflects a fundamental inconsistency in Locke's theory. Locke seems to have not one doctrine of forfeiture, but two.

Sometimes Locke presents the simple picture of forfeiture described above: criminals lose their rights, making punishment by any other person lawful. Criminals' rights simply disappear—for a time, that is; they presumably return when criminals have received just punishment, or perhaps when they are forgiven. This seems to be Nozick's version of Locke, and a version consistent with Locke's insistence that *all* persons in a state of nature have the right to punish criminals. At other times, however (and, indeed, in the most prominent passages on forfeiture—e.g., II, 23, 172), Locke talks as if the criminal's right is not simply lost, but is rather forfeited *to* or *with respect to* a particular party—namely, the victim of the crime. Victims are the only persons with the right to punish, although they may, of course, enlist the aid of willing assistants. This seems to be something like Rothbard's view. It implies, among other things, that if Morton wrongs Swanson, and I attempt to punish Morton for this, I wrong Morton by doing so, even if the punishment I apply to Morton is the one he deserves (or the one that would otherwise be lawful in kind and amount). Morton's moral barriers have been lowered only with respect to

[49] *Ethics of Liberty*, 80.
[50] *Anarchy*, 137–38. Notice that Ross, like Nozick, characterizes the right to punish as a liberty (*Right and the Good*, 61).

Swanson, not the rest of humankind. Locke also talks as if victims have the right *not* to punish criminals if they so decide, which seems to make room for the virtue of forgiveness.[51]

However we may feel about forgiveness, it has to be admitted that this second line on forfeiture conflicts with many of Locke's most important claims about punishment. It is inconsistent with his view that the natural right to punish a wrongdoer is held by all persons, and it implies that one person may forgive (or be lenient in response to) what is a "trespass against the whole species." And it conflicts with Locke's claim that the victim's special right, entailed by the right to preserve self, is a right to reparation. Nor is it a plausible position considered on its own merits. It has serious difficulty in cases where the victim is killed by the wrongdoer (who then has a right to punish?).[52] Further, punishment seems to be "owed" to the criminal, not to the victim;[53] the criminal does not deserve to be punished *by the victim*. Locke, by noting the victim's special right to reparation, has already taken account of what is unique about the victim's position. We must, then, reject this second line of argument about forfeiture in Locke, as both implausible in its own right and inconsistent with more important features of Locke's theory.[54]

I have spoken approvingly of the first Lockean line about forfeiture (where rights are simply lost for a time). But much about this line of argument remains unexplained (and goes largely unexplained by Locke and most of the libertarian authors who have followed his lead). For instance, it should be made clear how

[51] "If [the criminal deserving death] be once allowed to be master of his own life, the despotical, arbitrary power of his master ceases" (II, 172; see also II, 24). Locke also talks as if magistrates (II, 11) or rulers (II, 159) may decide *not* to punish the guilty (and they are, after all, also only exercising the natural executive right). The possibility of forgiveness might seem to modify an essentially Old Testament conception of punishment with some New Testament sentiments.

[52] Perhaps the solution might be that whoever inherits the other rights (i.e., property) of the deceased, also inherits the right to punish the killer. But this solution seems to conflict with the general limits on inheritance Locke elsewhere discusses (see below, 4.4). Warren Quinn has suggested to me that we might understand the victim to have tacitly transferred the right to punish the murderer in advance, as an obvious act of prudential rationality.

[53] Nozick, *Anarchy*, 138; Altham, "Reflections on the State of Nature," 142.

[54] This is not to say that the second line is without advantages of its own. In addition to those mentioned below (concerning exclusivity), for instance, the second line obviates some (but not all) concerns (also discussed below) about the *reasons* for which we may harm others. If unjust aggressors simply forfeit rights (not *to* anyone), *fellow* aggressors (who share their evil aims) may justly harm or kill the unjust aggressors, for whatever bad reasons they may have. I try to show below that the first line can handle such worries.

heavily this account relies not only on a theory of natural *rights*, but on whatever theory is used to determine what punishments fit the crime (a subject on which I will not even begin to comment here). As I have outlined it, the Lockean line on forfeiture makes central use of certain aspects of a retributivist theory of punishment; moral desert determines the degree of right-forfeiture that results from moral wrongdoing. Of course, this does not mean that the Lockean position just reduces to a pure retributivism, insofar as those who are rightly punishable are not simply those who *deserve* punishment, but only those who have also first violated the rights of another. (Thus, one who might seem to deserve punishment more than some minor violator of rights—such as one who constantly and deliberately humiliated others—might not be punishable on the Lockean account.) Desert determines only the extent of the forfeiture, by determining what constitutes an appropriate response to wrongdoing.[55] But only another's forfeiture of rights can give one (in Locke's language) a "commission" to punish. Forfeiture makes it legitimate to give wrongdoers what they deserve.[56]

This may still leave us wondering, however, about why the violation of another's rights causes us to lose our own (to the extent deserved). The answer is surely not obvious, as defenders of the doctrine of forfeiture seem to assume. It is the "mystery" or apparent emptiness of the idea of forfeiture that has led critics in this century to reject it (e.g., critics of Ross and other intuitionists). When asked why punishment is justified, defenders of forfeiture say: because criminals have forfeited their rights. But no account is forthcoming of *why* criminals lose their rights on this occasion. As a result it appears that saying criminals forfeit their rights is saying nothing more than that punishing them is justified.[57] But we naturally want to be shown why this is justified, not simply have it asserted in a mysterious way.

Locke would appear to have several accounts available of why

[55] This may, of course, be a more strongly retributivist view than Locke would have been happy with, given the consequentialist character of some aspects of his moral theory. It is possible to replace this retributivist account of the proper kind and amount of punishment with a consequentialist one, without altering the basic character of the Lockean program. But the result would, in my view, be a less plausible position.

[56] Of course, to the extent that retributivism is taken to include the views that neither punishability nor the authority to punish are to be determined simply by considerations of moral desert, this is a "retributivist" stance.

[57] Quinn, "The Right to Threaten," 332–33.

criminals lose rights. One is that God has granted us our rights and chooses to withdraw them when we violate His law.[58] Another is that rationality is a condition for being subject to natural law and a possessor of the rights that law defines. Since acting wrongly demonstrates some measure of irrationality (on Locke's view), it involves a loss of some part of the rights enjoyed by the fully rational. Neither line of argument is entirely persuasive. The first line, while it is clearly consistent with Locke's premises, will not help us in any attempt at a *secular* theory of forfeiture (and it retains a rather mysterious quality itself). The second line is unconvincing because wrongdoing is neither a necessary nor a sufficient condition for lack of (full) rationality.

But it is possible to give other accounts of forfeiture within a (secular) natural rights theory. Perhaps the most "natural" way to view forfeiture involves maintaining that any reasonable or fair system of protective rules (laws, conventions) must specify (explicitly or implicitly) that one's status under the rules depends on respecting them. Protection under the rules is contingent on our obeying them; any rights the rules may define are guaranteed only to those who refrain from violating them (independent, of course, of unanimous agreement to alternative arrangements). Surely we cannot reasonably complain of being deprived of privileges under rules we refuse to live by. Indeed, to extend such privileges to those who break the rules would seem to involve serious and straightforward unfairness to those who limit their own liberty by obeying the rules. Of course, considerations of fairness also seem to dictate that a minor violation of the rules results in only a minor loss of status under the rules, and so on; so that the protection we enjoy under the rules will be proportionate to our own conformity to them. Insofar as there are objective moral rules (defining rights) under which all persons (originally) stand, and protection under the rules depends on others' obedience to them, then, a proportional forfeiture of moral rights may be a necessary consequence of infringing the moral rights of others.[59] Valid moral rules do not

[58] If, as I will suggest below, Locke believes that rights are entrusted to us by God only for certain uses, it is perfectly natural that when abused, our rights return to God.

[59] Thus no consent to loss of rights (as in Hegel) is necessary to explain the idea of rights-forfeiture. The moral work in the account is done instead by the idea of fairness. The Lockean can as a result avoid Hegel's problem of having to claim that any inalienable right must also be nonforfeitable. See Wood (*Hegel's Ethical Thought*, 121) on Hegel's problem. For a related forfeiture account of punishment, see Goldman, "Paradox of Punishment," 43–45. Goldman seems to be discussing legal

extend protection to persons unfairly taking advantage of others' willingness to abide by them. Locke occasionally uses language that suggests an account of forfeiture based in natural fairness, as when he speaks of punishment as "the abridgement of anyone's *share* of the good things of the world."[60]

There is, of course, a Kantian rendering of this argument that seems particularly obvious. The style of Kantian position I briefly described earlier (1.3) prohibits our using persons merely as means to our own ends, in the same way that Locke believes we are not for one another's use. And when we violate protective rules under which all stand in ways that deprive others of their rights (or violate their rights), we seem to be using others in a straightforward way. We use their compliance and forbearance (which is motivated by their recognition of our equal standing under the law) as a means of securing greater advantage for ourselves.[61] Rights-forfeiture can thus be seen as what secures the possibility of natural fairness and what renders impossible ongoing but morally protected patterns of (ab)use of others.[62]

Even if these sketchy suggestions about the ground of forfeiture are found convincing or suggestive, of course, it may seem that serious problems for this account will be caused by the fact that the right to punish (as I have derived it) can only be a "liberty right," not a full "claim right." If my right to punish arises from another's forfeiture of right, the right to punish must be only a

rights in his account of forfeiture; it is not clear whether he would wish to extend his analysis to natural rights (along the lines I have suggested). Herbert Morris discusses punishment in terms of fairness in his well-known paper, "Persons and Punishment." But he is not trying to either analyze forfeiture or discuss natural punishment. See also Ross, *Right and the Good*, 60–64.

[60] King, *Life*, 1:110 (my emphasis).

[61] See Murphy's discussion of Kant's own views on the unfairness of not punishing the guilty (which is, of course, slightly different from the unfairness I describe here of persons enjoying full moral protection while breaching the rights of others), in "Three Mistakes," 167–68. Punishing the guilty, on this account, is not a case of using them as mere means to our ends; for punishment is both required by a moral principle of fairness (and hence is *not* justified simply by its consequences) and responds to the free choices of persons to violate binding rules with their preestablished sanctions.

[62] It is worth noting another reason for suspecting that Locke might have been happy to subscribe to this account of rights-forfeiture—that is, to an account that centrally utilizes the idea of "taking advantage" of others. Locke never suggests that those violations of natural law that involve only harm to *oneself* result in forfeiture of rights; only harm to *others* is said to have this consequence. But self-harming violations of natural law *are* contrary to reason and *do* endanger humankind (i.e., oneself as part of humankind), just like other-harming violations. The only feature of other-harming violations that self-harming violations seem to lack is their taking advantage of the sacrifices of others.

permission, the absence of an obligation to refrain. It does not imply, as a claim right would, that others must not interfere with my actions. That is, although wrongdoers' forfeiture of their right leaves me (morally) free to punish them, it does not obligate others to *allow* me to punish them. They, being also at liberty to punish, may "compete" with me to punish wrongdoers first. The situation would be slightly different on the second line about forfeiture (considered and rejected above). For on that account, only the victim has the right to (is at liberty to) punish; the victim's liberty right is thus an *exclusive* liberty, not in competition with the liberties of others. Others could not punish the criminal first (this would violate the *criminal's* rights), nor could they interfere with the victim's lawful punishment of the criminal (for that would infringe the victim's right of self-government—the right not to be hindered by others in lawful pursuits except by their *competition*). Thus, the exclusive liberty the victim would have on the second (unsatisfactory) account of forfeiture, would have moral consequences similar to the victim's having a full claim right to punish. It may seem a shame not to pursue this account further, for is not this kind of exclusivity of the right to punish (i.e., the guarantee of freedom from interference) exactly the property that we wish our *government's* right to punish to have? Most believe that legitimate governments have a right, in the full sense, to lawfully punish criminals, a right that includes an obligation on citizens not to interfere or try to punish the criminal before the state does (this is the so-called monopoly on force that governments claim and that excludes, among other things, vigilantism). We need to explore the potential of the first account of forfeiture (the one I have chosen to defend over the second account) to provide a solution to this problem of explaining the exclusivity of the legitimate government's right to punish.

Suppose (as the first account maintains) that Butch commits crime (moral wrong) C, for which punishment P is appropriate (according to natural law). Butch forfeits certain of his rights, making it morally permissible for me, or any other person to impose P upon him (subject to the limit that no more than a total punishment of P be imposed). Just how strong a "right" to punish does this liberty give me? Well, what kinds of justifications might another person, Chico, have for interfering with my imposing P on Butch? First, Chico might think Butch deserved punishment Q, instead of P, and as a result believe himself justified in imposing Q and resisting my imposition of P. Or he might think Butch innocent altogether, and feel justified in defending Butch against me. Or he might oppose punishment generally and argue that he was justified in stopping my punishment of Butch. Finally, Chico might want to punish Butch himself, and compete with me to impose P.

Only the last of these could be a successful defense of Chico's interfering with my punishing Butch with P; and even this would not justify Chico's physically impeding my punishing. Chico's only justification would be for *competitive* interference (where he rushed to Butch's home and punished him with P before I could get there). We must remember that we are not describing a Hobbesian state of nature, in which people have only liberty rights. In a Lockean state of nature, each person has a full claim right to freedom from (noncompetitive) interference, provided that person acts within the constraints of the moral law. Since my imposing P on Butch would be within those constraints, any interference by Chico other than competitive interference is morally indefensible. My right to punish, then, when combined with my right of self-government, rules out most kinds of interference, and constitutes a reasonably substantial right.

My remarks above have already suggested that I think the proper solution to the problem of competitive liberties is an appeal to the principle "first come, first served." This answer for the system of "open punishment" I have been describing is similar to the Lockean solution for a system of "open property." Where land or natural resources are unowned, those who labor on them first (subject to certain provisos) "make a property" in them. All are initially at liberty to claim parts of the common, and may use only competitive interference (i.e., taking first) in exercising this liberty.[63]

Nozick worries that if we allow the first punisher to preempt the field, sadists will compete to arrive first at the scene of the crime (to get in their licks while the getting's good). This possibility makes one uncomfortable, and not because (as Nozick supposes) the sadists will be hard to control (always imposing excessive punishment in the heat of passion). Sadists who thus lose control will

[63] The well-known Lockean provisos on the creation of property (II, 31–33) are necessary in that case, but *not* in a system of open punishment, because (obviously) being deprived of access to natural resources endangers one's life, while being deprived of chances to punish criminals (as long as *someone* does it) does not (in fact, it may even enhance one's life prospects). I return to the limits on property and to the liberty to make property in 5.4.

also be punishable. What makes one uncomfortable is the prospect of punishing being done by rational, responsible sadists—who punish only the guilty, and only with the proper kind and amount of punishment, but who delight in doing so. This brings us squarely up against a difficulty I have thus far avoided facing. If the criminal simply forfeits the right not to be harmed in certain ways, then *any* way in which this harm is imposed appears morally acceptable, *any* reason a person has for imposing it is good enough. If Butch and his gang roam the state of nature, cutting throats at random (just for the fun of it), and happen to cut the throat of a murderer (who deserves to be punished with a painful death, say), then that particular throat-cutting, but no other, might be morally acceptable. This seems a preposterous implication of the position I have been defending.[64]

We must remember first that punishment is the infliction of harm for (in response to, because of) wrongdoing.[65] At least part of what motivates those inflicting harm must be the belief that a wrong has been done and that the response they are making is morally (legally, conventionally) appropriate or deserved, or that infliction of harm cannot possibly count as *punishment*. Butch and his gang *punish* no one; neither do the rational sadists if part of their reason for acting is not the belief that punishment is appropriate. Punishers may have additional motives (beyond these beliefs)—anger, a desire to protect society, sadism, and the like. But these cannot be *all* that moves a person to inflict harm on another, if we are to count that infliction of harm as punishment.[66]

Of course, what we *call* the harm Butch and his gang cause is not very important or interesting. What is important is that it is not morally permissible. We are permitted to harm wrongdoers only for certain reasons. The situation parallels that of taking reparation for injuries another has caused. If I take property from one who, completely unbeknownst to me, had previously stolen *my* property, my taking is still theft (and morally impermissible)—

[64] Quinn, "Right to Threaten," 332–33.

[65] On Locke's commitment to this view, see Von Leyden, "Locke's Strange Doctrine," 121. For a recent general statement of this view of punishment, see Wood, *Hegel's Ethical Thought*, 108.

[66] Where institutional forms of punishment are concerned, matters are not so simple. A criminal can properly be said to be punished, for instance, even if the motives of some judge, jury member, or executioner are purely sadistic. What remains true, however, is that (what we might call) the overall "institutional" motive must reflect the notion of a justified response to wrongdoing if we are to count the institutional process as one of punishing.

even though the property I took from that person I might have been entitled to take, if I had taken it *as reparation*. Similarly, the throat-cutting Butch imposes is murder, not justifiable punishment, although he might have been entitled to kill if he had done so *as punishment*.

The main difficulty with this suggestion (as far as I can tell) is in motivating the revision it requires to the doctrine cf forfeiture. Criminals must be said to forfeit not rights not to be harmed in certain ways (simpliciter), but rather rights not to be harmed in certain ways *for certain reasons*. The criminal, after such a forfeiture, has no right to complain about harms done as punishment; the criminal still has every right to complain (although we will no doubt be less sympathetic than usual) about other kinds of harming. These claims seem to me not unbearably awkward or ad hoc, for we often voluntarily transfer to others rights to act only for certain reasons (e.g., you may give your doctor the right to act during your upcoming surgery as he thinks best—but only when he acts for medical reasons, as opposed, say, to his acting for financial reasons or to enhance his professional reputation). If we may voluntarily create a situation where others have rights to act only for certain reasons, it seems plausible to suppose that nonvoluntary forfeiture might result (as I have claimed it must) in rights to harm another only for certain reasons. And the fairness account of forfeiture defended above seems to push us naturally in just this direction. For the unfairness to others that would be involved in allowing the criminal to retain a full complement of rights is unfairness only to those who themselves obey the relevant rules. Butch (with others who harm for the wrong reasons) is not obeying the rules in the relevant sense—that is, he is not prepared to deliberately limit his own liberty according to his view of what is required by fair rules. Indeed, he demonstrates his unwillingness to obey the rules in the very act of attempting to inflict the harm (since he believes the act *not* to be one of just punishment). There is thus no unfairness to *Butch* in allowing a criminal to retain the right not to be harmed for *Butch's* reasons. Fairness (thus forfeiture) is at issue only in relation to those who *do* obey the rules (and attempt to harm others only for acceptable reasons).[67]

[67] This argument provides as well, I think, a response to many who have criticized certain aspects of forfeiture theories of the right of self-defense. David Wasserman, for instance, has claimed (following George Fletcher) that there are "serious and well-recognized drawbacks to a forfeiture approach" to self-defense rights ("Justifying Self-Defense," 361). Among these "drawbacks" is the alleged inability

Again there is, I think, a Kantian (and thus, to the extent elaborated earlier, a Lockean) motivation for this restriction on rights-forfeiture. Harming others (who deserve punishment) for the wrong reasons is morally wrong in the same way that disproportionate punishment of wrongdoers is wrong. Both fail to respond to persons and what they did, both fail to respect them. "An autonomous person has a right that his punishment be *addressed* to that status—to those unique features of his individual, responsible conduct which occasion the punishment"; otherwise, he is "being *used*" for whatever the purposes are that motivate the excessive punishment[68] (or, in my case, the wrongly motivated harming). Respect or responsiveness is not determined just by the brute, physical description of our acts, but also by our beliefs and intentions. Since the possession of rights is premised on autonomy and moral agency, forfeiture of rights is similarly restricted—we forfeit rights by our misconduct only to the extent that makes possible *respectful* punishment. Only the total forfeiture of personhood affects this restriction for Locke.[69] The same style of argument that Locke could use to justify his insistence on proportionality of punishment (II, 8), then, can be used to justify this limit on the reasons for which we may legitimately harm wrongdoers.[70]

If my claims to this point have been correct, a system of open punishment is a morally acceptable (and morally well-motivated) system.[71] But are there difficulties we have not yet considered for

of forfeiture accounts to explain why aggressors' lives may not be taken for just any reason, why they may be taken only by those responding defensively, and then only if such force is necessary to repel the attack (see Thomson's similar criticisms in "Self-Defense and Rights," 33–37). The style of argument presented above suggests that forfeiture theory has ample resources to deal with such problems.

[68] Murphy, "Cruel and Unusual Punishments," 234.

[69] Here Locke apparently disagrees with Vlastos, who claims that "the moral community is not a club from which members may be dropped for delinquency" ("Justice and Equality," 48).

[70] And Locke would here again be following Grotius, who restricts reasons for which one may punish (*De Jure Belli ac Pacis*, 468).

[71] Nozick, in his discussion of open punishment, very quickly gives up trying to understand how it might work, and retreats instead to a view according to which everyone jointly holds the right to punish (or to empower someone to punish). No one *individually* has such a right (*Anarchy*, 139). But his apparent retreat turns out to be only a strategic withdrawal. Nozick has good reason to *want* a system of open punishment to be indefensible (which explains his haste in disposing of it). For if everyone jointly holds the right to punish, but people disagree about who to empower to do their punishing, then the "dominant protective agency" operating in the state of nature has the best claim to do the punishing. For it represents a larger part of the "everyone" who jointly hold the right to punish, than any competing agency or individual. And since no individual has the right to punish, held separately, no individuals' rights are violated when the dominant protective agency

a system of open punishment (other than the obvious ones, like defending a theory of natural rights in the first place)? Admittedly, this account of the natural executive right leaves no room for a certain kind of mercy or forgiveness, understood as the right of any individual. While individuals can be forgiving in their hearts and can refrain from punishing, criminals can only be forgiven (in the performative sense, so that punishment is no longer rightful) if everyone agrees to forego punishing them. I accept this result without great discomfort. Perhaps someone might wish to argue that this is another reason for favoring civil society (where it will be easier for criminals to be forgiven); I do not. It may, finally, seem that in spite of the "strength" of this version of a right to punish (in terms of making interference by others impermissible), it is still too weak a version of the right to punish to satisfy Lockean ambitions. I will consider two ways in which this might seem to be so.

First, it might be claimed that a mere liberty to punish, even if protected from all but competitive interference, fails to capture the sense (occasionally suggested by Locke) in which punishment in the state of nature is not merely morally permissible, but a *duty*.[72]

---

does all of the punishing of criminals for us (i.e., for everyone). This is what allows Nozick to claim that the dominant protective agency has "some special legitimacy" and violates no individual's rights (ibid., 139–40).

If, however, the best way to understand the right to punish in a state of nature is in terms of the system of open punishment defended above, Nozick's main argument appears to fail. He can argue neither that the dominant protective agency has a special legitimacy nor that the rights of individuals (who will be prevented by the agency from punishing in their own way) will not be violated by its practices. Even Nozick must have been uncomfortable about suggesting that the right to punish must be held jointly, since he observed that this would make it the *only* right in a state of nature "possessed by people jointly rather than individually" (ibid., 139). This has the appearance of a position designed only to produce the desired results. See Postema's interesting and much more complete discussion of the difficulties with Nozick's main argument ("Nozick on Liberty"). Some portions of my presentation in this section parallel Postema's work, although we reach quite different conclusions. See also Altham, "Reflections on the State of Nature," 141–44.

[72] In the central sections on punishment (II, 7–13), Locke actually almost always talks of punishment as if it is permissible only, *not* a duty. His use of "may," "right," and "power" convey this sense. The quotation from Genesis (II, 11) stands out in quite dramatic contrast to this tendency. Punishment only seems to be a duty at all after government takes over and *agrees* to use the right to punish for the common good (making the duty in that case consensual in nature); and it is not always a duty even then, since the magistrate may rightfully decline to punish wrongdoers in some cases (II, 11) (see below, and note 51 above). The idea that we have no *duty* to punish seems to be central to Locke's arguments concerning resistance to oppressive government. If there is no duty to punish in Locke, this is further reason to favor our first (simple) line on forfeiture as the best reading of

If it is simply *permissible* to punish a thief, say, there seems to be no stronger moral reason to do so than there would be to hit an unruly dog (who also lacks the right not to be harmed). Punishment seems a matter of moral indifference. What this complaint overlooks is that in the case of the wrongdoer, but not in the case of the dog, the punishment is not only permissible but *deserved*. Where it is true both that someone deserves a certain treatment and that it is permissible for us to treat that person in that way, we have good moral reason to act. Thus, punishing the wrongdoer is not a matter of moral indifference on this account (even if it is not, strictly speaking, a duty either), for the mere absence (through forfeiture) of rights is not the whole of the story.[73] I believe that the natural right to punish, understood as it has been described in this section, captures all of the force of the intuition expressed earlier (in 3.1) about the justifiability of punishment in a nonpolitical state. But can it also be used to explain why a legitimate government has the *exclusive* right to punish, the other essential part of the Lockean project?

3.6. The Monopoly on Force

We can, I think, give a Lockean account of these matters (if not precisely Locke's own) that captures the main ideas Locke was concerned to defend—(a) that a legitimate government's right to punish can only be understood in terms of a redistribution of previously existing natural rights, and (b) that the natural right to punish *must* be sacrificed (i.e., freely alienated) by all members on entrance into civil society. The Lockean account I have in mind proceeds as follows: As per the revised Lockean position outlined in 3.3, each citizen must entrust to government that portion of the

---

Locke, since we can see now that it naturally yields no such duty. On the other hand, of course, the right to punish is derived by Locke from the right to preserve mankind—a right that is, as we have seen, also a duty. This strongly implies that punishment should also, at least often, be a duty. Perhaps Locke is attracted to a view like that of Grotius, for whom some punishment is required, while other is only permitted, so that forgiving the criminal is only sometimes acceptable (*De Jure Belli ac Pacis*, 489–91). But Locke seems never to take any explicit stand on this question.

[73] This point provides a partial answer to one of Allen Wood's criticisms of Hegel's account of punishment—for example, that Hegel shows how punishing is morally permissible, but can offer no positive moral reason *for* punishing the guilty. See *Hegel's Ethical Thought*, 116–17. To the extent that we allow considerations of deterrence to function in the account, of course, there is a further reason (the preservation of humankind) for punishing the thief, but not the dog.

right to self-government that is necessary for effective government (if that government is to be legitimate). The government then holds against each of us a right to interfere (including, particularly, by punishing) in our lives in the designated areas. But the government *cannot* obtain from us in this way an *exclusive* right to punish those crimes that are *moral* wrongs. For our rights of self-government do not include the right of exclusive control over our lives when we violate the moral law. Our right to be free of interference is only a right to be free *within* the bounds of natural law. By our wrongdoings we forfeit the right of control over our lives in some measure, making the interference of any other lawful. The government can be given by each of us only a right to interfere where we are *not* violating moral law, for only in those areas do we begin with a natural right of self-government. In cases of *moral* wrongdoing, the government has (given what has been said thus far) only the same liberty to punish that other persons possess.[74] It is thus in competition with private citizens where it seeks to punish acts that are *mala in se*. The simple transfer of our claim rights to noninterference cannot give the state an exclusive right to punish. This requires a remedy, if there is to be one judge over all citizens.

The obvious solution is that (in the Lockean spirit) each citizen must also surrender on entering civil society the natural liberty to punish wrongdoers. Each must agree not to compete with the state in punishing (moral) criminals.[75] In this way, and only in this way, can the government acquire an exclusive liberty to punish moral wrongdoers (the effective equivalent of a claim right), in addition to the claim right it receives from each consenting citizen to punish in other (necessary) areas.[76] The production of the exclu-

[74] Locke's sensitivity to these issues is best displayed in his early *Second Tract*, where he carefully distinguishes between the magistrate's powers in the areas of morally obligatory conduct (covering crimes that are also moral wrongs) and "indifferent" conduct (covering those areas in which our right of self-government originally left us free). Locke worries that if the magistrate is not free to legislate concerning "things indifferent," then the magistrate could only recommand and enforce the requirements of natural law, in which sphere "the power of the magistrate seems to be no greater than that of any private citizen" (228). This problem is solved by Locke in the *Second Treatise*, where both obligatory acts and indifferent acts bearing importantly on effective government are taken to be proper subjects for legislation. See also King, *Life*, 2:109–10; L, 126.

[75] More precisely, citizens in their *private* capacity must renounce the natural (liberty) right to punish, leaving citizens in their *public* capacities (possibly including self) free to exercise a (collectively) exclusive liberty to punish. The renunciation is thus *conditional* on not occupying a public executive office.

[76] Once the government has this right, citizens are no longer free to punish even those who somehow escape the punishment they deserve. This, however regret-

sive liberty for government, of course, is in some ways analogous to Hobbes' account of the origin of the sovereign's right to punish and to Locke's own account of how a father can come to have title as a prince.[77] But because the Lockean version of our natural condition also includes full claim rights that may be transferred, none of the Hobbesian difficulties about the obligating force of the sovereign's laws arise.

The force of this account might be captured more simply as follows. If it is ever morally permissible to punish wrongdoers (i.e., to coercively control them in certain ways) in the state of nature (and, of course, I have argued that, at least often, it is), then our natural rights of self-government must be taken (as Locke took them) to be limited to those areas of our lives where we operate *within* the bounds of natural law. The government cannot, then, obtain in the manner suggested in 3.3 (by a simple transfer of rights of self-government) an *exclusive* right to punish moral wrongdoers. If it tries to forceably exclude attempts by private citizens to punish wrongdoers, it invades their natural liberty to use competitive interference in punishing. In the absence of a Lockean "contract" of government, in which this liberty to punish is laid aside by citizens, leaving their governors free to legitimately exercise their liberty to punish (and to force citizens *not* to punish

---

table, must be understood as part of the price we pay for having one umpire over all citizens. If failure to punish the deserving is part of a deliberate, unjust program by government, of course, matters are changed.

[77] "And this is the foundation of that right of punishing which is exercised in every commonwealth. For the subjects did not give the sovereign that right, but only in laying down theirs strengthened him to use his own as he should think fit for the preservation of them all; so that it was not given but left to him, and to him only, and (excepting the limits set him by natural law) as entire as in the condition of mere nature" (*Leviathan*, chapter 28, paragraph 2). Locke similarly talks as if the father's children can simply "lay down" their rights to punish, leaving the father free to exercise his own executive right as an exclusive liberty (II, 74). The strategy I here suggest for Locke (and the Lockean) is similar to the "Hobbesian account" discussed and rejected by Schmidtz (*Limits of Government*, 36–37). Schmidtz appears to reject the account because it cannot justify state punishment with reference to independents (nonconsenters, nonclients), since the state's liberty to punish is exclusive only with reference to those who have surrendered or laid down their similar liberties. But since I take the (correct) Lockean position on legitimacy to be precisely that standard state practices (such as punishment) typically *cannot* be justified except to those who freely consent to those practices, independents must simply be accepted by the Lockean as remaining in the state of nature and as being beyond coercive assimilation into the state (see note 78 below). The problem for the Lockean, then, is not with this account of the legitimate government's right to punish; it is with the meaning of political consent and with the possible resulting truth of philosophical anarchism.

163

wrongdoers), any government's claim to a "monopoly on force" within its territories must be morally indefensible.[78]

However badly this account may fit with some of the details of Locke's own presentation, it surely captures the central spirit of his views. On the account I have sketched, the government's (exclusive) right to punish must be understood to be composed of its exclusive liberty to punish moral wrongdoers, plus its claim right(s) to control individual citizens (collectively) in other designated areas of their lives. Similarly, Locke insisted that governments could only rightfully punish if empowered in a fiduciary transaction between citizen and government—and that the rights transferred to government in this transaction must include both rights to control our lives and rights connected with the punishment of wrongdoers (II, 128–30). My agreement with Locke is, then, quite substantial. I agree that if there is a natural executive

[78] This conclusion does *not* follow, of course, if individuals can justifiably be deprived of or prevented from exercising their rights to punish *without* their consent (i.e., without actual wrongdoing on their part and without their free alienation or renunciation of those rights). Locke, of course, steadfastly opposes such "prescription" of natural rights (see my "Inalienable Rights," 178–79, 185). But Nozick has encouraged us to think instead about this question in terms of the *reliability* of methods of self-help enforcement of natural law, suggesting that the state (or a protective agency, or an individual) may justifiably prohibit and punish methods of enforcement by others that are unreliable, thus legitimately eliminating any conflict between its right to punish and that of those independents whose private punishing threatens its clients (*Anarchy*, 101–10). But Nozick really provides no justification for prohibiting independents from using reliable private punishing methods, or for doing any more than monitoring the use of even unreliable methods (and intervening only to prevent wrongful punishment). Since Locke's executive right is only a right to punish correctly, the proper use of that right by independents cannot be justifiably infringed without their agreement. Their consent to give up their executive rights is thus still necessary to secure for government a legitimate monopoly of force. I think, then, that Farrell is mistaken in insisting that on Locke's own terms the consent of the governed is *not* really required for legitimate government (see, for example, his "Punishment Without the State," 450; "Legitimate Government," 201–2; "Coercion, Consent," 528–29, 532, 536), both for the reasons suggested above, and because the legitimate Lockean state can *at most* prohibit self-help enforcement of natural law, *not* coercively bring independents under the requirements of civil law. Similarly, I disagree with Schmidtz's conclusions that the right to punish should really be understood as the right to punish only by the method that is least risky to others, and that this may require that independents let the state punish for them (*Limits of Government*, 38). For, in the first place, it is only *acceptably* risky methods of punishment that are morally permissible, not the *least* risky method in use (which might, of course, be far *too* risky to be allowed). And independent punishment *may* be "acceptably risky." Second, while no individual can be sure that he is a "Charles Bronson type," as Schmidtz rightly claims (ibid., 46), state punishment methods can surely not be taken to be exactly risk-free either (given corrupt and overburdened police and courts, crowded and dangerous prisons, etc.). For criticisms of Nozick's approach related to those voiced above, see Sayward, "Anarchism," 106–9.

right (and if it is possible to defend the theories of natural rights and desert on which the executive right depends), then this Lockean transaction between government and citizens is necessary for the moral legitimacy of the common practice of punishment within political communities. Since I am further persuaded that there are good reasons to support the natural right to punish, Locke's beliefs about the necessity of this transaction may well be justified.[79]

The results for which I have argued here seem to square well with the central intuition about the justifiability of "natural punishment" expressed in 3.1. But what of the apparently conflicting intuitions (e.g., that private citizens within civil society might also be justified in punishing unpunished wrongdoers)? I suspect that such beliefs arise largely from skepticism about Locke's claims that we have in fact given up our natural right to punish to our government in the kind of transaction he describes. And this skepticism may well be warranted. The Lockean account I have just defended is an account of what must take place if legal punishment is to be *legitimate*. We must not confusedly suppose that it is a *descriptive* account of what in fact occurs in most civil societies (although Locke himself, of course, seems to have supposed just this). It may be true that punishment in many or most civil societies is *not* legitimate, and that private citizens in these societies *are* entitled to punish wrongdoers who go unpunished (either within or without their societies).[80] Lockean consent may be necessary for legitimate

[79] I have not yet commented on the international implications of the Lockean position—for example, that (barring international covenants) each legitimate government has the right (i.e., liberty) to punish moral wrongs committed within the territories of other countries by citizens of those countries. This right is not, of course, a right to *interfere* with the legitimate processes of punishment that may be taking place within other countries, but only a right to punish alien wrongdoers who have gone unpunished. If even this limited right seems indefensible, remember the attitude of the Allies at the Nuremberg trials, where German war criminals were prosecuted for *moral* (not legal) crimes against German citizens, committed on German soil. Was it not within the rights of the Allies to punish the monstrous acts of these criminals? The Lockean view implies an affirmative answer. Legitimate governments have exclusive rights to punish wrongdoers within their territories, but these rights are held only against their own citizens, not against the world at large. Other governments have the right to punish moral wrongs that are left unpunished by the responsible government, although exercising this right will only be sensible and prudent when (as in the case of Germany) the wrongs in question are serious and numerous.

[80] If citizens retain their natural executive rights, of course, they may even have a right to punish wrongdoers *before* the state has a chance to institute legal proceedings. But there will often be good reasons for not doing so—for example, reasons of prudence, or the fact that it is best (even if not *obligatory*) to allow more experienced and better organized punishers to have the first chance to do the job.

legal punishment, but not sufficiently in evidence in real political societies to justify our actual practices.

There are, obviously, many other details of the Lockean program on punishment that need elaboration.[81] But anyone, I think, who finds the Lockean intuitions about natural punishment compelling, who believes in the possibility of a defensible theory of natural rights, or who thinks the arguments of this chapter not clearly defective will have reason to consider this program seriously. If it is not, in the end, an acceptable position, there is at least more to be said for it than most contemporary commentators have allowed. On the subject of punishment, then, some of Locke's own arguments point toward the proper position to incorporate in the Lockean theory of rights.

[81] For instance, it may seem to be an objectionable consequence of our Lockean account that legitimate governments have the right to punish *all* moral wrongs (including, for instance, those that are quite trivial and those that have not been made legal wrongs at all). The proper response to such worries is to note that the transaction necessary to create legitimate government involves not only a transfer of rights from citizens to governors. It also includes the specification of limits on the government's authority—most important, that it not violate the rights of any citizen and that it exercise its authority only for "the common good" (for example, II, 131). The latter requirement (that it use its power only for the common good) can be understood to constrain the government's exclusive liberty to punish moral wrongdoers. It establishes that governments can only rightfully punish moral wrongs that have been made legal wrongs by "promulgated, established laws" (II, 142) ("Or else that law would have been of no use: it being to no purpose to lay restraint or give privileges to men, in such general terms, as the particular person concerned cannot be known by" [I, 128]), that it should not make some moral wrongs (for example, simple promise-breaking) into legal wrongs, and that it should not punish trivial moral wrongs. To do otherwise would be to exercise its authority in ways clearly at odds with the promotion of the common good. As Locke argued much earlier than the *Treatises* (in 1667), magistrates may tolerate some vices if it is best for society that they do so (ECT, 183). And the government violates no one's rights by not punishing certain moral wrongs (at least where it provides equal protection from wrongdoing for all of its citizens). Of course, the promotion of the common good requires that punishment be frequent and effective enough to secure a safe and decent life for citizens, but this in no way implies that all moral wrongs must be punished.

FOUR

RIGHTS AND THE FAMILY

4.1. Wives, Husbands, and Servants

Locke's insistence on the artificiality of authority and our natural freedom may seem to face a substantial obstacle in the apparently *natural* structure of authority we acknowledge within the family (a point noted earlier by Filmer in his critique of contractual theories of authority). The authority parents wield over their children seems both justifiable and in no way to depend on the consent of the governed children (Hobbes' claims to the contrary notwithstanding[1]). Filmer's use of these facts to support a patriarchalist theory of political authority required a powerful response from Locke; so it is hardly surprising that the complex of rights (and duties) within the family receives more careful attention in the *Treatises* than any other of the special or general rights Locke discusses (with the possible exception of property rights). Both of the *Treatises* contain lengthy examinations of morality in the family. And by taking care to appreciate the real force of Locke's claims, I will contend, we can find in the *Treatises* the framework for a surprisingly liberal and intuitively appealing conception of the order and substance of natural familial rights and duties.[2] A Lockean position on this subject, developed along lines (sometimes) suggested by Locke himself, is, I think, compelling. While I will disagree with Locke's claims in a number of places, the correct positions will almost always result from extending arguments that Locke merely employed too weakly.

We will be here discussing only the moral dimensions of family life, not the emotional, social, legal, or other important aspects of it (all of which are, of course, related to one another in a variety of

[1] For discussions of Hobbes' views on filial duty, see Blustein, *Parents and Children*, 67–74, 107–8; and Meilaender, " 'Little Monarchy.' "
[2] A brief but sound introductory discussion of Lockean familial morality can be found in Tarcov, *Locke's Education*, 66–76.

fashions).[3] In certain ways, of course, the moral dimensions seem the least important features of family life. Talk of rights and duties seems to clash with the caring, committed mutuality, loyalty, and naturalness of the healthy family. Only when things are going very wrong in a family does moral language seem to become prominent. Wives and husbands claim their rights against one another during divorces. Parents are reminded of their duties (and of the rights of their children) when they are negligent, abusive, or overindulgent. Children are reminded of their duties (and of the rights of their parents) when they are disobedient, disrespectful, or unsupportive. Healthy family life seems to proceed without thought of rights and duties.[4] None of this, however, suggests that familial morality is an empty or uninteresting subject,[5] any more than the loyal, habitual, or unthinking behavior of most (happy) citizens shows that their rights and political obligations can be ignored. While these rights and duties may be actively appealed to only in times of stress and conflict, their existence as a recognized (if unformalized) background even in happy times seems undeniable.[6] Rights and duties within the family determine both the moral limits of familial relationships and the presupposed structure upon which our nonmoral commitments and attachments are formed.

It is important to emphasize, however, that accepting the existence of special duties and rights within the family need *not* commit one to a rejection of so-called impartialist,[7] neutralist,[8] or universalist moral theories, such as Kantian or utilitarian theories. It is currently popular to oppose those moral theories that treat all per-

[3] Actually, my focus may be even narrower than these remarks suggest. I will concentrate only on those rights and duties that are not based or grounded in *emotional* ties (although they may, of course, coexist with them). If there is more to familial morality than this (or even more to familial rights and duties), I do not touch on this remainder. On questions about the relationship between "caring" and familial morality, see Blum, "Gilligan and Kohlberg."

[4] Sandel, *Liberalism*, 112; Young, "In the Interests of Children," 188–89.

[5] See Melden, *Rights and Persons*, 67; and Wicclair, "Caring for Frail Elderly Parents," 172–73.

[6] See Waldron's defense of the need for rights in the family "to fall back on" (*Nonsense upon Stilts*, 188–89; "When Justice Replaces Affection") and Blustein's similar remarks in *Parents and Children*, 103–4. Railton also notes that recalling the moral dimensions of personal relationships may help us to distance ourselves and prevent powerful emotions from blinding us to what is best ("Alienation," 146–47).

[7] For an attack on "impartialism," see Sommers, "Filial Morality." Blum uses the same term ("Gilligan and Kohlberg," 472).

[8] Pettit and Goodin, "Possibility of Special Duties."

sons impartially to those that are sensitive to the special ties and obligations that exist between family members, friends, and others in special relationships. And surely when the opposition is portrayed in these terms, there can be little doubt where the truth lies. With the opportunity to save only one of the two drowning children before me, few would doubt that I ought to save my *own* child rather than the other, completely unrelated child.[9] The Kantian (or utilitarian) is, by contrast, supposed to recommend use of a perfectly impartial method of choosing between the children (perhaps the Kantian will quickly flip the coin carried at all times).[10] But thus portrayed, the dichotomy is a false one. Defenders of impartialist theories can with perfect consistency accept general moral principles that account as well for the existence of *special* moral bonds between family members, friends, and the like, in the same way that they can accept general principles that account for the special obligations of promises. An impartialist can acknowledge that if I have promised an inexperienced swimmer to watch over him while he is in the water, and the promisee and an unrelated stranger both begin to drown at the same instant, that my first obligation is to the promisee. Flipping a coin would amount to denying that my promise had any moral force whatsoever. Similarly, an impartialist may acknowledge general principles of gratitude or reciprocation, or defend special responsibilities toward those whose plights we cause, and let these principles explain our special ties to parents and children.[11] There is no need for "partial" moral principles to explain our special obligations.[12] Locke, I think,

[9] See Sidgwick on the force of such intuitive judgments of special obligation (*Methods of Ethics*, 246–47).

[10] Pettit and Goodin allow that Kant probably *doesn't* qualify as a neutralist ("Possibility of Special Duties," 659n), nor apparently do rule-consequentialists, although they are said to have problems of other sorts (658n). It looks as if only actconsequentialists may qualify, making true neutralists or impartialists a reasonably exclusive club. Act-consequentialists, of course, have always had problems explaining even the widely accepted special duties, such as those derived from promises (see below).

[11] Becker argues, for instance, that social distance almost always determines the extent of reciprocal relationships, so that the strength of moral bonds (under a general principle of reciprocation) will tend to vary with social distance (*Reciprocity*, 216–22).

[12] Pettit and Goodin try to ground special duties (in part) in general principles of *responsibility*, apparently without seeing that this involves an appeal to precisely the kind of general moral principle on which neutralists rely ("Possibility of Special Duties," 665). A view similar to the one I defend here is advanced by Gewirth, who claims that "ethical particularism" is *derivable from* "ethical universalism" ("Ethical Universalism"). See also Railton's efforts to derive particularist duties within another kind of universalist framework (in this case, a consequentialist one) ("Alien-

tries to handle the special rights and duties in families in this latter, impartialist fashion (contrary to Sommers' hesitant claim[13]). There is no need to search beyond the general impartialist principles Locke espouses to find a justification for the moral priority of the family in Locke.[14]

I begin my discussion of rights in the family with the consensual aspects of the family, which in Locke comprise the conjugal rights (and duties) of wives and husbands and the (economic) rights of masters and servants. In sections 2 and 3, I will consider the nonconsensual special rights (and duties) of parents and children; section 4 deals with property relations within the family, and in particular, with inheritance rights (as a preface to the more general discussion of property in chapter 5); in section 5, I briefly elaborate the political implications of a Lockean view of familial moral relations.

Conjugal society, Locke writes, "is made by a voluntary compact between man and woman" (II, 78). The rights of the husband (and the wife) are "founded on contract" (I, 98; II, 82–83), and are thus what I have called (in 2.3) consensual special rights. Locke is clearly speaking here of marriage as a *moral*, not a legal, relationship (II, 83; I, 123), and one whose terms are thus not to be thought of as constrained by any particular legal (or other) rules or conventions (II, 83). Husband and wife may promise to love, honor, cherish, and obey one another, or they may bind themselves by different and more specific agreements. The contract must be consistent with the ends of conjugal society, or else it cannot count as a *marriage* contract; but all else can "be varied and regulated by that contract which unites man and wife" (II, 83). There is thus a wide range of possible contracts between a woman and a man, ranging from purely economic (nonmarital) contracts, through "standard" marriage contracts, to quite individual and unconventional marriage contracts. For Locke, of course, the end

---

ation"); Buchanan's observations on the derivation of special, nonvoluntary obligations from voluntary undertakings of responsibility ("Assessing the Communitarian Critique," 873); and Wong's discussion of "impartial" and "particularist" moralities ("On Moral Realism," 107–12).

[13] "Filial Morality," 444.

[14] For Locke's more general defense of "impartialism," see 6.4 below. We must remember here that our subject is the *natural* rights that are possessed specially by members of families, qua members. Locke is trying to understand those aspects of familial morality that are logically independent of any law, custom, convention, or agreement (and of any *positive* familial rights or duties derived from such sources).

or point of conjugal society is procreation and the care of the "common offspring" (II, 78–83); so any marriage contract necessarily must be understood to include an agreement to care for and educate any children resulting from the union, and to "support and assist" one another during the time that the rearing of children takes place (II, 78, 83). For those of us who may disagree with this (or any other essentialist) account of marriage, however, Locke's contractualist view of marriage can still be accepted, with marriage contracts only exhibiting certain "family resemblances" to one another.[15]

Locke is, I think, correct in supposing that the rights (and duties) of spouses (or of any other persons involved in long-term, monogamous relationships) are primarily determined by consent, as the appropriate source of bonds between equals.[16] While there need not be anything so formal as a contract, voluntary agreements or understandings may distribute the rights and duties within the relationship as the partners please. That is the fundamental moral component of marriage. Religious and legal recognition of certain unions, the profound emotional ties that usually accompany them, and the function such unions play in social interaction do not alter this fundamental component, nor do other moral aspects of marriage that may add to it.[17] That marriage aims, in a sense, at overcoming the partners' preoccupation with their moral rights and duties with respect to one another, in no way suggests that they lack these rights and duties or that they are not based in a voluntary undertaking.[18] A more troubling problem, however, is that the "contractual" undertaking between wife and husband may be uninformed, seriously underspecified, or amorphous, leaving it uncertain just how the rights and duties within a marriage ought to be distributed. In such cases the natural solution is to favor equality between the parties; but it is in this context that Locke's least liberal (and most sexist) views on marriage are expressed.[19]

[15] Kant, for instance, claims that while the *natural* end of marriage is producing and educating children, this is not *essential* to marriage, since people may have other ends (*Metaphysics of Morals*, part 1, section 24).

[16] Again, see Kant, *Metaphysics of Morals*, part 1, section 26.

[17] See the discussion of reciprocity between spouses in Becker, *Reciprocity*, 186–95. I do not think that considerations of reciprocity can *override* the genuinely voluntary undertakings of spouses.

[18] Contrary to what Hegel seems to have thought (*Philosophy of Right*, section 163).

[19] Locke must receive mixed reviews on his liberality with regard to equality of the sexes. The passages I consider below (and Locke's views on paternal control of

While a husband has no *absolute* power (right, authority) over his wife,[20] Locke argues (I, 48; II, 82–83), he does have a certain "priority" over her (she "owes" him a limited "subjection" [I, 48]). Every husband has the right "to order the things of private concernment in his family, as proprietor of the goods and land there, and to have his will take place before that of his wife in all things of their common concernment" (I, 48). In disagreements between husband and wife, the man has the right of "last determination" in "things of their common interest and property" (II, 82). Why this priority of the man's will? Aside from references to God's punishment of women for Eve's transgressions (I, 47) (which, I argue below, Locke does *not* intend as a source of man's authority over woman), Locke says only this: when husband and wife disagree, it "being necessary that the last determination, i.e., the rule, should be placed somewhere, it naturally falls to the man's share, as the abler and stronger" (II, 82).

Even supposing (falsely) that men (individually or as a group) are "abler and stronger" than women, it is hard to see why Locke should have thought this fact a ground for unequal rights between husband and wife.[21] After all, other natural inequalities in strength or ability (those between adult males, for instance) do not seem to justify inequalities in *their* rights, on Locke's view (as we saw in 2.2). This apparent inconsistency seems easy to explain if we simply ascribe to Locke a firm commitment to the natural superiority and dominion of men over women, a prephilosophical commitment that his general philosophical principles cannot budge (even

---

property) make it easy to simply dismiss his views as thoroughly permeated with the deep and casual sexism of his age. (See, e.g., Clark, "Women and John Locke," 721–24; Seliger, *Liberal Politics*, 211–12.) But while Dunn is certainly right that Locke's sexual egalitarianism fought a losing battle with his acceptance of the radically inegalitarian conventions of his age (*Political Thought*, 121–22n), there was at least a battle. Locke's insistence on equal parental authority and his very liberal views on the free determination of nonconventional marriage contracts deserve some notice. And, as I argue below, other aspects of Locke's views on the rights of women deserve more charitable readings than they usually receive. See Yolton, *Locke*, 58.

[20] Locke's proof of this claim seems seriously confused (again involving a blurring of moral with physical "powers"). He argues that if the husband *did* have absolute power over his wife, "there could be no matrimony in any of those countries where the husband is allowed no such absolute authority" (II, 83). This seems to amount to the quite silly claim that if the state denies you exercise of a right to X, you cannot have a moral right to X (a claim, of course, which Locke emphatically and correctly rejects throughout the body of his work).

[21] I will concentrate here on the husband's right to decide in conflicts over their common concerns; wives' property rights—which they can acquire by "labor or compact" (II, 183)—I discuss separately in 4.4.

at the price of inconsistency). We could then argue that for Locke the "natural dominion of one sex over the other" is so obvious that it "does not even have to be justified."[22] Locke may *say* conjugal society is consensual; but given Locke's view of women's weakness and inequality, any contract of marriage would border on unconscionability.[23] In the end, the argument goes, Locke's real view is that men enjoy a *natural* (not contractual) dominion over women, both in and out of marriage. He should not be credited with having espoused a more "liberal attitude toward marriage and the relation of the sexes."[24]

This reading of Locke, I think, is unfair to him, for he quite specifically denies that man has any natural dominion over woman. God never gave him any such dominion: He never gave "any authority to Adam over Eve, or to men over their wives."[25] Women are not naturally subject to their husbands, although, Locke "grants," there is "a foundation in nature for it" (I, 47). What is this natural "foundation" for an artificial authority? It is quite clearly meant to be man's superior strength and ability—not as the source of his authority, but as a natural fact to which man's achievement of conventional authority is connected. What, then, is the relevance of this natural superiority? First, of course, it is natural (not *obligatory*) to defer in certain ways to those who are abler, stronger, wiser, older, or more virtuous (as Locke says elsewhere—e.g., II, 54). As a result, it is natural (and, subsequently, conventional) for women to *give* men greater authority than they reserve for themselves in their free marriage contracts. This is natural and conventional, not *necessary*—for Locke mentions instances in which women have elected *not* to give their husbands this authority (e.g., I, 47; II, 65). And *because* it is natural (and thus inevitably conventional), Locke assumes, if the marriage contract does not specify alternative arrangements, we may understand it to give greater authority to the husband. But Locke has, I think, a second reason for his belief that husbands typically have (limited)

[22] "Women and John Locke," 702–4, 708. See also Pateman, *Problem of Political Obligation*, 75.

[23] Clark, "Women and John Locke," 709–11. On unconscionable contracts, see my "Consent, Free Choice," section 5.

[24] Ibid., 721. See also Pateman, "Women and Consent," 152. While Locke never indicates any interest in considering, for instance, female citizenship, these assessments of his views still seem unduly harsh (for reasons specified below).

[25] The biblical text at issue merely "foretells what should be woman's lot" (I, 47); it does not *prescribe* it. Locke uses this same style of biblical interpretation on other occasions in the *First Treatise* (e.g., I, 118).

authority over their wives. In voluntary unions between persons that do not involve a precise specification of the methods for settling disputes, the right to determine the body's actions must be understood to lie with the greatest "force" in the body. This is an important principle for Locke, for it underlies his defense of majority rule as the understood rule of resolution for *political* unions: "it being necessary to that which is one body to move one way; it is necessary the body should move that way whither the greater force carries it, which is the consent of the majority: or else it is impossible it should act or continue one body" (II, 96). Locke's reasoning about the husband's right of "last determination" in a marriage proceeds similarly: this right must "be placed somewhere," so it "naturally falls to the man's share, as the abler and stronger" (II, 82).

Locke's argument is in neither case very convincing.[26] But the important point to note here is that he is in neither case arguing for a natural authority (of majorities or husbands). In both cases he is trying to give reasons for interpreting an inexplicit contract in a certain way, for understanding where the artificial authority to make decisions for a body must be taken to lie, when it has not been explicitly stated in the contract. And in both cases he allows that if there *has* been an explicit agreement on some alternative arrangement for decision-making, this agreement overrides the reasoning he has advanced. Thus, political bodies may "expressly agree" to require more than a simple majority for binding decisions (II, 99); and, presumably, this means they may opt for different procedures altogether (e.g., lottery, weighted lottery, plural voting for the more able, etc.). Similarly, *every* aspect of the marriage contract (except the responsibility to provide for offspring) may be varied by express agreement (II, 83). Wives may have the right of "last determination" themselves, if this is agreed on, or the mates may decide conflicts by lottery or by taking turns, and so on. The authority of husbands is neither natural nor necessary.

Where, then, does this leave a Lockean contractual account of

[26] In the case of majority rule, of course, there is nothing straightforwardly more authoritative or fair about this procedure than many alternatives (e.g., lotteries, votes weighted by intensity of preference, etc.). Even the physical analogy (right must follow force) will not help here, since an intense minority might be a "greater force" than an apathetic majority. In the case of marriage contracts, even if greater ability *were* a ground for greater authority, a right of "last determination" is far from the only way to implement this authority. And again, the "greater force" in a dispute need not fall on the side of the party possessing the greater physical strength.

"marital morality"? If we deprive the account of its false factual assumptions (about man's superior strength and ability), it seems not at all unreasonable or illiberal. Marriage contracts may distribute rights and duties between the partners as they specify. In the absence of explicit specification by or understanding of the partners, we should take the contract to have the conventional form.[27] In Locke's day, this meant a superior position for the husband; but the voluntariness and fairness of marriage contracts in Locke's day were typically undermined by the vastly inferior bargaining position of the woman (based on her economic dependency and social limitations).[28] Fairness, then, would have dictated that we interpret inexplicit contracts more equitably than the conventions of Locke's day would have suggested. Today, when conventions are more egalitarian and women's dependency on male approval less profound, the problem of unfair contracts is less dramatic. Women can, if they wish, accept a traditional or limited role in family decision-making; or they can insist on equal (or greater than equal) rights in this area as a condition of the marriage contract. Only unfairness and duress (etc.) involved in entry into a marriage will require us to question the terms of an explicit contract or interpret an inexplicit one in other than conventional terms.[29]

On the role of servants in the Lockean family, I shall in this chapter have considerably less to say. In seventeenth-century England, of course, servants were commonly treated as members of the families for whom they worked; the act of making oneself a servant "commonly puts him into the family of his master, and under the ordinary discipline thereof" (II, 85).[30] But Locke forcefully resists the consequently natural urge to treat the authority of fathers (and mothers) over their servants as paternal (parental) or even

[27] Sidgwick, *Methods of Ethics*, 256.
[28] Locke accepts the idea that unfair bargaining position can void an apparent contract (see, e.g., I, 42).
[29] I leave untouched myriad difficulties concerning degrees of voluntariness, social conditioning, "false consciousness," and so on, as well as questions about the term of marriage contracts (may they be renegotiated when one or both of the partners changes or grows in ways that make the initial specification unrewarding or inappropriate?).
[30] Locke himself was often regarded as a member of Shaftesbury's "family," in spite of being a gentleman and absentee landlord. On the servant's place in the family in Stuart England, see Schochet, *Patriarchalism*, 64–72; Macpherson, *Possessive Individualism*, especially 282–86, and "Servants and Labourers"; Ashcraft, *Revolutionary Politics*, 154–60.

despotical. The only rights a master possesses over his servant are those he acquires by contract between them.[31] A servant is a freeman, who gives rights to his master "by selling him for a certain time, the service he undertakes to do, in exchange for wages he is to receive" (II, 85).[32] Thus, "the turfs my servant has cut" are my property (II, 28), the contract between us specifying that he will provide for me these fruits of his labor in exchange for pay.

Much has been made of the significance of Locke's claims about servants to his overall views of property and economy.[33] I will return to those issues in 5.2. Here it is important to stress that, as in the case of husbands' authority over their wives, the authority of masters over servants is limited and contractual for Locke. Again against Filmer, Locke is quite clear on the distinction between slaves (who are not holders of equal [or any] rights) and servants (who, being equal rightholders, may freely contract with others) (II, 85). While he calls slaves "another sort of servants" (and occasionally seems to confuse the two in the case of *de facto* slavery[34]), the *de jure* distinction is clearly drawn. Again, as in the case of women's marriage contracts, the key issues for the viability of Locke's claims will be voluntariness and fairness (in the relative strengths of bargaining positions). Where servants must (as a result of need, intimidation, social conditioning, etc.) accept the terms offered by masters, Locke's description of the servant as free contractor will seem a case of blithe and self-serving deception. But if we read Locke's remarks (as I will argue we should) in the context of an understood acknowledgment that duress and unfairness are conditions that *limit* the bindingness of contracts, we can accept his description of the moral condition of servants as reason-

[31] For Kant's parallel claims, see *Metaphysics of Morals*, part 1, section 30.

[32] These "wages," of course, need not be in the form of money; other goods may be adequate compensation for the servant's services, both before and after the invention of money. See Seliger, *Liberal Politics*, 160–61.

[33] Briefly, Macpherson argues that Locke's claims show his acceptance of the wage relationship (even in the state of nature), and that thus defending the right to alienate labor for a wage removes moral obstacles to accepting (as Locke allegedly did) unlimited capitalist appropriation (*Possessive Individualism*, 214–21). Tully responds that Locke's master-servant relationship, far from being the wage relationship of capitalism, is actually inconsistent with capitalism (and unlimited appropriation). The servant sells a service or a task, not his labor (*Discourse*, 135–44). For a recasting of what is most plausible in Macpherson (and least plausible in Tully), see Shapiro, *Evolution of Rights*, 139–43.

[34] As in I, 130, where he writes of "servants" purchased by "a planter in the West Indies." Perhaps Locke finds it hard to refer to those who are clearly *unjustly* enslaved (by his own principles) as "slaves," however contentedly he may have profited from the slave trade himself.

able, and as a trivial consequence of a more general doctrine of economic liberty.[35]

4.2. The Rights of Parents (and the Duties of Children)

Parents are said at various times by Locke to have natural rights to respect, gratitude, assistance, honor, support, obedience, defense, reverence, and acknowledgment. Children have (under appropriate conditions) correlative natural duties or obligations to satisfy these claims. But the (noninstitutional) rights of parents (and filial duties) can in fact be divided neatly into two main classes: what Locke calls the "right of tuition" and the "right of honor" (II, 67). And these two (classes of) rights arise from very different sources. It is on this subject that Locke's remarks on familial morality are at their most plausible, and many contemporary writers have followed the Lockean line as a result. I will try here to summarize Locke's views and to motivate certain natural extensions of them, in order to defend a Lockean position on natural parental rights and filial duties.

Parental rights are for Locke, first, rights held by *both* parents. While he occasionally uses the more traditional term "paternal power" in place of "parental power" (e.g., II, 69, 170, 173),[36] Locke's view that these rights are shared is clearly stated in both *Treatises* (e.g., I, 6, 55, 61, 62; II, 52). This group of shared parental rights is divided by Locke (following Aquinas, and as suggested above) into two distinct rights (or better, subgroups of rights), each of which seems as well to have two parts, and each of which has a distinct ground.

What Locke calls the "right of tuition" is "a sort of rule and jurisdiction" (II, 55) or "temporary government" (II, 67) that parents have over their children, a right to rear them and control them in

---

[35] I do not mean by this remark to suggest that all who work for wages are equivalent to "servants" in Locke's view (as Macpherson supposes). The distinction between servants and other laborers played a very important role in the Putney debates and the Levellers' defense of manhood suffrage (and consequently in Locke, as Ashcraft has shown [*Revolutionary Politics*, 154–60]). I mean only that the servant's *moral* condition is only interestingly different from that of any other participant in economic activities by virtue of the specific terms of the contract under which he works.

[36] Schochet briefly discusses Locke's waffling in "Family," 85. Locke's emphasis on fathers' rights throughout his discussion is due (at least in part) to his polemical task, for he needs to refute Filmer's various claims about the nature and extent of paternal authority. Filmer, obviously, made no claims to refute concerning *maternal* authority.

ways which will ultimately result in the children's healthy independence and moral agency. It is a right to rule "paternalistically" (i.e., for the good of the one ruled[37]) over one's children, to help them through "the weakness and imperfection of their nonage" (II, 65) by informing their minds and governing their actions (II, 58). Locke should be understood here to have two kinds of rights in mind under the heading of the right of tuition. On the one hand, parents have a right to rear their children as they see fit (within the limits set by the *point* of that right—i.e., the good of the children), a right that is held against the world at large. This is a right not to have the job of parenting stolen or usurped by others. Natural parents have the right of "first try" in rearing their offspring. While Locke nowhere explicitly discusses this aspect of the right of tuition, it is clearly presumed (since Locke even denies the power of the state to overturn natural parental rights [e.g., I, 64]). The second aspect or part of the right of tuition is a right held not against society, but against one's children. Parents have a right to obedience from their children during their minority (at least when they are parenting properly). "The power of commanding and chastising" (II, 67) falls to parents, as those who are in charge of governing for their children's good, until the children "come to the use of reason" and are able to govern themselves (II, 170). The right of tuition, in both its parts, cannot be taken from a natural parent without cause. But it can be forfeited by parental incompetence, abuse, or neglect (whether from inability or from deliberate breach of duty); it can be alienated by the parents' decision to "put the tuition of [their child] in other hands" (II, 69); and it is naturally dissolved when children reach the "age of discretion."[38] It is thus a right that is far indeed from *absolute* dominion of parents over children (I, 51–53; II, 53, 64, 69, 74).

The second parental right is the "right of honor," a right held by parents against their children and one that must also be under-

---

[37] Locke does not seem to have in mind that parents must *maximize* the benefits they provide for their children. They must only refrain from harming their children and provide them with the necessary means to self-government (which includes, as I argue below, both satisfying their basic needs and providing reasonable comforts, where possible). Parental rule is limited at least to that authority which is consistent with the performance of these parental duties. The *Education* makes it clear that parental education and discipline must be aimed at making children capable of liberty—that is, rational, virtuous, and free.

[38] Locke's specifications of the ways in which parental power can (and cannot) change hands are, of course, important to his case against Filmer, since for Filmer political authority was an instance of paternal authority that had "changed hands" all down through the ages.

RIGHTS AND THE FAMILY

stood to have two parts. Its first part concerns the *nonmaterial* support and responses to which parents have a right from their children—that "honor" that is due parents "by the Fifth Commandment" (I, 64). Parents have a right to be respected and revered by their children (II, 67), to be shown gratitude and receive acknowledgment for the benefits they have bestowed upon their children. Deference to and compliance with parental wishes are appropriate even after children have matured and are self-supporting (II, 69). Second, the right of honor is also a right to *material* support from one's children, where this is needed and the children are able to supply it (*after* one's children provide for their *own* children, if any). Parents are entitled to "support and subsistence" (a "return of goods") from their children, and even have a claim to inherit from their children if there are no grandchildren with prior claims (I, 90). Like the right of tuition, the right of honor is imprescriptible.[39] Locke describes the right as "perpetual" (e.g., II, 67), but he clearly intends that it may be forfeited by parental neglect, at least in large measure.[40] Unlike the right of tuition, however, the right of honor cannot be alienated (transferred voluntarily).[41]

As should be plain by now, the right of tuition is a right parents have over children (primarily) in their minority, while the right of honor largely refers to the claims of parents against their grown children (although, of course, even young children should honor their parents in ways appropriate to their ages). As a result, the correlative duties or obligations of children are similarly divided by age, with the duties being "stronger on grown than younger children" (II, 68). Young children, then, have a duty of obedience to their parents' commands, correlating with (part of) the right of tuition (II, 65, 67). Even grown children may owe some obedience, although this seems to be thought by Locke to be part of the duty of honor (correlating with parents' right of honor), rather than being a simple extension of the young child's duty of obedience (II,

[39] To call a right "imprescriptible" is to say that it may not be simply taken away from the rightholder by some other party. See my "Inalienable Rights," 178–79.

[40] In I, 100, Locke first says this right can be forfeited "to some degrees" and later that "much" of the right can be forfeited. In II, 65, Locke suggests the stronger view that forfeiture of parental power can be total.

[41] Again, Locke is unclear about how *much* of the right of honor may be alienated. In I, 65, he doubts that the father "can alien *wholly* the right of honor that is due" (my emphasis); in I, 100, however, the father can "transfer none of it," making the right of honor in principle inalienable. I criticize this argument for inalienability in "Inalienable Rights," 186–87.

68). The duty of honor, then, is owed by grown children to their parents, and is a "perpetual obligation . . . containing in it an inward esteem and reverence to be shown by all outward expressions" (II, 66). It is a duty to "honor and support" one's parents (II, 68) in the ways just specified.[42]

What, then, are the grounds (source) of these parental rights and filial duties? By examining Locke's arguments for his claims, we will be led, I think, to make certain changes in the contents (scope) of the rights and duties just described. At times, of course, it appears that Locke wants to ground parental rights simply in the biological relation of parents to children (blood, as they say, is thicker than water). He refers to the ground of these rights as "nature" (e.g., II, 173) and calls their basis "the right of generation" (II, 52) or the "right of fatherhood" (I, 64); and the *First Treatise* is filled with apparent agreements with Filmer that mere "begetting" is sufficient to ground parental rights (e.g., I, 63, 74, 98, 101, 111). It is tempting here to compare the rights of parents over their children to the self-evident "right of creation" enjoyed by God over His creatures (discussed above in 1.2), and Locke did occasionally suggest this comparison.[43] But, of course, parents do not *own* their children in the way God owns His creatures (as Locke argued at length against Filmer's, and, e.g., Aristotle's, contrary claims[44]), and in the strict sense they do not *create* their children at all (and so cannot have a "right of creation" over them). Parents lack the knowledge and skills necessary for the creation of so remarkable and mysterious a creature as a child. Only God possesses these, and only God can be credited as the maker or creator of children (I, 52–54).[45] Parents are only "the occasions of life to their chil-

---

[42] There is one peculiar suggestion in Locke that these filial debts are paid (in large part) "by taking care and providing for [one's] own children" (I, 90). The idea that a debt owed by A (the child) to B (the parent) could be paid by rendering services to C (the grandchild) makes no sense at all, unless there is a clear understanding or agreement between A and B that this shall be an appropriate manner of paying the debt. Nonetheless, this odd suggestion is repeated by Olafson in "Rights and Duties." Olafson's claims are criticized in Melden, "Olafson," and in Schrag, "Children: Their Rights and Needs."

[43] See Colman, *Moral Philosophy*, 45–46.

[44] For a contemporary version of the parental ownership thesis, see Rothbard, *The Ethics of Liberty*, 99.

[45] See Tully's discussion of Locke's creationism in *Discourse*, 57–59. Tully claims earlier that Locke holds that parental rights and duties arise simply from begetting (that the relation of begetting may be "unpacked" to reveal these rights and duties)(34). I argue below that while this may be Locke's view of parental *duties*, it cannot be true for most of the parental *rights* Locke discusses. Melden defends a view similar to the one Tully attributes to Locke (i.e., that to identify one as a father

dren" (II, 66; I, 54). They are *procreators*, not creators, only depu-
ties and trustees for a higher authority.[46] Their rights must thus be
explained differently from God's (supposing that God's are even
capable of explanation).

Locke's considered opinion seems to be this. Parental rights (at
least for the most part) do not derive from mere begetting or biological relation at all (II, 65).[47] They must be earned by the provision of care and support to the child. The one kind of right that
mere begetting does in part ground is that portion of the right of
tuition that I called earlier the right of "first try." Natural parents
have first claim on rearing their own children, a claim held against
the world as a whole. Other parental rights belong only to those
who actually pursue parenting (i.e., those who do not abandon,
give away, or abuse their children). The distinction between the
two basic (classes of) parental rights with regard to their grounds
is simple: the right of tuition derives from parents' duty to care for
their children (II, 58, 67) and the correlative rights to care that
these children possess (II, 63, 67, 78; I, 89–90); the right of honor,
by contrast, is grounded in the provision of benefits by parents to
children, and is a right to a return that is proportionate to the extent of these benefits (II, 65, 67, 70; I, 100).

Let us examine these claims in order, beginning with the right
of "first try." In the absence of alternative arrangements to which
parents have consented, Locke is claiming, natural parents have
first right to rear and educate their children without interference
from others.[48] Unless they forfeit or alienate this right, they may
fashion their child's environment without the scrutiny or direction
of others who may disagree with their parenting decisions.[49] This
is a right possessed by all and only those who beget children. But

---

just is to identify the rights he has) in *Rights and Right Conduct*, 72, 77–78, 84. But
Melden does *not* mean by "father" simply "biological father."

[46] Ruddick, "Parents and Life Prospects," 126.

[47] Compare the opinion of Grant, who maintains that the parent's right to be
honored arises from the act of generation (*Liberalism*, 59, 62). This seems doubly
mistaken, since not only does Locke appear to reject the moral significance of mere
generation, but clearly bases the right to honor on parental benefaction, not mere
generation (see below).

[48] On the special problems connected with the authority to educate children
(which I cannot pursue here), see Gutmann, "Children," and *Democratic Education*;
Henley, "Authority to Educate"; Schrag, "Rights over Children"; Lomasky, *Persons, Rights*, 174–80.

[49] This amounts to a right to "a certain latitude," within the constraints set by
their duties to their children (Blustein, *Parents and Children*, 112–13). See Schoeman's description of this "latitude" in "Rights of Children," and Lomasky's in *Persons, Rights*, 172–81.

why should natural parents be supposed to be entitled to this sort of control? Locke's answer is that such parental rights are (what we called in 2.1) mandatory claim rights—they are rights to do what we have a prior duty to do (II, 58, 67). When a person has a duty or special responsibility to provide care for another (as natural parents do, for the reasons discussed below in 4.3), that person must be allowed by others to do that duty. They wrong that person if they prevent the fulfillment of responsibilities. It is thus the natural parents' special responsibility to their child that explains their right of tuition, a right that is simply a trivial consequence of their duty of tuition.[50]

The main difficulty with this view lies in its attempted derivation of claim rights from duties. As I argued above (2.1, note 25), while *liberty* rights do indeed seem a trivial consequence of duties, *claim* rights do not. We can see this most clearly in the case of unrelated promises made by two different people to do (or purchase) what only one of them *can* do (or purchase). The obligation of the first promisor may entail a liberty to discharge the promise, but it in no way entails a *claim* right (which would *exclude* the liberty of the second, equally bound, promisor).[51] Parental authority, however, must be more than a mere (competitive) liberty to rear one's children if it is to square with either a Lockean stance or common moral intuitions. Parental authority must consist of *claim* rights, which others have a duty to respect.

[50] Blustein has recently defended a "Lockean conception of parenthood" that argues for parental authority in precisely these same terms (*Parents and Children*, 111–13; see also the principle on which these views are based—ibid., 171). It may seem, as a consequence of this Lockean position, as if at least in *this* area of Locke's thought, natural duty is prior to or more basic than natural right (to return to an issue discussed in chapter 2). But if we remember that the duty of tuition is simply a logical correlate of the child's rights to care and (eventual) freedom (these rights often being spoken of by Locke as that from which the parental duty derives—e.g., II, 63, 67), we will see that there is no case to be made here for the priority of duty or for a derivative status for rights.

[51] This argument succeeds only if it is true that no third party has a right of control in the matter—that is, a right to decide which promisor shall have access and a right to grant that person a claim right. If, for instance, society had the authority to distribute parental rights, mere parental liberties might be converted into parental claim rights by society's exercising its authority. But Locke clearly assumes (as do I) that society can have no natural rights of control that might compete with individual natural parental rights, given that society's rights are merely composed from logically prior individual rights. Society's rights over children must be understood to be contractual, conventional, or in some other fashion positive, and so to presuppose a background of individual rights of control. Natural parental duties do not entail natural parental claim rights. That is the only point relevant to Locke's (and our) concerns here.

It is natural to try to justify such claim rights by appealing here to the labor expended in bearing the child (by the natural mother) or to the fact that both the father and the mother have contributed parts of themselves to produce the child. While these styles of argument are more commonly used to justify property in Locke (as we will see in 5.2), and we know parental rights cannot be property rights exactly, it may be possible to produce variants of Locke's property arguments that establish not property in the child, but rather only a special right to a large say in what is done with the thing to which one has contributed (the child). Along these lines, it seems reasonable to suppose that parental claim rights could be derived as follows. The duty of natural parents to care for their child could be conceded to entail only a moral liberty to do so, which is in competition with the liberties of others to rear the child. In situations of competitive liberties, however, the rule to follow in establishing claims is "first come, first served" (see 3.5 and 5.2). The way one "comes first" is by being the first to make things a part of one's projects or life plans: in the case of appropriating goods from the common, we "come first" by investing our purposive labor in the object (see 5.3); in the case of children, we "come first" by making them parts of our lives. Since the natural parents (or, at least, mothers) are always (barring exotic technology) the first to perform significant acts of commitment and concern for the child (such as carrying it to term, laboring to give it birth, protecting it after birth, etc.), natural parents have first claim on rearing their child (which is not the same as having property in the child[52]). Children are not only a physical part of (one of their) parents; they are a part of their lives. And since a child is best reared in a stable, dependable environment, those with the *first* claim should have the *only* claim, unless they forfeit or alienate

[52] Why parents do not own their children in Locke is not initially easy to see. Locke seems to answer that parents do not own their children because they didn't *really* make them (God did); but then the parents didn't *really* make the vegetables in their garden either, over which they *do* have property rights. And they labored in both cases. A more convincing answer is offered by Becker ("Labor Theory," 657–58; *Property Rights*, 37–39): since property rights in external goods are justified by appeal to prior rights over our bodies (and our labor), or to our prior right of self-government (as I will argue in 5.3), property in external goods must be consistent with these prior rights. Since owning other human beings is not consistent with their rights to their bodies and their rights of self-government, we cannot own human beings unless they have forfeited those foundational rights. Parents thus cannot have property in their children. Their claim rights over their children must be limited to that control consistent with their children's rights (see 4.3 below).

it (thus eliminating the possibility of others "getting their turns" to rear the child for a period).

While this style of argument may be the best of those that extend a secular strand of Locke's thought on parental authority,[53] the bases for several other arguments for natural parental rights are easy to find in Locke (even if they are far less compelling for most contemporary readers). Locke notes, for instance, both that God (the child's creator and owner) entrusts children to their parents, making them "accountable" to God for the care they bestow (II, 56), and that to "temper" parental power God has placed in parents "suitable inclinations of tenderness and concern" toward their children (I, 56; II, 63, 67, 170). The first point suggests that parental rights can also be thought of as the rights of *trustees*— limited claim rights granted in trust by the original rightholder or settlor (in this case, God). And the second point can form the basis for a plausible rule-consequentialist argument for parental rights (which, as we saw in 1.4, also is ultimately tied for Locke to a divine command morality, but which may be "detached" from such foundations by secular humanists). If the natural tenderness and concern of natural parents are likely (as a rule) to make them the best rearers of their children (which is certainly Locke's view), then humankind will be best preserved if biological parents have first right to rear their own children.[54] Add to this the fact that any alternative noninstitutional child-rearing arrangements will involve significant disutility (e.g., in the emotional costs of taking children away from their natural parents), and we have a reasonably plausible consequentialist argument for the same Lockean conclusion.[55]

---

[53] In the sense that it is perfectly compatible with secular accounts of the duties of parents and the moral rights of others. See Blustein, *Parents and Children*, 111–12.

[54] Whether or not it is true that natural parents are (as a rule) the best rearers of their children is discussed in Schrag, "Rights over Children," 99–100; and Schoeman, "Rights of Children," 11–12. I believe that it is true, although I will not here argue for the position.

[55] Additional considerations concerning the value of the family and intimate relationships can be adduced to support either the consequentialist or the deontological cases for natural parental authority. Schoeman, for instance, argues for "family autonomy" on the grounds that we ought to respect those relationships in which persons find meaning and intimacy (in this case, the natural family) ("Rights of Children"). And Schrag considers that rearing one's own children is "a great source of [the] happiness and dignity" of parents. An arrangement in which parental rights do not fall first to the natural parents will both deprive them of these goods and undermine "the intense passions that a close family life gives rise to [which] are considered precious in themselves" ("Rights over Children," 101). Lomasky also takes account of the importance to parents of rearing their own children

What of the other part of parents' right of tuition—their right to obedience, held against their children? Locke, as we have seen, derives this "power of commanding" (II, 69) from the duties of care that parents have toward their children.[56] Just as noninterference by others is necessary for parents to properly do their child-rearing duties, so is obedience by children. From the parents' duty of care is derived a right to do whatever is necessary to fulfill that duty. So parents have a right to filial obedience (unless they forfeit it by abuse or are released from it), and children have a correlative duty of obedience (II, 67–68).[57]

Now this attempted derivation of claim right from duty faces the same difficulties mentioned above. But there are additional reasons to be skeptical about filial duties and parental rights of obedience. Young children clearly lack filial duties of obedience because they lack those capacities necessary for minimal levels of moral responsibility, and consequently have no moral duties at all.[58] Grown children lack duties of obedience because they have

---

(*Persons, Rights*, 167). Other apparently consequentialist support for natural parental authority in fact makes that authority more customary than natural. For instance, insofar as we appeal to the unhappiness natural parents would experience (in having others rear their children), which is based on a frustration of expectations that are convention-dependent, we make parental authority depend on the presence of those conventions that generated the expectations. An argument for parental rights that are natural in the full sense can appeal only to harms or bad consequences that are themselves not the result of the presence and operation of contingent practices or conventions. Thus, Sommers, while rejecting relativism and accepting some natural rights ("Filial Morality," 453), ultimately defends "special obligations" (and the parental authority that correlates with some of them) in a way that really renders them in part customary only. For her case depends in the end on an argument from "conventional expectations" (446–47). (Daniels accepts a similar account of filial obligations in *Am I My Parents' Keeper?* 112–13.) In the absence of the relevant (contingent) conventions, natural parents would not have any special claims on their children. The rights parents *did* have on Sommers' account would be natural rights (in the sense given above in 2.3), for the ground would be given by a natural moral principle (with only the content of the right determined conventionally). But Sommers could not defend parental rights as natural in the stronger sense Locke requires—namely, as rights possessed by all biological parents.

[56] Obedience to their parents' rational commands prepares children for learning to obey their own reason (*Education*, 36, 61, 112). Again, Locke's line of reasoning here is duplicated by Blustein (and much earlier by Kant [*Metaphysics of Morals*, part 1, section 29]).

[57] Blustein, *Parents and Children*, 168–72. Children's duty is, according to Blustein, really best thought of as owed to children themselves, and to the parents only as "temporary trustees of the child's welfare" (169). Since children cannot release their parents from their parental duties, they have "a duty to facilitate or at least not prevent" their parents' discharging their duties (i.e., they must obey their parents) (171).

[58] See Tarcov, *Locke's Education*, 4, 74.

the same rights and duties as adults.[59] Only for children who are capable of understanding moral concepts and controlling their actions, but who are not yet mature, fully rational, or fully in control, does the ascription of a duty of filial obedience seem initially plausible. And Locke acknowledges that even in these cases, the duty is limited: "we are no doubt bound to comply with the orders of parents, but only in things lawful" (ELN, 203). Children have no duty to comply with immoral commands or with commands that conflict with the requirements of binding civil law (and parents may forfeit their rights of obedience if they issue such commands frequently).[60]

These facts may lead us to question whether even in other cases children have a moral obligation to obey parental commands. Even when parents command things that are neither immoral nor illegal, parental commands can still be unnecessarily restrictive, arbitrary, unreasonable, and pernicious. Children clearly do no moral wrong by reading Darwin in secret, contrary to their fundamentalist parents' orders (or by reading *Huckleberry Finn* if their parents are [misguidedly] liberal). Obviously, parents often command their children to do what is best (or at least good) for the children as well. But do we really want to say in these cases that the reason why children ought to do what they are told is "that their parents ordered them to"? Surely children ought to do what is best (or good) for them *because* it is best. We can allow that parents may reasonably *specify* the precise boundaries of vague issues concerning what is best (e.g., whether staying out too late, which is objectively bad for the child, means being home after 11:00 or 12:00 or 1:00). But this is far from acknowledging a general parental right to obedience.[61] Children often act wrongly in disobeying their parents. But the wrongness of their conduct seems to be explained by reasons that have force independent of any reasons for acting that the command itself might give. The wrongness is not a simple

[59] I will not comment here on exactly what qualifies a child as "young" or "grown." On these matters, see my "Obligations of Citizens," 77–78; Blustein, *Parents and Children*, 170–71; Woozley, *Law and Obedience*, 66–67; Slote, "Obedience and Illusions," 120.

[60] Blustein, *Parents and Children*, 171–72.

[61] Insofar as the parents' right of of obedience is derived from their duty to care for children, it can at best be a right to obedience that is genuinely *needed* for doing parental duty. This seems likely to limit severely the scope of children's obligations to obey (to matters in which there are *independent* reasons for children to act as commanded). *More* obedience from children than is strictly needed by parents might be *wanted* by the parents or convenient for them, but they have no *right* to it simply on the strength of their parental duties.

function of a parental command having been disobeyed. Parents can, of course, sometimes command their children paternalistically (indeed, it is their duty to do so). But this hardly shows that disobedience to their commands is wrong. In fact, it shows that this is *not* the case, since paternalism is permissible only toward those who are not fully responsible for their actions, and consequently only toward those who cannot act wrongly (at least in the matter in question). As long as they need their parents' care and support, of course, children may be prudentially "obliged" to obey parental orders (whatever their virtues). And children will often want to please and impress their parents with obedience, especially when parents are loving and reasonable in their demands. But Locke's worries about the force of unlawful parental commands should, I think, push us naturally to question the whole idea of a general filial duty and parental right of obedience.[62]

I turn now to the second (class) of Locke's parental rights—rights of honor, rights based in parental provision of benefits to children during the process of child-rearing. Parents have, we have seen Locke claim, a right to be revered and respected for the benefits they have bestowed, to be shown gratitude and supported materially (where necessary and possible) by their grown children. The "specific" return that is owed by children is whatever is appropriate to the benefits, care, and sacrifices that the parents provided (took, made) for their children. This return is what is due "in justice" (I, 90) or, more accurately (and following Aquinas), as "gratitude" (II, 68, 69) for past parental performance.[63]

[62] Slote and Woozley (see note 59 above) seem to agree that there is no general parental right of obedience. Becker, by contrast, tries to derive this right from the parents' right to restrict obligatory filial reciprocation (for parental benefaction) to obedience (*Reciprocity*, 213–15). This makes the parental right to obedience a matter of return for benefits (much as Locke derives filial duties of (limited) obedience for *grown* children from their duty of honor (II, 68). Because of my doubts (expressed below) about extensive filial duties to reciprocate for parental benefaction, however, I think Becker's account is bound to fail as an account of a general parental right. My discussion here has, of course, left unanswered many vexing questions about parental rights of tuition—for example, the specific content of their rights with respect to educating their children, training them in a religion, seeking medical treatment for them (if, say, the parents are Christian Scientists), and so on. Lockean answers to all of these questions must proceed by allowing parental discretion in such matters *only* when this is consistent with the child's successful development into a rational, autonomous adult, capable of living a free and happy life (as, for instance, denying the child needed medical treatment for parental religious reasons would seem *not* to be).

[63] See Wicclair's distinction between "duties of indebtedness" and "duties of gratitude," and his convincing argument that what we owe our parents must be thought of as a duty of gratitude ("Caring for Frail Elderly Parents," 174–76). I will

Just which benefits Locke has in mind as the ground of the filial debt of gratitude is not as clear as we might like it to be. He mentions that the child receives "life and education from his parents" (II, 170); and earlier "happiness or life" (II, 66; or perhaps only "life"), education (II, 68), and "the highest benefits he is naturally capable of" (II, 69) are referred to. But of life and education as parental benefits, Locke clearly has doubts about at least the former. For he acknowledges that merely begetting a child gives a father no power at all over the child (II, 65). And when we remember that it is God, not the parents, who really gives life to the child, Locke's reference to life as a benefit bestowed by parents seems curious indeed.

Locke's doubts about life as a benefit for which children owe a return to their parents seem sensible, even forgetting God's role in his theory. For while others have certainly defended the view that the gift of life grounds filial duties,[64] it is a view beset with quite obvious difficulties. In the first place, of course, whether or not life is a benefit depends very much on the quality of that life, on what else parents provide for their children. As Sidgwick puts it, "It may be said that a child owes gratitude to the authors of its existence. But life alone, apart from any provision for making life happy, seems a boon of doubtful value, and one that scarcely excites gratitude when it was not conferred from any regard for the recipient."[65] Add to this the fact that "we were certainly not the beneficiaries in the sense that *we* were made better off for getting [life] than *we* would otherwise have been: for we *would not* otherwise have been at all. Of course it also follows that the benefit in question is nonrefusable."[66] If we speak not of life itself, but of our

---

not try to deal here with alternative (and, I think, less plausible) accounts of the bases of parental rights. Some (e.g., Sommers) make these rights depend on the presence of certain conventions or customs (see note 55 above). Others ground some parental rights (under general duties of beneficence) in the parents' need for help (Daniels, *Am I My Parents' Keeper?* 32). Still others ground filial duties (and parental rights) in the presence of intimacy, friendship, or understanding between parents and their children (English, "What Do Grown Children Owe Their Parents?" 353–55). See my criticism of this last approach in "Obligations of Citizens," 79.

[64] Classically, Aristotle and Aquinas (among many others) held to it. And recently Belliotti has argued for a moral requirement of "care" toward those who help form our identities; since "my biological parents' genetic contribut [sic] provides a most enduring aspect of who 'I' am, I owe them certain moral requirements" ("Honor Thy Father," 153). Narveson subjects this position to convincing criticism in the article referred to below.

[65] *Methods of Ethics*, 248n.

[66] Narveson, "On Honouring Our Parents," 75; see also Jecker, "Are Filial Duties Unfounded?" 74.

specific genetic endowments as the benefits for which we should be grateful, similar responses seem appropriate. To which we can add that our parents, lacking any real control over how we turn out, cannot really have tried to endow us in any particular way.[67] Finally, it seems clear that none of these benefits (life or genetic endowment) was initially given to us in a way that involved any sacrifice on our parents' parts. It may even have been (indeed, we hope that it was) a pleasure, or worse, an accident. Any parental sacrifices come later than the initial "gift" of life and genes.[68]

But if life (and genes) is, as Locke saw, a dubious benefit on which to base parental rights and filial duties, it is also the only benefit given by all parents to their children. Beyond this, all other parental provision of benefits is quite variable. And if filial duties are to be proportionate to parental benefaction, it follows that some children will owe quite extensive debts to their parents while others will owe nothing at all[69] (which seems, in the end, to be Locke's real view, if, perhaps, one to which he was pushed reluctantly). The central question about the filial duties of grown children (and about the parental right of honor), then, will be a question of which benefits children are thought to owe a return for. And we have already seen some suggestions of general rules we might apply in deciding. A return is owed only for those benefits: which are given with "regard for the recipient"; which are refusable; which are given intentionally; which are given at some cost to the giver. These (and other) conditions on "debts of gratitude" are normally cited by those who resist altogether the idea that parental benefaction grounds filial duties of reciprocation; on these views parental benefits simply fail to satisfy the conditions under which such duties might be generated.[70] Those who think that parental sacrifices and benefits conferred on children are morally important

[67] Narveson, "On Honouring Our Parents," 75–76.

[68] If the benefit conveyed by the "gift of life" is alleged to be a soul, of course, although the benefit is no doubt precious, the relevant benefactor is quite clearly God, *not* our parents.

[69] See Daniels, *Am I My Parents' Keeper?* 31.

[70] English argues that parental sacrifice and benefaction are irrelevant to filial duties because only requested favors (not voluntary sacrifices) ground an obligation to reciprocate ("What Do Grown Children Owe Their Parents?" 352–55). Slote is skeptical about "any moral *duty* to show gratitude for benefits one has not requested" ("Obedience and Illusions," 320). And Blustein thinks both that "if parents have any right to repayment from their children, it can only be for that which was either above and beyond the call of parental duty, or not required by parental duty at all" (*Parents and Children*, 182); and that "it is also necessary that the benefits received be voluntarily accepted" (which "young children and infants" cannot do) (183).

(in grounding filial duties), generally resist (or ignore) the idea that these sacrifices and benefits are disqualified by such conditions.[71]

I have elsewhere explored at some length the limits on debts of gratitude and the conditions under which they may arise.[72] That analysis suggests that the standard blanket objections to filial duties of reciprocation for parental benefaction are misguided. While it is true that provision of benefits will create reciprocal obligation only when benefits are provided intentionally, out of regard for the beneficiary, and at some cost to the benefactor (etc.[73]), these conditions are normally satisfied in the parent's provision of benefits to the child. Further, the mere fact that the benefits parents provide are nonrefusable or not voluntarily accepted by children is not sufficient to show that these benefits do not require a return.[74] Nor does the mere fact that parents have a duty to provide many of these benefits disqualify them.[75] But this second concern comes closer, in my view, than the first to identifying the real problem with parental benefits (as a source of filial duties).

The care, attention, education, support, and healthy environment good parents provide for their children are undeniably real benefits that are typically supplied out of concern for the children and at considerable cost and effort on the parents' part. It is also clear that it is the parents' duty to provide at least many of these goods (see 4.3 below). But that it is the parents' duty to benefit their children in these ways does not by itself show that the children do not, as a result, have filial duties to reciprocate. Sometimes duty-meeting beneficial action requires reciprocation, sometimes it does not. If you are drowning a short distance from the pier and I ruin my new suit or incur some injury while saving you, few would maintain that you owe me nothing. Perhaps paying for the suit or tending to the injury would be appropriate as a return; if a serious risk were involved, perhaps more of a return would be fitting (if it were possible and agreeable to the benefactor). But what is clearly true as well of the situation described is that I did

[71] Among those who think parental sacrifices and benefits are important in this way are Sidgwick (*Methods of Ethics*, 248), Becker (*Reciprocity*, 210–11), Narveson ("On Honouring Our Parents," 74), Woozley (*Law and Obedience*, 65–66), Belliotti ("Honor Thy Father," 151, 153), Sommers ("Filial Morality," 446–47), and Lin Yutang ("On Growing Old Gracefully," 457).
[72] *Moral Principles and Political Obligations*, chapter 7 (esp. 163–83).
[73] See ibid., 178–79, for a full statement of (at least some of) the conditions in question.
[74] Contrary to the suggestions of Blustein, English, and Slote. See also Wicclair, "Caring for Frail Elderly Parents," 165–67.
[75] Contra Blustein and Daniels (*Am I My Parents' Keeper?* 30).

no more than my duty in saving you. Had I ignored your plight (perhaps out of concern for my suit), I would have been open to the most severe moral condemnation. There are, then, familiar cases in which the provision of benefits that it is our duty to provide nonetheless grounds obligations to reciprocate. There are obviously other kinds of cases in which it does not.[76] If I have a duty to pay you $10 (because I earlier borrowed it from you), you surely are not bound to reciprocate when I give you the $10. Now, which of these kinds of cases resembles that in which parents benefit their children (as they are duty-bound to do)? Any resemblance must surely be to the second case, for what is striking about the benefits parents provide is that the parents have themselves created the needs these benefits satisfy (by creating the child who has them). Parents not only have a duty to care for their children but are (normally) morally responsible for the necessity of caring for them. It is as if, instead of just pulling you from the water, I had first pushed you in (accidentally or intentionally), making me responsible for your need. In such a case, it is far less convincing to claim that anything is owed me as a benefactor; and by analogy it is unconvincing to insist that filial obligations arise from routine cases of parental benefaction.[77]

More, then, than simply caring for a child and seeing that its needs are met will be necessary for the generation of filial obligations. Perhaps extraordinary sacrifices by parents (those beyond the requirements of parental duty) will make a difference. And certainly nonbiological parents (or, say, victims of rape), who have voluntarily taken on a child's care (when not duty-bound to do so)

[76] See my *Moral Principles and Political Obligations*, 179–83, for a fuller discussion of these matters. Jecker argues that if a benefit is owed another as a matter of duty, no debt of gratitude will arise from its provision unless the benefit is very valuable, very burdensome to provide, provided in some praiseworthy way, or includes with it some supererogatory element ("Are Filial Duties Unfounded?" 74–75).

[77] Becker criticizes my analogy, suggesting that "the more apt (but still not quite right) analogy is the case in which I resuscitate you, thus creating an opportunity to live, and since the situation into which I have brought you is temporarily a perilous one (let's say we are stranded on an island), I take care of you until you are strong enough to fend for yourself. Obligations of reciprocity are perfectly intelligible in such a case, and also in the case of parent-child relationships" (*Reciprocity*, 396). But here the debt is at least partly owed for the resuscitation (and we have seen that the analogous "giving of life" to the child cannot plausibly be taken to ground a debt). Further, the benefactor in Becker's case is not responsible for the "perilous" situation in which the beneficiary awakens (as the child's parents are); if Becker's benefactor were responsible (say, the benefactor had kidnapped the person needing resuscitation, or wrecked the person's boat), our judgment of the beneficiary's duties would be very different.

will be owed more by their children than others would be. Even the "gift" of firm but loving guidance, so seldom and with such great difficulty given by parents but so crucial to the child's psychological well-being and potential for happiness, may (in conjunction with more routine benefits) ground special filial obligations.[78] This seems to me to be the proper explanation of the relevance of love to the moral component of the parent-child relationship. Genuine parental love, understood here as a deep emotional commitment to a painstaking and disciplined pursuit of the child's long-term happiness, is so difficult to give fully and wisely that it may count as the kind of benefit that is not simply a straightforward requirement of parental responsibility. If this is so, then filial obligations may be generated by the parent's loving care (although, as mentioned above, in the ideal parent-child relationship the child will not be motivated by any sense of duty or obligation).

The resulting position on parental rights and filial duties is not Locke's, but it can plausibly be described as Lockean, for it is motivated by concerns about and limitations on Locke's position that he himself expressed. Parental rights (and filial duties) are, on this account, less extensive than those suggested in the *Treatises* (there being no right to obedience, per se, or to a return for routine, obligatory provision of benefits). But it remains true that natural parents have a special (if limited and defeasible) claim to rear their own children, and that filial duties will be in some measure proportionate to the extent of parental care. Since (as far as I can see) the portions of Locke's position that are altered are less central to his overall stance than are those we have preserved, the revised account can be accepted as part of a more defensible Lockean moral theory (i.e., as part of the Lockean theory of rights).

4.3. The Rights of Children (and the Duties of Parents)

I turn now to the "other side" of the parent-child relationship. Locke does not refer often to the rights of children, but both of the

[78] We may thus both do our duty (for which no return is owed) and do more (for which it is) at the same time. Becker has also (incorrectly) criticized my account for ignoring this fact (*Reciprocity*, 395). See *Moral Principles and Political Obligations*, 180, for earlier comments on this point, and 182–83 for a brief discussion of the relevance of love to filial duties. I have, of course, made no efforts here to be very precise about which benefits parents owe their children as a matter of duty and which benefits go beyond parental duty, but have been content to suggest some broad guidelines. On the difficulties of precisely marking this distinction, see Wicclair, "Caring for Frail Elderly Parents," 168–69.

Treatises contain a few brief remarks on the subject. The primary rights of children seem to be two. First, children have "a right to be nourished and maintained by their parents, nay a right not only to a bare subsistence but to the convenience and comforts of life, as far as the conditions of the parents can afford it" (I, 89; see also I, 90; II, 78, 183). This right lasts until children "are able to provide for themselves" (II, 78). Second, and "founded in" the first right (I, 97), children "have a right of inheritance to their father's property" (I, 93; see also I, 88; II, 190) (about which I shall say no more until section 4). Locke also mentions that the child must be allowed "the privilege of his nature, to be free" (II, 63, 190). By this he seems to mean that children have a right not only to be kept comfortably alive, but to be reared in such a way that they will one day become responsible, rational agents (as we saw in 4.2). This means that they must be taught self-control, moral sensitivity, respect for reason, and so on. Children have rights (property), unlike lawful slaves; but the child is "incapable to manage his property" (II, 174).

Contemporary philosophers have recognized the difficulties in ascribing rights to infants and young children, who seem unable not only to "manage" their rights, but to assert, waive, or even understand their rights. How can one who lacks even a rudimentary understanding of the significance of moral rights and duties be said to be a rightholder? The whole point of rights seems to be to protect the pursuit of values and plans (2.2) that the infant lacks altogether. A similar tension concerning children's rights can be observed in Locke's work. Locke often writes as if there are two classes of beings in the world—those who are under the law of nature (to whom the law is given or promulgated), and those who are not under it. Members of the former class—persons or "men"—have the rights and obligations defined by the law of nature. Members of the latter class do not have either. But things cannot really be so simple for Locke, for there are at least four distinct groups of beings who are said at various times not to be under the law, but who seem to have quite different rights and duties. First, we have the "inferior" lower animals, "terrestrial irrational creatures" (I, 27), who have been given by God to mankind in common (II, 26; I, 24–29, 38–40, 60, 87). Lacking reason, they cannot be given the law (which is promulgated through reason), and so they have neither rights nor duties. They can neither do wrong nor be wronged.[79] Second, we have the warmakers and

---

[79] I will not even try to discuss here whether or not this view of the lower animals

lawful slaves (captured warmakers) who have quit the law of reason and forfeited all rights under it, making themselves like noxious beasts of prey (II, 16, 85, 172–73, 181). They are also said to be no longer under the law (II, 16). But it is doubtful that Locke intends to say that they, like lower animals, also lack duties. May people free themselves of all moral requirements by committing an awful crime, undoing the wrongness of all future crimes by committing a great enough crime in the present? I suspect Locke would say (although he nowhere does say) that warmakers and slaves have few or no rights, but that they do have (at least some) duties. Third, we have those suffering from "defects," who cannot now and may never be able to know the law or be guided by it—lunatics, idiots, innocents, and the insane (II, 60). "Nobody can be under a law which is not promulgated to him; and this [natural] law being promulgated or made known by reason only, he that is not come to the use of his reason, cannot be said to be under this law" (II, 57). Fourth, children are not under the law of nature (II, 59–60), until maturity brings the understanding and control (reason and will) that make them free.

We seem, then, to have at least two groups of beings who are not under the law of nature, but nonetheless have either duties (warmakers) or both rights *and* duties (children). How can this be explained, assuming (as Locke certainly seems to) that it is the law of nature that specifies all moral rights and duties? If warmakers and children were not under the law in the way that animals are not under it, we would seem to be allowed to confine, breed, and eat them, make clothes of their skins, and so on. Is there then more than one way to not be under the law of nature?

It might seem at first as if the answer must lie in the rights and duties of those who *are* under the law. For if peaceful persons have rights not to be harmed, must not warmakers have duties to respect those rights? And if parents have duties to care for their children, cannot the rights of children merely be the logical correlates of these duties? But this line of reasoning takes us nowhere, of course, for from our rights not to be harmed it in no way follows that tigers (who are not under the law) have duties not to harm us. Nor does our duty to care for a thing (e.g., another's pet or plant) entail that the thing cared for has a right to that care. The logical correlativity of rights and duties holds only insofar as du-

---

is correct. But it is worth noting that many ways of defending children's rights also entail rights for at least some of the lower animals.

ties are owed *to* other persons (and rights are held *against* other persons), and our question is precisely one about whether moral relations can hold between persons and those not under the law.

Perhaps we can appeal to the potential personhood (agency, rationality) of children to explain why they have rights without being under the law now (as so many more recent philosophers have done).[80] Children are, after all, "born to" reason, freedom, and equality (II, 55, 61). But this line of argument seems to be closed to Locke, for it seems to divide up the groups of beings not under the law in the wrong way. Animals lack this potential (on Locke's view), and so would not be rightholders according to a potentiality argument. But the same argument would seem to place many lunatics, idiots, innocents, and the insane (i.e., those who also lack potential) in the same moral camp with animals. Worse, it would also seem to make rightholders of warmakers and slaves, at least many of whom surely *do* have the potential to recover their rationality (as Locke can be taken to concede in his recognition that a lord can make a binding contract with his slave, thereby releasing him from his rightless condition). So warmakers would seem to fall in the same moral camp with children, contrary to Locke's repeated claims that while warmakers have forfeited all rights, children *have* rights.

The likeliest explanation of why human beings not under the law seem to nonetheless be allowed some moral standing in Locke, while animals (equally not under the law) are not, is that human beings are made by God in His own image, while animals are made by God for our use. This, of course, does not explain how beings not under the law can have rights and duties; but it may explain Locke's reluctance to class together all beings who are not under the law. But even on this theological model, things are far from clear. For "wherein soever else the image of God consisted, the intellectual nature was certainly a part of it" (I, 30). This would seem to imply either: (a) that those with no current "intellectual nature" (animals, children, warmakers, idiots) are not in God's image, and can be classed together, or (b) that those with no intellectual potential (most animals and idiots) are not in God's image, while those with it (most children and warmakers) are. So on the theological model, the problems above are merely duplicated in new terms.

Of the three groups of humans said by Locke not to be under

---

[80] For a reading of Locke in these terms, see Glenn, "Inalienable Rights," 94.

the law, warmakers are probably the easiest to deal with from a Lockean perspective (although we must in some ways revise what Locke actually says). Warmakers are those who have been given the law, and hence remain bound by its duties, but who have freely (and culpably) chosen to disregard the law in the most serious fashion. In thus taking advantage of the obedient behavior of their fellows, they forfeit their rights, but *not* their duties, under the law's protective scheme. They thus remain bound to comply with the law's requirements, but may be legitimately confined at hard labor (enslaved) or put to death (if required for the safety of others). We need not suppose, with Locke, that warmakers forfeit *all* rights. Locke seems to have thought that if one forfeits the right not to be killed, one must in the process have forfeited all other ("lesser") rights. He is far from alone in this view. But we may allow, contra Locke, that the warmaker retains at least some rights (e.g., the right not to be cruelly degraded), even while losing the rights not to be killed or used for labor.[81] Warmakers remain morally considerable beings on this account, and do not really qualify as beings who are not under the law of nature at all.

Children and idiots are harder to deal with in a way true to the spirit of Locke's claims. One thing that seems clear about children's rights, however, is that Locke almost always speaks of them simply as the logical correlates of parental duties. Parents, Locke tells us, are "by the law of nature, under the obligation to preserve, nourish, and educate the children they [have] begotten" (II, 56; see also II, 60, 67; I, 56, 88). And it is almost always in the context of such claims about parental duty that Locke goes on to speak of the rights of children. Children have, as a consequence of parental responsibilities, "*their kind* of right" (I, 88; my emphasis) to be preserved and supported. Notice that there is in the *Treatises* (as far as I know) no passage in which Locke mentions the rights of children held against the world—for instance, rights not to be killed, assaulted, raped, and so on. The picture that seems to emerge is one of children with quite limited rights only against their parents, but with none of the more general equal rights against one another possessed by mature persons.

If this is indeed Locke's view, we may begin to wonder whether Locke needs to defend children's rights at all, or whether he might

---

[81] This seems to be the idea, for instance, behind the restrictions on capital punishment to those forms that are not "cruel and unusual," and the bans on torture, public displays of punishment, and the like, even in the cases of those acknowledged to deserve death.

not simply leave children in the class of beings with no rights or duties.[82] For the objects of the child's rights of which Locke speaks (nourishment, maintenance, education) are things that it is the natural parents' duty to provide. Even, then, if children had no rights, we could still defend the claim that failure to provide them with nourishment (etc.) was wrong (although we could no longer say that this was owed to the children themselves). And we could still explain why it is wrong for others to harm children, for to harm them would be a wrong done both to their parents (who have the right to control them) and to God (who is the owner of the children).[83] But on this account of matters, it is initially hard to see why parents should be taken to have duties to the nonpersons (nonrightholders) they bear. We have no duties toward other kinds of nonpersons (rocks, trees, animals, etc.). Why should our children be any different? Locke, of course, has at least two answers to this question. First, God has entrusted the child to the care of its natural parents. He has "laid on man" a duty to preserve offspring (II, 60, 63; I, 89) and made us accountable to Him for their safety (II, 56). Parents are made by God "instruments in his great design of continuing the race of mankind" (II, 66). Parents thus have a duty owed to God to care for their children, much as a babysitter has duties to parents. Second, however, Locke's language frequently suggests that natural parents are responsible for caring for the children they beget because it was their free act that brought a needy individual into the world (e.g., I, 88–89, 93; II, 80). Parents have done something that makes them responsi-

[82] There are, of course, straightforward implications of his commitment to children's rights for Locke's political philosophy: for example, (a) if children have rights, parents do not have absolute authority over them; it is then impossible to argue (with Filmer) that the king has absolute authority over his subjects *because* he has paternal authority over them; (b) if children have rights, conquerors (even just conquerors) cannot gain absolute authority over a whole people by the use of force; for while the conqueror may gain absolute authority over those who aggress against him, the rights of the aggressors' children limit the authority he can acquire. But I think that Locke could probably still defend these aspects of his political theory without appeal to children's rights, by arguing (a) that parents have duties toward their children (laid on them by God), and (b) that the rights of aggressors' wives (and those of other noncombatants) limit the just conqueror's authority.

[83] Animals, of course, were also originally owned by God. But they may be harmed where necessary, because God gave them to us for our use. Nothing made by God may be harmed or destroyed needlessly. But God may be understood to have given His permission to constrain or to destroy things where it is necessary for our best preservation. Thus, children may not be harmed or killed (it not being necessary to humankind's effective preservation). But animals and (sometimes) warmakers may be harmed (where failing to harm endangers oneself or others).

ble.[84] Now either of these two answers looks sufficient by itself to explain parents' duties to their (nonperson) children. God's assigning duties of child-rearing (the first answer) would be adequate to explain parental duties even if the parents had done nothing (even if the conception had been "immaculate," or a stork had left the child on their doorstep). But only the second answer could bear any weight in a secular Lockean account of family morality; so it is worth considering the second answer a bit further.

I suggested above (4.2) that parents are (normally) morally responsible for meeting their children's needs, having created the children who have those needs. This is more than a claim of causal responsibility (which can be made about all natural parents). It is rather a claim that by creating a needy and dependent child through one's voluntary actions, one creates as well a moral duty for oneself to care for the child. We bear moral responsibility even for the unintended or undesired consequences of our voluntary actions, provided these consequences are reasonably foreseeable. As Kant puts it, we have brought children into the world without their consent.[85] Our actions put children at risk, bringing them laden with needs into an inhospitable environment. Parental duty is not just a special case of the general duty to give aid to (or not to harm) others, which the biological parent just happens to be in a better position than anyone else to discharge;[86] nor is it just a case of a duty to help those who are dependent on us.[87] Parental

[84] Locke sometimes seems to suggest a third answer: that parents must preserve their children because children are "a part of themselves" (I, 97), and parents are "by a like obligation bound to preserve what they have begotten, as to preserve themselves"(I, 88). I do not here discuss this suggestion, for it would seem to involve claims of parental property in the child that are inappropriate for Locke.

[85] Kant, *Metaphysics of Morals*, part 1, section 28: "the act of generation [is] a process by which a person is brought without his consent into the world, and placed in it by the responsible free will of others." For a slightly more sinister reminder of the duties of creators, recall the monster's words in Mary Shelley's *Frankenstein*: "You, my creator, detest and spurn me, thy creature, to whom thou art bound by ties only dissoluble by the annihilation of one of us. . . . Do your duty towards me, and I will do mine towards you and the rest of mankind" ([New York: Bantam, 1981], 83).

[86] Sidgwick notes that parental duty may be "partly" accounted for by "duties arising out of special needs": "the parents, being the cause of the child's existing in a helpless condition, would be indirectly the cause of the suffering and death that would result to it if neglected." But he also acknowledges that this general duty cannot fully serve "as an adequate explanation of parental duty" (*Methods of Ethics*, 249). Parental duty must be understood as a special moral bond. See Wicclair, "Caring for Frail Elderly Parents," 170–71.

[87] Blustein bases parental duty primarily on the duty to satisfy the needs of those dependent on one (*Parents and Children*, 116–17). But he sees that this cannot determine why the *parent* is specially bound. We can add that dependency is a more

198

duty is not a general natural duty we have the bad luck to be called to perform (like the solitary walker on the beach where another is drowning). It is a moral requirement based in a special relationship established by parents' voluntary actions, analogous sometimes to a contractual duty of care, sometimes to the duty (of reparation) we create for ourselves by carelessly harming another, and sometimes to the duty (of extensive care) we create for ourselves by secluding an injured person (and thus preventing others from helping to give care).[88] Many such voluntary actions by parents are not at all like promises or commitments; they may be perfectly unintentional. But like promises and commitments, they ground special moral requirements.

We can describe a rough range of cases and the corresponding kinds of responsibility grounded in parental acts (or nonacts). Thus, at one extreme we have cases involving fully informed, fully voluntary decisions to procreate (or to assume responsibility for the care of a child—as with step-parents, adoptive and foster parents, or guardians). Here the parental duties that result most clearly resemble those resulting from other voluntary undertakings of obligations.[89] Next, we have cases where the child's conception resulted from carelessness or "bad luck," where this con-

---

or less interesting moral property depending on how one came to be dependent. Becker criticizes dependency accounts like Blustein's (he also criticizes voluntarist accounts, although the sort I sketch below seems untouched by his complaints) (*Reciprocity*, 200–201).

[88] In American law, one can be obligated to rescue or care for another in all of these situations: if there is a valid contract requiring care, if one puts another in peril by one's own careless act, or if one secludes a person in need from others.

[89] O'Neill, "Begetting, Bearing, and Rearing," 26. I am less inclined to agree that not aborting a child counts as a voluntary undertaking of duties (as Ruddick seems to suggest in "Parents and Life Prospects," 27), particularly in cases where initial conception involved force or deceit. Blustein argues that the decision to procreate only counts as an undertaking of responsibility in the context of societal expectation of child-rearing by biological parents. Similarly, the consequence of the child's eventual need for parental care only counts as reasonably foreseeable (my second kind of case, below) where society makes no alternative arrangements for rearing children (*Parents and Children*, 144–56). This seems to me to place too strong an emphasis on custom in explaining parental duty. Societal practices may relieve natural parents of the responsibility of care for their children (by society's undertaking to replace natural parents, as adoptive parents do). But parental responsibility does not depend on the absence of such practices. If a couple decides to have a child (and conceives it) in a society that practices communal child-rearing, but are later stranded on an island (with several strangers) and give birth, it would be hard to argue that they have no more responsibility for (or rights over) the child than the strangers with whom they are stranded. The decision to procreate commits one to caring for the child "until relieved" (which relief one may have a reasonable, but defeasible, expectation of receiving).

199

sequence was an unintended but foreseeable possible result of voluntary acts aimed at some other end (e.g., sexual gratification).[90] Here again, there seems little doubt that the acts are of a type that often ground special responsibilities (as in the case of civil liability for negligence).[91] One's voluntary actions risk eventually putting another (the child) at peril. In a third class of cases, such as those involving force, rape, or deception, conception is not a result of voluntary acts (or ones with foreseeable risks) at all, for one party. But in such cases, the other party (the aggressor or deceiver) clearly *is* responsible for the child's eventual predicament, having acted recklessly or negligently with regard to the conception (and possibly also wrongly with regard to the sexual act itself). We can, finally, imagine a fourth class of miraculous (or science fiction) cases in which conception results from no one's risky voluntary acts.[92] In such instances, the natural "parents" (i.e., sperm and egg contributors) would have no more responsibilities for the child than would any unrelated person, confronted with a child in need (i.e., only general duties would apply).

It is natural to ask in response to such a voluntarist account of special parental duties: to whom are these duties owed? In Locke, of course, we have the same moral overdetermination here that we saw in examining the ground of parental duties. Parental duties are owed both to God (as settlor) and to the child (as another rightholder). In a secular Lockean account, however, the first answer is closed to us. And if we try to do without children's rights in our account altogether (as we began by trying to do), the second answer is closed as well. Parental duties, as a result, will seem to be owed to no one—neither to the interacting party (as in the case of special duties) nor to humankind as a whole (as in the case of general duties)—and it is hard to understand duties that make no "contact" with other persons. So while Locke himself may be able to scrap rights for children, a secular reconstruction or extension of Locke, it seems, cannot.

The awkwardness of this conclusion for a Lockean account of rights lies in the fact that there are reasons to want children *not* to be rightholders within such an account. The Lockean account of persons and rights emphasizes (as we saw in 2.2) agency, ratio-

---

[90] Locke mentions that conception is "most commonly without the intention, and often against the consent and will of the begetter" (I, 54).

[91] Olafson, "Rights and Duties"; Lomasky, *Persons, Rights*, 165–67.

[92] This class may also include cases in which parents are non-negligently ignorant of the connection between sexual intercourse and conception.

nality, having a will, purposiveness, acting (in the strict sense), autonomy, self-consciousness, and the like. All of these are traits or capacities that infants and young children seem not to possess at all, and which children acquire only very gradually. It seems natural, then, for a Lockean to try to argue that young children are not persons and have no rights, and that older children acquire personhood and rights in gradual stages (culminating in a threshold reached at maturity). Many contemporary philosophers who argue against children's rights do so in these terms.[93]

But it seems that the (secular) Lockean line needs children's rights, both to explain the wrongness of abusing children and to make sense of special parental duties. Even (the nonsecular) Locke has, as we have seen, problems with children's rights. Even if parents have their rights and duties from God's entrusting children to them, and children have their rights "by donation" or "by the appointment of" (I, 89) God, we are still left with beings who are not under the law of nature but nonetheless have rights. And unless children also get duties (beyond obedience to their parents) in the bargain, their status as rightholders without (significant) duties violates the (so-called) doctrine of the moral correlation of rights and duties.[94] If, instead of God's donation being the source of children's rights, we try to analyze them simply as the logical correlates of parental duties, we render unintelligible those parental duties. For it is only insofar as the infant is already a morally considerable being (one with rights), that a parent's responsibility

[93] Hart thinks we should "not extend to animals and babies whom it is wrong to ill-treat the notion of a right to proper treatment," apparently because babies (and animals) cannot claim, waive (or release others from the duties that correlate with) their rights ("Are There Any Natural Rights?" 180–81). For Frankfurt, young children are "wantons" who lack the second-order volitions (and rationality) necessary for personhood ("Freedom of the Will," 10–12). Wilkes describes infants as "fuzzy persons" (*Real People*, 56). According to Gewirth, "possession of the generic rights must be proportional to the degree to which [individuals] have the abilities of agency" ("Basis and Content," 54–55), so that children cannot possess full rights (*Reason and Morality*, 141). And Murphy denies that young children (and the severely retarded) have "autonomy rights," because they "certainly are not fully rational and autonomous" ("Rights and Borderline Cases," 237). It is also common because of children's lack of these traits or capacities, to refer to (at least some of) their rights with such terms as "rights-in-trust" (Feinberg, "Child's Right," 125–26), "rights by analogy" (McClosky, "Rights"), "preparatory rights" (Gewirth, *Reason and Morality*, 141), or rights in "future interests" (Morris, "Persons and Punishment," 316–17), or to say that children have genuine rights, but with some of the "conceptual linkages" missing (Melden, *Rights and Persons*, 72–73).

[94] Which is stated (and rejected, precisely *because* of the case of infants, etc.) in Benn and Peters, *Social Principles*, 89, as follows: "the enjoyment of rights . . . is conditional on the performance of duties."

for its plight can explain a parental duty of care. If the infant comes into the world rightless, parents seem to have no more duties to it than they would to a frog they created from leftover frog parts in a laboratory. It is by virtue of being *God's* that children enter the world as morally considerable beings in Locke's account of the matter. And it is because they are *God's* that they can be "morally considerable" even without having rights. Locke could, then, coherently deny rights to young children (although he should also acknowledge a gradual accumulation of rights and duties for the growing child, rather than the "moral avalanche" at maturity that he seems to favor). Natural parental rights and duties would still be easy to ground, either (directly) in God's entrusting the child to parents or (less directly) in simple rule-consequentialist arguments (concerning the best means for preserving humankind).

What, though, can Locke in his secular moments (or the secular Lockean line, which *needs* children's rights) do in these matters? The natural account of children's rights to attempt is one that is "forward-looking"—that is, one that somehow anticipates the child's future status as an autonomous, rational agent, capable of planning, self-control, and moral action. Kant argues that we must understand rights not just as rights to *be* autonomous, but to *become* rational, autonomous beings.[95] Locke similarly argues that for the child, "the privilege of his nature, to be free" is best understood as a right to be helped in reaching the condition where reason guides actions (II, 63). While such arguments are sometimes cast in terms of the child's status as a *potential* person,[96] they are more plausibly developed by a Lockean as claims about the child's present capacities or identity. Children have the capacity for rationality and autonomy, although they will not be able to exercise it until later, which makes them persons now. They are the same persons they will be as adults (in most cases). It is precisely because we adults are continuous with our child-selves that it matters now to each of us how we were treated when we were children.[97] Respect for persons entails respect for them even when

[95] Kant, *Metaphysics of Morals*, part 1, section 28.

[96] On the use of this notion of potentiality, see Wilkes, *Real People*, chapter 2. Locke, however, seems to ridicule the idea of deriving current rights from future status in his attack on Filmer's distinction between "habit" and "act" (I, 18–20). He accepts derivations of rights from present identity.

[97] See Lomasky, *Persons, Rights*, 157–62; and Blustein, *Parents and Children*, 134–35. On the capacity for autonomy, see Feinberg, *Harm to Self*, chapter 18. Melden also argues that rights must be assigned according to what one *is*, not according only to the characteristics one exhibits at all times ("Do Infants Have Moral

they are children, as yet unable to exercise the capacities that distinguish them from nonpersons. Treatment appropriate to the nature of children must be responsive to their capacities; children, like the adults they become, are entitled to such treatment.

I will not try here to develop this (or any other) account of the rights of children.[98] I will only point to a difficulty faced within a Lockean perspective by the alternative "potentiality" account of children's rights. The difficulty is that the purest form of this account (i.e., the form in which it is not simply equivalent to the "present capacity" account sketched above) has a very hard time explaining the child's right not to be killed. Insofar as we explain children's rights in terms of the status of the adults they will become or in terms of the effects of our current treatment of them on those adults, we seem to lack an explanation of their rights in those cases where the adults in question will never exist. The natural next move is to try to explain the child's right not to be killed in terms of that child's *current interest* in becoming an adult rational agent.[99] But this is a move that involves shifting in midstream away from the previous emphasis on choice, reason, will, self-consciousness, and the like, as the bases for rightholding. Interests are possessed by a much wider class of beings than persons (or agents or beings with wills); and focusing on interests in a theory of rights indicates a quite different set of concerns than focusing on reason or freedom. While we have seen (in 2.3) that Locke embraces unqualifiedly neither a choice (or will) theory of rights nor a benefit (or interest) theory, he would surely be uncomfortable with at least some of the consequences of the shift to a focus on interests at this point in the argument.[100]

Rights?" 215–18); young children count as persons *now*, in virtue of their continuity with their future selves (*Rights and Persons*, 221–23).

[98] If rule-consequentialist arguments can establish rights, of course, there is an alternative Lockean argument for children's rights: since mankind is best preserved if children are preserved, there is a duty to preserve children and a corresponding right of children to be preserved (both positively and negatively) by all others (and not merely by their parents).

[99] See Wilkes, *Real People*, 53. This problem is quite well illustrated in Lomasky's argument for children's rights. Some of the child's rights (and all of the rights of normal adults) are defended in terms of the rightholder's special status as "project pursuer" or "future project pursuer." But the child's right not to be killed is defended in terms of the child's interests (*Persons, Rights*, 162–63).

[100] Consider, for instance, Feinberg's argument that because rightholders must be capable of being harmed or benefited and being represented, "the sorts of beings who *can* have rights are precisely those who have (or can have) interests" ("Rights of Animals," 167). This class of beings clearly includes not only very young children, but at least many lower animals as well (ibid., 161–67; see also

I do not pretend that the "present capacity" account of children's rights is easy to defend. But the only other obvious alternative compatible with a secular and genuinely Lockean theory is to try to explain the duties at issue—the general duties not to harm children and the special duties of parents—in a way that does not depend on children being persons or rightholders (and which appeals neither to God's will nor to His entrusting children to parents). This is obviously an even harder task than the first.

4.4. The Family and Property

Locke's theory of property (the subject of chapter 5) comes into contact with his account of familial morality chiefly on issues concerning inheritance and bequest. The time Locke spends discussing inheritance (primarily in the *First Treatise*) is, of course, important to his critique of Filmer, since it is by inheritance that Adam's power is alleged by Filmer to descend to kings. But in the process of answering Filmer, Locke creates a puzzle of his own. His remarks on inheritance and bequest leave his reader not at all clear on the status of property within the Lockean family. At times Locke seems to say that the father's property is his own, to dispose of as he will. At other times, however, the rights of children (and wives) to (all or a share of) this "paternal property" seem to be emphasized. The following question emerges: "Which is to prevail—the testator's liberty to bequeath his property as he wills or his dependents' natural right to the inheritance?"[101] This question, of course, is just a more specific form of two more general puzzles: Is property in the family essentially individual or familial? Does the property holder's right of free alienation or the dependents' right to support have priority in Locke?

There is ample textual evidence to support the first interpretive option—that in Locke property is individual with free alienation and bequest having priority.[102] Of the father's property, Locke

---

Feinberg's "Child's Right," 127; and Blustein, *Parents and Children*, 163). Now interest theories of rights (or of the possible subjects of rights) are not without problems of their own (some of which are discussed in White, *Rights*, 79–85). But the point to note here is that an appeal to interests at this stage of the argument will make rightholders of very different classes of beings than Locke wanted; indeed, it will make rightholders of *all* of the beings said by Locke *not* to be under the law of nature.

[101] Waldron, "Locke's Account," 40.

[102] Strauss reads Locke in this way (*Natural Right*, 247n), as do many others: for example, Tyler, *Family Provision*, 1; Pangle, *Republicanism*, 233; Wood, *Capitalism*, 79–80. Both Waldron ("Locke's Account," 41, 47) and Grant (*Liberalism*, 60–61)

RIGHTS AND THE FAMILY

writes: "that possession, *if he disposed not otherwise of it* by his positive grant, descended naturally to his children, and they had a right to succeed to it, and possess it" (I, 87; my emphasis). Fathers have the power to "bestow their estates on those who please them most" (II, 72). The natural reading of such passages is that the father may dispose of his property as he pleases. His dependents have a right over unrelated persons to inherit what remains at his death. But their rights in no way limit the father's right of free alienation (and bequest).[103] And this may seem as it ought to be in a theory that appears to many to emphasize the right of free alienation as an important component of property.

It is not, however, at all obvious that free alienation is central in this way to Locke's theory of property. There are many things one clearly may not do with one's property in Locke—harm oneself or others, deny the needy, and so on (see 5.1 and 6.3). Such limits should make us wonder about free bequest. Even if we accept the claim that free alienation is essential to property in Locke, however, nothing would follow from that about the priority of paternal bequest. Locke could defend free alienation and still defend the priority of inheritance (dependents' rights) in several ways. First, provided that the property that may be freely alienated is conceived as joint property, held by all of the family members together, paternal alienation or bequest will have no priority (indeed, it will have no moral force at all). Second, even if property is individual, free alienation is compatible with having committed or partially alienated one's property to those with whom one enters into a special relationship—such as those relationships created by marriage or procreation. The rights of dependents might thus have priority over (or at least be in conflict with) the later right of paternal alienation.

It is appropriate, then, to explore the other possibility—that property is essentially familial or that inheritance and the rights of dependents have priority (in family settings) over paternal prerogative. This latter view of Locke has been (too) vigorously defended by Tully, who argues that for Locke "any family man's property is not his property at all; it is the common property of the whole family. . . . The standard form of a right of property is not an individual right for Locke. . . . The reason for this unique familialisation of property is to preserve mankind by preserving its basic

have claimed that while this is indeed Locke's view, he gives no adequate justification for it.
[103] This is Clark's reading of Locke ("Women and John Locke").

unit: the family (I, 88, 89). Locke destroys the very foundation of individual rights."[104] Inheritance, then, cannot be "justified in terms of a father's right to dispose of his property as he pleases, since it is not wholly his property."[105]

Now there is clearly textual evidence on this side as well. "Men are not proprietors of what they have merely for themselves, their children have a title to a part of it, and have their kind of right joined with their parents" (I, 88). And the wife participates in a "community of goods, and the power over them" (I, 83) with her husband. Her title to her share may be gotten by either "her own labor or compact" (II, 183). But there is no doubt that both wife and children have "a title to the goods [the father] enjoyed, and their shares in the estate [the father] possessed" (II, 183).

The source of the wife's title is no mystery, as we have seen. She has a general right, of course, to the products of her labor. But her basic conjugal rights (including her rights in the "community of goods") are *"contractual"* (4.1). It is thus not possible to say precisely what she is entitled to without a knowledge of the contract (or understanding) that underlies her marriage (although we can assume that she is entitled to at least "maintenance" [II, 83]). The source of the child's right to inherit is slightly more mysterious, since Locke seems to suggest at least four distinguishable accounts of it in the key passages on inheritance (I, 88–98) and yet another in the *Second Treatise*.

(1) In I, 88, Locke argues that human beings have "a strong desire . . . of propagating their kind" and that *"this* gives children a title, to share in the property of their parents, and a right to inherit their possessions" (my emphasis). Read by itself, this argument is incoherent. At most, even accepting the style of reasoning used in I, 86–88, the "strong desire" to propagate could ground only a right to propagate (and a duty to respect this right in others), not a right of children to inherit. We should thus read the argument as elliptical and take it to "point" to (2).[106]

(2) Later in I, 88, Locke suggests (more reasonably) that from the

[104] Tully, *Discourse*, 133.

[105] Ibid., 134. See also Waldron: Locke's "primary *economic* unit is the *family*. Although it is individual labor that gives rise to property entitlements, the entitlements to which it gives rise are familial, not individual" ("Locke's Account," 43). For a classic defense of a similar view of familial property (and of the resulting limitation on the right of paternal bequest), see Hegel, *Philosophy of Right*, sections 170–80.

[106] Contrary to, for example, Pangle, who takes this first argument to be Locke's only argument for the child's right to inherit (*Republicanism*, 232–33).

obligation of parents "to preserve what they have begotten," we can infer that children have a right to their parents' goods (these being necessary to their maintenance). He also (although later, in I, 97) maintains that the child's right to inherit is "founded on" this right to goods needed for subsistence and comfort. This seems, on the face of it, a reasonable derivation. If the parental duty of care can require (as it clearly does) parents to exercise prudence with regard to future contingencies during the parents' lives—for example, by requiring them to take care that food and shelter will be available to the child tomorrow, as well as providing it today—then that same duty of care can be plausibly interpreted as requiring that they provide resources for the child's well-being in the event of their deaths. If the parents have a duty to make this provision, their children have the correlative right to it (which is simply equivalent to the right to inherit).

(3) Locke awkwardly (and unnecessarily) attempts (in I, 89) to complete argument (2) by claiming that the parents should be "understood" to have wished to leave their property to their children, even "though the dying parents, by express words, declare nothing about them." Argument (2), however, as elaborated above, is quite adequate without these "understandings" of parental intentions. Indeed, (3) undercuts the argument in (2), making the child's right to inherit the correlate *not* of the parents' duty of care, owed to the child, but of the obligation grounded in the parents' (understood) decision to leave their property to the child. Presumably, an express statement that they did *not* wish their child to inherit would eliminate the child's right to inherit. (3) thus provides better support for parental free alienation and bequest than it does for the child's natural right of support.

(4) Several paragraphs later (I, 93), Locke states that it is "by the *dependence* they have on their parents for subsistence, [that children] have a right of inheritance to their father's property" (my emphasis).[107] This looks like the suggestion of an argument of the following form: children need and are entitled to support; children happen to be dependent on their parents, who are specially placed to provide support; therefore, children are entitled to support (and to an inheritance, as in [2]) from their parents. Thus, children have a general right to support (and others a general duty), which is "focused" on the parents by virtue of their being in the best position

[107] Note that here "dependency" seems to ground "rights"; our dependency on God, by contrast, grounds *obligations* (and rights for the God on whom we are dependent).

to provide the support (as one with a general right to needed aid might have a specific claim on the people who are nearby when aid is needed). If this is indeed Locke's intended line of argument, it cannot be rendered consistent with other aspects of his position on familial morality. For it makes parental duties and children's rights into *general* duties and rights, not *special* ones based in the special nature of their relationship. The moral relationship between parent and child (as we saw in 4.3) cannot be captured by the observation that parents are simply in the best position to help their children (if for no other reason than that parents are not *always* in the best position). Parents owe more to their child than does a well-positioned stranger. I propose, therefore, to reject (4).

(5) Finally, there are hints in the *Second Treatise* that inheritance is "taken care for" in any compact of marriage (e.g., II, 81). An agreement (understood or explicit) between spouses to provide an inheritance for their children would seem, at first blush, only to explain parental duties owed to each other to leave property to their children, not any duty owed to the children. But insofar as the children are the direct, intended beneficiaries of these parental duties, some theories of rights will allow that the children have, as a result, a right to inherit. Since I take argument (2) to be Locke's primary line on the right to inherit, however, I will not pursue this rather different approach any further.

We have now considered Locke's primary claims about paternal freedom of bequest (and free alienation of property), on the one hand, and the rights of wives and children to a share of property on the other.[108] There seems to be textual evidence to support both the priority of paternal bequest and the priority of dependents' rights. And there seem to be good Lockean arguments available on both sides. Reasoning as a rule-consequentialist, humankind

[108] I have commented not at all on Locke's rejection of attempts to derive the right to inherit from consent (I, 88) or his arguments against the doctrine of primogeniture. With respect to the latter, Locke seems clearly to reject arguments that order of birth should determine possession or nonpossession of the right to inherit (I, 91–101, 111–19), and (less clearly) to reject gender as a determining factor (Grant, *Liberalism*, 60; Waldron, "Locke's Account," 43; Ashcraft, *Locke's Two Treatises*, 93–96). From the rule-consequentialist perspective, of course, primogeniture is a silly doctrine; for it is precisely the youngest child whose needs are likely to be greatest (although perhaps the oldest who is best able to manage the estate) (see Waldron, *Private Property*, 244). But we should remember that Locke's rejection of primogeniture may not be complete (see Wood, *Capitalism*, 79–80). For he allows that the eldest brother "has the greatest part of his father's estate" (II, 202) and elsewhere seems not to object to the eldest son's having a larger portion than his brothers (I, 114–15). On the relation of Locke to the Levellers on this issue, see Ashcraft, *Revolutionary Politics*, 283.

seems likely to be best preserved if those who have natural affection for the needy (their parents) are made responsible for caring for them (since parents will work harder at it, resent it less, etc.). Of course, it also seems true that people will work harder to make property (which benefits all humankind) if they will be free to use that property (and alienate it) as they please. There are similar deontological arguments for both the special responsibilities of parents and husbands (based in their voluntary performances) *and* the right to control that property which is a natural extension of oneself and a part of one's projects and plans. In the face of such conflicting arguments, the natural resolution for the Lockean is some position that accepts the strength of the arguments on both sides.

A likely compromise is a position that acknowledges the freedom of the father to dispose of his property as he pleases, so long as he also (a) provides for the needs of his dependents (to whom he owes special duties), and (b) honors his contractual duties to his wife. This position gives a limited priority to the rights of other family members, but it does not (a la Tully) make property essentially familial and thus does not do away altogether with individual property within the family. It simply acknowledges all of the claims on the individual property produced by the father. And I believe that something like this is precisely the position Locke wished to defend: "a father may dispose of his own possessions as he pleases, when his children are out of danger of perishing for want" (II, 65). While a certain level of inheritance is required or expected, "yet it is commonly in the father's power to bestow it with a more sparing or liberal hand" (II, 72). Notice also that the claims of children are always said to be claims to a "part" or a "share" of the father's property, not claims to joint ownership of it. The father, then, may freely dispose of *his* share as he pleases, his share being that which is not owed to other family members as *their* shares.

One might object to this reading of Locke, pointing (as we did initially) to the passage in which Locke says that property "descended naturally to his children" if the father had "disposed not otherwise of it by his positive grant" (I, 87).[109] Now we can explain

[109] Waldron, "Locke's Account," 45–46 (these arguments are repeated in *Private Property*, 241–51). Waldron also argues that a proper Lockean position would (a) limit rights of inheritance to what is needed by dependents, and (b) deny that there is any natural right of bequest at all (bequest being only, if anything, a civil right) (48–50). I discuss the possibility of (a) below. But (b) seems both indefensible as a reading of Locke and quite unappealing (and unnecessary) within a Lockean perspective.

this passage in a variety of ways, without rejecting the proposed interpretation. Perhaps Locke was just careless or genuinely ambivalent. Better, perhaps Locke is trying to say here simply that whatever the father has not disposed of (from within the father's own share) descends naturally to the child, along with the child's share. But the likeliest and most literal reading of the passage makes it an acknowledgment that there can be conflicting claims to the father's property. Where the father does not leave or promise his property to another, it descends naturally to the child. But if the father does make other arrangements, property descends not naturally, but in conflict. We have seen already (in the discussion of II, 183 in 1.4) that Locke allows other rights to conflict with rights of inheritance—in particular, the just conqueror's right to reparation for injuries done him by the father. There is no reason to be suspicious, then, of the claim that the father's positive grants might also yield rights to his property that conflict with the rights of his wife and children (and, of course, such conflicts were not, and are not, uncommon in the law).

We know, of course, that the father should not promise away property to which his wife and children have a claim. But what if he does do this? What is the moral result of such a promise? The answer depends on our answer to the more general question: when a person makes two conflicting promises or commitments (i.e., promises that, as things turn out, cannot both be performed), can these result in conflicting rights, or must the first promise always take priority? The answer is far from obvious. Are second promises always "negated" in conflict situations? In at least one place Locke seems to answer "yes," for he denies that "oaths to any foreign power" could bind citizens who have already given their consent to their own society's authority (II, 134). On the other hand, there is reason to believe that Locke would have been troubled by this position had he thought much about it. For on the line suggested in II, 134, one would expect Locke to argue that in the case of warmaking fathers and just conquerors, the father could not give the conqueror a right to reparation by his wrongdoing that would conflict with the claims of his wife and children. For they had the prior claim. Locke, however, allows in such cases a genuine conflict of rights. And he may well also believe that the father's grant can generate rights that conflict with the rights of wife and children. Such conflicts (I argued in 1.4) are to be resolved by direct appeal to the fundamental law of preservation. Thus, the resolution will almost always favor the wife and children, since mankind is best preserved when those who are neediest are supported. This again, then, affirms the (limited) priority of the rights of the family members over the father's right of bequest. But it does nothing to suggest that this latter right is illusory or insignificant.

The limits are not all on the right of bequest, however. It is natural to suppose, within a Lockean framework, that the right to inherit should be limited as well (although Locke nowhere suggests this).[110] The most obvious limitation can be derived from the very structure of the right itself.[111] Insofar as the right to inherit is founded on the child's right to support from parents, it can be no more extensive than that foundational right. The child's right to support is a right to basic necessities plus reasonable comforts (where the parents can afford them). The child cannot, then, have a right to inherit any more of the parents' property than will make reasonable comfort possible. The surplus[112] of wealthy parents' holdings should not descend to the children, but to the common, to be shared by all (as in the case of parents who have no living children or parents [I, 90]).[113] Such limits on inheritance, of course, seem appropriate for other reasons as well. Because inheritance is one of the most pernicious causes of enduring (and unmerited) material inequalities in society, and because genuine (not merely formal) equality of opportunity seems to depend in important ways on material equality, the goal of equal opportunity (and such

[110] I do not here discuss limits on the wife's right to inherit, since these are presumably determined contractually.

[111] Locke seems in the *First Treatise* to set other, quite general limits on the right to inherit. In I, 74 (also I, 98, and elsewhere), Locke appears to argue that no one can acquire (from another) a right to anything "without doing that upon which that right is solely founded." Locke states this as a principle about inheritance (in order to block claims to the inheritance of paternal power), but it looks like a more general limit on alienation, or on any means by which rights change hands. This principle, if taken seriously, would appear to make both alienation and inheritance of property impossible, since property is "solely founded" in laboring, which only the laborer does (see Grant's similar remarks in *Liberalism*, 61–62). We would expect Locke to say, as a result, not only that a man's property dies with him (Waldron, "Locke's Account," 39–40), but that he can also never give it away or sell it during his lifetime.

[112] This same surplus (the amount beyond what is needed for comfortable preservation) is, I believe, what the needy have a right to when they cannot support themselves. See my discussion in 6.3.

[113] Waldron argues that any property beyond what is strictly needed by wives and children cannot be inherited by them, but reverts to common ("Locke's Account," 47). It is hard to see why the father is entitled to enjoy the comforts of life at all, on Waldron's line of reasoning, although Locke clearly allows this. And if parents can enjoy these comforts, why can't children inherit them (since their right to support includes rights to comforts [I, 89])?

goals as social solidarity and fraternity, unalienated labor, efficient utilization of social resources, etc.) may be advanced by reasonable limits on the right to inherit (as many contemporary authors, often inspired by Rawls, have insisted).[114]

4.5. The Family and Political Society

I will briefly discuss here only two (or three) of the ways in which Locke's account of familial morality touches his views on the proper structure of political life: the political implications of his theory of inheritance, and his rejections of patriarchalism and paternalism.

Locke's theory of inheritance has political implications primarily because governments must have the right to "regulate" property within their boundaries.[115] Insofar as governments are entrusted with the task of securing the property of their citizens, they must have jurisdiction over the land within the territories of the commonwealth in order to discharge this task. But it follows from this, Locke believes, that "whoever . . . by inheritance . . . or otherways enjoys any part of the land, so annexed to and under the government of that commonwealth, must take it with the condition it is under: that is, of submitting to the government of the commonwealth, under whose jurisdiction it is" (II, 120; see also II, 73, 116–17). Governments have the power to require submission as a condition on the inheritance of land within their domains. How did they acquire this power? Apparently they acquired it by transfer from the original owners of the land, who, on incorporating themselves into the commonwealth, also joined their property to that society.[116] This joining of property is viewed by Locke as a

---

[114] See, for instance, Haslett's argument that inheritance is inconsistent with capitalist ideals (like distribution according to productivity, equal opportunity, and freedom) in "Is Inheritance Justified?" Nozick now acknowledges that the inequalities reproduced by free bequest seem unfair, and so he favors the "simple subtraction rule" for bequests, on which only additions one makes to one's inherited wealth can be passed on to one's children (*Examined Life*, 30–31).

[115] I use the term "property" here as neutral between "land" and "possessions." Whether Locke intends to claim that governments acquire rights over all possessions (of external goods), or over land only, is not entirely clear from the text. I opt here for the latter reading. While Locke frequently speaks of joining possessions to the commonwealth (II, 116, 117, 120), he seems to have in mind only possessions in land (Mabbott, *John Locke*, 161). See 6.1 below for my defense of this reading.

[116] Locke also argues that commonwealths do not permit "any part of their domains to be dismembered, nor to be enjoyed by any but those of their community" (II, 117). But since the rationale for this power is presumably just that allowing dismemberment (or discontinuous, "swiss-cheese" boundaries) would make secur-

necessary and understood part of any act of joining a civil society, since it is necessary for securing property (which is the end of joining society) (II, 120). Would-be citizens give society a kind of partial right over their land (which is in turn entrusted to that society's government)—a right to regulate that property and to limit alienation of it to others who are citizens. This partial (but permanent) right in each citizen's property is what Locke calls *jurisdiction* (which should not, of course, be confused with public *ownership* of citizens' land[117]). And this partial right over the land gives society the power to limit the natural right of inheritance (by placing conditions on it—namely, submission to society and its laws and government).

It seems possible, however, to argue that this position conflicts in at least two ways with other aspects of Locke's theory. First, if children need the estate they (otherwise) stand to inherit, and the government forces them to submit as a condition on inheritance, is not the government guilty of using their need in order to get submission? Yet Locke claims that "a man can no more justly make use of another's necessity to force him to become his vassal [or "subject" (I, 43)] . . . than he that has more strength can seize upon a weaker, master him to his obedience, and with a dagger at his throat offer him death or slavery" (I, 42). At least two lines of response to this worry seem available to Locke. First, he could claim that while children cannot inherit without submitting to society, children are still entitled to sell their parents' estate or to receive from the state a fair price for it (thus satisfying their needs) should the children decide not to become subjects (and hence abandon the land to the society's commons). Second, Locke could argue that the case in question represents a conflict between the rights of the needy children and the (contractual) rights of society (received from the original owner of the land), and that the conflict

---

ing a citizen's property very difficult, the argument is not independent of the one considered in the text. We should remember that Locke is not appealing to what original owners of land actually agreed to, but rather to what we must *understand* their agreement to commit them to. His appeal thus depends on a factual assumption that a state that permitted "dismemberment" or "internal boundaries" ("internal emigration") could not secure its citizens' property (so that original owners can be understood to have agreed to eliminate this possibility). But this factual assumption is by no means obviously true, as I argue in "Voluntarism," 28–30. Again, see 6.1 below.

[117] As, say, in Rousseau, where property owners are really only "trustees for the commonwealth" (*Social Contract*, 1.9, paragraph 6). See Gauthier's discussion of Locke's argument and of the distinction between jurisdiction and ownership in "Role of Inheritance," 38–41. I return to these issues in 6.1.

should be resolved (as we saw earlier) by direct appeal to the fundamental law of preservation. Since allowing "dismemberment" of society's territories endangers all citizens, and since the needy children can be supported in other ways than by allowing them (unregulated) possession of the land, the proper resolution of the conflict of rights will favor society's right to limit inheritances.

A second concern about society's right to limit inheritances is the possible consequences of this right for Locke's theory of conquest.[118] It is the rights of dependents to inherit the property of the vanquished warmakers that seem to stop a just conqueror from acquiring political power by conquest. The just conqueror acquires no rights over the dependents of the conquered, nor can he acquire rights over the land of the conquered (II, 179, 182–84); the rights of dependents take priority over the conqueror's right to reparation. But if the warmakers' society (government) had a right to demand submission as a condition on their dependents' inheritance, and if the government had this right by virtue of its jurisdiction over the land, why couldn't the just conqueror acquire this jurisdiction over the land from the defeated government, and then acquire political power over the warmakers' dependents by requiring submission as a condition on their inheritance? Locke emphatically denies that even a just conqueror can in this way acquire jurisdiction or political power (II, 192). But, we might argue, he should not have done so. Locke *should* have said that an aggressor commonwealth forfeits its right of jurisdiction to the just conqueror, so that the conqueror has the same standing (and can similarly require submission as a condition on inheritance) as the conquered government formerly did. To deny this, Locke must say that the conquered government's right of jurisdiction merely reverts back to its original holders—the people of the commonwealth—or, in the case of the warmakers themselves, descends to their heirs.

But is not this latter position precisely the one Locke *must* adopt? For it is essential to the idea of civil society for Locke not only that political power be limited and of a particular kind, but also that it remain in *the same hands* that the people put it in (II, 216–17). Only a new consent of the people can place it in new hands. In this respect at least, political power is personal (although it is not, of course "personal" in Filmer's sense [II, 151]). Since all political

118 Gauthier, "The Role of Inheritance." The arguments in this paragraph are all Gauthier's.

rights are given in trust, they cannot be forfeited by the trustee, but return on the trustee's demise or enslavement to the settlor of that trust—that is, the people. This is as true of jurisdiction as of any other political right. Those among the people who themselves participated in or aided the unjust war, forfeit all rights and are no longer incorporated in the society—for only free individuals (right-holders) can be members of civil society. Jurisdiction (with all other entrusted political rights) thus reverts to the remainder of the people who did not participate in the war. The conqueror can no more acquire jurisdiction by forfeiture than you can acquire a right to my daughter's trust fund when the trustee of that fund negligently injures you. In the (bizarre) instance that all members of a society participate in an unjust war, the conqueror can acquire ownership of all that society's territories (there being no innocent person with prior claims). But this is not jurisdiction over territory; it is simply property. Over the vanquished, the conqueror can acquire only despotic, not political, power.

There may, then, be no serious or irresolvable conflicts between Locke's theory of inheritance and other aspects of his moral and political philosophy, although we have seen that the part of Locke's position on familial morality that deals with inheritance clearly does have important political implications. The more direct and obvious political implications of his views on familial morality, however, lie in Locke's rejection of patriarchalism and paternalism in government. Indeed, this rejection is clearly one of the most important contributions to political thought made by the *Treatises*. It establishes the character of Locke's work as distinctively liberal and amounts to a convincing refutation of a very influential way of thinking about authority. Locke's arguments on this subject, however, have also been commented on at length by generations of Locke scholars. I will, accordingly, be brief in my remarks on this aspect of Locke's thought, without, I hope, creating the impression that my brevity is a measure of my estimation of its importance.

The form of paternalism rejected by Locke is governmental interference (by standing laws or arbitrary decrees) aimed at promoting or protecting the good of the governed without their consent.[119] The form of patriarchalism Locke rejects is what Schochet

---

[119] Gerald Dworkin's more general definition of paternalism is: "interference with a person's liberty of action justified by reasons referring exclusively to the welfare, good, happiness, needs, interests or values of the person being coerced" ("Paternalism," 108). I shall not comment here on any of the important recent work on

has called "moral patriarchalism"—that is, the view that political authority is a kind of (or identical to) paternal authority, so that the obedience owed magistrates is of the same kind as the obedience owed fathers.[120] This latter doctrine was taught in Locke's day by the Church of England, which based it on an interpretation of the Fifth Commandment.[121] And it was, of course, the view of Locke's Tory opponents, and in particular, of Filmer.[122] Paternalism and patriarchalism are obviously related positions, although (just as obviously) they are far from identical. While patriarchalism makes political power "paternalistic" in one sense, it is compatible with quite "unpaternalistic" views of the nature of paternal power (e.g., Filmer's absolutist view, on which paternal power need not be exercised for the good of the one ruled). And paternalism (as defined above) does not need to derive the right of a government to act paternalistically in the same way that it derives parental rights to govern children. Locke's attack on patriarchalism (which I will discuss first) is quite central and obvious in the *Treatises*. His rejection of paternalism (to which I return shortly) is more entailed by than specifically formulated in the argument of the text.

The heart of Locke's attack on patriarchalism can be captured by noting the conclusions of three arguments. (1) Paternal and political power, although "confounded" by many (II, 169) are completely different in both origin and extent (e.g., I, 48; II, 65, 71, 74, 77, 86, 173–74). There is thus no Fifth Commandment ground for political authority or obligation (e.g., I, 64–65; II, 52, 65–66, 69). (2) Even if political power *were* paternal, political power would not be absolute (e.g., II, 53, 64, 69, 74). (3) Parents cannot bind their children to any commonwealth. "For every man's children being by nature as free as himself," children are free to decide for themselves which society to join (II, 73). This establishes the necessity of consent as the basis of all political authority and obligation. In defending these three conclusions, Locke decisively undercuts the main contentions of Filmer's patriarchalist theory.

paternalism, but only direct the reader to Feinberg, *Harm to Self*; Van DeVeer, *Paternalistic Intervention*; Kleinig, *Paternalism*; Sartorius, *Paternalism*. Many of the helpful articles on the subject (which are too numerous to list here) are referred to in these longer works.

[120] Schochet, *Patriarchalism*, 10–14; Tarcov, *Locke's Education*, chapter 1.

[121] Ibid., 6, 14–16, 73–81. Locke's predecessors and opponents in the debate are discussed by Schochet in chapters 6–12. See also Ashcraft, *Revolutionary Politics*, 232–33; and Leites, "Locke's Liberal Theory of Parenthood."

[122] For Filmer, all political rights are simply identical to the natural rights of fathers (*Patriarcha*, I, 8–9; III, 11), which is to say that they are rights of absolute dominion (rights of life and death) over children (ibid., I, 4).

Locke also, of course, concedes several of the patriarchalist's claims. He allows that monarchy is the simplest and most natural form of government, being appropriate for simple people with little property (who will thus be worried more about foreign invasion than about their own ruler's excesses).[123] Monarchy is the form of rule to which they have been accustomed in the family (II, 107). And Locke allows as well that it is natural for fathers to become princes (II, 64). There is thus a natural change from family to political life. None of this shows, however, that the patriarchalist is correct. For it is "only by the consent of his children," not by any paternal right, that the father comes to be prince. His grown children stand aside and let the father exercise his natural executive right unimpeded (II, 74), as they were used to seeing him do when they were young. It is thus only "by an insensible change" that fathers become "politic monarchs" (II, 76), and their grown children give only a "tacit and scarce avoidable consent" to this change in status (II, 75, 110). But while the *observable* condition of parents and children changes very little in moving from family to patriarchal monarchy, their *moral* condition changes dramatically.[124] The child's obligation of filial obedience is now the freely undertaken, consensual obligation of free person and citizen. And the paternal authority, once based in the father's duty of care (which ended with his children's maturity) and paternal benefaction,[125] is now political power, held in trust from a society of equals consisting of father and grown children (along with adult relatives, servants, etc.).[126]

It is essential to keep this consensual dimension in mind as well in thinking about Locke's attack on paternalism. Otherwise, it may seem that Locke has no real objection to paternalism, in light of (for instance) his acceptance of executive prerogative—a right to

[123] Filmer, of course, takes the "naturalness" of monarchy to show that God intends us to be governed in this way (e.g., *Patriarcha*, II, 9–14).

[124] Schochet, *Patriarchalism*, 55–56, 256–61.

[125] Which continues, on Locke's view, as a source of quite *independent* (and nonpolitical) filial obligation.

[126] See Grant's discussion of whether such patriarchal monarchies can really count as legitimate governments (given their absence of standing rules, any separation of legislative and executive powers, etc.) (*Liberalism*, 86–87). There are also questions to be raised about just how distinct the grounds of paternal and political power really are. Tacit consent is tied closely to the enjoyment of benefits in Locke. Given that it is also the receipt of benefits that is supposed to ground (some) parental rights, the border between consensual and paternal authority is considerably blurred.

act "arbitrarily" for the public good (II, 159–68).[127] Locke even compares prerogative to the power of a father, "watching over [the people] for their good" (II, 162). When we remember, however, that even executive prerogative is really only a trust from the people, a result of their consenting to what is necessary for effective advancement of the end of government (securing their persons and property) (II, 163–64), we see that the use of prerogative is not paternalistic. Prerogative is a consensual, limited right, far indeed from a right to interfere paternalistically in all areas of citizens' lives (e.g., their personal or religious lives).

Paternalism is appropriate for (young) children, idiots, and the insane (II, 60). He who "has not understanding of his own to direct his will, he is not to have any will to follow: he that understands for him, must will for him too; he must prescribe to his will and regulate his actions" (II, 58). But when persons acquire the understanding and control to know the law of nature and keep their actions within its bounds, they are no longer subject to paternal authority. They are then free and equal rightholders, subject to no authorities but God, those appointed by God, and those they make by their own consent (precisely which classes of beings have by these standards a right to be free of paternalistic intervention is, of course, more of a problem than Locke's remarks suggest[128]).

[127] It may also seem that because each person has a natural duty to preserve self, and the government has the right to enforce natural law, governments may intervene paternalistically to require persons to care for themselves. Locke does not address this line of argument, I believe, because of a confusion about correlative rights. Consider the following, equally Lockean argument: My duty to preserve myself seems to correlate with no other person's rights; government's job is to secure our rights (preserve our property); therefore, my government should not require me to preserve myself. Is the job of government in Locke to enforce natural law or to secure our rights? Locke answers in both ways because he thinks of natural duties as correlating with natural rights. But at the same time he accepts duties of self-preservation that seem *not* to correlate with rights (perhaps a further reason to be suspicious of such duties—see 1.5). This is simply more evidence of the fence Locke straddles in his moral theory (see 2.4 above). And, of course, it introduces a similar problem about the punishment of those who try to harm themselves (see note 128 below; and chapter 3, note 62 above).

[128] Older children (or even exceptional young children) may well possess these capacities (see Schrag, "Child in the Moral Order"). As far as I can see, Locke is committed to no criterion of (biological) age in distinguishing children from free individuals. It is even less clear what we are to say about two other classes of beings. Warmakers, who are also not under the laws or controlled by their reason, might seem to qualify for paternalistic care rather than punishment. Locke, of course, nowhere expresses any sympathy for this view—perhaps because warmakers have knowingly (when they *did* have control) *quit* reason, and forfeited any title to consideration. On my view, warmakers are under the law (4.3). A final worry concerns the possibility of paternalism for those who harm or attempt to harm

It is not appropriate for government to "take care of" free persons, interfering with their choices solely for their own good. Politics is unlike medicine, except in this: that the patient must consent to the surgery before the cutting begins, even if the surgery is in the patient's best interests.[129]

We have already seen (in 2.2) one important Lockean argument with apparent antipaternalistic implication: the presumptive argument for natural moral equality among persons. There are, according to this argument, no reasons why any person should be taken to begin with a special right to interfere in the life of another person (whether for good or harm). But the moral equality of all persons is in fact quite compatible with *everyone's* having the right to interfere paternalistically (even if it rules out *some* having a *special* right in this regard). Since each has a duty (and hence a right) to preserve others, might not each have a right to interfere paternalistically in the lives of other adults? Locke needs more than the presumptive argument to attack paternalism.

We can, in fact, find suggestions of two (by now familiar) lines of antipaternalist arguments in Locke—one Kantian (deontological) and one rule-consequentialist (although neither is concisely stated, as far as I know). The first (Kantian) argument is suggested throughout Locke's discussion of the limits of paternal power, and is simply this: paternalism for normal adults is degrading and inappropriate. It treats them as if they were children, showing no respect for their freedom, equality, and dignity.[130] This argument is just an instance of the more general Kantian line (sketched in 1.3) that wrongdoing involves failing to respect others and failing to treat others as what they manifestly are (and are conceded to

---

themselves. It is common enough in our societies for those who attempt suicide or pursue other obviously self-destructive courses to be confined and treated (hopefully paternalistically). Yet on Locke's view, such individuals have (perhaps knowingly) breached the law of nature, which requires that we preserve ourselves (1.5). Presumably, this calls for punishment, not paternalistic care, but Locke never mentions any cases of *self*-harmers forfeiting rights. Self-harmers, of course, do not breach the rights of others, nor does punishment seem necessary for either reparation or restraint (i.e., to protect others). It seems likely that Locke would class attempted suicide cases as lunatics, who qualify for paternalism. But he needs an account of how *their* forfeiture of rights, or the justifiable temporary abridgement of their rights, is brought about without justifying punishment. Interestingly, Kant also opposes suicide because we are God's property, God's creations. But he allows that those who violate the suicide prohibition *do* deserve punishment (*Lectures on Ethics*, 153–54).

[129] See Windstrup, "Freedom and Authority," 259.

[130] *Education*, 40–41. See Parry, *John Locke*, 79–80; Tarcov, *Locke's Education*, 9, 114–16.

be). Just as the father wrongs the grown child by treating "him still as a boy" (II, 69), the paternalistic prince wrongs his subjects. The second (rule-consequentialist) argument against paternalism is more familiar from Mill's antipaternalist stance in *On Liberty*: "mankind are greater gainers by suffering each other to live as seems good to themselves, than by compelling each to live as seems good to the rest."[131] Since all persons, according to Locke, are equal and adequately endowed by nature for their "business" (each being "no better than other men" [I, 41]) and people are likely to know best their own concerns and welfare, humankind will be best off (*as a rule*) leaving people a significant realm of personal liberty to pursue their own good in their own way.[132] Paternalistic interference by government is likely not only to be done wrongly (since government is unlikely to know the particulars of an individual's case), but is likely as well to encourage more of the same by setting a dangerous precedent. In the case of young children and the insane, of course, we can be confident in the superiority of our judgment about what is best for them; but as the threshold of maturity (or rationality) is approached, our justification for confidence in the superiority of our practical wisdom to theirs diminishes sharply. Both of Locke's arguments against paternalism make points that I believe are essentially correct.

While the *Two Treatises* is a great antipaternalist document, Locke's explicit rejection of paternalism is probably even clearer in others of his works. In *A Letter Concerning Toleration*, for instance, he writes:

In private domestic affairs, in the management of estates, in the conservation of bodily health, every man may consider what suits his own convenience, and follow what course he likes best. No man complains of ill-management of his neighbor's affairs. . . . The care, therefore, of everyman's soul belongs to himself, and is to be left unto himself. But what if he neglect the care of his soul? I answer: what if he neglect the care of his health or of his estate, which things are nearlier related to the government of the magistrate than the other? . . . Laws provide, as much as is possible, that the good and health of subjects be not injured by the fraud and violence of

[131] *On Liberty*, chapter 1, paragraph 13. Other aspects of the argument outlined below are at chapter 4, paragraphs 4, 12; and chapter 5, paragraph 20.
[132] Parry, "Individuality," 166, 170.

others; they do not guard them from the negligence or ill-husbandry of the possessors themselves. (L, 136–37)[133]

Similarly, Locke's hard line on charity (discussed below in 6.3) is motivated largely by the recognition that charity is an inappropriate response to the status of a free person, capable of rationality and industry.[134] The rejection of paternalism has obvious consequences for Locke's views on toleration and charity; but we will see that it also affects his more general theory of property, the subject of chapter 5.

[133] The magistrate should only protect citizens "from being invaded and injured by others," not "force them to a prosecution of their own private interests" (ECT, 176).
[134] Parry, "Individuality," 175.

F I V E

PROPERTY RIGHTS

5.1. Natural Property Rights

Most of what has been written about Locke's theory of rights concerns the theory of property defended by Locke in chapter 5 of the *Second Treatise*. There is a sense in which this concentration is perfectly appropriate, for Locke characterizes all of a person's rights as "property" (as we have seen). But the "property" that is Locke's chief concern in chapter 5 is property in a sense more familiar to contemporary readers: rights in external goods (such as consumables or land). Our rights in external goods, of course, play an absolutely central role in Locke's arguments in the *Treatises*,[1] and, as a result, so much has been written about this feature of Locke's position that it is hard to imagine being able to say anything really new about it. My ambitions in this chapter will, accordingly, be even more modest than those pursued elsewhere in this volume. I will try to locate Locke's position and arguments more clearly, finding (as before) that he relies exclusively on neither purely theological nor purely secular arguments (but a liberal mix of the two), and that the position to which he argues amounts to neither a defense of unlimited capitalist appropriation and a conservative acceptance of all existing property relations nor a defense of purely conditional property and radical redistributionism. The Locke that emerges from his theory of property is again pluralistic and moderate.[2] I will also argue that plausible bases for

[1] One work (among many) that stresses this centrality is Wood, *Capitalism*, especially 49. But as Tully nicely demonstrates (in the most important work yet produced on Locke's theory of property), exactly how we understand the point of Locke's central use of the concept of property depends on a host of broader interpretive issues bearing on the reading of the *Treatises* as a whole (*Discourse*, especially 146–51). A recent and very important addition to the literature on Locke's theory of property is chapter 6 of Waldron, *Private Property*.

[2] My reading of Locke thus falls between traditional readings and the newer "revisionist" readings, largely because I find working in Locke at once both older and more modern conceptions of property. Others who find in Locke a similarly mod-

many of Locke's claims about property rights can in fact be articulated, that the labor theory of property acquisition Locke defends is much more interesting and promising than is usually allowed. These are large topics, more suitable for a book than for a chapter. I must aim more, then, at care and clarity in what I do discuss here than at the thorough treatment my topic deserves.[3]

There has been no more widespread or enduring intuition about property rights than that labor in creating or improving a thing gives one special claim to it.[4] We feel that those who innocently work to discover, make, or usefully employ some unowned good ought to be allowed to keep it (if in so doing they harm no others), that it would be wrong for others to take it away. It is the strength of this intuition that keeps alive the interest in Locke's labor theory of property acquisition, despite generations of criticism of Locke's arguments. However badly he defends his views, we might say, surely Locke is on to something. It is not just law or convention or agreement that gives laborers special claim to the fruits of their labors. There is something natural about this claim, something it would be somehow wrong for law to contradict.

Locke's theory of property exploits fully this intuition of "naturalness" in the relation between labor and property. The "property" of which Locke writes in chapter 5 of the *Second Treatise* is a moral, not a legal or civil, ownership;[5] and this moral relation is conceived of by Locke as a natural relation in the strongest possible sense—it is sanctioned by natural law and presupposes no agreements or conventions.[6] Remember (from 2.3) that for Locke

---

erate stance include Schwarzenbach, "Locke's Two Conceptions," 142, 146; and Wood, *Capitalism*, 16.

[3] I will say nothing here about the considerable influence of Locke's theory of property on more recent philosophers (e.g., the early socialists or contemporary libertarians); and my discussion of the historical setting for Locke's theory and the intellectual background against which he wrote will be as minimal as care and clarity permit. The best source for a thorough treatment of these latter concerns is again Tully, *Discourse*, especially chapters 1–4.

[4] See Becker, "Moral Basis," 204–5. As an indication of just how widespread such intuitions are, remember that even Marx and Engels wrote (in *The Communist Manifesto*, 232) "we by no means intend to abolish this personal appropriation of the products of labour, an appropriation that is made for the maintenance and reproduction of human life."

[5] Day, "Locke on Property," 208; Medina, *Social Contract Theories*, 36; Ellerman, "On the Labor Theory," 294.

[6] Rapaczynski, *Nature and Politics*, 306–7; Waldron, *Private Property*, 19–20, 138. Steiner's contrary view ("Natural Right," 43–44) is a simple function of his (on my view and Locke's, mistaken) belief that no right that arises from someone's act can count as a *natural* right. Locke's appeal to natural law, in addition to reflecting his view of the obviousness of the connection between labor and property, fits well his

a right is a natural right if its binding force is nonconventional and it could be possessed in the state of nature. Locke's property is not only a natural right in this sense, but a *nonconsensual* natural right. His theory can thus be usefully contrasted not only with natural right theories in which property is a consensual right (e.g., the compact theories), but also with all conventionalist accounts (like Hume's) and all accounts on which property can only be a civil, legal, or political right (such as the theories of Hobbes and the later positivists).[7] Property is for Locke neither just a useful arrangement for the division of goods on which humankind informally settled nor a right created solely by civil law. For if property is a consensual, conventional, or legal notion, the rules of property can change as consent, conventions, and laws change, making our rights in effect subject to whatever constraints society deems proper. Our property is then not secure (defeating part of the point of having civil society).[8] Locke's need for a natural, nonconsensual ground of private property rights, then, was clear; and labor seemed, then as now, an obvious choice.

Labor is not, of course, the only ground of private property allowed by Locke. It is the sole ground of *original* exclusive property

---

theoretical and practical needs. He can at once answer Filmer's critique of natural law theories of property and avoid the absolutist pitfalls of previous natural law theories (such as the "compact theories" of Grotius and Pufendorf). See Tully, *Discourse*, 54–55. It is nonetheless excessive to say that for Locke "labor is the only title to property which is in accordance with natural right" (Strauss, *Natural Right*, 236). Aside from the other titles to property noted by Locke (see below), even prepolitical compact (as in Pufendorf) would ground property in a way consistent with natural right. Locke's view is not that a compact among the original commoners would not be sufficient to ground property rights. Locke claims only that such a compact is not *necessary* for private property (for if it were necessary, people would starve, contrary to God's plan). Compact would have been a ground for original exclusive rights only if very unusual circumstances had held (i.e., if the consent of all the commoners *had* been practically obtainable). Note that Locke himself does elsewhere offer hints of a contractual theory of property (in the manuscript on "Morality"): "man at his birth can have no right to anything in the world more than another. Men therefore must either enjoy all things in common or by compact determine their rights. If all things be left in common, want, rapine, and force will unavoidably follow. . . . To avoid this estate, compact must determine people's rights" (MS c28, fol. 140).

[7] In Hobbes' state of nature there is "no propriety, no dominion, no *mine* and *thine* distinct; but only that to be every man's that he can get, and for so long as he can keep it" (*Leviathan*, chapter 13, paragraph 13).

[8] If property is what is bestowed by the king, for instance, then it can be withdrawn by the king as well, giving him absolute power over the lives of his subjects (this concern, of course, was central in the minds of Locke's audience, who worried that James planned to repossess former monastic lands). See Seliger, *Liberal Politics*, 199; Parry, *John Locke*, 52; Minogue, "Concept of Property," 19; Waldron, *Private Property*, 152–53, 162; Vaughn, *John Locke*, 81.

rights, the way in which something previously unowned can become owned. Chapter 5 of the *Second Treatise* is concerned primarily with the defense of a theory of original appropriation, so naturally labor is the central concept at work there. But once a property has been established by labor, subsequent title to that property can be acquired in a variety of ways (not prominently discussed in chapter 5):[9] (1) *inheritance* (as we saw in 4.4) can give subsequent title, either consensually (as in inheritance based on spousal contract) or "naturally" (as in filial inheritance); (2) *need* can give title to the surplus of another's property, as we will see in 6.3; (3) one may acquire title to another's property as *reparation for injuries* done to one by that person. The right to take reparation is (as we saw in 3.2) part of each person's natural executive right, based on the forfeiture of rights suffered by wrongdoers; (4) *alienation* of property rights (by gift, sale, or trade, for example) can also give subsequent title to what was first acquired by labor.[10] Thus, common libertarian summaries of Locke's position are misleading when they suggest that while original property rights rest on nonconsensual grounds (i.e., labor), subsequent rights are based on consent. For Locke accepts at least three nonconsensual bases for subsequent rights: filial status, need, and forfeiture.

In addition to these ways of creating property in external goods, each person for Locke is *born* to a right with regard to external goods. What I have called "the right of self-government" includes for Locke the rights to preserve and control one's own life; and these rights entail a moral power (and consequent liberty) to make property in unowned (common) nature by one's labor, as well as a claim right not to be excluded by the efforts of others from taking by labor one's fair share of the resources given in common to mankind by God (see 2.1 and 2.3 above).[11] Thus, each person "begins"

[9] Tully mentions only inheritance and charity (need) as grounds for subsequent title to property in Locke, neglecting (3) and (4) below (*Discourse*, 131–32). All rights acquired in the ways specified below can be held either as natural rights or as civil rights in political society. I thus disagree with Ashcraft's claim that the right to subsistence is the only natural right to property in Locke (*Locke's Two Treatises*, 126), probably because we disagree about what should be counted as a natural right in Locke (see 2.3 above).

[10] Mabbott oddly accuses Locke of inconsistency for saying that gift or legacy (which involve no labor on the part of the recipient) can ground property (*John Locke*, 148). This charge involves a fairly basic confusion of the grounds for *original* rights and the grounds for *subsequent* rights.

[11] Although Tully does characterize this "inclusive right" as a "power" (*Discourse*, 76–77), he also insists that it is chiefly to be thought of as a right to *use* the common property of mankind (ibid., 61). Since the kind of "use" Locke has in mind counts as labor, and labor grounds exclusive property, it seems more accurate

with a "right to property" (the morally protected power to create property in up-to-a-fair-share of common nature), but not with a right in any particular external goods. Particular exclusive rights (to *this* apple or *that* piece of land) arise only from labor (on unowned nature) or from one of the four grounds of subsequent title mentioned above, not directly from any "grant from God."[12]

Given that a central theme of most contemporary writings on property or ownership has been the variety of possible forms of property, it seems important to ask at this point just what Locke means when he speaks of "property." The primary sense Locke gives to the word "property" is that of "a (moral) right." My property is simply whatever I have a right to.[13] Locke defines property in the *Essay* as "a right to anything" (E, 4.3.18), and those justly made slaves (those who are rightless) are described in the *Treatises* as "having no property" (II, 174) or "stripped of all property" (II, 173). One's property (propriety, *suum*) is thus whatever is one's own, what is proper to (belongs to or is part of) oneself,[14] what is

to describe the inclusive right as a right to make or take property (up to one's share), and not to be prevented by others from doing so. This is *not* the right of a commoner to use the commons and consume the product *without* making exclusive property in it (as Tully misleadingly suggests). For Locke, use of the original commons *can* create exclusive property, even if this property can only be used in ways consistent with God's law. Further useful discussion of the distinction between exclusive property rights and inclusive (commons) rights can be found in Macpherson, "Human Rights," 95–97.

[12] Others who are careful to distinguish the general power to make property from particular property rights include Tully, Rapaczynski ("Locke's Conception of Property," 306), and Lemos (*Hobbes and Locke*, 140–41; "Locke's Theory of Property," 228). Ashcraft argues (with Tully) that labor is *not* what makes rights to property. It is rather fulfilling our natural law obligations that gives us a right to subsistence (*Locke's Two Treatises*, 130). On my reading of Locke, we are *born* to a general right to subsistence (although failure to perform our obligations can forfeit it); it is *labor*, however, which grounds specific property rights in particular things.

[13] Tully, *Discourse*, 7, 113–16; Parry, *John Locke*, 49; Laslett, "Introduction," 115–16; Seliger, *Liberal Politics*, 165–66; Rapaczynski, *Nature and Politics*, 180. As Olivecrona notes, Locke in fact uses "property" to refer both to the right itself and to that to which I have the right (the object that is my property) ("Appropriation in the State of Nature," 219). See also Cherno, "Locke on Property," 51; Tully, *Discourse*, 61; Honoré, "Ownership," 128. I follow Locke in this usage, since I find it not so much an inconsistency in Locke (as Olivecrona does) as a reflection of *ordinary* usage (according to which "X is my exclusive property" and "I have an exclusive property in X" are equivalent expressions, despite the fact that "property" refers first to the object and then to the right to the object. Compare "X is my right" and "I have a right to X."). As Tully notes, Locke is "clearly aware" of this "equivocity" (ibid.).

[14] Tully, *Discourse*, 7, 112; Olivecrona, "Appropriation in the State of Nature," 218–19, and "Locke's Theory of Appropriation," 222–25; Schwarzenbach, "Locke's Two Conceptions," 145.

private.[15] Other frequently noted features of property are intended
by Locke not as definitions of property (as is often claimed), but
as statements of characteristics or components of property (rights
that are part of property). For instance, Locke often writes of one's
property as that which cannot be rightfully taken without one's
consent:[16] "I have truly no property in that which another can by
right take from me, when he pleases, against my consent" (II,
138); "the nature" of property is "that without a man's consent it
cannot be taken from him" (II, 193; see also, e.g., II, 140, 194).
Here, however, Locke means not to define property, but to point
to one of its constituent rights: the right of security or nonexpropriation. All property (moral right) is secure from "prescription"
in the form of laws or acts of expropriation (I, 6, 63, 116). Similarly,
Locke sometimes characterizes people's property as that which is
"at their own dispose . . . or else it is no property" (II, 194), suggesting to some an intention to define property as that over which
one has a right to decide how it will be used.[17] But again, Locke
only points here to one important constituent of property: the
right to use and manage. The only definition of property offered
by Locke and the only one that is consistent with all of his claims
about property is "that which one has a right to." Property thus
conceived is capable of further analysis into the constituent or
component rights that make up the moral relation of property.

It is correct, then, to insist that "property" has only one *meaning*
in Locke;[18] but it is far from confused to claim that Locke uses
"broad" and "narrow" senses of the term in his work, as so many
have claimed.[19] For Locke does use the word "property" to refer
to larger and smaller classes of rights over things, as his argumen-

[15] Yolton, *Locke*, 68. There is this further reason to be suspicious of Tully's claim
that standard cases of property are *familial*, in addition to those reasons adduced in
4.4.

[16] Ryan, "Locke and the Dictatorship," 246; Dunn, *Political Thought*, 176n; Tully,
Discourse, 114–16.

[17] Parry, *John Locke*, 49–50. Mabbott takes this idea to extremes, claiming that for
Locke "to say anything is a man's property is to say that he can do what he likes
with it" (*John Locke*, 147). In light of the many restrictions Locke places on how we
may use our property (discussed below, primarily in 5.4 and 6.2), the problems
with this view are obvious.

[18] As do Tully (*Discourse*, 116) and Richards, Mulligan, and Graham (" 'Property'
and 'People,' " 37–39).

[19] For example, Macpherson, *Possessive Individualism*, 198, 230, 247–50; Gough,
Political Philosophy, 85; Olivecrona, "Appropriation in the State of Nature," 219;
Goldwin, "John Locke," 496; Parry, *John Locke*, 49; Plamenatz, *Man and Society*,
1:215; Laslett, "Introduction," 115–17; Lemos, "Locke's Theory of Property," 227;
Medina, *Social Contract Theories*, 32.

tative needs require. And while this does not exactly constitute a confusion on Locke's part,[20] it is certainly a habit that is confusing for his readers and obscures some important points he wants to make. Often, of course, Locke uses the word "property" to refer simply to all of our rights—our rights over our selves, our actions, our land, our external goods, and so on. Locke famously summarizes the things over which we have rights as our "lives, liberties and estates, which I call by the general name, property" (II, 123; see also, e.g., II, 87, 173, 222). It is this largest class of rights that Locke has in mind when he claims that "the great and chief end . . . of men's uniting into commonwealths and putting themselves under government is the preservation of their property" (II, 124; see also, e.g., II, 87, 134, 222). Governments are instituted to secure and enforce our rights to life and liberty, not simply our rights to land or money.

At other times, however, Locke uses "property" to refer to smaller subclasses of our rights. In chapter 5 of the *Second Treatise*, for instance, property refers almost exclusively to our rights in external things (or in "the several parts of that which God gave to mankind in common" [II, 25])—our "goods" (II, 173), "estates" (II, 123), "possessions" (II, 36), "the fruits of the earth . . . , the earth itself" (II, 32), and the products of "invention and arts" (II, 44). I say "almost exclusively," of course, because Locke also speaks briefly in chapter 5 of the property each has "in his own person . . . the labour of his body and the work of his hands" (II, 27). But the primary use of "property" is clearly to refer to our rightful possessions in land and moveable external goods.[21] Elsewhere the class of rights to which "property" refers narrows even further. The prominent discussion of property and allegiance at the end of chapter 8 (§§116–22), for instance, clearly intends by "property" and "possessions" to refer to our rights in land only (see 6.1 below and 4.5 above). So Locke at different times uses "property" to refer to all of our rights, our rights in all external goods, and our rights in land. There is no logical difficulty here (since all classes of our rights, however large or small, are equally property), but

[20] As Macpherson claims it does (*Possessive Individualism*, 220, 247–48). See also Cherno, "Locke on Property," 51.
[21] Cherno, "Locke on Property," 51. As Day rightly observes, Locke often suggests that the rules (e.g., for taking, use, limits) of property are the same for all external goods (e.g., II, 26, 32, 38), making no real distinctions among land, products of the earth, and human artifacts ("Locke on Property," 207).

these shifts in usage have caused serious confusions among Locke's interpreters.[22]

Assuming (as I shall henceforth) that Locke means by property (all or some of) our rights over things (internal or external), we have still not been sufficiently precise in specifying the content of Locke's concept of property. For to say that I have a right over something is not to say precisely what *kind* of moral control over the thing I possess. My rights over different things (or different kinds of things) may consist of quite different ranges of constituent or component rights (claims, powers, or liberties). It has now become a commonplace, for instance, to observe that property is best thought of as a bundle or cluster of constituent rights, rights that are logically separable and are often separated in fact in existing systems of property. The result is the possibility (and actuality) of a wide range of forms of property or ownership, depending on which constituent rights make up the bundle that comprises the "property right" in some particular instance, system, or society.[23] We can, for instance, contrast the rights that make up the classical paradigm of modern (capitalist) private property, with the rights at issue in "the new property,"[24] feudal dominion, or (more communal) property in many tribal societies. A well-known article on ownership distinguishes eleven leading "incidents" of the liberal concept of "full ownership." Among these are the constituent rights to possess, use, and manage the thing, rights to the income, to capital, to security, transmissibility, and absence of term in one's possession of it.[25] It is probably fair to say that the central constituents of standard instances of property are the rights to use

---

[22] I will discuss one such confusion (about what kind of property is "joined" to the commonwealth) in 6.1. Another is Macpherson's overemphasis on material property (especially land) in his analysis of Locke's arguments, leading to his assertion that Locke favored greater political rights for landowners. Macpherson believes that Locke refers to the narrowest class of rights as "property" when discussing the limits on governmental authority and the right of resistance. As a consequence, "the people" is taken to be the propertied class only. For an effective refutation of Macpherson's reading of Locke on property, see Ryan, "Locke and the Dictatorship," especially 247.

[23] The most effective presentation of this position is in several papers by A. M. Honoré. See his "Ownership" and "Property, Title." For elaboration, see, for example, Snare, "Concept of Property," 204; Marvodes, "Property," 261; Becker, *Property Rights*, 18–22, and "Moral Basis," 205–7; Waldron, *Private Property*, chapter 2.

[24] Reich, "New Property." See Waldron's remarks on the difference between property systems generally and private property in particular (*Private Property*, 31–46).

[25] Honoré, "Ownership."

the thing, to alienate it, to exclude others from using it, and to nonexpropriation of it. But it seems reasonable to ask at this point to what extent *Locke's* concept of property conforms to such "standard" cases—that is, what are the constituent rights that make up Lockean property?

It is clear that property rights in Locke cannot amount to absolute rights over a thing,[26] for Locke accepts (as we will see in 5.4) many limits on our use of property. Nor, I think, can Locke's property even be the "full ownership" Honoré describes (which, of course, includes prohibitions on harmful uses of property), for Locke allows (among other things) that property in external goods must continue to be used by the owner, else it returns to common and may be taken by another (II, 38) (contrary to the "full ownership" rights to the capital and to absence of term).[27] Indeed, it may be difficult to specify any *one* set of constituent rights in which property consists for Locke at all. For while it seems likely that Locke would accept the modern view of property as a bundle of rights,[28] he might well insist that property consists in different component rights depending on the *kind* of property in question. The law of nature that defines our rights, remember, commands the best preservation of mankind, and it seems natural to argue that which *kind* of property (e.g., in our selves, our land, our artefacts, etc.) is at issue will bear importantly on the question of what extent of control over the thing will best facilitate mankind's preservation.[29] Nonetheless, Locke clearly seems to have in mind at least certain rights as necessary components of all kinds of property. The rights to possess, use, and manage the thing, to exclude

[26] Shapiro, *Evolution of Rights*, 146–47. On absolute ownership of or dominion over a thing (i.e., unlimited, perfect title), see Reeve, *Property*, 18–19.

[27] That Locke does not aspire to a defense of "full ownership" provides him with some measure of defense against those who have convincingly argued that the labor theory (which Locke embraces) cannot yield full ownership rights. See, for example, Becker, *Property Rights*, 39–44; Gould, "Contemporary Legal Conceptions," 227–28; Christman, "Can Ownership Be Justified?" 160–62, and "Self-Ownership," 39.

[28] Sartorius, "Persons and Property," 203.

[29] This constitutes the beginning of a response to Lomasky's claim that a Lockean will have a problem with the idea of property as a bundle of rights (*Persons, Rights,* 119). How, he asks, could one get less than complete ownership of an acorn? Property rights can vary in extent only if they are socially determined, Lomasky argues. But the Lockean response must be that natural, nonconventional property rights can vary in extent if their justification (e.g., in terms of the best preservation of humankind) requires variation (as it seems plausible that it should, since my right to, e.g., alienate acorns will affect humankind quite differently than my right to alienate my self or my labor).

others (at least where they have no prior or more weighty title—as the needy do to our surplus goods), and to security or nonexpropriation (similarly qualified) seem to be essential constituents of all property for Locke.[30] Similarly, some rights that make sense only with respect to external goods (such as transmissibility) seem uncontroversial as features of Lockean property. Beyond this, however, the question of the precise content of property for Locke becomes more difficult to determine.

Does property in Locke include, for instance, the "standard case" rights to alienate or destroy the owned thing? Tully appears to argue that it does not, and is especially forceful concerning the right of alienation: alienation rights are no part of the common property given us by God, no part of any natural rights to land, and no part of our property in our lives and liberty; "alienation is not an analytic feature of the concept of property for Locke."[31] But there are good grounds for questioning Tully's view. Early in Locke's writings on society and morality he argues that "both ownership and the rights of property (are), in general entirely free, it being open to everyone individually either to harvest his wealth or to give away his riches to anyone else and, as it were, to transfer them" (Second Tract, 229). Later he claims that "propriety and possession" involve for owners "the right . . . to dispose of them, as they please" (Education, 105), and he speaks frequently in the Treatises of the property holder's right to "dispose of it by his positive grant" or to "transfer" it (e.g., I, 87–88). Now one might, of course, suppose that Locke intends to defend only the alienability of our rights in external moveable goods, while still maintaining (a la Tully) that property in land, in our lives and liberty, and our common use rights do not include the right of alienation. But this view is hard to defend as well. For, to begin with land, it is hard to understand how parents could leave land to their children or join land to the commonwealth (both activities being described by Locke as occurring in the state of nature), if our natural property in land is not alienable. Indeed, Locke says of the father's land: "that estate, being [the] father's property, he may dispose or settle it as he pleases" (II, 116). Second, I have argued at length elsewhere that those rights that we possess over our lives and liberties are consistently treated by Locke as in principle alienable; while Locke is in certain ways confused about the implications of his

[30] See Schwarzenbach, "Locke's Two Conceptions," 168n.
[31] Tully, Discourse, 113–14, 99, 114, 88.

own moral theory, the position he actually seems to defend is that
all rights (property) are alienable, whether these are rights in ourselves, our moveable goods, or our land.[32] Finally, our "inclusive"
common rights are either distinguished by Locke from "property"
or are taken by him to be alienable as well.[33] I take Locke's view to
be that property *does* include a constituent right of free (harmless)
alienation.

What about the right to destroy our property? It may seem that
Locke could hardly have in mind a right to destroy our selves, our
liberty, or the land, opposing, as he does, suicide, voluntary enslavement, and waste. And this analysis is, of course, partly correct. We cannot have rights over ourselves, others, or nature to do
that which jeopardizes the effective preservation of mankind (ourselves or others). But this is not to say that the rights (property)
we *do* have do not include a constituent right to destroy the
thing.[34] Locke does not, I think, help us much with his very few

[32] "Inalienable Rights." The key to this reading of Locke's texts is that according
to Locke we simply do not *have* rights to kill or severely endanger ourselves. Those
rights we *do* have over ourselves (our property in ourselves and our liberty) are all
alienable. Others who take alienation to be a component right of property in Locke
(although often for quite different reasons than my own) include Strauss and Macpherson (and their respective followers); Parry, *John Locke*, 52; Laslett, "Introduction," 116n; Snyder, "Locke on Natural Law," 733; Schwarzenbach, "Locke's Two
Conceptions," 149, 168n; Andrew, *Shylock's Rights*, 94–95; Den Hartogh, "Tully's
Locke," 659–64. The alienation of property is, of course, a bit of a puzzle on one
understanding of Locke's arguments. For if labor literally joins part of the agent
(the agent's labor) to the object, how do the agent and the object ever become
sufficiently "unjoined" for another to acquire clear title to the object by alienation
(Rapaczynski, "Locke's Conception of Property," 306–8)? As we will see below (in
5.3), however, Locke need not take labor to be our property in the sense that it
(and what it is joined to) remains ours forever. Rather, it is ours in the sense of
being rightfully under our control (to keep or alienate). Labor must be understood
as *purposive* activity, so that our plans for it (and what it is joined to) will partly
determine the extent and duration of our rights.

[33] It is worth noting that in the central passages in which Locke discusses what
God has given to mankind in common, he seems to contrast, not equate, the gift
we were given with "property" (see Rapaczynski, *Nature and Politics*, 183–85). In I,
87, for instance, the "right in common" is contrasted with "property," as it is in II,
25. I return to this point below in 5.2. Most of Tully's case against property's essential alienability rests on his observation that "men cannot alienate the world which
is their property in common" (*Discourse*, 88). But this is because people do not *have*
a right in (or to) the world that they might alienate. They have, rather, the right to
use and thereby make property in their fair share of the world (and the right *not* to
do this, unless failure endangers themselves or others who have a claim to support). There is no textual evidence in Locke that suggests that he takes *that* right
(the common right to make property) not to be alienable, whether or not he wishes
to call the common right "property."

[34] Day, for instance, takes the right to destroy to be a constituent right of property in Locke ("Locke on Property," 211).

pronouncements about the right to destroy one's property. At one point he suggests that "nothing was made by God for man to spoil or destroy" (II, 31); but at another he says that "a right to destroy any thing by using it" is "the utmost property man is capable of" (I, 39), suggesting perhaps that there are different forms of property some of which do and some of which do not include a right to destroy the thing. Later, however, Locke claims that "property . . . is for the benefit and sole advantage of the proprietor, so that he may even destroy the thing that he has property in by his use of it, where need requires" (I, 92). From these passages we are entitled to conclude no more than this: the right to destroy what one has property in is at least often a constituent part of property, but this is not a right to destroy the thing frivolously. We have a right to destroy things we own only in our *use* of them for "the comfortable preservation of (our) beings" (I, 87).[35] The right to freely destroy our property for whatever reason we choose may be part of the liberal concept of "full ownership," but it is not a component of Lockean property.[36]

We will gain a fuller understanding of the content of Locke's "property" along the way, as we proceed to discuss the ground of and limits on property that Locke acknowledges. First, however, we should try to be clear about how we are to understand Locke's arguments in chapter 5 of the *Second Treatise*. Given that the "property" Locke there discusses is the right (or bundle of rights) described above, what is Locke trying to tell us about it? One view is that Locke is simply offering us a justification of private property.[37] At the opposite extreme is the view that Locke is not trying to

[35] I, 53 seems to suggest that one who truly creates a thing "might indeed have some pretence to destroy his own workmanship." But I doubt that even here Locke has in mind a right of pointless or frivolous destruction.

[36] Ashcraft attributes to Locke "a prohibitive injunction against any humanly advanced claims to exercise a right of destruction over God's 'property'" as part of an effort on Locke's part to respond to Filmer's absolutism (*Revolutionary Politics*, 260–61). There are, however, enough other limits set in Locke's theory, both on what we can have property in and on how we can use our property, that he can refute Filmer's conception of "absolute property" without needing to deny outright that property sometimes includes a constituent right to destroy what God has made.

[37] Indeed, Macpherson contends that Locke is not only justifying property, but unlimited appropriation and the unrestrained acquisitiveness of capitalism. Locke's strategy, on this view, is to defend property in traditional natural law terms and then show how the natural law limits on acquisition can be overcome (*Possessive Individualism*, 221–31). Others who see Locke's project as a justification of property include Day ("Locke on Property," 207), Rapaczynski (*Nature and Politics*, 182–85), and Cherno ("Locke on Property," 51).

233

justify (or explain the origin of) property at all. One could argue, for instance, that Locke is only defending the particularization of the commons, trying to show how what God gave in common to mankind can be lawfully divided to give exclusive rights. But the rights in question, far from being rights that permit unlimited accumulation, would only be exclusive rights "to use and enjoy God's property for God's purposes" (as part of a conditional trust from God).[38] I will maintain that neither view accurately captures Locke's intentions and that the opposition between them suggests an opposition that is no part of Locke's understanding of the problem of property. There is for Locke no conflict between thinking of labor as grounding exclusive rights to keep and accumulate goods and thinking of persons as trustees or stewards of God's property. Locke is justifying private property, explaining how the common can be particularized, and defending limits on property, all at the same time. He aims to present a full theory of original natural property rights (and a position on the relation of natural property to property in civil society). This includes: (a) an explanation of the origin of property and a justification of the rights in question, (b) an account of the extent of the property created by any appropriative act, (c) an account of the limits on our use of our property, and (d) an account of the limits on total accumulation of property.

Before I can proceed to Locke's theory, however, I must answer one last question: why bother? This is not just the question put by the natural rights skeptic (2.5), but a deeper and more troubling one. Apart from its historical interest, why should we care about the content of a theory of original natural property (i.e., about how unowned things can become owned, and to what extent)? It may seem that such a theory has no contemporary relevance, for we never seem to mix our labor with unowned nature anymore. Force and fraud have long since upset any lawful distribution of goods, and our knowledge of the history of that process is so inadequate that theories of original appropriation are not even useful for deal-

[38] Tully, *Discourse*, 3, 99–105, 122. See also Yolton's less dramatic (and more accurate) claim that Locke's "main concern" is explaining "how particularisation of the common is possible" (*Compass*, 187–95). I will reject Tully's suggestion that Locke's conception of this problem of particularization results in Locke's maintaining that labor grounds no rights over one's goods (ibid., 131) and that individual property in land is not possible (ibid., 122–25, 153–54). See 5.2 below; and the convincing responses to Tully in Ashcraft, *Revolutionary Politics*, 271n; Mackie, "Review of Tully," 92; Waldron, *Private Property*, 156–57, 208n, 220; Den Hartogh, "Tully's Locke," 656–64; Cohen, "Marx and Locke," 381–86.

ing with problems of contemporary rectification of past injustices. So a theory like Locke's may seem of no interest at all, except as a scholarly move in response to other theories like Locke's.[39]

While these complaints have some justification, they badly exaggerate the extent to which our current concerns about property are distant from concerns about the natural roots of property (if any). For we still have a serious interest in possible moral justifications (or condemnations) of current property systems; and to the extent that such systems can be thought of as a series of moves (legitimate or illegitimate) from a state of affairs in which unowned goods were taken (roughly) in proportion to labor, we can gain moral insight into these systems. When we see the ways in which current forms of property *fail* to distribute according to labor (and fail to respect other natural limitations on property), for instance, we can see more clearly the nature of the need for different and further justifications of current holdings. We need not have full information about the history of all holdings from Adam to Donald Trump to see that some arrangements reliably yield distributions of rights that contradict principles of natural property, and which are for that reason morally suspect. Nor is it possible to deny that even within a complex property system in a time when few goods are unowned, our intuitions about property rights may still conform fairly closely to the principles of natural property espoused by Locke—for instance, in cases of noninstitutional discoveries or inventions, simple handcrafts, and small holdings of a variety of sorts. Add to this the fact that we often forget that there *are* vast tracts of unowned land and unused resources still available to humankind, not only within the territories of organized political communities, but external to them (as in Antarctica and on other bodies in our solar system). While takings in these areas are governed by domestic law and international treaty, it is far from uninteresting to ask what the rights and duties of individuals and nations would be *independent* of such conventional arrangements. Any assumption that such questions are irrelevant must rest upon the (unwarranted) assumption that all domestic laws and international treaties are legitimate and binding not only on all nations

[39] This is a charge often brought against Nozick's entitlement theory. For accusations of contemporary irrelevance leveled specifically at Locke, see Mautner, "Locke on Original Appropriation," 267–68; Held, "Introduction," 5–6; Lodge, "New Property," 235–37; Waldron, *Private Property*, 258–59; Minogue, "Concept of Property," 20; Whelan, "Property as Artifice," 103–4; Lomasky, *Persons, Rights*, 115–16. For opposing views (closer to my own), see Schmidtz, *Limits of Government*, 28; and Lemos, "Locke's Theory of Property," 226.

but on all individuals (terrestrial or alien). Once the question of illegitimacy is raised, the success or failure of a theory of natural property rights has quite direct contemporary interest. For all of these reasons, then, I enter my discussion of Locke's (and the Lockean) theory of property without undue concern that the enterprise may be of only academic interest.

5.2. Labor: The Arguments

We should begin where Locke begins: with "the original community of all things amongst the sons of men" (I, 40), which is the result of God's gift to mankind. God, as creator of the earth, enjoys the "right of creation" over it. He is "sole Lord and proprietor of the whole world" (I, 39). Although God retains His rights over the world in the last analysis,[40] He has "given the world" (along with "all the fruits it naturally produces and beasts it feeds") "to men in common . . . for the support and comfort of their being" (II, 26). As a result of this "gift" (which, as we will see, is really more in the nature of a trust), mankind shares a "dominion in common" (I, 29), a "right and power over the earth and inferior creatures in common" (I, 67). This common right initially excludes any *private* dominion, either for Adam (I, 24) or any other person (II, 26).[41]

The problem Locke sets for himself in chapter 5 of the *Second Treatise* is this: how is it possible from this "original community of all things" for any person to come to possess "a private dominion" (II, 26) in any thing (a "private possession" [II, 35])? How can persons "make . . . distinct titles to several parcels of [the world] for their private uses" (II, 39)? Further, Locke agrees with Filmer that he must deny himself one popular answer (used by Grotius and Pufendorf, for instance)—that private property derives from the

[40] "The goods of fortune are never so much ours that they cease to be God's" (ELN, 203). See Ashcraft, *Locke's Two Treatises*, 85. I discuss the "right of creation" further below, in connection with Tully's "workmanship model" (and above in 1.2).
[41] Adam's original private dominion, of course, is urged by Filmer and opposed not only by Locke, but by Grotius and Pufendorf as well. McNally argues that in denying Adam's private dominion, Locke faced the disagreeable alternative Filmer described: that (a la the Levellers) all modern property must be illegitimate, modern inequalities constituting an obvious theft of God's common gift (given equally to all). So Locke must avoid both Filmer's absolutist position and the Levellers' rejection of inequality ("Locke, Levellers and Liberty," 27). I will suggest below (in 5.4) that Locke is more attracted to egalitarian, leveling conclusions than McNally allows.

consent of the other commoners. Locke will "endeavour to show how men might come to have a property in several parts of that which God gave to mankind in common, and that without any express compact of all the commoners" (II, 25). It is important here to distinguish between the "commons" *outside* of the territory of a legitimate civil society (such as the *original* community of things or the wilderness in America in Locke's day—"in the beginning all the world was America" [II, 49]), and the "commons" *within* some polity (such as "the land that is common in England," which is "the joint property of this country or this parish" [II, 35]). In the former case only, Locke tries to show that persons may appropriate parts of the commons for their private property without the consent of the other commoners. In the latter case, where things are left common "by the law of the land," "no one can enclose or appropriate any part without the consent of all his fellow commoners." What is "left common by compact" can only be made private by a new compact (II, 35).[42]

Locke's problem, then, is how "the private" can lawfully emerge from that which is naturally common. Indeed, Locke makes it clear that his problem would remain the same even if he chose to disregard the revelation of God's gift to mankind. Both "natural reason" and "revelation" suggest our common right to use the earth, its fruits, and the "inferior creatures" for our preservation (II, 25). So even a secular project on property rights must begin with the community of all things (thus allowing Locke to think of *his* project as the heart of *either* a theological *or* a secular approach to property). Locke is aware, however, that the idea of a natural community of things is not an unambiguous notion. A common right suggests that persons must be equals (against Filmer's derivation of rightful absolute government from *unequal* property in the earth). But persons may be equals in a variety of ways. Pufendorf, for instance, distinguishes between a "positive community" of possession (where all are equals by jointly holding property) and a "negative community" of possession (where all are equals by having no property, but only an equal liberty to use).[43] We can distinguish at least four ideas that might be intended by "the original community of all things":

[42] Locke has in mind here primarily the land as remaining common. The commoner in Locke's England could without wrongdoing harvest certain goods from the commons (without the necessity of obtaining the consent of the other commoners), while the land remained common.

[43] Pufendorf, *De Jure Naturae et Gentium Libri Octo*, 4.4.1–9.

(1) *Negative community*: all persons are at liberty (morally) to use the world and its products, but none has a protected liberty or exclusive right to anything (hence, there is no property, which requires at least an inclusive right). Pufendorf accepts a version of this, as does Hobbes (whose "right to every thing" is simply an unprotected moral liberty). This has been as well the standard interpretation of Locke's "original community."[44]

(2) *Joint positive community*: all persons jointly own the world, each holding an undivided proportional share (as in instances of contemporary "concurrent estate," such as "joint tenancy"). Grotius may have this idea in mind, and Locke is occasionally read as intending this form of "original community."[45]

(3) *Inclusive positive community*: each person holds an inclusive use right to the common; the common belongs to all only in the sense that each has a protected right (a claim right) to free use of the common for support and comfort.[46]

(4) *Divisible positive community*: each person has a (claim) right to a share of the earth and its products equal to that of every other person. Each may take an equal share independent of the decisions of the other commoners; each has property in the sense of a claim on an equal share (but not possession of or a claim on any particular share).[47]

[44] See, for example, Seliger, *Liberal Politics*, 188–90; Rapaczynski, *Nature and Politics*, 181–85, and "Locke's Conception of Property," 309–10; Parry, *John Locke*, 51–52, 78; Goldwin, "John Locke," 486; Kelly, " 'All Things Richly to Enjoy,' " 284n; Schwarzenbach, "Locke's Two Conceptions," 143; Waldron, *Private Property*, 155; Ryan, *Property and Political Theory*, 29–30; Winfrey, "Charity versus Justice," 430.

[45] See, for example, Thomson, "Property Acquisition," 664–65. Others take seriously the idea of joint positive community as the proper view of original community, quite independent of any interpretation of Locke. See, for example, Roemer, "Challenge," where what I call joint community is called "public ownership" and contrasted with mere "common ownership" (which, for Roemer, involves mere rights of access or use, conditional on noninterference with others, as in my option [3] below) (697–99, 700, 705). Cohen also distinguishes in the same way joint and common ownership ("Self-Ownership," 129).

[46] This is how Tully believes Locke intended to "redefine" positive community (*Discourse*, 126–29).

[47] Steiner seems to understand our original common rights in this way and to read Locke as agreeing with him ("Natural Right," 48–49): the "spirit" of Locke's claims "is captured in the requirement that each individual has a right to an equal share of the basic non-human means of production" (49). Steiner begins with di-

Which of these forms of "original community" did Locke believe was created by God's gift of the earth to mankind? The textual evidence seems inconclusive. On the one hand, as we have seen, there is significant support for the "negative community" reading in Locke's apparent unwillingness to characterize mankind's common rights as "property." Indeed, in the key passages (e.g., I, 87; and II, 25) our common rights seem to be contrasted with "property" (suggesting that there is *no* property prior to individual appropriation).[48] And in I, 86 our property (in the creatures) is said to be "founded upon" (not "identical to") the common right of use (I, 92 suggests, similarly, that property is derived from, not identical to, the right of use—property's "original is from the right a man has to use"). Locke's efforts seem more designed to establish human precedence or favored status in the world (e.g., I, 40) than our "property."[49] On the other hand, there are reasons to be unhappy with reading Locke as a simple "negative community" theorist. First, of course, Locke indisputably accepts some individual property as an original consequence of God's creation and donation—namely, our property in our persons, our bodies, and our labor (II, 27).[50] Second, a negative community alone would seem to establish no limits on the kind or extent of appropriation that is permissible.[51] And Locke clearly intends to impose limits on ap-

---

visible common property because he believes that one must have rights in shares of the common if one is ever to derive private property in particular things. Property cannot come from nothing. As Mack correctly observes, however, one can begin with negative community (only moral liberties with respect to the world) rather than positive shares, provided one allows (as Locke seems to) that we each have property in our own body and labor ("Distributive Justice," 140–43).

[48] See Shapiro, *Evolution of Rights*, 92; and Rapaczynski, *Nature and Politics*, 183–84. Rapaczynski takes our shared right to be just a liberty of using the fruits of the earth. Property, however, involves more than this; in particular, he claims, it involves rights of control (185).

[49] Tully's efforts to discount these facts are unsuccessful. I, 28 does not characterize property as "the dominion of the whole species," as Tully claims it does (*Discourse*, 60). "Property" is not used in I, 28. Nor does Locke call the "right" in I, 41 "property," let alone give it as his "definitive formulation" of mankind's property (as Tully claims, ibid.). And Tully misreads I, 23 as reporting Locke's agreement with Selden (ibid.), when the point is clearly made by Locke only *arguendo*.

[50] Contrary to (e.g.) Hobbes' acceptance of the "right to every thing" extending "even to one another's body" (*Leviathan*, chapter 14, paragraph 4). For a vigorous defense of natural property rights in our bodies, see Wheeler, "Natural Property Rights," especially 273–74.

[51] Fressola, "Liberty and Property," 319–20. Fred Miller seems to suggest that Locke must have had a positive community in mind, since his acceptance of the Lockean proviso is necessary only if others have a *right* that appropriation might violate ("Natural Right to Private Property," 283–85). I will suggest below, how-

propriation (as we will see in 5.4). Finally, it is simply indisputable that the common right to use the earth and the inferior creatures (I, 24, 67, 86, 87) is still a *right*, and Locke characterizes all rights as "property" (suggesting that there must be original common property).[52]

This problem of interpretation suggests another problem: the imprecision (or nonexhaustiveness) of the distinction between positive and negative community. Our common right to use the world and not be excluded from it *is* property; but it is not property in any particular thing. It is (I have claimed) a moral power (correlating with the duties of others to allow its exercise) to make property in up to a fair share of what God has given us. Our original condition for Locke can thus reasonably be described as either one of "negative community" (there being no property, either joint or individual, in any particular external thing), or one of "positive community" (each person having the right to be allowed to create property). In any event, I suspect that "divisible positive community," as described above, probably comes closest to Locke's intentions, providing we remember that mankind's common right is only a *power* to take property.

We may wonder why Locke is not clearer about his intentions. One possibility is that he simply did not know what kind of "community of things" he was working with in his arguments. But a more charitable answer is possible. It may be that it seemed to Locke not to matter which conception of community he employed in his arguments, that he believed his central claims could be sustained regardless of whether the original community was negative or positive (and so regardless of whether one was arguing in theological terms, which generally favor positive community, or secular ones, which usually favor negative community). Locke's problem, remember, was to show how private property could be rightfully derived from original community, without appeal to a compact among the commoners. And to deal with this problem, Locke employs two main claims. The first is the religious proposition that God must have intended private property to arise from original community without consent, since private property is needed for our preservation and a general consent of the commoners would have been impossible to obtain (II, 26, 28; see below). On this reasoning, it does not matter what kind of community we begin with; it must be possible to derive property from it, since

---

ever, that division of even a *negative* community may need to be constrained by considerations of equality and fairness.

[52] Tully, *Discourse*, 112–13.

this is God's will. The second claim is the neutral (i.e., neither essentially theological nor essentially secular) proposition that appropriation without prior consent is lawful (rightful) if no other person is harmed by the appropriation (II, 33; see 5.4 below). The acceptance of this claim can also be taken to render moot the issue of what kind of original community we accept. If the community is negative, appropriation requires no consent of the commoners, because no person can claim to be harmed when another takes what that person had no property in (right to, claim on).[53] And even if the community is positive, Locke believes (I will contend), it is at least sometimes true that taking no more than one's fair share harms no one, and so requires no prior consent from the commoners. Sometimes taking one's fair share of even undivided joint property is permissible, if doing so does not make the common worse for the other commoners. This is the point of Locke's contrasting the English common with the original common. Enclosure of the English common (which is, remember, "*joint* property" [II, 35; my emphasis]) is impermissible without the consent of the commoners, and one of the reasons Locke gives for that fact is this: "the remainder, after such enclosure, would not be as good to the rest of the commoners as the whole was, when they could all make use of the whole: whereas in the beginning and first peopling of the great common of the world, it was quite otherwise" (II, 35). The implication of the passage seems clear. Even a positive community of property may be divided without consent if it harms no others, as would be the case in the early ages of humankind (I return to this claim below and in 5.4).[54] So again whether the original community of things was positive or negative seems not to matter to Locke's derivation of the private from the common independent of compact.[55]

[53] See Parry, *John Locke*, 50–51. Gibbard argues that from a state of initial equal use rights (negative community), no consent is necessary to reduce the opportunities of the other commoners; but consent is necessary to reduce their rights, as happens when one claims an exclusive right to part of the common ("Natural Property Rights," 237–38). Locke's view (which seems to me substantially correct) appears to be that *this* kind of reduction of right (the loss of the right to use the appropriated object) constitutes no harm to any person, provided that person is left a fair share for appropriation.
[54] Locke's obvious willingness to accept enclosure and appropriation without consent on the original common counts strongly against Tully's reading of Locke as defender of the common and opponent of permanent, alienable property in land (*Discourse*, e.g., 99, 122–25, 169; see also Ryan, *Property and Political Theory*, 35–36). See 5.4 below.
[55] Becker suggests that in cases of genuine joint ownership "the decision to allocate specific shares at all must be a joint decision" (*Property Rights*, 25); this is Cohen's view as well ("Self-Ownership," 129). If correct, this view implies either that

The private emerges from the common, according to Locke, as a result of labor. It is labor that "put a distinction between [the appropriated objects] and common. . . . The labour that was mine, removing them out of that common state they were in, hath fixed my property in them" (II, 28). This is, as we have seen, a compelling suggestion, although by no means one that was original with Locke. What *is* original is the justification (or rather, *justifications*) that Locke offers for his belief that labor is the sole ground of original private property. One traditional reading of the *Second Treatise*, which seems to me substantially correct, is that the text contains two main lines of argument purporting to justify private property through labor.[56] The first line of argument simply applies Locke's divine will theory of morality (sketched above in chapter 1) to the issue of rights in the earth and its products. This is the argument from human needs and God's intentions. The second line of argument is more purely conceptual in nature and proceeds from prior rights that each possesses in person and labor to prop-

---

Locke is mistaken in his views about nonconsensual division of positive community or that Locke is thinking of a negative original community. But I think that Locke is correct in thinking that sometimes joint property is best thought of on the model of "divisible positive community" (see 5.4). And it is worth remembering that even in cases of *legal* joint property (concurrent estate, say), when the owners disagree about use of the property, courts may institute a compulsory (i.e., nonconsensual) partition process. These points constitute the beginning of a response to claims that joint ownership of the world is inconsistent with the Lockean thesis of self-ownership (see, e.g., Cohen, "Self-Ownership," 113).

[56] Macpherson finds these two lines of argument in the text, characterizing them as arguments from (1) the right of self-preservation and (2) the right to one's body and labor (*Possessive Individualism*, 200–201). Cherno's and Plamenatz's readings are similar ("Locke on Property," 51–52; *Man and Society*, 1:244–45), as is the more recent interpretation offered by Drury, who sees both arguments as proceeding from the "right to life" (divided into our rights *over* our life, limb, and actions and our rights *to* preserve our lives) ("Locke and Nozick," 32). There are, of course, hints of many other arguments in chapter 5 (all of which I discuss in the text below); but these two are the only ones that are plainly intended by Locke. Waldron finds five arguments (or hints of arguments) in Locke's text: arguments from (1) need, (2) efficiency, (3) the labor theory of value, (4) desert, and (5) mixing ("Two Worries about Mixing One's Labour," 37–39). (1) and (5) are the arguments on which I concentrate here, while I find (2), (3), and (4) to be simply parts of (1) or (5). Becker finds two arguments for the significance of labor in Locke: from prior rights in self and labor (the mixing argument) and from "return for pains" (*Property Rights*, 33–36, 41; "Labour Theory," 656). Mautner also finds two: from "fusion and accession" (mixing) and from "incorporation" ("Locke on Appropriation," 261–62). Snyder calls the argument from incorporation the "slippery slope" argument ("Locke on Natural Law," 736). I treat both the fusion and the incorporation arguments as parts of the mixing argument. Schwarzenbach distinguishes three arguments in Locke: the arguments from (1) taking (need, common right, incorporation), (2) making (workmanship model, desert, mixing), and (3) initiative (return for pains) ("Locke's Two Conceptions," 150–51, 154–55).

erty in the goods altered by labor. This is the mixing argument. It is easy enough to consider the second argument as simply part of the first.[57] But it is not presented as such, by Locke. It is presented as having force entirely independent of the first argument; and, indeed, it neither makes a natural conclusion to the first argument nor relies on that argument's premises. The mixing argument is both logically detachable from the first argument and the most prominent justificatory argument offered by Locke in chapter 5. These facts constitute strong reasons for treating it as an independent justification in Locke's theory, a justification that is notable for its ability to be incorporated into either a theological or a secular theory of natural property rights. Once again, it seems plausible to read Locke as embracing the "moral overdetermination" of parallel routes to the same conclusions. This should become clearer as we examine more closely the two lines of argument.

1. The Argument from Human Needs and God's Intentions

We can, Locke argues, infer God's intentions for humankind with respect to property from several facts. God wills the preservation of mankind (this is the fundamental principle of natural law, itself a conclusion in Locke's "demonstration" of morality), and God has given the earth to mankind in common. From the original community of all things, of course, there might, for all we know, be no way to rightfully acquire exclusive property (it has seemed "to some a very great difficulty" [II, 25]). But we know that God wills our preservation. And we know that we must be able to take things as our exclusive property "before they can be of any use, or at all beneficial to any particular man."[58] So "there must of neces-

---

[57] Or as simply an aberration on Locke's part. Those who treat the mixing argument as just a part of the first argument include Tully (*Discourse*, 131) and Snyder ("Locke on Natural Law," 734–75, 736–37). Schwarzenbach treats the mixing argument as part of the argument from making (a la Tully) ("Locke's Two Conceptions," 150–51). Waldron sees the mixing argument as "an independent line of argument," but finds the argument more of a "distraction" than a substantial contribution to Locke's case ("Two Worries," 38–39). Plamenatz takes the mixing argument to be a simple non sequitur (*Man and Society*, 1:245).

[58] On its face, this claim seems false. Why access or use rights would not serve just as well as exclusive property rights in allowing beneficial use of nature is not at all clear (see Waldron, *Private Property*, 168–71). Would Locke be willing to allow that where things *can* be beneficially used in common (as he seems to think is true of air and water), that they must be *left* common? These problems suggest an avenue for developing Locke's arguments (see 5.3 below): while beneficial use may not require private property, pursuit of our projects and purposive activities *does* require it. It is our right of self-government generally, not merely our right of self-

sity be a means to appropriate them" (II, 26), since we need the goods of the world to preserve ourselves. Consideration of human needs and God's intentions, then, seems to show that there must be a way to make private what was common.[59]

It is important to see that this is not yet a complete argument for property rights. The argument as stated shows only that God wills that we have private property, that property is necessary for our preservation. It follows from this that we must have a right (indeed, a duty) to *make* property in ways consistent with the preservation of mankind—that is, that each has a moral power (and liberty) to make property in up to a fair share of the common, correlating with the duties of others not to prevent exercise of the power (this is the inclusive "right to property" to which each is born, a part of the "right of self-government," which includes the right of self-preservation). The argument from need thus yields a right to make property (and, as we will see in 6.3, a right to the surplus of the property of others, under certain conditions). But the argument still doesn't show *how* we can make property, *why* any particular method yields rights (why laboring on a field gives rights to it, but pointing to the field and saying "this is mine" does not). While the ultimate justification of property thus lies in human needs and God's will, there must be a *specific* justification for labor's claim to ground property rights. Why is labor the answer to Locke's puzzle and not something else? It is easy to see why some alternative methods must fail, although Locke himself explains only the failure of consent or compact as the ground of exclusive property: if the consent of the other commoners were the source of property, "man had starved, notwithstanding the plenty God had given him" (II, 28), such consent being impossible to obtain. Since God wills that mankind not starve, "common consent" is an answer to Locke's puzzle (how to get the private from the common) that contradicts God's will (and hence cannot be adequate). But why is "labor" the answer that Locke accepts?

There are several reasons Locke might give that seem consistent with the overall line of argument. The most obvious is that we

---

preservation, which requires natural property rights. See the related argument in O'Neill, "Nozick's Entitlements," 318.

[59] The best statements of this "argument from need" are in I, 86–87 and II, 25–26, although it is implied in many other passages. For discussions of various aspects of this argument, see Tully, *Discourse*, 3–4; Colman, *Moral Philosophy*, 190; Olivecrona, "Appropriation in the State of Nature," 221–22, and "Locke's Theory of Appropriation," 221–22; Waldron, "Enough and as Good," 324–26, "Locke, Tully," 100, and "Two Worries," 37.

have been *commanded* to labor, that this is the positive revealed will of God.[60] "God, when he gave the world in common to all mankind, commanded man also to labour, and the penury of his condition required it of him" (II, 32); "God commanded and [man's] wants forced him to labour" (II, 35). It may seem at first that God's command establishes only a *duty* to labor, not a *right* to the products of the labor (which is what Locke is trying to justify). But if private property rights are necessary for our preservation (as we have seen Locke believes), and God wills our preservation, then the *right* to the products is necessary to doing our duty and hence is also willed by God.[61] So the moral power to make property is in part, at least, a mandatory power (i.e., a power that we have a *duty* to exercise).

But there are two obvious problems with the argument as developed above. First, only some of the products of our labor ("products" here being used to mean what is labored *on* as well as what is added to it) are actually necessary to our preservation (or the preservation of our dependents, the poor, etc.). Yet Locke clearly allows that our labor grounds property even in those goods that are only for our convenience or comfort, not just in those necessary for survival. Why should labor give title to things that are not necessary to our preservation? (Even if we have a duty to labor and "subdue the earth" [II, 32] beyond what our personal needs require, why do we have *rights* in those products of our labor that are beyond our needs?) Second, and more telling, is the following difficulty: why does labor establish property in the *fruits* of *our* labor? True, we have both a duty to labor and a need for goods from the earth to preserve ourselves. But why should it be the particular goods we have labored to produce to which we gain title (so they can be used by us for our preservation)? Why not some other goods, unrelated to our labor, but equally good for preserving us (such as the goods produced by some other person)? The argument as specified thus far cannot explain the significance of labor in grounding rights to the *particular* products of one's labor. Even

[60] See Dunn, *Political Thought*, 219–20, 222–24, 250–51; Tully, *Discourse*, 109–10; Ashcraft, *Revolutionary Politics*, 261–62, and *Locke's Two Treatises*, 134–35; Wood, *Capitalism*, 58; Kendall, *Majority-Rule*, 70–72.

[61] Obviously, this same conclusion can be reached independent of the above revelation, since one can infer a duty to labor directly from the duty of self-preservation and the facts of the human condition. Ashcraft suggests that Locke wants to argue as well that since land is valueless without labor, we can presume that God wouldn't have given it except with the intention that we labor on it (as II, 34 might suggest) (*Locke's Two Treatises*, 134).

allowing that God favors "the industrious and the rational" (II, 34) and wants them to profit from their labor,[62] the reason for God's wanting them to profit by ownership of the particular products of their labor remains obscure.

Perhaps the idea is that those who labor deserve a reward for this, and the product of their labor is the best measure of what they deserve. So each deserves to have a right to the product of one's own labor (this right being the fitting return for the labor).[63] Locke does say that one who "meddled" with what another had labored on plainly desired "the benefit of another's pains, which he had no right to" (II, 34), suggesting, perhaps, that we have a right to what we have taken pains over because we deserve it. The laborer, after all, creates *value* by labor (as we will see), and it is common to suggest that value-creating activities merit reward. And no other is harmed (i.e., deprived of what might otherwise be enjoyed) by giving laborers the product of their labor, since the value they create would not exist at all for others had the laborers not produced it.

There are, however, serious obstacles to completing Locke's justification of property with this argument from desert. In the first place, this argument is not only not obviously in Locke's text, it is entirely *independent* of the argument from human needs and God's intentions. The argument from desert is completely unrelated to concerns about the preservation of mankind or our need for the goods of the earth (and so, if it were indeed in the text, it might count as another argument equally useful within a purely *secular* theory of property). In the second place, the desert argument in fact fails to solve the problem we introduced it to deal with. Even if the product of our labor were the best measure of the rights we deserve to acquire (which it is not), our desert claim could be perfectly well satisfied by providing us with an equivalent measure of

[62] There is, of course some controversy over whether Locke wanted to identify "the industrious and the rational" in his own time with all of the landowners (Macpherson), the gentry rather than the idle, wasteful large landowners (Ashcraft), or neither. I suggest below and in chapter 6 that Ashcraft's reading is the most plausible.

[63] Miller calls this argument "the most obvious way of reconstructing Locke's argument [and] one for which there is some support in the text itself" ("Justice and Property," 6). Ryan also seems to take this reading of Locke seriously (*Property and Political Theory*, 28, 33, 37, 44). Becker characterizes it as the best reformulation of the labor theory, but *not* the argument Locke intended to make (*Property Rights*, 47, 49). For fuller presentations of the desert argument, see Becker, *Property Rights*, 47–56, and "Labor Theory," 655–56; and Christman's critique in "Can Ownership Be Justified?" 166–67.

goods (and rights to them), rather than the particular products of our labor. Those who deserve a fitting return generally deserve not specific goods, but a particular kind or level of well-being. Finally, the desert argument actually conflicts with many features of Locke's theory of property. Those who labor most (or hardest, or most thoughtfully, etc.) deserve the most return; but the products of one's labor seldom correspond to the best measure of one's desert. How productive one's labor is frequently depends on luck (on the weather for farming, the richness of the vein for mining, the abundance of fruits and game for gathering and hunting, etc.); what one deserves depends (on this account) on effort. Locke's theory (of a right to the product) accepts fortune as a determinant of property in a way no desert theorist could allow. Similarly, for Locke only the *first* laborer has a claim on what is improved by his labor (provided he continues to use it, etc.). But a desert theory will have a hard time not counting (as equally productive of rights) later labor on what has been previously improved, since later labor seems just as deserving of reward. And Locke would be able to accept neither a theory of property transfer based on desert (rather than his own theory, which allows consent, inheritance, need, and forfeiture as bases for transfer) nor the very severe limits on possible holdings that a properly framed desert theory would impose.[64] All of these problems point to a more basic gap between rights and desert, and to more fundamental problems with desert theories of property rights.[65]

The best way to understand how Locke wished to complete the argument from human needs and God's intentions, I believe, is to follow the interpretive strategy outlined above in 1.4: we can derive the specific content of natural law (which includes the rights and duties of natural property) by rule-consequentialist reasoning from the fundamental law of nature. We can ask "by general conformity to what rules will mankind be best preserved?" and our answer will give us the content of natural law for Locke. So if

[64] See Miller, "Justice and Property," 6–7; and Becker, *Property Rights*, 54–55.

[65] See Waldron's similar rejection of the "desert interpretation" of Locke's arguments (*Private Property*, 201–7). Regardless of how we read *Locke's* theory of property, a desert theory of property rights must be able to respond to at least these two fundamental concerns: (1) Isn't there a significant difference between deserving to have a right and actually having one? That there is a difference seems clearest precisely in the case of rights that involve practices (such as property or promising); (2) Aren't desert claims based on what we do using assets in which we have property (to which we are "entitled"), making property a more fundamental notion than desert (and so not capable of being explained or justified in terms of desert)? See Nozick, *Anarchy*, 224–26.

Locke can show that a system in which laborers receive title to the products of their labor (within the limits mentioned below in 5.4) is the best system for preserving mankind, he will have justified what needs justifying. He will have shown why labor (rather than something else) grounds property, and why the particular products of our labor (rather than something else) are what our labor grounds property in.

Now Locke famously argues that labor increases the stock of goods for all (e.g., II, 37, 41–42). It seems, then, that the system that most effectively encourages labor will be likely to be the one that most effectively preserves humankind (and hence does God's will). Here we have the start of a rule-consequentialist argument to the conclusion that laborers should have title to the specific products of their labor. For one good way of encouraging (inducing) labor is to reward the laborer with title to the product, thereby (indirectly) encouraging the laborer to do what is best for all (as, for instance, Hume, Paley, and Bentham later argued).[66] And, of course, laborers who receive more for greater labors will be able to better preserve themselves and their dependents. Rewarding laborers with title, then, will enable them to better perform their duties.[67] But why reward laborers with the *particular products* of their labor, rather than with some proportionate good unrelated to their labor? The simplest answer is that there *are* no goods lying about to be distributed. It is our labor that makes the earth and its products useful for our preservation; nature provides only things that are "rough and unfitted to our use,"[68] our labor transforming them into useful goods. So the only goods available for rewarding laborers are those produced by the labor. A system of immediate transfers (e.g., where I earn title to the products of your labor, and vice versa) is obviously not only hopelessly impracticable, but ignores factors like the emotional investment of laborers in the product of their labor. Rule-consequentialist reasoning from the basic principle that humankind is to be preserved, then, seems to lead naturally to the conclusion that laborers have property in the par-

[66] See Reeve, *Property*, 116–22; and Gibbard, "Natural Property Rights," 238. Notice also that while Gauthier justifies our rights to use our bodies and powers, and our rights to the effects of our labor (or compensation for them) by appeal to his Lockean proviso, he founds rights of possession in the fact that exclusive rights provide more benefits for all (*Morals by Agreement*, 209–10, 211, 216–17).

[67] Parry, *John Locke*, 49; Ashcraft, *Revolutionary Politics*, 264–66, 270, and *Locke's Two Treatises*, 135–36, 141–42.

[68] King, *Life*, 1:162.

ticular products of their labor (I return to this argument in 5.3 below).

This reading of Locke gives a special point to all of the passages in chapter 5 of the *Second Treatise* that emphasize how important labor is to the well-being of humankind (and how large a percentage of what is valuable for the support of life is the result of labor) (especially II, 40–43, but also, e.g., II, 36).[69] On this reading, the point of these passages is to support Locke's rule-consequentialist reasoning by showing that whatever encourages labor encourages the best preservation of humankind (as a *rule*—in particular instances, of course, rewarding labor with the product may not have this effect). That reading seems preferable to interpreting these passages as an independent effort to justify property in the products of labor. Nozick, for instance, considers the possibility "that laboring on something improves it and makes it more valuable; and anyone is entitled to own a thing whose value he has created."[70] On this line, adding value will create property in the improved thing and "over-balance the community of land" (II, 40). But there is no very good reason to attribute such an argument to Locke. It is not, in the first place, even a complete argument; for when we ask why adding value should give property, the natural answer is: we have a right to what we have created. This, however, merely asserts a "right of creation," which is itself the core of another style of argument purporting to justify property (see below). Second, Locke never comes even close to explicitly mentioning or defending this argument, and many of Locke's examples of labor establishing property (particularly, the examples of picking and gathering) seem very difficult to describe as instances of labor adding value to a thing.[71] Finally, the value-adding argu-

---

[69] The sections I, 40–43 are what Olivecrona calls "the second part" (or "section B") of the chapter, and he suggests that they were probably added to the text after Locke completed the rest of the chapter ("Locke's Theory of Appropriation," 233–34). My reading of the sections as supplying support for Locke's argument (without being themselves a critical justificatory argument) would make sense of a decision on Locke's part to add them to a previously composed chapter. I will not discuss here Cohen's convincing arguments that Locke is mistaken in his claims that labor is responsible for virtually all of the use value of the world ("Marx and Locke," 374–78).

[70] *Anarchy*, 175.

[71] Remember that Locke's claim is that the moment I pick up the acorn, my labor has made it mine (II, 28). Is the "acorn on the ground" really interestingly less valuable than the "acorn in my hand" that my labor creates at the moment I grasp the acorn? See Olivecrona, "Locke's Theory of Appropriation," 226, 232; Waldron, *Private Property*, 193; Drury, "Locke and Nozick on Property," 32; and Mautner, "Locke on Original Appropriation," 263.

ment is not a very convincing argument, even if we accept a right of creation. For laboring on something may not add value to it (indeed, it may make it less valuable); and it is hard to see, in any event, why adding value to something should give the laborer title to the entire improved thing, rather than just to the value created by the labor.[72] Only a rather uncharitable reading of Locke, then, would take him to be using the value-adding argument to directly justify property in the products of labor (taking "products" here, as elsewhere, to include the things labored upon).

So we should read the "labor-value passages" (i.e., chiefly II, 40–43) not to be advancing a new justification for property, but as supporting one step in the argument from human needs and God's intentions. But these passages obviously have other important roles in Locke's argument as well. The most important of these is their role in Locke's defense of enclosure of unowned (i.e., naturally common) land. Locke identifies laboring on the land (tilling, planting, improving, cultivating, subduing, sowing, ploughing, and reaping are examples of such labor used by Locke) with *enclosing* it ("He by his labour does, as it were, enclose it from the common" [II, 32]); and he takes enclosure to be the means of appropriating land ("he cannot appropriate, he cannot enclose" [II, 32]).[73] Locke makes it clear that enclosure is the best use of unowned land, for it transforms what is "waste" into what is useful and productive. "Land that is left wholly to nature" is worth "little more than nothing" (II, 42; "it would scarcely be worth anything" [II, 43]). Enclosure (private appropriation of land that is naturally common) is thus to be encouraged, since it "does not lessen but increase the common stock of mankind" (II, 37).[74] Private property in land (acquired by one "who appropriates land to himself by his labour" [II, 37]) is clearly regarded by Locke as a natural (and beneficial) feature of prepolitical life.[75] On the other

---

[72] Nozick, *Anarchy*, 175.

[73] Olivecrona, "Appropriation in the State of Nature," 226–27.

[74] An apparent reversal of Locke's earlier view that "it is impossible for anyone to grow rich except at the expense of someone else" (ELN, 211). Tully's argument that Locke is opposing enclosure and defending the common (*Discourse*, 99, 122–25, 168–69) is, in the face of this textual evidence, impossible to sustain; and it has been convincingly criticized in, for example, Ashcraft, *Revolutionary Politics*, 271–72, and *Locke's Two Treatises*, 136; Shapiro, *Evolution of Rights*, 94–96; Wood, *Capitalism*, 57–58, 62–66, 82–83; McNally, "Locke, Levellers," 28–31.

[75] Tully's claim that for Locke "fixed property in land does not have a natural foundation" (*Discourse*, 122) seems to be based largely on Locke's maintaining (a) that improved land that is no longer used reverts to common (ibid., 123–24), and (b) that (a) is just one example of how Locke makes property "conditional upon its

hand, Locke seems to oppose enclosure of land left common by compact (i.e., within political societies), both because of the obligation to respect the compact, and because (as we have seen) enclosure would make the other commoners in this case worse off than they were before the enclosure (II, 35) (the "common stock" is lessened, not increased by enclosure of land left common by law).[76]

The "labor-value passages" are used not only in this defense of enclosure, but also as support for Locke's related contention that dividing the original common is fair to all and requires no consent. Appropriation by labor is not "to the prejudice of others," who are, if anything, better off as a result (II, 37). And none can complain of harm or wrongdoing when I take what I create 99/100 of the value of (II, 40) (or 999/1000 [II, 43]); since land in common is worthless and the value I take in appropriating would not exist but for my labor, no other is harmed by my appropriation (I return to this argument in 5.4).[77] So here we have further support for Locke's view that taking one's share of the "original community of all things" does not require the consent of the other commoners.[78]

---

use to perform our positive duties to God" (ibid., 124; see also 99). It is true, of course, that property in land is limited in various ways (see 5.4 below) and that property is forfeitable by wrongdoing (failure to perform our duties). But all of our natural rights (not just property rights in land) are limited by the value of preserving mankind and forfeitable by wrongdoing. So if being limited and forfeitable is what deprives property in land of its "natural foundation," Tully might as well have claimed that natural rights do not have a natural foundation for Locke, a claim that is transparently false. Rights that are merely limited and forfeitable are not thereby non-natural or conditional (in Tully's sense). Add to this the fact that Locke allows many innocent uses of land (and property generally) that are not specifically required by duty (e.g., uses for our "comfort" and "convenience").

[76] It is important to distinguish here, as McNally argues, between what is left common by law and what is simply open to enclosure with "no legally enshrined common rights" at issue. It is only enclosure in the former case that Locke explicitly opposes. See "Locke, Levellers," 31.

[77] Olivecrona, "Locke's Theory of Appropriation," 232–33; Ashcraft, *Locke's Two Treatises*, 141–42. Note that even in the case of what is left common by law (within civil society), the second point still holds (by enclosure I create 99/100 of the value); but the first point (that none is made worse off by enclosure) apparently does not hold (II, 35).

[78] Locke is often, however, taken to be doing more still in the labor-value passages. Since labor creates value and increases "the common stock of mankind," and since enclosure makes *all* better off (II, 37), it would seem that none can complain even if nearly all of the available land has been enclosed (appropriated) by others (as Locke supposes will happen after the invention of money in populous regions or nations [II, 45]). Even those who have to work on land owned by others (there being none available for their own appropriation) seem to be compensated for this disadvantage by the benefits enclosure produces for all. Macpherson takes this to be Locke's way of showing that the requirement of leaving "enough and as good

We have been primarily concerned in this section with Locke's arguments for the claim that labor grounds property, exploring thus far various aspects of the argument from human needs and God's intentions. But there are two other arguments frequently attributed to Locke that we have not yet examined: the argument from the right of creation and the mixing argument. Both arguments have been seen as parts of the argument from human needs and God's intention; but it is important to see that both are *conceptually independent* of that argument. Neither our right over our creations nor our ability to mix our property in ourselves with nature has any special connection with considerations of what we *need* for our survival. Both arguments retain their own force whether or not we *have* any need for what we have created/mixed our labor with. I will thus treat both arguments as independent justifications, discussing them both separately and in their connection to one another.

2. The Mixing Argument

Where the argument from human needs and God's intentions justifies property in our labor's products by appeal to the right (and duty) of preserving oneself (and others), the mixing argument appeals to our right of self-direction (another aspect of our right of self-government). While it is possible to read the mixing argument as merely completing the argument from human needs and God's intentions, this is *not* how Locke presents the mixing argument (in II, 27–28).[79] It is presented as a free-standing justification for property; and nothing in either argument requires the other for its completion. If anything, the mixing argument is given a much more prominent and explicit presentation than the other, and thus looks

---

in common for others" when we appropriate (II, 27) has been overcome in contemporary societies, thus portraying capitalist accumulation as rational, productive, and favored by God (*Possessive Individualism*, 211–13). My reasons for doubting that these are Locke's intentions I reserve for 5.4.

[79] Tully takes the mixing of labor not to justify anything, but only to be "a means of identifying something as naturally one's own" (*Discourse*, 131). This reading seems to me to make utterly superfluous Locke's quite elaborate (and purely conceptual, nontheological) explanation in II, 27–28 of why labor makes property. None of this is necessary to Locke's argument, on Tully's reading, making Locke's central presentation of it appear foolish or deliberately deceptive. Another reading that similarly simply disregards Locke's elaborate efforts to explain "mixing our labor" is offered by Schwarzenbach ("Locke's Two Conceptions," 151). Waldron sees that the mixing argument appears to be "meant to stand up on its own" ("Two Worries," 38; *Private Property*, 139–40).

to be taken by Locke to be his central argument (as many philosophers writing after Locke, not to mention generations of Locke scholars, supposed[80]). Indeed, once all of the main justificatory argument of chapter 5 has been presented by Locke (and prior to his shifting to a discussion of money and civil property), he summarizes his case by direct reference to the mixing argument (with no mention of the argument from human needs and God's intentions): "Man (by being master of himself, and proprietor of his own person, and the actions or labor of it) had still in himself the great foundation of property" (II, 44). Locke's use of the phrase "the great foundation of property" should warn us to take seriously the argument that explains it (the mixing argument), and to consider the possibility that he intends the argument to independently justify property, not merely to complete some much more basic and important line of argument (how much more basic can one get than a "great foundation"?).

If this is not reason enough to take the mixing argument seriously (as an important part of Locke's project), there are others. First, the mixing argument constitutes an indispensable step in the realization of Locke's theoretical ambitions. It provides him with an answer to Pufendorf's question of how a mere "corporal act" could limit the rights of others (as the creation of a property does).[81] And it explains better than any of Locke's other arguments how permanent, alienable property in land is possible. It is hard to see how any other parts of Locke's argumentative apparatus could justify permanent property in land;[82] but the mixing argu-

---

[80] William Paley, for instance, takes the mixing argument to be "Mr. Locke's solution" to the problem of property (*Principles of Moral and Political Philosophy*, book 3, part 1, chapter 4). This reading has become extremely unfashionable since the work of Dunn, Tully, Ashcraft, and others of the most recent generation of Locke scholars.

[81] Pufendorf, *De Jure Naturae et Gentium Libri Octo*, 4.4.5. The answer is that labor is *not* a mere corporal act; it involves extending our prior property to include parts of nature, by mixing them together. It is not, then, the corporal act that limits the rights of others, but the extension of our own rights. See Seliger's discussion of Pufendorf's query in *Liberal Politics*, 193–95.

[82] This fact may explain Tully's belief that Locke is really only defending the common, given Tully's rejection of the mixing argument. Similarly, Schwarzenbach is forced to invent for Locke an "argument from initiative" (she grants "that this argument remains rather sketchy in Locke's thought" ["Locke's Two Conceptions," 154]) in order to justify fixed property in land, because she has already mistakenly subsumed the mixing argument (the obvious tool for the job) under the arguments from taking and making (ibid., 150–51). Further support for the view of Locke as defending fixed property in land (in addition to that noted above) can be found in Mackie, "Review of Tully," 92–93; Schwarzenbach, "Locke's Two Conceptions," 153–54; and Miller, "Justice and Property," 6.

ment appears to easily explain this (since land on which we labor cannot be taken without taking what is indisputably ours—i.e., our labor). Finally, I explore throughout this work Locke's pluralism, pointing to his frequent use of quite different argumentative styles to reach the same conclusions. If there is any force at all to my claims of Lockean pluralism, there is good reason to look carefully at the mixing argument as an argument intended by Locke to provide an alternate route to the same conclusion reached by the argument from human needs and God's intentions. Indeed, the first words of chapter 5 of the *Second Treatise* can be viewed as announcing Locke's plan to argue along more than one route. Viewed in this way, the mixing argument is especially interesting in being compatible with either a theological or a secular perspective on property. All aspects of the mixing argument are capable of being stated in purely secular, but still recognizably Lockean, terms: the starting point of original community is derivable by "natural reason" (II, 25); our property in ourselves can be derived from our natural equality of jurisdiction (which can itself be derived, on Locke's view, by a purely conceptual, nontheological argument, as we saw at the start of 2.2); the idea of "mixing" is straightforwardly secular; and the limits on appropriation are derivable (as we will see in 5.4) from considerations of natural fairness. I do not mean to argue here that Locke *intends* the mixing argument to be purely secular. But the dual conception of our property in ourselves that Locke *does* intend (or so I argue below) clearly points to the potential of the mixing argument for secular natural rights theory.

Let us begin, then, with a more careful statement of the mixing argument as Locke presents it in chapter 5. II, 27 and 28 actually present two rather different arguments (the difference between them not being mentioned by Locke), but both involve the idea of making something external a part of one's protected personal (private) sphere. In II, 27, labor (which is private) is mixed with what is external; in II, 28, what is external is mixed with what is private (one's body). In both cases what was common is made private by laboring on it.

In II, 27 Locke tells us that "every man has a property in his own person," and by extension in "the labour of his body and the work of his hands." When a person "removes" a thing from its natural state, he has "mixed his labour with and joined to it something that is his own, and thereby makes it his property. . . . For this labour being the unquestionable property of the labourer, no man but he can have a right to what that is once joined to." The idea, then, seems to be that by mixing what is yours (your labor) with what is available for appropriation, you make any other's taking of that thing without your consent unlawful; for by taking the improved thing, that person also takes your labor "which another had no title to, nor could without injury take from [you]" (II, 32). By laboring you extend your natural property in yourself (by mixing, joining, or annexing it) to things external to you.[83]

Where II, 27 uses the ideas of fusion and accession, II, 28 relies in part on some idea of "incorporation."[84] In II, 28 Locke begins by claiming that "nobody can deny" that acorns or apples that you picked in the woods are yours once you have eaten them (they are now literally part of your body, which is private to you[85]). But, moving backwards in time, it seems obvious that if they are yours once eaten, they were yours while being prepared for eating; and if the latter is true, they were certainly yours while being carried home for preparation, and so on back to the actual picking. So it is plain "that if the first gathering made them not his, nothing else could." There is a continuum between the gathering and the point at which nobody could deny a property, and there is no intermediate point on the continuum where it seems to make sense to deny that there is property.

I think that the second mixing argument (of II, 28) must in fact be taken at least in part to rely on the first (of II, 27). For while it may be true that physical incorporation of a thing (mixing what is external with your body) serves as an independent source of undeniable property (although only in a rather odd sense, since the new "property" loses its identity as it is incorporated), it is cer-

---

[83] For other summaries of this argument, see, for example, Olivecrona, "Appropriation in the State of Nature," 223–24, and "Locke's Theory of Appropriation," 225–26; Mautner, "Locke on Original Appropriation," 261; Waldron, "Two Worries," 39–40; Becker, *Property Rights*, 33–34.

[84] Mautner, "Locke on Original Appropriation," 261–62. On Hume's account of "accession," both of Locke's arguments employ this idea, since for Hume things are acquired by accession "when they are connected in an intimate manner with objects that are already our property, and at the same time are inferior to them" (*Treatise of Human Nature*, 3.2.3).

[85] "The fruit or venison which nourishes the wild Indian . . . must be his . . . i.e., *a part of him*" (II, 26; my emphasis). Wheeler essentially makes the two arguments of II, 27 and 28 into one argument, by arguing that (a) you have rights over your body, (b) you have the same rights over what becomes part of your body, and (c) you have the same rights over anything that can be used *like* a body part (such as a house). So "your property *is* your body" ("Natural Property Rights," 273–82). The price Wheeler pays for this strategy is making nonsense of the idea of a "body." See Christman, "Can Ownership Be Justified?" 170.

tainly *not* true that one could not intelligently deny property in the acorns or apples at some earlier point on the continuum. While the acorns may be yours once you are eating them, I see nothing odd about denying that they are yours while you are cooking or carrying them. What makes the acorns yours at these earlier stages can only be that to take them would be to rob you of your labor (which you mixed with them). But now we are back to the first mixing argument (involving mixing what is private with what is external).

While there are, of course, very real difficulties in understanding just how labor can be "mixed" with an acorn (say), I want to reserve comment on those matters until 5.3. There is another (prior) problem of interpretation we face in analyzing the mixing argument: how are we to understand Locke's claim that each has property "in his own person" (labor, etc.)? There are a number of quite distinct possibilities (of which I will discuss only two), but any reading of Locke's claim must deal centrally with the fact that only twenty-one paragraphs earlier in the *Second Treatise*, Locke plainly states that all people are *God's* property (II, 6). It seems unlikely that Locke forgot about that statement, but it seems at first blush not a little confused to claim both that each of us is God's property *and* that we all have property in our own person.[86] How we resolve this apparent conflict for Locke will dictate much of our understanding of the mixing argument.

One resolution involves appealing to the "workmanship model" of property. On this model, all property—God's in us, ours in ourselves, and ours in external goods—is explained by reference to the "right of creation" or "maker's rights." We saw in 1.2 how God's "right of creation" seems to be taken for granted (or regarded as self-evident) by Locke as the final explanation of our obligation to obey God. The workmanship model[87] draws an analogy between God's creative power (and subsequent rights) and ours (we having been made in God's image): as God created the world and made property in it, so we create our own world

[86] Day not only finds these two claims "incompatible" but also thinks that it makes no clear sense to say of a person that he "owns himself" ("Locke on Property," 215–19). Parry follows Day in this (*John Locke*, 50–51). Mansfield (not very plausibly) suggests that Locke is deliberately laying a false trail and *really* means that people should regard themselves as their own property ("On the Political Character," 29–33).

[87] As described by Tully, *Discourse*, 4, 8–9, 105, 108–10, 116–21. Others who see the "right of creation" at the center of Locke's theory of property (rights) include Shapiro (*Evolution of Rights*, 96; "Resources," 49–51), Ashcraft (*Revolutionary Politics*, 258–59), and Colman (*Moral Philosophy*, 186–90).

through our laboring activities and in the process make property in our creations. We should act as much as possible like God. Further (and more directly to the present point) both God and we can claim "rights of creation" with respect to various aspects of our selves. God made us; but we make our *own* persons and actions (or labor).[88] We are thus both our own and God's, with no inconsistency. Our property in ourselves "is the right to use and preserve what is essentially God's property, similar to a tenant's property."[89] Using our property in ourselves, we transform the world with our labor, making *new* things out of the material with which God provided us. This creative/transformative activity consists of gathering (for natural products), catching, domesticating, or killing (for animals), and cultivating (for land).[90]

Both the workmanship model and the interpretation of Locke's theory of property in terms of it face serious objections. As we saw in 1.2, appealing to the right of creation does not really explain the rights of creators at all,[91] nor is this right easy to justify within an exclusively theological moral theory. If all duties and rights derive from God's will, did God will the right of creation? And where did God get the authority to do this, if His right to command *derives* from His right as creator? If the "right of creation" is simply self-evident, on the other hand, then morality does not all depend on God's will, and the theory of property that relies on the right of creation (as Locke's allegedly does) can be presented intact with no mention of God (if we are *really* creators of our actions and makers of *new things* in the world). But we do *not*, of course, create as God creates. Analogies between God's makings and ours are *very* extended, since the most interesting feature of God's makings are the acts of creation *ex nihilo*. We merely modify existing things (see below), whether we work on ourselves, our actions, or external things. Victor Frankenstein did not create life as God does (indeed, the point of Shelley's tale is precisely how wrong it is to believe oneself capable of and to aspire to God-like creation[92]); neither do human parents or human gardeners.

[88] Tully, *Discourse*, 105, 108–9. Similar readings are advanced by Colman (*Moral Philosophy*, 189–90), Yolton (*Locke*, 69–70), Herzog (*Without Foundations*, 70–72), and Waldron (*Private Property*, 178–80).

[89] Tully, *Discourse*, 114.

[90] Ibid., 116–21.

[91] See also Reeve, *Property*, 126.

[92] "Frightful would be the effect of any human endeavour to mock the stupendous mechanism of the Creator of the world" (*Frankenstein* [New York: Bantam, 1981], xxv).

More important for our purposes here, however, are the problems involved in trying to portray Locke's theory of property as essentially an application of the workmanship model. Locke says nothing explicit (or even highly suggestive) in the *Treatises*, as far as I can see, which suggests that he believes human beings create their persons or labor, or that when they labor they gain property because they are creating "new things." He only says that they *have* property in their persons and labor (actions), and that they *make* property in other things by labor.[93] And even in the *Essay*, where Locke talks of "owning" actions as "our own" (i.e., "appropriating" them or accepting responsibility for them, seeing them as *our* actions, rather than someone else's—as he does primarily in E, 2.27), Locke's language is not explicitly "creationist." While these are the passsages always cited by those who advocate extending Locke's theological creationism to his theory of human property, there is really nothing in the passages that dictates this reading (which should make us a bit reluctant to then extend that very constructive interpretation to cover the *Treatises*, where no such things are said).

While it is easy enough to see how we might be said to "create" our actions (although this involves an extended sense of "create"), Locke does not elaborate on it; and it is extremely difficult to see how we could be said to create our persons. Do we really labor (with "maker's knowledge") to produce our *persons*? As Locke seems to describe things in the *Treatises*, it is our parents who are primarily responsible for guiding us through the change from mere human beings to persons (i.e., "men" in Locke's *moral* sense of the word) (e.g., II, 63–64). He would probably say similar things about some teachers.[94] Of the many traits, capacities, or other properties that constitute one's person, some are innate, many are unintentionally acquired or learned, and some are the product of thoughtful (intentional) "labor." This does not make us the *creators* of our persons (unless every change we accomplish counts as a new creation), and Locke nowhere says that we are. Efforts to show that Locke really means that we create our persons (and not just that we *own* them) invariably appear strained.[95]

[93] Ryan, *Property and Political Theory*, 28–29; Waldron, *Private Property*, 198–200.

[94] Notice that while Yolton claims in one place that we make our own persons (*Locke*, 69–70), he rightly notes in another that it is the task of education to "produce persons"; education is the source of developed reason, hence personhood (Yolton and Yolton, "Introduction," 15, 18–19, 25–26).

[95] In the one paragraph Tully devotes to "defending" this claim (*Discourse*, 109), nothing is said that establishes anything except that our persons are our property.

The problems are, if anything, even more severe in trying to portray the "right of creation" as the heart of Locke's theory of property in external things. Again, Locke speaks not at all about creating or making new external things as the source of our property in the *Treatises*.[96] Locke's examples of appropriation are almost all of hunting, gathering, and agriculture, with very few examples of handicraft or manufacture.[97] Hunting and gathering neither create nor transform the objects of labor.[98] Agriculture no more involves creation than does parental procreation. God creates children and entrusts them to their parents' care, but this trust is specifically distinguished by Locke from *property* (indeed, this is a central theme of the *First Treatise*). We *do* have alienable property in the crops we grow, but *not* in the children we grow. The reason for this is *not* that we create the former, but not the latter, for we have no knowledge of the real essence of either to employ in creation. The reason, I will contend, is that the trusts we exercise in the two cases are very different (the former involving significant discretion that the latter excludes).

Human property in Locke, I think, is not essentially a matter of creation or making. Even when we design things, we seldom create them; even if you know the real essence of the thing you design (a chair, say), you do not know the real essence of the thing

---

But *that* point is not in question. It is our *creation* of our persons as the source of our property in our persons that Tully is asserting; and none of his arguments or citations supports *that*. Similarly, Colman can only show that Locke believes we make our thoughts, not that we make our persons or the consciousness that constitutes them (*Moral Philosophy*, 189).

[96] Tully acknowledges that Locke does not use the word "create" (creation being God's province), but says Locke "consistently and repeatedly" speaks of "making" (*Discourse*, 120). As far as I can see, however, almost all of Locke's uses of "making" in chapter 5 concern "making" use of a thing, "making" it one's own, or "making" a property in it. The only thing we are said to make by laboring (other than our *rights* over what we labor on) is the "greatest part of the value of things" (II, 42; see also II, 40); and these remarks occur long after the central passages in which Locke is discussing the justification of property. See Waldron's similar observations (*Private Property*, 199–200).

[97] Among those who have seen this (and, for the most part, been led to question the creationist analysis of Locke) are Olivecrona ("Locke's Theory of Appropriation," 225–26, 232), Mautner ("Locke on Original Appropriation," 263), Fressola ("Liberty and Property," 315–16), and Snyder ("Locke on Natural Law," 737).

[98] Tully claims that these activities transform "earthly provisions" into "manmade objects of use" (*Discourse*, 117). But it is awfully hard to believe that Locke thought picking up an acorn to be sufficiently like God's acts of creation to generate rights under the same creationist principle. Making something useful is not like making the thing itself. I can make a tree useful to me (as shade) by moving under it; but I do not thereby create a new thing (in any sense interesting enough for Locke to have thought of it as similar to God's creation).

you build (a *wooden* chair, say). (If we could design children, by manipulating sperm and ovum, would we have a maker's rights over them?). Human property is not so much a matter of creation as a matter of extending the person (which is indisputably ours) into the world. By our labor we alter the world and make it useful to us. But even when this involves no physical transformation (let alone creation) of a thing (as in picking up acorns), it brings about a fundamental *moral* change in the thing upon which we labor. For our property, what is private to us, is extended by our labor to include labor's object.

Consider an alternative, noncreationist account of human property in Locke, one that also explains how God and I can both have property in myself. God, as our true creator, has original property in us and all that "grows" from us (including our persons, labor, etc.). But God entrusts us (rational, corporeal beings) with extensive control over ourselves and the uses of ourselves. We have property in our persons and labor, not as creators of them, but as trustholders with respect to them. We can, however, view our property in ourselves from two perspectives. First, with respect to God, our property in our persons and labor is not "unquestionably ours" except in the sense that we are the clear holders of a strong discretionary trust from God.[99] The trust (and its limit) is to care for ourselves in ways consistent with the best preservation of mankind. We have seen (in 1.4 and 2.1), however, that the rules for the best preservation of mankind include allowing each significant liberty to pursue personal nondestructive goals (i.e., those which do not involve imperiling self or others). And caring, for oneself involves taking seriously one's own plans and projects, since failing to do so will cause frustration, boredom, or other nonproductive conditions.[100] The trust we enjoy from God, then, imposes

[99] Viewed in this way, our property is a form of "ownership in trust" or "stewardship". On the importance of the "stewardship" model in Locke, see Ashcraft, *Revolutionary Politics*, 263n; Schwarzenbach, "Locke's Two Conceptions," especially 145–46; Stell, "Dueling," 16; Ryan, *Property and Political Theory*, 29, 31–32, 45. Schwarzenbach describes Locke's view of our property in life, limb, and freedom as "gift property," which involves a "loose" obligation to abide by the will of the donor ("Locke's Two Conceptions," 146–47). The obligations limiting property are sufficiently strict, however, that the idea of a *trust* (rather than a gift) seems to make better sense of Locke's intentions. The idea of trust is also, of course, one that Locke uses centrally in his theories of government and revolution, so it might reasonably be called one of the central concepts at work in the *Treatises*.

[100] Tully's characterization of "Locke's 'property in' " as "the right to use and enjoy God's property for God's purposes" (*Discourse*, 122) is thus slightly misleading. We may use God's property for our own purposes, since doing so is consistent with God's purposes.

limits on our freedom (it is not "license" [II, 6]), but also gives us a "robust zone of indifference" within which we may pursue our own harmless goals (again see 1.4 and 2.1). As trustees we enjoy a wide range of discretion to use ourselves and our powers as we please. Breach of this trust (exceeding its limits), however, entails loss of control over ourselves. Breach entails forfeiture of rights, justifying either paternalistic intervention (where harm is done to oneself) or punishment (where harm is done to others) (although Locke mentions only the latter case).

We can also, however, describe our property in ourselves with respect to other persons. From this perspective, we are masters of ourselves (II, 44). Our property includes a clear right to be free of the control of others; no other can rightfully use our body, mind, or labor without our consent.[101] Our freedom and "unquestionable" property in our person and labor (II, 27) are often characterized negatively in this way by Locke (as the right *not* to be used by others). Man has "a right of freedom to his person, which no other man has a power over, but the free disposal of it lies in himself" (II, 190). One's property in one's labor means "no man but he can have a right to what that is once joined to" (II, 27); it is something "another had no title to, nor could without injury take from him" (II, 32). The trustee has clear rights of noninterference held against others. Viewed more positively, our property in ourselves is the right to pursue our plans, to invest our actions and labors, to extend our sphere of rightful control (that which is private) into the world, and to alienate our rights in the pursuit of innocent projects.[102] With respect to other persons, our property in ourselves is simply obvious or "unquestionable."[103]

[101] See Becker, *Property Rights*, 37, 39; Ashcraft, *Locke's Two Treatises*, 128–30; Machan, *Individuals and Their Rights*, 139–40; Reeve, *Property*, 123–5; Christman, "Self-Ownership," 39.

[102] I have already suggested (in 5.1) that Locke sees all property as alienable, since property is limited to rights whose possession and transfer is nondestructive. It follows that our property in ourselves and our labor is also alienable. This does not mean, however, that we can destroy or give another absolute power over ourselves or our capacity to labor, for our rights in ourselves and our labor are only rights to use, control, alienate (etc.) them in ways that do not endanger ourselves or others. We have property in ourselves only within limits. We can rightfully do what makes us unhappy, but not what kills us. We can give up our freedom of action for a period and in certain respects, but we cannot become slaves by alienation. We can alienate our labor, but not if doing so endangers us (for we had no right in the first place to use labor or to refrain from using it in ways that endanger ourselves or others).

Labor *is* alienable (see Day, "Locke on Property," 212; Wood, *Capitalism*, 34; Schwarzenbach, "Locke's Two Conceptions," 149). It follows that labor can be sold

A related account can be given of the property we acquire in external things. God, the sole original proprietor of the earth He has made, has given it to mankind to use as we please in the exercise of our rights over ourselves. We may make property in parts of the earth (and inferior creatures), provided these takings fall

---

for a wage. As we have seen (4.1), Macpherson takes this fact to indicate Locke's acceptance of the wage relationship and unlimited appropriation even in the state of nature (*Possessive Individualism*, 214–21). Tully, by contrast, argues that it is anachronistic to find capitalist relations in Locke and that, in any event, Locke could not accept capitalism because it is coercive (*Discourse*, 142–43, 136–39). The first charge (of anachronism) is hard to sustain (see Wood, *Capitalism*, 44–45; Shapiro, *Evolution of Rights*, 141–44; Rapaczynski, *Nature and Politics*, 194; Cohen, "Structure, Choice," 305–6). What of the second charge? The debate revolves around Locke's remarks on the transactions between servants and their masters (e.g., II, 28, 85), so the question becomes: just what is the servant selling, and is it sold freely?

Tully claims that Locke's servants do not sell their labor power, to be directed by the master, but only sell a specific service to the master (as II, 85 seems to say). Free servants selling services are acceptable to Locke, but *not* wage laborers. On the other hand, Locke *does* say in II, 85 that the servant sells his service "for a certain time," and he specifically mentions "day labourers" in II, 41. One might try to maintain, of course, that the servant sells not his labor, but only the *product* of his labor (to which he is naturally entitled). Tully, for instance, claims that the servant who cuts the turfs (in II, 28) has natural property in them, which he alienates contractually to the master (*Discourse*, 140). But this is a hard view to maintain, given that servants often (indeed, typically) labor on lands or things that are *already owned* by the master; and it is only the *first* labor on something that makes natural property (I cannot come to own the chair you build by waxing it later on). Locke seems in II, 28 to say that the servant's labor belongs to the master ("the labour that was mine"), so that by "service" (in II, 85) Locke means not some "craft," a la Tully, but rather only labor for a certain time and purpose, within limits set by contract. Whether or not Locke's acceptance of the sale of labor is an endorsement of capitalism, it does seem to leave this open as a morally permissible possibility. But it is important to see that the sale of labor is not for Locke the alienation of freedom or of one's "labor power" in its entirety. We can sell our labor (capacity to labor) for a time (within limits on its use), for we can alienate parts of our "self-government." But we cannot alienate rights we lack, and we lack the right to entirely give up our freedom or labor power, since these are essential to our preservation. So it is, as Tully rightly claims, impossible to alienate our labor in *this* sense (although it is only morally, not "logically" impossible; see Tully, *Discourse*, 142, 138. See also Shapiro, *Evolution of Rights*, 140–41; Seliger, *Liberal Politics*, 163–65; Schwarzenbach, "Locke's Two Conceptions," 168n).

Is selling one's labor for a wage inherently coercive? Tully claims that wage laborers have no choice but to sell their labor power. Since Locke (in I, 42) says that agreements compelled using another's need are coercive and unjust, there can be no sale of labor. The servant is a freeman, and must have a free choice *not* to be a servant; if he has no such choice, he must be given relief, not forced to accept some master's terms (Tully, *Discourse*, 137–38). Wood responds by claiming that in I, 43 Locke allows that the choice (of the "needy beggar") to accept subjection rather than starvation *is* free and hence binding (Wood, *Capitalism*, 89–90).

Neither Wood nor Tully has read I, 42–43 carefully enough. Contra Wood, I, 43 is not condoning the "compact" into subjection of the needy beggar, but only arguing that *at most* only a contract, not *property in land*, could give one authority over

within the range of our entrusted rights. This means that the taking and use of external things must be nondestructive (i.e., consistent with the rules requiring the best preservation of mankind), accounting for the limits on property described by Locke: that we take no more than our fair share (or less than we need), that we not waste (or frivolously destroy) useful things, that we not use our property to harm others (or ourselves) (see 5.4 below). Within these limits, however, we may by mixing extend our private sphere to include external things, giving us the full Lockean package of rights over those things.

Viewed with respect to God, our property rights are not particularly strong guarantees, for God retains moral control over all of our property (and as settlor of the trust that gives us our rights, may withdraw the trust). Viewed with respect to others, however, our property rights are strong claims to freedom of action and to be allowed to (fairly and innocently) make and use property as we please. We are *neither* owners *nor* trustees or stewards. We are *both*.

> In respect of one another, men may be allowed to have propriety in their distinct portions. . . . Yet in respect of God the Maker of heaven and earth, who is sole Lord and proprietor

---

other men. Locke clearly condemns such compacts (in I, 42). But contra Tully, I, 42 does *not* say that if you have no choice but to work for another, you are entitled to charity; it says only that you must receive charity if you have *"no means* to subsist otherwise"* (my emphasis), and that you cannot be forced by need to become a "vassal" of another (Locke's contrast is throughout between servants, on the one hand, and slaves or vassals, on the other. See Cohen, "Structure, Choice," 306n). But a wage laborer is not a "vassal" in Locke's sense (although Tully seems to equate them—*Discourse*, 141), and he *does* have "means to subsist" (namely, the labor he sells). Indeed, Locke seems to accept as morally permissible the arrangement in which servants sell themselves to "drudgery" (service for a specified period of time, and limited by the master's duty not to kill or maim the servant); for this drudgery is *not* the same as *slavery* (II, 24) (see Waldron, *Private Property*, 226–29). Tully's claim that Locke worries about coercive economic arrangements is perfectly correct. But Locke clearly does not worry enough about this. For while Locke rightly assumes that the alienation of labor need not be coercive, he does not consider the full range of ways in which economic relations may be coercive.

[103] Secular versions of Locke's argument (such as libertarian ones) routinely begin with this premise as incontestable (since with respect to other persons, it is hard to see who could have as good a claim to a person and that person's labor as the person proper). Only *nonhuman* resources are "up for grabs" (an especially apt expression for making the point). This is a common position as well in popular debates about abortion, organ donations, and the like (see Reeve, *Property*, 123–25), and it is widely acknowledged to be "compelling" (Cohen, "Self-Ownership," 111). There are, however, competing views—such as Rawls' view that natural human assets should also be regarded as common property of the community, with rights over them to be determined. See Rawls, *Theory of Justice*, 102, 179; and Nozick's reply (*Anarchy*, especially 228–29). See also Miller, "Natural Right," 276.

of the whole world, man's propriety . . . is nothing but that
liberty to use . . . which God has permitted. (I, 39)

For Locke there is no inconsistency between the pictures of persons as holders of strong property rights and persons as stewards
or trustees for God. We are not *just* tenants on God's property. We
are also free, independent rational beings with moral worth and
"capable of dominion" (I, 30) of our own. These two pictures of
our property are for Locke one picture. Nor is this surprising,
given the transitional nature of Locke's moral-conceptual framework (as we saw in 2.4). Morality (and hence property) is for Locke
both between man and God *and* "between man and man" (II, 181).
By emphasizing both God's dominion over us and the rule of reason as the guide between persons, Locke provides the material for
both theological and secular derivations of the same conclusions
about property. Reading Locke in light of only one of these emphases neglects his true standing as an important transitional fig-
ure in the history of moral and political philosophy.[104]

5.3. Labor: Replies and Reconstructions

We have now seen the structure of Locke's two central arguments
for property in the products of labor. Of the first argument, the
argument from human needs and God's intentions, I will say relatively little. For, in large measure, it will stand or fall with Locke's
moral theory generally (as described in chapter 1), facing the same
problems that theory faces (e.g., weaknesses in the proof of God's
existence, in the inference to His intentions from human nature
and the nature of the earth, and in the use of rule-consequentialist
reasoning to derive specific duties and rights).[105] There are, however, two additional factual claims made by Locke in the argument
from human needs and God's intentions that seem to be at least
badly underargued (if not just obviously false). The first is the
claim that we require exclusive property in the earth's products
before they can be of any use to us in preserving ourselves (II, 26).

[104] It is thus not so much mistaken as onesided to read Locke as Tully does, or to
read Locke as utterly rejecting the "stewardship" view of property (as, e.g., Pangle
does, in *Republicanism*, 159). See Schwarzenbach's discussion of the "two conceptions of property" in Locke ("Locke's Two Conceptions").

[105] I do not mean by this to claim that a secular version of this argument cannot
be constructed, beginning with (say) negative community and trying to derive
rights from human needs. But the resulting argument would not, in my view, be
especially convincing even in its new secular form.

It seems so clear that use rights or access rights would also allow us to preserve ourselves, without any exclusive property rights, that we may wonder what Locke could possibly have in mind. I will take him to be trying (not very clearly) to make two points: (a) that self-government, not just self-preservation, requires exclusive property (see below and note 58 above), and (b) that mankind is best preserved with exclusive property. Point (b) is immediately related to the second controversial factual claim made by Locke in the argument from human needs and God's intentions: that labor and enclosure increase the "common stock of mankind" (II, 37). This is by no means obviously true (even as a *rule*), since (a) the benefits accruing to individual laborers and enclosers need not "trickle down" to those who have least, possibly creating an unused surplus rather than a greater "common stock"; and (b) a smaller number of large holdings, worked indifferently, need not yield more than a larger number of small holdings, worked intensively.[106] Further, however, there is no guarantee that mankind is best preserved by any arrangement that simply improves the lot of all (Pareto preferability is not Pareto optimality). Mankind might be best preserved if appropriation were limited sharply, leaving persons free to improve their position beyond what could be assured by widespread enclosure. I return to these questions in 5.4 below.

Criticisms of the mixing argument are more familiar from the literature on Locke, but they tend to focus on the argument of II, 27. I begin here, however, with the less discussed "incorporation" argument of II, 28. I have already claimed that this latter argument relies on the former for at least some of its force. But it is important to notice that it is also not obvious that one acquires a *right* even to what is ingested and incorporated into one's body (as Locke seems to suppose in II, 28). If I steal your banana and eat it, I do not acquire property in the banana simply because it has become part of me. You cannot get your banana back, of course. It no longer exists. But the situation is not different morally from one in which I burn the stolen banana, rather than eating it, thereby destroying it in a different way. The mere fact of incorporation is not morally interesting. If the banana somehow remained whole and undigested within me, but could be forcibly removed (without

---

[106] Labor increases the common stock only in the sense that laborers use less of the common stock to support themselves. But this, by itself, says nothing about what is in fact available for needy others. See Cohen, "Marx and Locke," 380–81; and Vaughn, *John Locke*, 105.

great harm to me), you might be able to lawfully invade my body to recover your banana. (If talk of bananas seems too silly, imagine that I stole from you a large diamond, subsequently swallowing but never incorporating or eliminating it.) The only thing of interest accomplished by the incorporation of stolen goods, is that it typically renders irrelevant the issue of recovery of (although not compensation for) the good.

The incorporation of unowned goods (the "fruit or venison" of II, 26, or the acorns or apples of II, 28) is no more of an incorporation than the incorporation of stolen goods. But incorporation of unowned goods is legitimate and would morally preclude the taking of those goods by force, even if this were possible. It follows, of course, that incorporation is not an independent, legitimate source of property, and that for it to be a legitimate act at all, it must be preceeded by a legitimate taking of the good subsequently incorporated. Legitimate taking, though, is accomplished by mixing our labor, which is already ours, with what is common, and so must be logically prior to incorporation as the source of property rights. Others may not remove from your mouth the acorns you are eating (or the acorn mush from your stomach) *not* because the acorns are then incorporated, but only because the acorns were previously legitimately taken. The acorns are just as much yours prior to your eating them as after; it is as wrong to take them from your pot as from your stomach (barring the harm done by the latter act, which could be completely eliminated by using a "transporter beam" to harmlessly remove the contents of your stomach, or partially eliminated by using a stomach pump). Ingestion does not make something *more* yours. It only makes issues of redistribution (by theft or law, say) less matters of practical concern and issues of compensation more central. It follows from these points, of course, that Locke's argument in II, 28 is confused, since he there tries to reason backwards from the obviousness of our property in the ingested good to cover less obvious property in what has only been taken from common. But ingestion simply does *not* make property more obvious.

What, then, of the labor-mixing argument of II, 27, which concerns the legitimization of takings from common? This argument has been subjected to withering criticism from all sides.[107] I recount below the most important counterarguments.

[107] Some of these attacks seem to me to clearly fail. Day, for instance, claims that Locke's central argument equivocates on "work" or "labour," conflating the sense in which this is an "activity" and the sense in which it is an "achievement" ("Locke

(1) "The idea of the mixing of labour is fundamentally incoherent"; some sort of category mistake is involved in speaking of literally mixing one's labor with an object. Actions (labor) cannot be mixed with objects.[108]

(2) "Why isn't mixing what I own [my labor] with what I don't own a way of losing what I own rather than a way of gaining what I don't?"[109] Locke cannot just *assume* that ownership of our labor continues after we employ that labor. Mightn't our property in it simply end once we use it?[110] We do, after all, "lose our labor" when we labor fruitlessly, so why not in other cases?

(3) Why shouldn't the *second* labor on an object ground property in it as reliably as the *first* labor? Locke seems to limit property to the first laborer, but subsequent laborers on the same object may labor more or more productively than the first.[111] Should subse-

---

on Property," 208–9). But if we try to take seriously the idea that what is ours (our labor) is invested in or mixed with nature, so that others would take what is ours if they took what we labored on, no equivocation on "labor" is necessary to make Day's version of Locke's argument valid. Day also, of course, attacks the idea that we might be meaningfully said to own our person or labor (ibid., 209–19). But we have seen above (5.2) and will see below that these Lockean claims make perfect sense, if they are read as simple restatements of our rights, within the limits set by the best preservation of humankind, to noninterference and self-government. In another attack on Locke's argument, Sartorius (following Epstein) claims that the labor-mixing argument is simply superfluous. For if mere *possession* of your body (and labor) gives you ownership of it, why shouldn't mere possession of external goods give you ownership of them? Why the requirement of mixing labor with external goods to ground property? ("Persons and Property," 204). The answer here must have two parts. First, since "taking possession" of a thing for Locke involves mixing labor with it, "possession" *is* sufficient for ownership (within the obvious restrictions and limits). Second, however, mere possession of one's body (and labor) is *not* what gives one property in it for Locke. As we have seen, this property can be derived either from God's trust or from its necessity for equality and self-government (noninterference) with respect to other persons.

[108] Waldron, "Two Worries," 37, 40–41 (the main arguments of this paper are repeated in *Private Property*, 184–91). See Hume, *Treatise of Human Nature*, 3.2.3.: "we cannot be said to join our labour to any thing but in a figurative sense."

[109] Nozick, *Anarchy*, 174–75. See also Becker, *Property Rights*, 40–41; "Labor Theory," 658–59; Miller, "Justice and Property," 6; Waldron, "Two Worries," 42; Sartorius, "Persons and Property," 204; and Fressola, "Liberty and Property," 315.

[110] Waldron argues that since I can't use or control my labor after I mix it with some object, my right to my *labor* is not really protected by giving me property in the improved object. Once my labor is freely used, it is no violation of my *liberty* (which is all the "ownership" of labor really amounts to) to take the object on which I have labored ("Two Worries," 43–44). In response to the first point we can note that if my right to my labor includes the right to keep it and exclude others from using it (as Locke supposes), then property in the improved object *does* protect that right (even if the expended labor can no longer be directly used or controlled, but only indirectly used through use of the object). As for the second point, we will see (below) that taking the object on which I have labored *may* be a simple violation of my right of self-government.

[111] Plamenatz, *Man and Society*, 1:246–47.

quent laborers not be entitled at least to compensation for their labor?[112] Locke seems to say that only with the owner's (*first* laborer's) consent is a subsequent laborer entitled to anything (except, perhaps, punishment for trespass). But isn't the second laborer's labor mixed with the object on which he labors as surely as the first's? Does not the original laborer take what is another's (i.e., the added labor) when he *keeps* an object upon which subsequent labor has been expended, just as much as the subsequent laborer would take what is another's (i.e., the first labor) were he to *take* the object from the original laborer?[113]

(4) Why should mixing one's labor with an object be thought to give one *full* ownership of the object (including the rights to exclude and alienate, say), rather than some more limited rights over the object (e.g., just a right of usufruct)?[114] If others are also denied full title to the object, the laborer's labor will not be "taken" or given to another as "right" or "title" (II, 27, 32).

(5) Locke's mixing argument also faces what we can call "the boundary problem." It is not obvious that labor can ground a clear right to *anything* if it is not possible to specify the boundaries of what is acquired by labor. But exactly what does labor get mixed with when one labors on what is common? When I enclose and grow a field of corn, I seem to acquire property in the fence and the enclosed land. Yet I actually touch or work on only some of the enclosed land. The ground between the furrows and between the field and the fence seems not to have my labor mixed with it. Can others rightfully come and use (or cart away) what my labor is not mixed with? If my labor mixes with what I have not actually worked on *within* my enclosure (so that others *can* be excluded), what stops it from mixing with land *outside* my enclosure (so that I get more than I bargained for)? And the boundary problem now has interesting applications that it did not have fifty years ago, since there is now a point in asking what one comes to own by labor (or *would* come to own, barring binding international treaties) when one's labor is mixed with the surface of the moon (or Mars, etc.). These are not easy questions to answer.[115]

[112] Seliger, *Liberal Politics*, 201.
[113] Waldron suggests that arguments from laborer's desert or the right of creation will be of no use to Locke, since they allow that entitlements may arise when one labors on what is already owned by another ("Two Worries," 38). Here, however, we see that the same problem seems to face the labor-mixing argument.
[114] Parry, *John Locke*, 52; Waldron, "Two Worries," 42.
[115] Could the United States have come to own the Sea of Tranquility by enclosing it and continuing to work it? If I plant my furrows of corn six yards apart instead

(6) Locke himself uses examples (e.g., in II, 43) that point to the social nature of production. But if the skills, tools, or inventions (etc.) that are used in laboring are not simply the product of the individual's effort, but are instead the product of a culture or a society, should not the group have some claim on what individual laborers produce? For the labor the individual invests includes the prior labor of many others.[116]

In the face of these many particular challenges to the mixing argument, it is natural to try to advance a more general challenge to the whole anticonventionalist program of Locke's labor theory of property acquisition. For conventionalists think their theory can explain not only the appeal of the labor theory but the reasons for its apparent weaknesses, thus offering a preferable overall conception of property rights. Property, on this alternative conventionalist account, is a purely conventional relation, not a natural one, with rules for acquisition, boundaries, and transfers (etc.) all determined solely by the conventions on which persons have actually settled. These conventions, of course, are not purely arbitrary, for people naturally tend to settle on those which are most useful for all concerned (see Hume's *Treatise*, book 3, part 2, for an approximation of this kind of conventionalist theory of property). But property could not exist *without* the establishment of such con-

---

of six feet apart, do I still own the whole field? Versions of this "boundary problem" critique are offered in Nozick, *Anarchy*, 174; and Mautner, "Locke on Original Appropriation," 261. Admittedly, the boundary problem seems a problem more for property in land than for property in moveables, since moveables have "natural boundaries" that might serve as "obvious" limits to appropriation (Olivecrona, "Locke's Theory of Appropriation," 227–28). For land, however, it seems a serious difficulty for the mixing argument. But might land, too, be thought to have "natural boundaries," like a cliff, an unfordable river, or a very steep incline? Olivecrona discusses enclosure and cultivation as if they are adequate for solving the boundary problem (ibid., 228), but we have seen that this cannot be the case if the mixing argument is taken seriously. It is also worth remembering that one can labor on land (and so, presumably, make property in it) without either enclosing or cultivating it (as in lumbering or strip mining).

[116] Grant, *Liberalism*, 112–13. Shapiro notes a related problem: that the development of productive capacities may depend in part on the labor of other individuals, such as spouses ("Resources," 57–58; see also Andrew, "Inalienable Right," 549–50). Day regards cooperation as an "insuperable difficulty" for Locke because of the problem of determining shares of a joint product from the amount, intensity, and skillfulness of the labor invested by various parties ("Locke on Property," 210–11). The truth is that Locke simply never discusses any cooperative ventures but those whose terms are settled in advance by the consent of the parties. Joint labor, in the *absence* of prior consent, would seem likely to generate joint property, with subsequent division (if any) to be determined either by consent or by some rough notion of natural fairness (based, I assume, on a sense of marginal productivity). We can only guess Locke's view on these matters.

ventions among persons. Labor seems a natural source of property, the conventionalist can concede, but this feeling of naturalness can be perfectly well explained by our internalization of the conventions on which property rests. These conventions are, for instance, enforced by law within civil society, so that we learn about the concept of property in terms of the conventions. But the conventional nature of what we learn is hidden from us, making the conventions seem (to people like Locke) to be laws of God and nature. Further, the conventionalist can concede that Locke is right (and the positivists wrong) about the possibility of property rights preceding or existing independent of the provisions of positive law, yet still deny that this makes property a natural relation. For conventions can arise prior to or independent of civil society and its legal system. Finally, the conventionalist claims to see why Lockeans have such a hard time supplying the details of a theory of property within the context of natural rights theory. These details are all matters of convention, not of natural moral relations. The boundary problem is a difficulty for Locke, for instance, because the boundaries of our claims are settled as a matter of convention. We cannot say how much land our labor on the moon would give us simply because there are as yet no clear conventions governing nontellurian appropriation.

Locke can accept, of course, the conventionalist's claim that the rules of property will be the most useful rules for mankind, for his own argument from human needs and God's intentions relies upon this claim. For Locke, however, usefulness (in preserving mankind) is related to doing God's will, not suiting human sentiments; and Locke's is an *ideal* rule-consequentialism, not a *conventional* rule-consequentialism like Hume's.[117] Locke can also, as we have seen (in 2.3), accept some conventional or legal *specification* of general moral rules: while God's law "forbids the vice, . . . the law of man often makes the measure of it" (ECT, 182–83). This seems to leave open the intriguing possibility of property rights whose *ground* is natural, but whose precise *content* is determined by convention or law.[118] But Locke can accept no more than this of the

---

[117] For Locke, the rules of natural law are the *best* rules to follow for preserving mankind (this is a maximizing consequentialism). For Hume, the rules of property are those actually accepted (conventionally determined) by humankind; while the rules are useful, they need not be ideal (maximizing) to be binding.

[118] While Tully's frequent pronouncements that for Locke property in civil society is conventional, or determined by positive law (see 6.1 below), create a different impression, in one place Tully says that in Locke "the particular rights men have

conventionalist theory of property. If he is to defeat the conventionalist challenge, his labor theory of natural property acquisition must be more clearly stated and better defended.

A plausible reconstruction of Locke's mixing argument must begin by specifying more carefully just what "labor" is. What, to take the first step, did Locke mean by "labor"? The examples of labor used by Locke involve a wide variety of free actions, such as gathering, hunting, cultivating, and reaping, and Locke seems in places to equate "the actions or labour of" a person (II, 44). Many of these actions (such as picking up acorns) involve no hard work (strenuous or demanding labor), so labor is not confined to what we might normally describe as "toil."[119] Nor is mere physical exertion, even if it is strenuous, sufficient to count as labor, since then animals (or perhaps machines) could labor and make property.[120] It is our "intellectual nature" that makes us "capable of dominion" (I, 30); the laborer must be acting freely and intentionally, not merely behaving. Labor for Locke, then, is action that is free and intentional,[121] aimed or purposive (in the sense of intending to produce a result of use to self or others).[122]

Not all free, intentional, purposive action can count as labor for Locke, however, for he seems to want to contrast labor at least with play or recreation.[123] One can make property *for* play, it seems (e.g., carve a bat from wood, or make a ball from hide and sawdust), but not *by* playing. Labor must be aimed at satisfying human needs or making human life more comfortable or convenient, in a way which play typically is not. I cannot make property in land merely by playing ball on it (although perhaps I might make property in the land by clearing and marking out part of my

---

in society are conventionally determined, albeit in accordance with natural principles" (*Discourse*, 171).

[119] Olivecrona, "Appropriation in the State of Nature," 224, and "Locke's Theory of Appropriation," 226; Christman, "Can Ownership Be Justified?" 172; Cohen, "Self-Ownership," 122.

[120] Rapaczynski, *Nature and Politics*, 186–87; "Locke's Conception of Property," 307.

[121] Labor must be *chosen*, and choice is only a possibility for rational ("intellectual") beings. This does *not* mean that the idea of "forced" or "coerced" labor is unintelligible. *Coercion* is consistent with freedom in this sense (the robbery victim may *choose* to hand over his money, even though the choice is made at gunpoint), but physical manipulation and compulsion (which produce bodily movement but *not* action) are not.

[122] Movements of my body caused by disease or the actions of others, say, or accidental conduct could thus not count as labor. See Becker, "Labor Theory," 654.

[123] In Locke's letters to Grenville, this contrast is clear. See Tully's discussion of this point (*Discourse*, 109).

fair share of land to serve as a baseball diamond). Nor can I make a property in land by simply walking over or occupying the land, unless I add to that occupation my labor on the land.[124] Labor must be aimed at a useful result.

But while labor must thus be intentional and purposive, labor cannot consist simply in *having* the intention to use a thing or a purpose for it. Intending to take X, thinking of X, declaring X one's own, wanting X, pointing at X, and seeing X first are all ways of *not* laboring on X. Labor must show enough seriousness of purpose to "overbalance" the community of things. In situations of competitive liberties (e.g., where anyone may make property in a thing by labor), the Lockean rule is "first come, first served." But to count as "first comer," an appropriate act must be performed; and for things of use the appropriate act for claiming them is to use them (i.e., labor on them to produce a result of use). One's labor need not be completed to "begin a property," but it must (to abuse legal language) constitute a real "attempt" and not "mere preparation." The hunter who chases the hare "has employed so much labour . . . as to find and pursue her" and "has thereby removed her from the state of nature, wherein she was common, and hath begun a property" (II, 30). Although the hare has not yet been caught, the hunter has invested sufficient labor in the hunt that another's taking it would constitute an injury, robbing the hunter of his labor.[125]

Some labor, it may be objected, constitutes such a small investment that it is hard to see how it is more of an injury to deprive a laborer of his product than, say, a planner of the object of his plan. One might easily spend more time and effort planning how to use the acorns in front of one than in actually gathering them. Why should "picking up" give title to a thing, but not "figuring out how to use" (or even "pointing to")? Locke's answer must be, I think, that picking up (and other kinds of labor) brings things within the immediate range of *use* for our purposes, in a way that thinking of or pointing to does not. Labor gives property because when we labor on a thing "we are so situated with respect to it, as to have it in our power to use it."[126] Physical *touching* may not be

---

[124] See Olivecrona, "Appropriation in the State of Nature," 225; and Ryan, *Property and Political Theory*, 33. Ashcraft notes that Locke's refusal to accept mere occupancy as a ground of property was also a rejection of the claims of idle, aristocratic holders of large estates (*Revolutionary Politics*, 281–82).

[125] Compare Locke's view with that of the Supreme Court of New York concerning the fox in *Pierson v. Post* (see Becker and Kipnis, *Property*, 28–32).

[126] Hume, *Treatise of Human Nature*, 3.2.3.

necessary (I can own the water in my pail, or the gold nuggets just uncovered in my mine); but one must have begun the physical process of making deliberate, productive use of one's property (body, labor) by altering nature. And to use a thing is to actually incorporate it into one's ongoing projects and pursuits.[127]

Let us try to think of labor in Locke's texts, then, not as a kind of substance, to be literally mixed or blended with an object, but as a kind of purposive activity aimed at satisfying needs or supplying the conveniences of life.[128] Labor in this sense can include (be mixed with) external things in a fairly straightforward way. As we think about, choose, or carry out various aspects of our life plans (our projects and pursuits), external things are often central to them. Indeed, control over certain external goods is a prerequisite for almost any typical life plan. We may first labor "internally" to produce a plan, idea, theory, or invention; but we must eventually labor on what nature provided to realize the plan (merely having the plan at most gives us property in the plan, not in the physical stuff necessary to realize it). We bring things within our purposive activities ("mixing our labor" with them) when we gather them, hunt them, enclose them, and use them in other productive ways. Grazing my cattle on a pasture counts as mixing my labor with it, for by doing so I bring it within the scope of a legitimate plan for use. This is why Locke can say that "the grass my horse has bit" is "my property," and explain it by claiming that "the labour that was mine" has "fixed my property" in the grass (II, 28). Labor and its product is thus not only an expression of and necessary condition for individual autonomy,[129] but a process of "objectifying" oneself in the world by making concrete what was abstract (as Hegelian and Marxist views of labor or property sometimes suggest[130]). "Mixing labor" in this way need not, of course, bring about any physical change in the object on which one labors. Gathering and catching mix labor and give property, but often don't change their objects. The object is changed only in the sense of being brought within my life and plans, by being made "a part of me," by being brought within the protective sphere of my prop-

---

[127] McNally, "Locke, Levellers," 30; Fressola, "Liberty and Property," 320–21.

[128] Becker, *Property Rights*, 33–34; Scanlon, "Thoughts about Rights in a State of Nature," 10. The account sketched below follows Scanlon's in many important respects.

[129] Rapaczynski, for instance, emphasizes that property is not just for consumption in Locke, but for self-sufficiency and autonomy (*Nature and Politics*, 172–75). See also Polin, "Justice," 269.

[130] See Wood, *Hegel's Ethical Thought*, 106.

erty (rights).[131] What I "add" to the thing on which I labor (II, 28) is its role in my purposive activities and the consequent right over it that I acquire.

Locke, of course, says none of this explicitly, but it helps to make better sense of what he *does* say. As we have seen, where the argument from human needs and God's intentions affirms a natural right of self-preservation, Locke's mixing argument begins with a broader right of self-government (control over one's body and labor), which is, of course, in part just a right of noninterference with respect to other persons. This emphasis on self-government, including control over one's plans and projects, is explicitly in Locke's texts. And property is an indispensable condition of self-government. Property does not, then, just insure survival; it is also the security for our freedom, protecting us against dependence on the will of others and the subservience to them that this creates (I, 41). Our "intellectual nature" makes us "capable of dominion" precisely because each is naturally free and the equal of any other; property secures that freedom and equality. Those who emphasize that property is essential to choice, freedom, or agency, then, capture an important part of the spirit of Locke's theory of property.[132]

Understanding labor as a kind of purposive activity, and the mixing of labor with an object as bringing the object within the activity, allows the Lockean to better respond to the attacks on the mixing argument noted earlier. While the mixing metaphor may not be the most felicitous way to express the idea, the *literal* mixing of labor that seemed so problematic (argument [1] above) is now replaced with a perfectly intelligible notion of "mixing labor." And

---

[131] Here the ideas of "mixing labor" and "incorporation" can be seen to come together. I have both invested my labor in the object (moved myself "outward") and brought the object within my own realm (moved it "inward"). The full variety of ways in which one can usefully employ nature is perhaps not adequately suggested by Locke's examples. I may use a tree, for instance, not only as lumber to build with, or as a source of nuts, but as an elaborately carved monument to my love for Claudette Colbert, as shade for my yard, as a model for my painting, and so on. All of these ways of "mixing labor" might give property, provided the use continues and others are not in need of the tree. That you could make better use of it than I am doing is simply irrelevant, unless you need it and it is surplus for me. It may seem that my examples involve "recreation," not labor. But if I may create a property in the baseball bat I carve (from unneeded wood) for use in recreation (as Locke would surely admit), then other work I do to make life more convenient or comfortable should create property as well.

[132] See, for example, Plamenatz, *Man and Society*, 1:249; Hospers, "Property," 271; Machan, *Individuals and Their Rights*, 142–46; Wheeler, "Natural Property Rights," 284–86; Gould, "Contemporary Legal Conceptions," 231–32.

mixing our labor cannot be a way of losing what we own, rather than acquiring what we do not (as argument [2] suggests), because what we own (our labor) is never "separated" from us. Our plans and projects, insofar as they continue, include those natural resources in which we have "invested our labor." Our purposive activities are inseparable from us. But why does only the *first* labor ground property, not subsequent labor on things already taken by another (as argument [3] above asks)? Because the right of self-government, from which property in external things is derived, is a right shared equally with all other persons. It is, as a result, a right only to such freedom as is compatible with the equal freedom of others. To try to control for one's own projects external goods that have already been incorporated into the legitimate plans of others, would be to deny to others that equal right. We may make property with our labor only in what is not already fairly taken as "part of the labor" of another.

Similarly, questions about the *extent* of property are better answered with the present understanding of labor and labor mixing. Labor grounds *exclusive* property rights, and not mere use rights, for instance (as argument [4] suggests), because property is not merely for self-preservation, but also for self-government. Self-preservation requires only rights of use or access, not exclusive property. Self-government is only possible, however, if the external things necessary for carrying out our plans can be kept, managed, exchanged (etc.) as the plans require.[133] Use rights will not suffice for any even moderately elaborate plans or projects. As for the social nature of production (the concern of argument [6]), the present line of argument can acknowledge that to the extent that our labor uses what is the property of others, it can create at best only a limited property of our own. (If I build my house with your axe and out of your wood, I cannot gain a clear title to the house.) If we use tools, skills, inventions, and the like, which are owned by society, society will have rights in the products of our labor. Even in contemporary society, however, many of these means to our ends are fairly purchased (e.g., education, with fees or tax dollars), given freely by parents, or simply parts of the collective wisdom of a society. And to suppose that society *owns* its collective wisdom seems to make nonsense of both the ideas of society and

---

[133] As Lomasky puts it, things that are *immune* are essential to our projects (*Persons, Rights*, 120–21).

of ownership. Such shared knowledge is no one's property and may be freely used by all.

Finally, this version of the mixing argument must address "the boundary problem" (the concern of argument [5] above). But our problem is no longer to specify what labor (as a "substance") has been literally mixed with; rather it is to specify the nature of our purposive activities. The amount of property that we make by our labor is determined by the nature of the activity.[134] We can take that which is necessary to our projects (and perhaps reasonable windfall products of those activities), but our property runs only to the boundaries of our implemented projects (and not to just whatever we might envision): it is "the spending [labour] upon our uses" that "bounds" our property (II, 51). Planting a field of corn gives one property not only in the corn, but in the land between the furrows and a reasonable amount around the boundaries (and perhaps as well to the gold nuggets uncovered while plowing); for these things are necessary to (or reasonable windfalls from) the activity of growing corn for the support of life. Laboring on the moon would give such property as was necessary to the activity in question. But it is important to see that the nature of our purposive activities specifies only the *maximum possible* extent of the property labor creates. Lockean property rights are subject to serious limits, all of which can be seen to be easily motivated by the present account of labor and labor-mixing.[135] For the right of self-government, from which property in natural resources is derived, is itself limited (to what is compatible with other natural equals being similarly entitled). The natural limits on property determined by the right from which it is derived are two: (1) One may only have property in what has been made a part and continues to be a part of one's purposive activities. We can make property only in what is actually labored on and continues to be used in our projects; what is spoiled, wasted, or lying unused is not anyone's property, but returns to (or remains) common.[136] (2) One may only appropriate by one's labor a fair share of the common. Taking property must not harm others, and taking too large a share of natural resources will make it impossible for others to

[134] Becker, "Labor Theory," 654.
[135] Contrary to Shapiro's claim that appropriate limits to property claims cannot be explained or motivated within a secular theory of property ("Resources," 56–58).
[136] Thus, of the three possible limits of property in Locke noted by Macpherson—the spoilage limitation, the sufficiency limitation, and the labor limitation (*Possessive Individualism*, 201–20)—the first and third can actually be cast as just *one* limit.

make property with their labor (and thus secure self-government). Some takings would constitute an "encroachment on the right of others" (II, 51). Fuller discussion of these limits follows in 5.4.

Now this has obviously been only the barest sketch of an account of natural property in the products of labor. But even in skeletal form, one consequence of the account is readily apparent. Insofar as the right of exclusive property in external things is derived from the right of self-government, justifiable property must be far more severely limited than is demanded by most existing (positive) systems of property. Most current systems of property permit exclusive rights in things that are *not* being used by their owners and in things that are in no way centrally related to the good of self-government. And most such systems permit levels of accumulation that guarantee dependence and subservience for the less fortunate, less ambitious, less talented, and less acquisitive. These aspects of legal property cannot be justified by appeal to a right of self-government (or even a right of noninterference), but would appear to require a *conventional*, non-natural justification (if they are to have any justification at all).[137] Our new question, then, must be this: how does Locke understand the natural limits on property, and how, if at all, can they be taken to permit the moral justification of modern legal property systems?[138]

[137] See Scanlon, "Nozick on Rights," 1–3; and "Liberty, Contract," 246–47.

[138] I have not yet included in the skeletal account above even the bare bones of a theory of property transfer or exchange. And, as Scanlon has noted, this continues to be a serious problem for the account of labor discussed above ("Thoughts about Rights in a State of Nature," 20–24; see also Waldron, *Private Property*, 260–62). For if we regard my transfer of property as the end of its role in my projects, the property simply reverts to common (rather than the right in it transferring to the one I intend to be the new owner); but if we take the transfer and subsequent use to be *part* of my plan for the property, then the new "owner" really has the property only on a kind of irrevocable loan from me (rather than acquiring full title). It is not, however, objectionally odd to suppose that a good's role in my projects and its role in the projects of one I intend as new owner might slightly "overlap." That is, my plans might include the successful transfer of property to its new owner, my rights in the property ending (only) when that plan is completed by the incorporation of the property into the new owner's projects. While this is still not exactly a transfer of my right to the new owner, the process does not leave the property at any point in common, nor does my property right in the object continue. This, I think, makes sufficient sense of the idea of transfer (which is not, to begin, a particularly perspicuous notion) to avoid dramatic counterintuitiveness.

As we will see, the limits on Lockean property (discussed below) may have to be applied to transfers as well as takings. Indeed, it seems far easier to justify limiting transfers than takings, since holding and using property typically seem more integral to self-government than exchanging it (see, for instance, Plamenatz's insistence on the need for a separate justification in Locke for the right of bequest [*Man and Society*, 1:244]; and Christman's observations about the relationship between

5.4. The Limits on Property

A full theory of natural property rights would specify (or deny) limits of at least three sorts on our property in external goods: (1) limits on the extent of any particular appropriation (i.e., how much we can acquire by laboring on some particular occasion); (2) limits on the total amount of property we can accumulate (which might include further limits on appropriations, limits on transfers and inheritances, etc.); and (3) limits on legitimate uses of our property. Locke discusses prominently (if nonetheless obscurely) the first and second of these types of limits, referring to them as the "bounds" of our property: "the same law of nature that does by [labor] give us property, does also bound that property too" (II, 31). And it is with the first and second kinds of limits on property that we shall be chiefly concerned in this section (and in chapter 6). The only limit on our *use* of property (our third kind of limit) suggested by Locke is the obvious one: we must use our property only in ways consistent with the requirements of natural law.[139] Within this limit, we may use our property as we please.[140]

Why, we might ask, should Locke recognize any limits (bounds) on natural property rights at all? Or better, why should the only

---

self-ownership and rights to benefit freely from exchanges ["Self-Ownership," 39]). Locke seems to worry relatively little about transfers, apparently taking consent to be sufficient for transfer and taking the *content* of property (its constituent rights) to remain constant across transfers (unless conditions are specifically annexed). But Gibbard seems correct in claiming that any argument Locke can advance in favor of perfectly free exchange will actually support not just "extreme ownership" and *pure* free exchange, but also much less dramatic (and more restrictive) market price systems ("What's Morally Special?" 21–25). Finally, I will not deal here with broader questions about when it might be morally wrong to *exercise* rights of transfer (e.g., to sell my Van Gogh or my cure for cancer to someone I know will immediately destroy it or hide it away forever).

[139] Ashcraft, *Locke's Two Treatises*, 85–86. Waldron is right to insist that this sort of limit should not really be thought of as a "property rule" at all, at least in its obvious applications. That I must not use my knife to murder you is not best regarded as a rule of the system of *property*, but rather as a specification of the more general *non*property rule that I must not murder (by any means) (Waldron, *Private Property*, 32–33, 49). Of course, to the extent that *all* rights are thought of as property, all rules forbidding the violation of rights can be counted as property rules (in the most general sense of "property").

[140] This is *not* to say that we may use our property as we please provided only that we do not directly harm others in the process ("My property rights in my knife allow me to leave it where I will, but not in your chest" [Nozick, *Anarchy*, 171]). Natural law for Locke sets limits on, for example, bequest (as we saw in 4.4) and imposes "positive" limits by requiring charity (see 6.3 below). Its limits on use of property are thus far more extensive than a mere prohibition of direct harm.

"limit" on our property not be the extent of our ability (or desire) to labor and appropriate?[141] We have already seen the start of an answer to this question. Labor is only "mixed" (in the proper sense) with what is made a part of and continues to be a part of our purposive activities; so there are natural limits (within a labor theory of property) set by the nature and extent of those activities. Further, however, since all persons possess *equal* rights to make property and not be excluded by others from doing so, additional limits on property are set by the conditions necessary for *all* to exercise these rights.[142] This second rationale for limits on property suggests another way of understanding Locke's thoughts about them: we can analyze the limits on natural property in Locke in terms of his conceptions of natural fairness and "shares" of the common.[143] Whatever a person takes that is beyond the "bound" on property set by the law of nature "is more than his share and belongs to others" (II, 31). The ideas of "shares" and a fair division of the original common (a division that allows all to freely labor and appropriate) appear over and over in chapter 5 of the *Second Treatise*, and it is worth being more explicit about just how these ideas motivate the Lockean limits on property.

The earth, remember, was given to mankind in common, no person having any exclusive rights in "parts" of the earth (and its resources), but all having the right to labor and appropriate such parts. Now suppose, first, that the "original community of all things" is intended by Locke to be a *negative* community. The earth can then be taken as unowned "manna from heaven"; and even so ardent an antiegalitarian as Nozick recognizes that justice or fairness seems to demand equal shares of manna for all involved.[144] Each may appropriate up to a fair share of what is made available to all, for all being natural equals, no other division

---

[141] What Macpherson calls "the supposed labour limitation" (*Possessive Individualism*, 214) and takes to be "overcome" by the alienability of labor (ibid., 214–20). See also Seliger, *Liberal Politics*, 145–47. I have already suggested, in a way consistent with Macpherson's point, that one's labor may be mixed with (one's projects may include) things actually altered by others (e.g., one's servants or one's horse). The "labour limitation" is thus not a limit set by what one actually touches or alters, but by what is made part of legitimate projects (what one "mixes one's labor with").

[142] Thus, there *does* seem to be a single, coherent rationale for all three of the commonly accepted limits (sufficiency, spoilage, labor) on property in Locke, contrary to Mautner's claim ("Locke on Original Appropriation," 261).

[143] On the idea of one's share of the common, see Tully, *Discourse*, especially chapter 5.

[144] *Anarchy*, 198, 219. See Waldron, *Private Property*, 279.

would as well respect the natural moral standing of everyone.[145] Further, however, principles of fair acquisition would not allow persons to take and hold what they cannot or do not use, for such appropriation (or holding) deprives others of the opportunity to use those goods. Frivolous appropriation of what others would put to use fails to respect the ends and projects of others and so is inconsistent with acknowledgment of their equal rights to self-government. We may, then, take only what we can use, up to a fair share of the whole of what is common. Where people's needs are not equal, fair shares may not be equal shares. But there is, in any event, a clear rationale for limits on natural property if the common with which we begin is taken to be negative.

Suppose, however, that Locke intends the original community to be *positive*, perhaps even as strong a positive community as joint property for mankind. What can be said about the possibility of fair division of joint property? Is not consent by all the commoners required for fair division, contrary to Locke's desire to preclude consent or compact as the foundation of property? Imagine that you and a group of friends pool your money (each contributing an equal amount) to buy a car. After purchasing the car there is still money left (perhaps a greater fiction than one's imagination can tolerate), and with the remainder your group purchases a large bag of macadamia nuts. May this joint property be justly divided without the unanimous consent of the owners? If you try to carry off your "fair share" of the car (the transmission, say, or the wheels), the other owners will be wronged by your action. For the car will be made by your appropriation far less useful for the others than it was when it was held intact by all jointly. The car is thus like the common in political society (of II, 35), which "would not be as good to the rest of the commoners as the whole was, when they could all make use of the whole." In such cases, unanimous consent by the owners is required for fair division. But what if you try to carry off or consume your fair share of the bag of nuts? Taking your share of the nuts leaves the shares of the other owners just as good as before you took yours (assuming, as seems reasonable, that a full bag has no special significance for anyone). None of the other owners is harmed by your appropriation of your share, so their consent to this division seems unnecessary to legitimate it.

The earth and its resources, according to Locke, are like the bag

[145] See Arthur, "Resource Acquisition and Harm," 345.

of macadamia nuts; "for he that leaves as much as another can make use of, does as good as take nothing at all" (II, 33; see also, e.g., I, 37 and II, 36). As long as each takes no more than a fair share of the earth's resources, the rest remains unspoiled for others, no other commoner is harmed, and no consent by the others is necessary. Whether the original community is negative or positive, though, appropriation must be limited to one's fair share to avoid wronging the others. Locke's acceptance of the fair division (without consent) of joint property is most clearly illustrated in his remark about "cutting the meat":

> By making an explicit consent of every commoner necessary to anyone's appropriating to himself any part of what is given in common, children or servants could not cut the meat which their father or master had provided for them in common, without assigning to everyone his peculiar part. (II, 29)

The meat, once given by the master, is the joint property of the group of servants. But each may take a fair share without the consent of the others, for no other is harmed by such appropriation. Here Locke again strongly suggests that he is thinking of the "original community of all things" as (what I called in 5.2) a "divisible positive community."

Whether Locke's original community is negative or positive, however, he is committed to the idea that lawful appropriation from the common must be limited to what we can use and to what is no more than our fair share. This is the core idea with which Locke begins. But the conclusions of his arguments are complicated by a variety of factors: the arrival on the scene of subsequent generations of would-be appropriators, the consequent increased demands on a relatively fixed pool of resources, the invention of money. We will need to see how these complications affect Locke's basic ideas about the fair division of the common.

But it may be that (this reading of) Locke faces a more immediate problem, for there seems to be more than one notion of a "share" at work in chapter 5. We have identified two distinct limits on natural property in Locke, and two quite different conceptions of "one's share of the common" would seem to be generated by them. The first limit is that set by the equal rights of others to appropriate and is usually referred to as "the Lockean proviso," "the sufficiency limitation," or "the no-harm requirement." It appears in the text as Locke's claim that labor gives property "at least where there is enough and as good left in common for others" (II,

27; see also II, 33). This limit would seem to define one's "share" as "a portion of the earth's resources as large and as good as the best share which could simultaneously be privately held by everyone with a right to appropriate." Here a "fair share" is (roughly) an equal share.

The second limit is that set by our own use of the good in question, and is commonly characterized as the "spoilage," "spoliation," or "nonwaste" limit.[146] Locke introduces this limit by saying that property is only given to us "to enjoy" (II, 31; see also I, 40): "as much as anyone can make use of to any advantage of life before it spoils; so much he may by his labour fix a property in. Whatever is beyond this is more than his share and belongs to others. Nothing was made by God for man to spoil or destroy" (II, 31; see also II, 37, 38, 46). This limit defines one's "share" as "whatever one can *use*," where "use" includes not only employment to satisfy needs and preserve oneself, but also use for whatever "might serve to afford him conveniences of life" (II, 37; see also I, 41). To take more than one can use is not only "dishonest," but "foolish" (II, 46) or "useless" (II, 51), for it both deprives others of opportunities and wastes one's own labor.[147]

The difficulty here, of course, is that the first limit seems to set one's "share" by its size (and quality) relative to what others can take, while the second limit sets one's "share" only relative to one's own capacity to use it. And there is no reason to believe that these two conceptions of one's share will even often dictate the same limits on appropriation. We may choose to solve the problem by simply rejecting the first limit and its associated notion of a share—that is, by arguing that Locke either never intended to defend or should never have attempted to defend the first limit (see below). For, among other things, Locke seems to say in one place, that one's share has nothing to do with its size (or quality): "the exceeding of the bounds of his just property not lying in the largeness of his possession, but the perishing of anything uselessly in it" (II, 46; earlier in this passage Locke seems to refer to "his just property" as "his share"). So perhaps the Lockean proviso, so central to so many readings of Locke, is not really a limit on property intended by Locke at all.

[146] For a brief general discussion of this limit, see Waldron, *Private Property*, 207–9.
[147] The text here (and elsewhere) directly contradicts Pangle's claim that avarice and unlimited acquisition in Locke are only imprudent, not sinful (*Republicanism*, 162).

In fact, the two notions of one's "share" described above are less distant from one another than the evidence thus far examined suggests, and I will argue that both notions are in fact intended by Locke as limits on property. We can begin to see this by asking of Locke's first limit, "enough and as good in common" *for what*? The answer is: enough and as good for others to *use*. Appropriation within one's share was not "any prejudice to any other man, since there was still enough and as good left, and more than the yet unprovided could *use*" (II, 33; my emphasis). Both notions of a share are relative to use. One is relative to what the taker can use; the other is relative to what must be left if others are to be free to use things similarly. These are obviously still distinct notions of one's share of the common, but they are related notions and can function together consistently (and were, I believe, intended by Locke to function) as follows. The freedom of others for similar use sets, as it were, the outside limit of our share; the most that we can legitimately appropriate is a "fair share" of the common, in our first sense of "share" (i.e., a portion that leaves enough and as good for all others). The inside limit of our share is set by our own capacity to use what we appropriate; whatever is wasted *within* the outside limit is also more than our share. Violating either the outside or the inside limit is unjust (wrong).

In chapter 5 of the *Second Treatise* Locke uses the idea of our "share" primarily to refer to the inside limit. The reason for this is that he is writing primarily about original appropriation, which took place at a time when there were plenty of resources available to any who wanted them. The outside limit was simply not an issue, since no person was at that time capable of appropriating enough for it to be "any prejudice to any other man" (II, 33; see also, e.g., II, 37). Once land and other external goods began to become scarce, however, the outside limit (on "largeness of possession") *did* become an issue, and people's titles to large shares became as a result unclear (as we will see below). Why, then, does Locke say (in II, 46) that the "bounds of just property" concern only waste (our inside limit) and not "largeness of possession" (our outside limit). First, of course, because he imagined that the "invention" of money (the concern of II, 46) took place in a time of plenty, when the outside limit was not yet an issue. Second, however, Locke (in II, 46) essentially equates *useful* things with *perishable* things, and the "largeness of possession" that Locke there denies as a limit to just property is explicitly largeness of possession of *useless* (i.e., nonperishable) things. Now since the outside limit on property is set by others' freedom to use the earth's resources, the "heaping up" of useless things is simply irrelevant to concerns about leaving enough and as good for others. We need not, then, read II, 46 as denying the outside limit on natural property. And there are, of course, good reasons to believe that Locke would not have wanted to discard the outside limit. For Locke cannot really want to claim that a person who was simply able to *use* all of some nonperishable resource could legitimately hoard all of it against future needs, regardless of what sort of resource was at issue. One who appropriated (and subsequently managed to use) all of the earth's supply of salt, coal, or oil (*useful* nonperishable resources) would surely be working contrary to God's plan (to give the earth to mankind for the comfortable preservation of all).

If one finds textual support for both limits on property (i.e., "nonwaste" and leaving "enough and as good"), as I do, it is easy to understand why both should be present, given the moral theory (or theories) with which we have seen Locke operates. For both limits (and their corresponding notions of "shares") can be easily motivated by either deontological or rule-consequentialist reasoning (concerning the best preservation of humankind). The deontological arguments for these limits from natural fairness and the right of self-government we have seen already; they are, of course, closely related to the Kantian objectives of treating all persons as equals (respecting others) and avoiding using others as mere means. Rule-consequentialist arguments for both limits are also simple to construct. For waste is clearly contrary to the best (i.e., most efficient) preservation of humankind, as is the exclusion of some from the right to appropriate their fair share of nature's bounty, when others have more than enough for their own needs. Central to both styles of justification and to both limits on property in Locke is this idea: that no person should be *dependent* on others for preservation, unless that person is incapable of self-support.[148] God never intended for persons to have to "depend upon the will of a man for their subsistence," but rather gave each the right to provide for self from "the materials whereof [God] had so plentifully provided for them" (I, 41). For Locke, preservation and self-government (independence) are what property is for, and they consequently determine as well the limits on property. To see this more clearly, I want to look more carefully at both limits and at the

[148] See Tully, *Discourse*, 169.

ways in which they are complicated by the increasing shortages in natural resources and by the invention of money.

(1) *Waste.* I will deal first with what I have called the second limit, for it is in certain ways less confusing and controversial than the first. This limit sets the bounds of natural property at what we can "enjoy," "use . . . to any advantage of life before it spoils" (II, 31), or employ to afford ourselves the "conveniences of life" (II, 37). One kind of "use" explicitly permitted by Locke is the accumulation of goods we do not plan to use ourselves, but which we will trade (before they spoil) for goods that we (or our families) *will* use (II, 46). (Presumably, after such bartering, the responsibilities for not wasting the goods at issue simply change hands along with the goods.) This limit on property is often taken to limit our just holdings to those goods we *need* (or will trade to others who need them for other goods we need),[149] but Locke quite explicitly allows accumulation for comfort and convenience, not just need-satisfaction.[150]

Locke writes as if he takes the requirement of use to be equivalent to the demand that nothing "spoil" or "perish" in our possession. Indeed, all of the central passages in which this limit is discussed (II, 31, 37, 38, 46) state it both in terms of use and in terms of spoilage. But these two requirements clearly are not equivalent. Natural resources that do not spoil (like coal or oil) can still clearly be wasted (i.e., not used at all or destroyed frivolously).[151] Locke's real concern, I think, must be with *productive use* (and waste), *not* spoilage. For goods are only a part of our purposive activities when they are *used* by us. It is productive use of a good that brings the right of self-government into play in the first place, since it is no limitation of my self-government for you to take what I will not use. Further, some productive uses of goods involve *allowing* them to spoil (some foods and beverages are made in this way, and some agricultural techniques involve allowing crops to "rot on the ground" or "perish without gathering" [II, 38]). Locke cannot have intended to ban such uses of natural resources. It is not, then, *spoilage* that should be prohibited by this limit on natural property, but *waste*—where waste includes not only holding without using, but frivolous destruction (both of which deny others the

[149] See Lemos, *Hobbes and Locke*, 148, and "Locke's Theory of Property," 235; and Ashcraft, *Locke's Two Treatises*, 131–33.
[150] As Seliger rightly notes (*Liberal Politics*, 151).
[151] Reeve, *Property*, 157.

opportunity of productive use). We must not "waste the common stock" (II, 46).

It is initially hard to see why wasting resources should be not just foolish but also wicked, and further, why it should be taken to "rob others" and "invade our neighbor's share" (II, 31, 37, 46).[152] It is, of course, not the best use of resources to waste them and we know God intends for them to be used for our preservation and comfort (which perhaps establishes the wickedness of waste). But if enough and as good is left for others, why should my waste be taken to harm them in any way? If I waste what others would otherwise use, I deny them the opportunity of productive use (and show that I do not respect them or their projects). Since their right is to make property by their labor in whatever fair share of the common they choose, I infringe their right by precluding their choice of the goods I waste.[153] One who has wasted resources has thus "offended against the common law of nature" and is "liable to be punished" (II, 37). Waste harms others, even in conditions of relative plenty (where even after the waste there is still enough and as good in common for others to use).[154]

Lady Masham tells us that Locke's personal attitudes matched his philosophical convictions about waste: "Waste of any kind he could not bear to see . . . nor would he, if he could help it, let anything be destroyed which could serve for the nourishment, maintenance, or allowable pleasure of any creature."[155] We know (from the same source) that Locke abhorred idleness. The idle holding (or destruction) of what could be used by others, then, whether the held goods spoil or not, will be morally objectionable. Land, of course, doesn't "spoil" in any very literal sense when it lies unused; the grass may or may not rot on the ground (depending on the climate and the kind of grass). But land can be *wasted*

---

[152] Among those who have expressed skepticism about Locke's claims on this score are Ryan (*Property and Political Theory*, 36–37), Olivecrona ("Appropriation in the State of Nature," 228), and Mautner ("Locke on Original Appropriation," 264).

[153] Legitimate appropriation likewise denies others the opportunity of productive use; but it does not infringe their rights, for it removes the appropriated objects from the common, and the rights of others are only to take freely from what is common. Waste makes taking some of what is common (the wasted goods) physically impossible or very difficult (or dangerous), and so violates others' rights of free access to the common.

[154] This seems most obviously true where the "plenty" that remains is inconveniently located (e.g., in America). Locke thus has an answer to those who claim that the "spoilage" limit is either irrelevant (in conditions of plenty) or inadequate (in conditions of scarcity). For this criticism of Locke, see Plamenatz, *Man and Society*, 1:242–44; and Goldwin, "John Locke," 490.

[155] Fox Bourne, *Life*, 2:536.

(e.g., by the idle rich) by lying unused. Locke's concern is not that we may squander our labor[156] (which is only foolish) or that something may spoil in our care (which may or may not be bad). His concern is with the waste of natural resources, the waste of all that can be made useful for the support of life.[157]

Some questions remain about how the "waste limit" is actually to be applied in practice. For instance, are we to take it as a limit on taking (appropriation) or on holding? Does the waste limit require that I only take by my labor as much as I can reasonably expect to use? Or does it allow me to take as much as I will, but establish the forfeiture of my property rights in anything that I do not actually use (i.e., whatever I stop using or never incorporate into my plans at all)? Locke is less than clear on this point. In II, 31 he writes in introducing it as if the waste limit is a limit on *taking*: "so much he may by his labour *fix a property in*" (my emphasis). But other passages strongly suggest that a person might take "as many . . . as he could" of the earth's resources and thereby "acquire a property in them," but that what "perished in his possession without their due use" or lay "waste" reverted to common "and might be the possession of any other" (II, 37–38). Each "had a property in all that he could affect with his labour. . . . He was only to look that he used them before they spoiled" (II, 46). I suspect that Locke intended the waste limit as a limit on both taking and holding; and such a position is perfectly consistent. We may take only so much as we can reasonably expect to use (for any of our projects, barter included), for to take more deprives others of the opportunity of using what will almost certainly turn out to be in excess of our needs. But further, if any of what we took and reasonably expected to use was not *actually* used by us, or is no longer being used by us, we forfeit our rights over it; for, again, to hold it unused is to deprive others of the opportunity of productive use of this idle surplus.[158] Reading the waste

---

[156] As Rapaczynski claims (*Nature and Politics*, 212–13).

[157] This should include as well the waste of useful *nonperishable* things (although, as we have seen, Locke seems not to recognize in II, 46 that there exists such a class of things). That point, of course, suggests that Locke *should* be prepared to condemn the waste of money (by, say, profligate spending). Money, although useless and nonperishable in itself, is exchangeable for what is useful for the support of life. Its waste thus qualifies not only as foolish, but as wrong. See Ryan's remarks on the waste of money (*Property and Political Theory*, 38); and note 196 below.

[158] It is not clear, on this "other-regarding" rationale for the waste limit, that I do wrong if I waste what no one else wants or what would go unused even if I did not take and waste it. Waste even in these circumstances, however, is contrary to God's plan (although *why* God would condemn such waste is unclear).

limit in this way as a dual restriction on property, then, not only follows naturally from Locke's justifications for taking waste to be wrong, but makes as well the best sense of Locke's various remarks in chapter 5.[159]

(2) *Enough and as Good for Others.* I have read this limit on natural property rights (our "first limit," above) as a limit set by the equal rights of others to appropriate. The point of property rights being to secure preservation and self-government for all mankind, we may appropriate by our labor only our fair share of the common, leaving for others their shares and the opportunity to appropriate within them. For that reason, I will call this limit the "fair share limit," and will understand the requirement that enough and as good be left in common for others as limiting each to appropriation only within a fair share of the common. This is, however, a controversial interpretation and requires extensive defense. Indeed, it needs to be shown that Locke intended the "enough and as good" clause as a restriction on appropriation at all, before we try to understand just what kind of a restriction it is. My defense of the above interpretation will thus proceed in that order.

Some have seen the "enough and as good" limit as the most important limit on property in Locke (although they would *not* describe it as a "fair share limit"), a limit that renders the waste limit pointless or of distinctly secondary importance.[160] This is at best an odd reading of the *Second Treatise*, given how prominently the waste limit is presented and repeatedly stated throughout chapter 5. The fair share limit, by contrast, is mentioned only in passing in the early portions of chapter 5. Those facts alone seem to limit the plausible readings of the text to two: that Locke intended that *both* limits be taken as serious restrictions on appropriation,[161] or that he intended the waste limit to be the *only* restriction on appropriation.[162]

[159] Tully may hint at such a "dual restriction" reading of the limit (*Discourse*, 121–22). Mautner notices the problems discussed in this paragraph and charges Locke with an inconsistency; but the "inconsistency" depends on Mautner's (mistaken) contention that for Locke labor must be a sufficient condition for appropriation ("Locke on Original Appropriation," 264–65).

[160] Nozick provides the most prominent example of this view (*Anarchy*, 175–76). See also Lemos' claim that spoilage is to be defined in terms of what is enough and as good (*Hobbes and Locke*, 148; "Locke's Theory of Property," 235), and Drury's comments on this point ("Locke and Nozick," 29).

[161] This reading is favored by Macpherson, Seliger, Ryan (*Property and Political Theory*, 17, 36), Snyder ("Locke on Natural Law," 739–40), Reeve, (*Property*, 133), Shapiro ("Resources," 49), Medina (*Social Contract Theories*, 37), and many others (listed in note 2 of the paper by Waldron discussed below).

[162] This reading is defended by Strauss (*Natural Right*, 239–40), Plamenatz (*Man and Society*, 1:219–20), Polin ("Justice," 269), Waldron ("Enough and as Good"),

I have suggested that the former view is correct. But the latter has also been ably defended. It can reasonably be argued that the enough and as good clause was never intended by Locke as a limit on or necessary condition for property acquisition; Locke presents it rather only as a *sufficient* condition for labor to ground property, with the waste limit as the only real restriction on appropriation.[163] "That there is enough and as good left in common for others, is seen by Locke as *a fact about* acquisition in the early ages of man, rather than as a natural limit or restriction on acquisition."[164] Locke is *not* saying, the argument goes, that appropriation wouldn't be legitimate if there were *not* enough and as good left for others. The fact that there was always enough and as good left after a taking is a fact that changed with the conditions of scarcity in later ages. But this change (and the limits on our options that it introduced) has to be accepted, since others' having taken more than would leave enough and as good for us was not immoral.[165] Further, if the enough and as good clause *had* been intended by Locke as a limit on property, it is not clear how this limit could be overcome once the abundance of the first ages was no more. Macpherson's answer is inadequate, and no other candidate readily suggests itself.[166] But if Locke did not intend this clause as a limit in the first place, he needn't say anything at all about the problem of scarcity in later ages.

The problem with this reading, is that Locke *does* seem to want to say things about the problem of scarcity. He says, for instance (as we will see below), that mankind has consented to the inequality of later ages through their consent to the use of money. But it is unclear why Locke would think such consent necessary to justify inequality if there were in the first place nothing naturally unfair about or wrong with the distribution of resources in these later times of scarcity. Indeed, Locke's basic position on property, as I

McNally ("Locke, Levellers," 28), Mautner ("Locke on Original Appropriation," 260), and Drury ("Locke and Nozick," 32–34).

[163] Waldron, "Enough and as Good," 320–21; *Private Property*, 211–18.

[164] Ibid., 321–22. See also Mautner ("Locke on Original Appropriation," 260) and Olivecrona ("Locke's Theory of Appropriation," 229–30). Drury distinguishes between what is called "the natural limit on appropriation" (that in the "first ages of the world" people were physically incapable of taking so much that enough and as good would not be left) and what is called "the moral limit" (which is just the waste limit) ("Locke and Nozick," 33–34).

[165] Waldron, "Enough and as Good," 322–24.

[166] Ibid. Some have dealt with problems of scarcity by saying that Locke just falsely assumes a continuing condition of bounty in the world. As far as I know, the only author who claims that Locke assumes the opposite condition of permanent *scarcity* is Parsons ("Locke's Doctrine of Property," 405–7).

have described it above, seems to require him to say that even when abundance of natural resources is no longer part of our condition, individuals are *still* naturally permitted to take no more than their fair share of the available common. Even if my fair share of the bag of nuts is less than I'd like or could use, I am still at liberty only to take my share. To take more robs others (or makes necessary their consent to the process). Under conditions of scarcity we may take only small shares of the common; or scarcity may (as many Levellers argued) make appropriation altogether illegitimate. If it is possible to productively use the undivided common, but impossible to use it productively if it is fairly divided among all those with claims, it must remain common (imagine a fair division of available land that leaves each with a lot one yard square). No person is naturally entitled to be the one who enjoys a large share, while others have none. (This, as we have seen, seems to be part of Locke's point in II, 35, when he denies the legitimacy of division of the common within contemporary political societies.) All of this is true, however, only if the commoners have not consented to different arrangements. And Locke notoriously argues that they *have* so consented in their consent to money. It is this consent that Locke uses to legitimize appropriations in later ages that exceed our fair share of God's bounty.[167]

Nor is this all that can be said in favor of reading the fair share limit as a natural restriction on property in Locke. It is certainly correct to claim that Locke regards there being enough and as good left in common for others as a fact about appropriation in the first ages. But its being a fact in no way precludes its also being a

---

[167] Even, then, if no acts of appropriation in a world of scarcity would satisfy Locke's fair share limit, as is claimed by, for example, Thomson ("Property Acquisition," 666) and Waldron ("Enough and as Good," 325), it does not follow that the fair share limit is not a natural moral limit on property (i.e., one that holds in the absence of consent to different rules). Nor does it follow, as Waldron claims (ibid., 325–26), that the limit must be contrary to God's intention that mankind be preserved, since it would require nonappropriation in conditions of scarcity. Locke never really considers conditions of extreme scarcity, since he takes God to be a bountiful provider. But in conditions of *genuine* scarcity (where all will die if goods are divided fairly—as in "lifeboat ethics" cases), it is not obvious that on Locke's view God would prefer that some save themselves without regard for the rest (or, for that matter, save some others without regard for themselves). He might well prefer that all consent to some useful rule for dividing the limited stock of goods. Indeed, if the fair share limit did not bind people in such situations of scarcity, one person might legitimately take food that could keep two alive, since (as we will see in 6.3) Locke holds that we are otherwise entitled to take and keep enough to keep ourselves *comfortably* alive (supplying needy others only out of what is beyond this amount).

natural moral limit on property. Indeed, Locke's actual remarks about appropriation in times of abundance suggest that the enough and as good clause is intended by Locke as a limit of some sort. Locke suggests again and again that it is because of the abundance of resources in the first ages that "there could be *then* little room for quarrels or contentions about property" taken by labor (II, 31; my emphasis). "There could *then* be no reason of quarrelling about title, nor any doubt about . . . largeness of possession" (II, 51; my emphasis), "no doubt of right, no room for quarrel" (II, 39), no "reason to complain, or think themselves injured by this man's encroachment" (II, 36). The clear implication is that in later ages, when scarcity *is* a problem, there is room for doubt about titles, rights, and largeness of possession.[168] The satisfaction of the fair share limit is a natural condition for clear, indisputable title to the products of our labor. Taking only our share is like taking nothing (II, 33). Taking more than our share without the consent of the other commoners injures others; it sets up a conflict between our property in the labor we have invested and their right to take a fair share of what God gave to all in common. Claims based on labor then become unclear and need to be settled (see 6.1).

It is not enough to say that there are other, stronger restrictions on accumulation in Locke that will do the same job as the fair share limit, so that Locke does not really need the limit.[169] While Locke does say that we must help those in need, the requirement is only that we satisfy their basic needs (see 6.3 below). The fair share limit, by contrast, assures no one what is needed, but does secure for each a fair opportunity to acquire property—including the opportunity to acquire not only what is needed, but also what will provide comfort and convenience, allow the pursuit of personal projects, and stimulate the moral development that accompanies these.[170] The right of charity secures for each a claim on what is needed. The fair share limit preserves for each an opportunity for independence and self-government, not just self-preservation.[171]

---

[168] Waldron claims that this does not follow logically from Locke's other claims (*Private Property*, 210), which is, of course, correct. But it is possible for a conclusion to be clearly implied without being logically entailed (as, I maintain, is true in this case).

[169] Waldron, "Enough and as Good," 326–28.

[170] See Freeden, "Human Rights and Welfare," 499.

[171] This is presumably why so many have taken the Lockean proviso to be abso-

When Locke suggests that our appropriations must do no "harm" or "prejudice" to others (e.g., I, 37; II, 33, 36, 37), then, I take him to mean we must leave others free to exercise their rights of self-preservation and self-government (note that "prejudice" seems to mean "intrenching upon the right of another" in II, 36). We must initially leave others free to appropriate a fair share of the common. In this sense of "injury," anyone can take what injures no other.[172] Locke is obviously not, then, prohibiting just any appropriation that worsens another's situation in *any* way. *Any* appropriation makes some other worse off in some way, if only in the loss of the opportunity to appropriate that particular thing.[173] Locke is prohibiting appropriation that denies others an opportunity equal to one's own for self-preservation and self-government.[174] Such appropriation is naturally wrong (or unjust), and only the consent of the other commoners can justify it.

Locke, then, initially seems to be defending what has been called a "stringent" version of the Lockean proviso.[175] "Someone may be made worse off by another's appropriation in two ways: first, by losing the opportunity to improve his situation by a particular appropriation or any one; and second, by no longer being able to use freely (without appropriation) what he previously could."[176] A stringent proviso prohibits both ways of worsening another's situation; a weak proviso prohibits only the second.

---

lutely essential for the plausibility of any labor theory of property acquisition (see Becker, *Property Rights*, 46).

[172] Thomson, "Property Acquisition," 665–66.

[173] Parry, *John Locke*, 55–56; Gauthier, *Morals by Agreement*, 202–3; Schmidtz, *Limits of Government*, 20. Cohen argues that Locke in fact means to require appropriators to leave enough and as good as others had access to before the appropriation, *not* just to leave as much for all others as is appropriated ("Self-Ownership," 124–25n). But he acknowledges that the "enough" in Locke's "enough and as good" makes little sense on his reading. If, however, "enough" is read to mean "enough for similar use," as on my reading, Locke's use of "enough" makes perfect sense.

[174] The fair share limit is thus crucial in restricting ownership of the means of production (see Becker, *Property Rights*, 34, 43; "Labor Theory," 662). It might be argued that having a system of property at all could constitute an injury to some, such as the severely handicapped, since they will lose their liberty to use the whole of the common while gaining no advantage from the property system (Gibbard, "Natural Property Rights," 239). But if restrictions on appropriation are sufficient to insure that their opportunities for self-preservation and self-government are not lessened by the appropriation of others, as Locke believes, private property will not count as an injury to them of the relevant sort.

[175] The terminology is Nozick's. Nozick in fact concedes that Locke "may have intended" a stringent proviso, despite Nozick's own preference for a weaker version (*Anarchy*, 176).

[176] Ibid.

With only the weak proviso in force,[177] we are prohibited from doing things that make others materially worse off; but this is compatible with appropriating in ways that preclude *their* appropriations altogether, provided only that they are compensated for this loss. Those who favor a stringent proviso[178] insist that others must be left free to make similar appropriations, to protect their full range of opportunities and prevent their dependence on those who appropriate first. It is easy to see why Locke might be thought to be defending either of these positions. His emphasis on independence and self-government clearly favors reading Locke as defending a stringent proviso. But his apparent acceptance of the "plight" of contemporary, landless freemen, who must earn a living working on the property of others, favors a reading of Locke that includes only the weaker proviso (as in Macpherson's interpretation, for instance).

We need not choose between these readings, however, for we do not yet have before us the full range of possible positions. Locke's true position on the fair share limit falls between and is more plausible than either of these two extreme readings. What must be protected from encroachment by the appropriations of others, remember, is my rights of self-preservation and self-government. This is *not* identical to claiming that I must be left free to appropriate land or other natural resources. If my rights can be secured *without* my freedom to appropriate, I may still have my fair share of God's bounty. What must be guaranteed to each person is the opportunity of *a living*[179]—a condition of nondependence, in which one is free to better oneself, govern one's own existence, and enjoy the goods God provided for all. This requirement is weaker than the stringent proviso, since it is consistent

---

[177] As favored by Nozick and, for example, Gauthier (*Morals by Agreement*, 203–4). Macpherson favors the weak proviso as a reading of Locke, although not, as far as I can see, as a defensible moral rule. Winfrey also accepts a reading of Locke in which Locke defends only the weak proviso ("Charity versus Justice," especially 435), as does Kymlicka (*Contemporary Political Philosophy*, 111).

[178] Among those who seem to favor more stringent versions of the proviso are Bogart ("Lockean Provisos," 833–34), Sarkar ("Lockean Proviso," 53), Christman ("Can Ownership Be Justified?" 175), Cohen ("Self-Ownership," 127–29), and Kymlicka (*Contemporary Political Philosophy*, 112–13). Drury ("Locke and Nozick," 33) and Rapaczynski (*Nature and Politics*, 208–9) read Locke as intending the stringent proviso.

[179] See Ryan, *Property and Political Theory*, 17, 45–46; *Property*, 69. I am not sure that my characterization of a "living" in terms of nondependence is what Ryan has in mind; but we will see further support for this reading in 6.3. For related views, see Macpherson, *Possessive Individualism*, 212; Vaughn, *John Locke*, 107; and Schmidtz, *Limits of Government*, 26–27.

with one's being unable to appropriate. But it is stronger than the weak proviso, for it requires not only an unreduced level of material well-being, but independence and opportunity. In the first ages, nature supplied the material for a living to all. In later ages, where some were denied access to land and resources, titles to the products of labor became unclear. By "consent" to the use of money, all consented to unequal holdings of natural goods; but none consented to *dependence*. What must be guaranteed to contemporary free persons, in order to satisfy the fair share limit, is no longer access to a *fair* or *equal* share of goods (their "consent" modified that requirement). It is instead, according to Locke, access to an independent livelihood. Locke far too optimistically assumes that this has been (or could easily be) secured in his own society, for he dramatically underestimates the constraints on independence that are imposed by the superior economic position of others (thus, he can blithely characterize servants as freemen who sell their services to others, but who are not really under the others' control [II, 85]). But the requirement that appropriation leave others the opportunities for self-preservation and self-government seems in itself a plausible candidate for a natural moral limit on property, regardless of how inadequately Locke may have attempted to apply this limit in evaluations of his own society.[180]

Much has been written about the problem of the "baseline" for comparisons in applying the Lockean proviso: appropriation must make "people no worse off than they would be *how*?"[181] This is not, however, a problem for Locke. Each appropriation must simply leave enough and as good of the relevant goods in common for others, if there is no alternative way to secure the rights of others to self-preservation and self-government. The only relevant baseline is the condition of others prior to the appropriation. Appropriation must initially leave others with no less opportunity to exercise their rights (to a fair share) than they had before the appropriation took place. After consent to the use of money (and the resulting inequality), appropriation must leave all at least able (if not perhaps as able as before) to preserve and govern themselves.

[180] Waldron argues that a principle of acquisition of property by labor brings onerous obligations into the world for us, on the basis of the unilateral actions of others; it is thus not a principle to which rational contractors could agree (*Private Property*, 267–78). But Locke's strong fair share limit guarantees that the obligations imposed on us (to respect the property acquired by others) will *not* be intolerably onerous (as Waldron may concede—ibid., 281–83).

[181] Nozick, *Anarchy*, 177, 180–81. The fullest discussion of the baseline problem of which I know is Arthur, "Resource Acquisition and Harm."

This is not, however, to say that the idea of leaving others enough and as good is otherwise an especially clear notion. On the contrary, full explication of this idea is quite extraordinarily difficult. Neither the quantitative nor the qualitative aspects of the requirement wears its meaning on its face.[182] And however these are read, the practical difficulties of calculation in determining when enough and as good has been left are bound to be enormous, if not insuperable.[183] But the fair share limit can still seem a theoretically clear (or clarifiable) limit on natural property rights, an objective measure of lawful accumulation. Even this limited possibility for clarity seems threatened, however, when we raise the questions of just who the "others" are for whom our appropriations must leave enough and as good in common, and when these common goods must be available to them. At least three possible answers suggest themselves. We must leave enough and as good:

(a) for all persons existing at the time of the appropriation to have the opportunity to acquire their fair shares (i.e., no appropriation at time t can bring my total holdings above roughly $1/n$ of the total natural resources, shares being adjusted for quality, and n being the total number of persons existing at t)

(b) for all existing persons who *want* some of what I appropriate to be able to have their fair shares,

(c) for all persons who will *ever* exist (or who will ever *want* the good) to be able to have their fair shares[184]

(a) and (b), of course, can be made to read not only as limits on appropriation, but also as limits on holding and/or transfers (i.e.,

[182] First, of course, a "fair share" is at best only a roughly equal share, so that "enough" for others' use will not simply be the same amount for all. Second, it is unclear whether what is left for others must be the same kind of thing one appropriated, or only something that will serve as well to satisfy their needs or plans (plums might be "as good as" apples for them). Third, it is hard to be very confident about what makes even the same kinds of things "as good as" one another. An apple that is six inches farther from me than the one you picked is in some sense not "as good"; if it is six miles away, or across the ocean in America, the apple is quite a lot less good. Where on this continuum another otherwise equally good apple ceases to be "as good" is hard to say without sounding arbitrary. Indeed, even specifying thick, gray lines on the continuum is far from easy. (See, e.g., Spencer's similar worries about what makes something "as good" in *Social Statics*, chapter 10, 126–28.)

[183] See Fressola, "Liberty and Property," 319.

[184] Steiner, "Justice and Entitlement," 382; "Natural Right," 45. But see Steiner, "Slavery," 250–53.

one cannot legitimately hold what was once lawfully appropriated but later came to be more than one's fair share).[185] And if we read "enough and as good" in either manner (a) or (b), natural resources can legitimately be appropriated in their entirety ("closed out") at some point in history (the point at which everyone's actual appropriation is equal to a fair share), so that future persons must inherit, purchase, or simply do without those resources. If n existing persons all labor to appropriate $1/n$ of the land in the world, the next person born (person $n + 1$) may have to live on land owned by others (since person $n + 1$ was not among those existing at the time of any of the prior appropriations of land). Interestingly, such a reading of the fair share limit might be used (conservatively) to justify larger holdings of property for older families (these holdings being passed down generation to generation); for in each succeeding generation of persons, a fair share of the unowned common will tend to be smaller, there being more people and less unappropriated resources.

By contrast, on reading (c) resources cannot be closed out. The fair share limit would now best be understood to allow each to appropriate up to a "current" fair share of the common, but require redistribution as more persons are born (who do not inherit a fair share) or as disasters reduce the total supply of resources. Person $n + 1$ could now claim a share of what others had previously legitimately appropriated. Alternatively, (c) might be taken to only allow appropriation that would never be more than a fair share of the total resources. But this reading implausibly requires for current appropriation impossible calculations concerning the number of persons who will live in the future, future patterns of transfer (especially including inheritance), patterns of consumption, possible changes in the pool of resources, and the like.

In which of these ways—(a), (b), or (c)—should we take Locke

---

[185] As in cases involving a decrease in the total supply of some resource without a corresponding decrease in the relevant population—like Nozick's waterhole: "Thus a person may not appropriate the only water hole in a desert and charge what he will. Nor may he charge what he will if he possesses one, and unfortunately it happens that all the water holes in the desert dry up, except for his" (*Anarchy*, 180). Nozick seems in the end to opt for a variation on (a), but modified to cover holding and transfers (ibid., 178–82). The "variation" I refer to here is, of course, significant. Nozick requires only that appropriation (plus compensation) leave others no worse off materially than they would be had the appropriation (or class of appropriations) not occurred. For criticisms of Nozick's version of the proviso, see Held, "John Locke on Robert Nozick," 175; Steiner, "Natural Right," 45–47, and "Slavery," 252–53; Sarkar, "Lockean Proviso," 51–59; Bogart, "Lockean Provisos," 829–32, 835; Cohen, "Self-Ownership," 132.

to understand the requirement that we leave enough and as good for others? On the one hand, if various resources are closed out (as [a] and [b] permit), this threatens to leave some dependent for their preservation (and their opportunity for self-government) on the good will of others. This points toward (c) as the proper reading of Locke. Similarly, Locke sometimes writes (e.g., II, 36, 48–50) as if it is the use of money that makes natural resources (especially land) "close out"; but because we have consented to the use of money, we cannot complain about this result. This creates the impression that without the consent, it would be wrong for appropriators to close out resources, again pointing to (c) as the best reading of the fair share limit.

On the other hand, it seems possible that mere population increase, even *without* money, could eventually close out resources (or bring an end to legitimate appropriation). (Notice that Locke does mention "the increase of people and stock" as a source of scarcity [II, 45].) And given that God has commanded mankind to be fruitful and multiply, it is hard to believe that it becomes contrary to God's will (hence natural law) to labor on and make useful natural resources simply because of a population increase. Indeed, we have seen (in our examination of the waste limit) that Locke is sensitive to possible differences between the conditions for taking (appropriation) and those for holding; so he could easily subscribe to (a) or (b), modified for plausibility to limit holdings and/or transfers as well as takings.[186]

We might try to push Locke back toward (c) by observing that future people are as much a part of the "humankind" to whom God gave the earth as are present appropriators.[187] But Locke never mentions future people (or their rights and opportunities) as a consideration relevant to present appropriation. And in I, 42, Locke strongly suggests that the "fairness" of acquisitions (and continued holdings) is *relative* to the time at which they occurred, as (a) and (b) insist ("the fair acquisitions of his ancestors descended to him"—see 6.2 below). On its face, then, the evidence seems to support a reading of Locke's fair share limit like (a) or (b). Even without our consent to money, significant inequalities in holdings may be fair, since fairness of shares is relative to the number of persons existing at the time of appropriation. The older families of the working rich, then, might have been entitled to take

[186] Contrary to Miller's suggestion ("Natural Right," 283).
[187] Schmidtz, *Limits of Government*, 24.

and pass down larger shares than families whose holdings extend less far into the past. Still, those born into a world in which resources have been used up or closed out by prior fair appropriations, are nonetheless born to the same rights of self-preservation and self-government as earlier generations. And they have also been given the earth by God, since they too are part of mankind. They are entitled to their fair share of God's bounty.

Fairness, then, seems to generate a conflict. Fair acquisition may result in resources being closed out (or in the requirement that any remainder of them be left common, thereby eliminating rightful appropriation). But fairness also demands a share for later persons. Governments must settle such conflicts. But these conflicts need not be insuperable, since later persons can get their share by getting access to a living. Fairness does not necessarily require the redistribution of initially fair acquisitions. It requires only that persons who cannot appropriate a share are not denied access to their share or room to exercise their rights of self-preservation and self-government. Where these latter goods *are* precluded, later persons must be allowed to appropriate the property of earlier ones. This conception of a "fair share limit" on appropriation, holding, and transfer seems to me a plausible addition to the mixing argument. For Locke, however, all of this concerns only the fairness of shares *independent* of the use of (and consent to) money. To see the whole of Locke's final position, we must explore that last piece of the puzzle.

5.5. Money

Money is first introduced into Locke's discussion of property in II, 36–37 to explain why the "rule of propriety . . . that every man should have as much as he could make use of" no longer "holds" in the world, as it did in the first ages of humankind. Then, no matter how much persons appropriated by their labor, they could do no injury to anyone else; for no one was capable of laboring on and using more than a "small part" of the world. "The same plenty was still left" to others after each appropriation (II, 37). Locke's remarks here touch on what I have called the "outer" limit on property (the fair share limit). The "inner" limit (the waste limit) was all that was relevant in the first ages; but money (along with "the increase of people and stock" [II, 45]) "made land scarce," so that one person's appropriation could "prejudice" others (as with the contemporary common in civil society). It seems natural to ask two questions about this process: (a) How did money make land scarce, given that there is twice as much land in the world as would "suffice" for its inhabitants (II, 36)?; (b) Why were the appropriations that made land scarce not a wrong to others? We have already seen part of Locke's answer to (b); we can see the rest only after first discussing (a).

Money is defined by Locke as "some lasting thing that men might keep without spoiling, and that by mutual consent men would take in exchange for the truly useful, but perishable supports of life" (II, 47).[188] Not being in itself useful for the support of life, money has no real or "intrinsic" value; "the intrinsic value of things . . . depends only on their usefulness to the life of man" (II, 37).[189] Money has only a "fantastical imaginary value" (II, 184). "Fancy or agreement" has put on it the value it has.[190] It is only because others will take it in exchange for useful things that money has any value beyond its tiny "fancy" value as a thing of, say, "pleasing colour" (II, 46).[191]

As Locke describes the process in II, 46, money arises naturally from barter.[192] Most goods useful for the support of life are perishable; and since we may not waste what we appropriate, we may only take of these goods what we (our families, others we support) will actually use. Barter allows division of labor, of course (I can now gather twice as many apples as I can use and trade them for your corn, instead of having to grow corn myself). But we are all still confined by the perishability of useful things and the moral requirement of nonwaste. We want to transcend this limit and

[188] For a useful general discussion of Locke's views on money, see Vaughn, *John Locke*, 32–43.

[189] See Yolton, *Compass*, 193–94; Vaughn, *John Locke*, 42, 86. Locke does say elsewhere that money (silver) has "intrinsic value," but he there seems to mean by "intrinsic value" what he calls in the *Treatises* "fancy" or "fantastical" value (see below): "The intrinsic value of silver . . . is that estimate which common consent has placed on it, whereby it is made equivalent to all other things" (*Further Considerations Concerning Raising the Value of Money*, 139; see also *Some Considerations of the Consequences of the Lowering of Interest and Raising the Value of Money*, 22).

[190] Locke seems to mean here that money has value both because it is pleasing and because of its conventional (consensual) exchange ("marketable") value (see Ryan, *Property and Political Theory*, 39). Of these, the latter value is clearly of vastly greater importance.

[191] See Kelly, " 'All Things Richly to Enjoy,' " 278. As Kelly notes, this is not a labor theory of exchange value (ibid., 291; see also Waldron, *Private Property*, 192), in spite of Locke's earlier claims that labor is the source of virtually all of the value of things (II, 40–43). Locke probably intends to claim that almost all of the "real" or "intrinsic" value (the use value) of a thing derives from labor. This seems a coherent view, not a confusion (as Kelly claims).

[192] For a clear summary of this process, see Waldron, *Private Property*, 218–25.

have more property—not so much from greed or miserliness, but for self-sufficiency, comfort, security, freedom for other activities, and so on.[193] But trying to take more is both foolish and wrong if that surplus is wasted.

We can get some accumulation of goods by trading for less perishable ones (I can pick fifty-two weeks' worth of plums [which last only a week] and trade them to others for fifty-two weeks' worth of nuts [which last a whole year] [II, 46]). But we are still severely limited: "What reason could anyone have there to enlarge his possessions beyond the use of his family, and a plentiful supply to its consumption, either in what their own industry produced, or they could barter for like perishable, useful commodities, with others?" (II, 48). We could, of course, within the limits set by natural law gather perishables and trade them for heaps of nonperishables (metal, shells, pebbles, diamonds). But since nonperishables are almost always useless, this seems a mindless activity. All facing the same problem, people agree (consent) to accept some useless thing in trade for useful things. The medium of exchange must be sufficiently durable and rare ("lasting and scarce" [II, 48]) to function as such, but its value derives not from its durability or rarity. It derives from the consent of persons to take it in trade for useful (perishable) things.[194]

The result of this agreement, of course, is that we can take far more perishables than we can use, exchanging the surplus for money (which, being in itself useless and nonperishable, cannot be wasted[195]). Further, of course, we can take more land than we

[193] See Rapaczynski, *Nature and Politics*, 207; Vaughn, *John Locke*, 103.

[194] See Ashcraft, *Revolutionary Politics*, 277 and Olivecrona, "Locke's Theory of Appropriation," 230. Olivecrona characterizes this as a kind of revival of the compact theory of property ("Appropriation in the State of Nature," 229); but that seems unfair, given that Locke has solved his primary problem (deriving private property from common) without any appeal to consent or compact. It probably is fair to complain that Locke to some extent runs together conventional value, imaginary value, and the value of the qualities that make gold and silver suitable as money (Kelly, " 'All Things Richly to Enjoy,' " 290). But Locke does elsewhere display a relatively clear conception of exchange value (see Parsons, "Locke's Doctrine of Property," 390). And in the essay "Venditio," Locke defends a theory of value based on demand, market-price, and the like (see Dunn, "Justice," 72).

[195] It sounds odd to say that money can't be wasted, given that wasting money seems to be a favorite activity of contemporary life. And I suspect Locke would not put the point so bluntly. Merely saving (or hoarding) money does not count as waste for Locke, for it can still be used later (by oneself or others) for the support of life. But throwing money in the sea or melting it down and sprinkling it over the earth might well count as a kind of waste prohibited by natural law. And it would be easy as well to use the waste limit to condemn the extravagant purchases of the idle rich. On wasting money in Locke, see Seliger, *Liberal Politics*, 157.

can use, hire others to work it for us, and sell the products we do not use. People found in money a way in which "a man may fairly possess more land than he himself can use the product of, by receiving in exchange for the overplus gold and silver, which may be hoarded up without injury to anyone, these metals not spoiling or decaying in the hands of the possessor" (II, 50). So "larger possessions" (II, 36) do not violate the waste limit (provided the surplus goods resulting from them are exchanged for money); and they will immediately result wherever money is used (II, 49). Larger possessions and more people will also, of course, make land (and some other goods) scarce.

What shall we say about those who must accept unequally small shares (or no shares at all) of natural resources as a result of the scarcity caused by money? Have they not been wronged in some way? A variety of positions seems to be available to Locke. The first we have already seen: even independent of the invention of money, some inequalities may be fair, if fairness of acquisition (and subsequent holding) is relative to the number of persons and common resources in existence at the moment of acquisition (as Locke's remarks suggest). This argument, however, seems unlikely to justify anything like the exceptionally large and pervasive inequalities that exist(ed) in contemporary society. A second position we have seen (in 5.2) is suggested by Macpherson: Locke overcomes the natural law restriction on inequality (i.e., the requirement of leaving enough and as good in common for others) by arguing that money encourages enclosure of land, which increases the common stock and benefits even of those who are left with much less (or no) land. All are in fact made better off by inequalities in shares of natural resources and money.[196] Thus overcoming the natural limits on property is Locke's "astonishing achievement" (which, in effect, "destroys" Locke's natural law system);[197] as a result, he can maintain that no person in civil society is wronged by prior appropriations of common goods simply because none is left for that person's appropriation.

[196] Macpherson, *Possessive Individualism*, 211–13; see also Parry, *John Locke*, 55–56. Notice that this argument could at best justify those inequalities (or kinds of inequalities) that actually *do* contribute to the well-being of all. It could not provide (as Macpherson seems to believe) a blanket justification for "unlimited capitalist appropriation" and the wasteful holdings of the idle rich. Schwarzenbach also rightly notes that this argument would show *not* that natural law limits have been overcome in civil society, but that those limits are satisfied in civil society ("Locke's Two Conceptions," 152).
[197] *Possessive Individualism*, 199; "Natural Rights," 232–33.

There are, however, good reasons for believing that these claims by Locke (about enclosure benefiting all) are not true[198] and that Locke did not intend to employ them as Macpherson suggests.[199] For one thing, Macpherson's reading takes Locke's fair share limit to be concerned only with levels of material well-being, so that any appropriation that does not lower that level for others is acceptable. I have argued, however, that Locke's chief concern is with material goods only as means to securing basic rights of self-preservation and self-government. It is thus not only levels of material well-being that must be insured, but opportunities to better oneself and pursue one's projects (i.e., access to material goods and to the means of creating wealth[200]). Each must have access to a "living." But if this is Locke's concern, his showing that "a day labourer in England" lives better than a "king" in America (II, 41) will hardly show the fair share limit to have been "overcome" in Locke's England. For the day laborer may have far less in the way of opportunities and access than the American, even if the laborer eats and dresses better.[201]

The only justification for material inequality (and for the appropriations that produce scarcity) explicitly offered by Locke is quite different from the two we have considered (and rejected) thus far. It is, Locke claims, our *consent* to the use of money (the cause of large holdings) that justifies unequal possessions and the consequent disadvantages for some. It is "the tacit agreement of men" to the use of money that "introduced (by consent) larger possessions, and a right to them" (II, 36); "men have agreed to disproportionate and unequal possession of the earth," making "an inequality of private possessions . . . practicable . . . only by . . .

---

[198] We saw several such reasons in 5.3. Others are offered by Waldron ("Enough and as Good," 323), Christman ("Can Ownership Be Justified?" 167–68), and Shapiro (*Evolution of Rights*, 94). Add to these that Macpherson must attribute to Locke central reliance on passages that Macpherson admits were probably late insertions by Locke into the text of chapter 5 (*Possessive Individualism*, 212).

[199] See Waldron, "Enough and as Good," 323–24; and Rapaczynski, *Nature and Politics*, 208–9.

[200] Kelly, " 'All Things Richly to Enjoy,' " 289n.

[201] Not to mention the American's simpler tastes (which are more easily satisfied), higher social standing, and purer lifestyle, all of which suggest that the American may lead a "better life" (see Ryan, *Property and Political Theory*, 41–42). It is interesting to consider, however, that at least some of the opportunities enjoyed by the American (e.g., to appropriate a share of the common in America) are shared by the English day laborer, even if they are more difficult for the latter to take advantage of. There was still in Locke's day plenty of "waste" land in the world (see, e.g., II, 36). As far as I can see, however, Locke never uses this fact as evidence that there is still enough and as good left for other Englishmen to appropriate (thus justifying the large holdings of the rich). As I argue below, Locke seems to appeal throughout (including II, 36) to consent as the justification for inequality.

tacitly agreeing in the use of money" (II, 50). Locke could hardly be clearer about what he thought justified inequality. We consent to the use of money, so we consent to the natural consequences of the use of money (large appropriations, scarcity, inequality).[202]

While possessions were always unequal in some ways (due to different levels of industry across humankind [II, 48]), Locke holds, private possessions were before money broadly equal, in that all were small (II, 36, 107). Money makes large possessions and substantial inequalities. Such inequalities *look* illegitimate until we see that they have been consented to by all concerned.[203] Macpherson's reading of Locke makes the appeal to consent utterly superfluous (hence mysterious); for why would the appeal to consent be necessary if no persons would be wronged by the appropriation of large holdings? After all, no consent to the division of the original common was required precisely because that division wronged no one. The only plausible explanation for Locke's appeal to our consent to money is that Locke believed the kinds and extent of material inequality in contemporary political society would not be justifiable independent of that consent.

Unfortunately for Locke (although perhaps fortunately for his own defense of human dignity), the consent argument in fact justifies existing inequalities no better than the arguments we examined previously.[204] For, in the first place, universal consent to participation in a scheme does *not* justify every act or state of affairs that flows from that scheme. Results that are unforeseen, immoral, or otherwise distant from the initial harmless intent of a scheme may not be legitimated simply because everyone freely entered into the scheme. The original point of money was to facilitate exchange and to free persons from the burdens of "hand to mouth" existence, according to Locke. Presumably few if any of the first users of money had in mind that it should be used to eliminate for some the opportunity to appropriate from the common. Subsequent users of money seldom, if ever, took themselves to be consenting to such outcomes either. Nor is it obvious that even our own consent could justify depriving us of access to a living (which is why Locke is so eager to characterize servants as freemen not under their masters' control). "Consent" to the use of money might reasonably be taken to justify greater inequality than would

---

[202] See Winfrey, "Charity versus Justice," 432–33; and Kelly, " 'All Things Richly to Enjoy,' " 292.

[203] Kelly, " 'All Things Richly to Enjoy,' " 282.

[204] Which may explain why Macpherson disregards it. For objections to this argument similar to my own, see Waldron, *Private Property*, 223–25.

be otherwise justified; but it will not justify *everything* that flows from the use of money, and, in particular, it will not justify forcing some into a condition of dependency (i.e., denying them their right to self-government).

Second, even if consent to a scheme could justify all of what that scheme produces, this would do Locke little good. For many, their "consent" to the use of money is not given freely, despite Locke's insistence that such consent is "voluntary" (II, 50). Even if the wealthy do not force their servants to exchange their labor for money (and so to consent to the use of money), their servants typically have no real choice but to do exactly that (having no access to common goods that they might appropriate).[205] Consent need not be coerced to be nonbinding. For most others, their "consent" to money really only amounts to "going along with" a scheme that is clearly not chosen by them (even if not opposed by them either). Indeed, Locke emphasizes that the consent at issue is "tacit" only, involving no "compact" (II, 50) (although it really resembles much more closely a Humean convention[206]). But mere acquiescence in or conformity to an externally imposed scheme (what Locke elsewhere calls "natural consent" [ELN, 161–65] or "common practice" [II, 88]) *cannot* justify what would otherwise be wrong. Locke could, for instance, easily have appealed to this kind of weak, tacit consent to justify the division of the original common (a la Grotius). But he chose not to do so, arguing instead that getting a *real* consent to the division from all persons would be impossible (for mankind would starve while trying to get it). A weak, tacit consent (acquiescence) would, by contrast, have been easy to get; but such a consent would not seem to justify anything. So Locke refrained from the appeal to weak "consent" at that point in his property arguments. He would have done well to refrain as well at this point (i.e., in the attempt to justify inequality through consent to money).[207]

[205] Ryan, *Property and Political Theory*, 40; Replogle, *Recovering the Social Contract*, 205.

[206] For Hume, gold and silver acquire their exchange value not by *consent*, but by *convention* (*Treatise of Human Nature*, 3.2.2).

[207] By contrast with the reading of Locke offered here, Tully's Locke says most of what I have suggested Locke *should* have said, and considerably more (in a similar spirit) besides. According to Tully's reading of the texts, Locke holds that while money arises from consent, money is also the root of all evil and the source of man's fall. Money creates or extends the unnatural desire for more than is needed or can be used, encouraging covetousness and hoarding. Money is responsible for ending the "Golden Age" (of II, 111), a time when people were motivated by need and convenience, and for creating the problems that we need governments to solve (*Discourse*, 147–51). Since money has "disrupted the natural order," governments

We can conclude that Locke has available to him no very good justification for the large, extensive, and oppressive material inequalities of his day (or of ours). Locke is attempting, here as elsewhere, to occupy the middle ground, calling neither for unfettered accumulation of property nor for radical redistribution of holdings.

---

must reorder property relations to bring them back "in line with God's intentions" (God's will for our nondependence) (ibid., 154). Once money creates large possessions and some are as a result excluded from their rightful shares of the common, natural property principles no longer hold and "no appropriation is justified" (ibid., 152). It is not the case that the natural limits on property somehow cease to bind us or are transcended or overcome after the invention of money. Rather, the violation of these limits brings morally legitimate appropriation to an end (as many leveling arguments contended).

Unfortunately for Tully's reading, Locke actually says almost none of this (although we have seen that he *should* have said some of it). Locke does, of course, at times seem to regret the loss of the "poor but virtuous age" of small possessions (II, 110), although it was not only the absence of money, but also "want of people" (II, 108) that created the simplicity of that age (and Locke is clearly *not* morally opposed to increases in population). The "little properties" (II, 75) people had in those days made simple monarchy a natural and acceptable form of government (II, 75, 105, 110); the larger properties of later ages necessitated more limited governments, with more extensive restraints on the ambitions of princes (II, 111). But Locke *never* suggests that these larger properties are illegitimate or that the appropriate remedy is to redistribute holdings to recreate a simpler, more virtuous age. Neither does he claim that money is the source of the main problems that governments are needed to solve. Money does create a certain unclarity in titles to external goods. But money has no essential connection to any of the chief problems of life in the state of nature, listed by Locke as the sources of our need for civil society (in II, 124–26). Want of a "settled, known law" (II, 124), want of a "known and indifferent judge" (II, 125), and want of "power to back and support the sentence" (II, 126) are all clearly problems of life in the state of nature that would exist even if money did not. Money no doubt aggravates these problems by creating new sources of contention and controversy (and temptation to aggress against others). But there were still plenty of people to conflict with and plenty of holdings to covet even prior to money's invention.

The real problem for Tully's interpretation, however, is that Locke clearly says that by virtue of our consent to money, larger possessions and material inequality are made "fair," "practicable," and of "no injury to anyone" (II, 50); people who acquire larger possessions (by the use of money) have "a right to them" (II, 36). This is hardly the language of moral condemnation (see Ashcraft, *Revolutionary Politics*, 271, 273; Seliger, *Liberal Politics*, 149; Wood, *Capitalism*, 77–78; Snyder, "Locke on Natural Law"; Drury, "Locke and Nozick," 35). Money is said by Locke to prevent waste (II, 45), to encourage beneficial enclosure (II, 48), and to promote trade and production. All of this looks distinctly like an attempt to justify, not to condemn, the use of money and the material inequalities that result from that use. At the very least, one must admit that for Locke such inequalities must be accepted as morally permissible, if perhaps regrettable (see Dunn, *Political Thought*, 248; Ryan, *Property and Political Theory*, 30–31, 39–40; Waldron, *Private Property*, 221). Locke may have had a genuine preference for simpler times and ways of living. He certainly condemns covetousness (contrary to the claims of Strauss, *Natural Right*, 247), and there is no indication that he intends to defend a right of *unlimited* accumulation. But neither does he take the use of money and its creation of substantial inequality to be contrary to God's will, or to end all legitimate appropriation under the rules of natural property (see Mackie, "Review of Tully," 93).

But while we can reconstruct for Locke a plausible variant of his theory of original appropriation (thus incorporating into the Lockean theory of rights the mixing argument and the fair share limit), we cannot accept Locke's attempted use of the theory to condone real social injustice. The social reforms required by the Lockean theory of rights need not have involved leveling redistributions of property; but at the very least the creation of genuine avenues of opportunity (to secure for all the right of self-government) was (is) required. Appropriation even after the invention of money should still be conditioned by the fair share limit (remembering, now, that this limit may permit *some* inequalities). Money may "raise" the "inner limit" on property (since waste is not typically an issue in the accumulation of money); but it cannot render nonbinding the "outer limit" (all must still be allowed access to their fair share of the common, for that is necessary for self-preservation and self-government). Locke seems, even in his best moments, only dimly aware of these consequences of his own basic principles. Locke *is* aware, at least, that larger possessions and the use of money create certain moral problems—problems with unclarity of title and problems with guaranteeing access to resources for all. It is in the *limited* but nonetheless substantial role as solution to these problems that government becomes a player in Locke's account of property rights. And it is to government's role that I turn first in chapter 6.

S I X

JUSTICE AND CHARITY

6.1. Property in Political Society

Achieving social justice is primarily a matter of morally proper distribution of basic rights and goods within society. What counts as a just arrangement in political (civil) society, then, will depend crucially on what and what kinds of property rights persons in that society are taken to have. That issue is the first question for this chapter: what changes in the rules for and holdings of property (if any) are accomplished on Locke's view in the transition from a state of nature to civil society? Answering this question will complete both the analysis of property undertaken in chapter 5 and the discussion of that transfer of natural rights that for Locke is necessitated by entrance into a legitimate polity (chapter 3).

Locke tells us very little in the *Treatises* (or elsewhere) about how he understands the principles of natural property to be affected by the institution of political society (and thus Locke creates the immediate impression that he does not take the effects to be especially momentous). Locke does say again and again (most prominently in II, 123–24) that the point of having political society is the more effective preservation of our property (including estate), suggesting that society's laws should simply enforce the rules of natural property and secure the holdings of citizens that are legitimate under those rules. On the other hand, we have seen (in 4.5 and elsewhere) that Locke also claims that when one consents to join a commonwealth, "by the same act . . . he unites his possessions, which were before free, to it also; and they become, both of them, subject to the government and dominion of that commonwealth" (II, 120). This passage suggests that a more dramatic change in the rules for and status of property may accompany the transition to political society.

The slightly more precise (but still very sketchy) story Locke tells about this transition (with respect to property) runs roughly as follows. As people incorporate into distinct groups, joining their individual holdings in land together, these groups come to occupy particular territories. "By compact and agreement" these groups formalize this division of the earth ("settle the bounds of their distinct territories" [II, 38]), agreeing "on limits between them and their neighbors" (II, 38) that then constitute internationally accepted boundaries. In the process, nations give up the claims they might have had by natural right on one another's territories ("either expressly or tacitly disowning all claim and right to the land in the other's possession" and giving up "their pretences to their natural common right, which originally they had to those countries" [II, 45]). By these remarks we can assume Locke means (at least) that (a) each nation agrees not to pursue contested titles to land within the territories of other states (i.e., agrees to let each government settle its own property controversies), and (b) each nation agrees not to try to appropriate land that remains common within the territories of other nations. This common ground is now allowed by all nations to be the joint property of the citizens of the particular nation within whose boundaries it lies (II, 35).[1]

All of this, of course, concerns only the distribution of rights *between* nations. *Within* each political society, Locke claims, each member's property is under the "jurisdiction" of that society's government (II, 120–21). Laws in the society "regulate" property (II, 3, 45, 50, 139) and "settle" the "properties of private men of their society" (II, 38, 45), while "the possession of land is determined by positive constitutions" (II, 50; see also II, 30, 136). All members, in the act of joining the commonwealth, give society certain rights over their property, as well as giving up any claims they might have on land that the society decides should be held by all in common.

How shall we understand the true force of Locke's occasional remarks on this subject? One broad school of interpretation contends that these remarks are Locke's way of saying that the original rules of natural property are replaced in civil society by positive, legal rules of property. All of our natural property rights are

[1] Notice that this agreement cannot bind those not party to it. While all civilized nations seem (to Locke) to be at least tacit consenters to the arrangement, those individuals still in the state of nature clearly are not. Thus, an American could have come to Locke's England and made a legitimate claim on part of the English common, unless that common was such that any appropriation of it would count as an injury to all the commoners (as Locke suggests in II, 35). But this happy feature of the English common is surely not a necessary feature of all common land within the territories of civilized nations.

surrendered to society on our incorporation, including the right to make new property by labor within the territories of the community. These *natural* rights are replaced with *civil* (legal) property rights, granted by society to each citizen, conditional on the citizen's performance of social duties, and secured by legal enforcement.[2] Locke's theory of appropriation, on this interpretation, is only relevant or applicable in prepolitical or nonpolitical conditions.[3]

One version of this position (the version best represented by Kendall) takes it to follow from the more general view that political consent in Locke involves the surrender of *all* rights to society. This entails, of course, that consent involves surrendering all natural rights in external goods (i.e., land and other possessions). A more sophisticated version of this position is Tully's. We have seen (in 5.4) Tully's view that money, by upsetting the natural order of property, necessitates a new basis for property rights. The original rules of property, Tully claims, were replaced by civil law in political society, so that property was thenceforth conventional. And these new rules were binding and legitimate because they were justified by the consent each member gave on joining society.[4]

According to Tully, each citizen of a legitimate Lockean civil society must surrender all personal possessions to the community, entrusting as well natural rights of appropriation to (the majority of) society, so that appropriation by the natural rules of property is no longer legitimate. The "regulating," "settling," and "determining" of property in civil society to which Locke refers is taken by Tully to indicate a fundamental reconstituting or reordering of property on a new (consensual, legal) basis. There is no *strictly* private property; civil property is always held only conditional on the performance of one's social functions (indeed, this was true of *natural* property as well).[5] Governments, however, cannot simply

---

[2] Some examples of this kind of reading of Locke (in addition to those discussed below) can be found in Von Leyden, *Hobbes and Locke*, 106–7; Wood, *Capitalism*, 54; Yolton, *Locke*, 70; Dunn, "Consent," 37–38; Olivecrona, "Locke's Theory of Appropriation," 231; Parsons, "Locke's Doctrine of Property," 399; Pangle, *Republicanism*, 169; Grady, "Obligation, Consent," 283n; Cherno, "Locke on Property," 52–53; Scanlon, "Nozick on Rights," 3–4; Drury, "Locke and Nozick," 36; Christman, "Can Ownership Be Justified?" 163–64; Schwarzenbach, "Locke's Two Conceptions," 152–53, 156.

[3] This, of course, allows one to think of property, as on economic models, as the product of a kind of bargain. Property would be purely contractual once people had incorporated.

[4] *Discourse*, 98–99, 158–61, 168.

[5] Ibid., 164–65, 158–60, 161, 99–105.

reconstitute property as they please. They are bound by natural law to reorder property in a certain fashion: property should be distributed so as to be proportionate to the "labour of each for the public good," and the distribution should guarantee that each member has the means for comfortable subsistence and is able to labor and enjoy the fruits of labor.[6] Unlimited rights of accumulation (a la Strauss, Macpherson, et al.) are, according to Tully, no part of this plan. The role of government is to guarantee the independence of each member by reordering property (and thus undoing the damage done by the invention of money) so that each can again enjoy a share of what God gave for the preservation and comfort of all.

Let us begin with the claim that all natural property rights are given over to society on joining a legitimate commonwealth. The primary textual support for this reading of Locke is in his discussion of the process of "uniting" one's possessions to the commonwealth (chiefly in II, 116, 117, 120). But the passages in question cannot bear the interpretation given them by Tully (et al.). Locke clearly claims that the citizen joins "person and possession" to the commonwealth in the same way and to the same extent (II, 120). But Locke obviously does *not* intend to claim that citizens give themselves to society, that each becomes society's property (only forfeiture of rights can make one human the property of another, not consent or contract). It follows, of course, that Locke cannot mean that each citizen simply gives personal possessions over to society either.[7] Our property is given to society only in the way our person is.

But in what way *is* our person and property given (or, as Locke actually says, "submitted") to society? Just as we give up only some of our rights over ourselves, we give up only some of our rights over our possessions. In both cases, we surrender those rights that must be surrendered for effective government to be possible. Citizens "must be understood to give up all the power necessary to the ends for which they unite into society" (II, 99) (each gives up rights "so far forth as the preservation of himself and the rest of that society shall require" [II, 129]). "And therefore the magistrate cannot take away [the] worldly things from this man or party and give them to that; nor change propriety amongst fellow-subjects (no not even by law), for a cause that has no rela-

6 Ibid., 166–67, 168, 169.
7 See Waldron's stunningly decisive refutation of Tully's position ("Locke, Tully," 105); see also Cohen, "Marx and Locke," 386.

tion to the end of civil government" (L, 153). But which rights with respect to our natural property do we give to society? How are our possessions "submitted" to government?

It is important, first, to see that by the term "possessions" (in II, 116, 117, 120) Locke clearly means possessions of *land* (as I argued briefly in 4.5 and 5.1). The "condition" on inheritance with which Locke is concerned in II, 116–17 (namely, submission to government) is said specifically to be annexed "to the *land*" (II, 116; my emphasis), or to the "enjoyment" or "possession" of the land (II, 73), not to possessions generally. While Locke refers to "possessions" in II, 117, the argument there makes sense only if "possessions" means "land"; for the argument concerns the dismember-ınent of the territories of the commonwealth (to which possessions other than land are utterly irrelevant). It follows that when Locke speaks of "uniting" or "submitting" our possessions a few paragraphs later (in II, 120), he is best read as referring only to our possessions in land (as, indeed, the text there clearly indicates[8]). Thus, Locke should not be taken to suggest in these central passages that membership in the commonwealth involves any surrender of personal property (i.e., moveable property, chattels) at all. As we have seen, the dominant language of the *Second Treatise*, which demands the protection or preservation of property, should have pointed us toward this conclusion. For the property that Locke wants to see protected seems to be precisely the natural property we bring with us to society: "to avoid the inconveniences which disorder men's properties in the state of nature, men unite into societies, that they may have the united strength of the whole society to secure and defend these properties" (II, 136). Unless "properties" shifts meaning within this sentence, Locke *cannot* mean that we must give up our natural property, receiving society's distribution of legal property (which may be quite different), on entering society.[9]

What, though, are we to make of Locke's claims that land must be "united" with and "submitted" to society? What Locke seems to have in mind is that each member must give society (and its

---

[8] II, 120, lines 6–12, makes it plain that Locke refers there to land ("for it would be a direct contradiction for anyone to enter into society . . . and yet suppose his *land* . . . should be exempt from the jurisdiction of that government"; my emphasis), as does II, 121, lines 1–4 ("the government has a direct jurisdiction only over the land").

[9] See Waldron, "Locke, Tully," 98, for further citations in support of this position. See also Gough, *Political Philosophy*, 73–75; Rapaczynski, *Nature and Politics*, 198–200; Den Hartogh, "Tully's Locke," 660; Cohen, "Marx and Locke," 386–87.

government) a limited set of rights over the land that the member
brings into society. That set of rights is what Locke calls "jurisdiction" (e.g., II, 120–21). But jurisdiction over land is plainly not
equivalent to public ownership of land.[10] The two central rights
that constitute a government's jurisdiction over its territories, on
Locke's view, are these: (1) the right to enforce the valid laws of
the commonwealth on that land (the land is "subject to the government and dominion" of the commonwealth [II, 120], as is all
other property); the territories of the state thus comprise "all parts
whereof the force of its law extends" (II, 122); (2) the right to refuse to permit alienation of land by members (by sale, bequest,
gift, etc.) to any parties who will not agree to submit themselves
and their acquired land to the laws of the commonwealth (II, 73,
117, 191) (as we saw in 4.5). These are the rights over land that
Locke takes to be necessary for effective government and are consequently the rights over land that members must be understood
to surrender to the society as a condition of membership.[11] But
these members still retain their *ownership* of their land. Any clear
title to property that a person brings to political society either remains that person's without conditions (in the case of moveables)

[10] See Gauthier, "Role of Inheritance," 38–41; Bennett, "Note," 231–32; Parry,
John Locke, 53, 98–99, 105; Beitz, "Tacit Consent," 495; Mackie, "Review of Tully,"
93; Wood, *Capitalism*, 80–81.

[11] This is an important point for several reasons. Locke argues that the land is
bound to the state in these ways, so that no person can own or enjoy (e.g., travel
on) the land without being subject to the state's laws (II, 119). No person has the
option of remaining in the state's territories *without* being bound to obey its laws.
Now one might respond by asking *how* the land became bound to the state forever.
Locke seems to want to suggest that the founders of the commonwealth (and any
who subsequently added their lands to it) have agreed to give the government the
right of jurisdiction over the relevant territories (see Beitz, "Tacit Consent," 491–
93). Further, Locke wants to say that *any* legitimate government enjoys such a right
of jurisdiction. But surely, we may respond, whether or not such rights have been
transferred to government in any particular society is a matter for *historical* inquiry,
not a priori pronouncement. And, in any event, there are serious questions to be
asked about whether the founders of a commonwealth have the *right* to transfer to
government perpetual interests in their land (since this transfer may harm subsequent generations—ibid., 498–500). Both objections, however, can be answered by
Locke's conceptual point. No historical inquiry is necessary if we accept two points:
(1) that all political consent necessarily includes a transfer of all rights necessary for
government to preserve a just, peaceful society; and (2) that states cannot subsist
if citizens have the right to "dismember" their territories (by sale, bequest, etc., of
their land to nonsubjects). If (1) and (2) are both true, as Locke believes, the rights
of jurisdiction are necessarily conveyed to government by political consent. Further, no transfer of perpetual interests in land is required by Locke, for each generation's enjoyment of its land is by itself sufficient to give a tacit consent, which
necessarily includes a transfer of the rights necessary for jurisdiction. My own view
(for which I will not argue here) is that neither (1) nor (2) is in fact true.

or is subject only to the jurisdiction of the government (in the case of land).

Nothing in the text points to any stronger view about the transfer of property.[12] And much suggests the position just articulated. The property enjoyed by citizens in a newly formed (or other legitimate) commonwealth is the *same* property whose rules (for appropriation) and limits are defined by the law of nature. The "original law of nature for the beginning of property in what was before common still takes place" even where civil law is in effect (II, 30). The positive laws of commonwealths must be "made conformable to the laws of nature" (I, 92; see also II, 135) (the law of nature may be used to "regulate" and "interpret" the "municipal laws of countries" [II, 12]). The law of nature (which defines the rules of natural property) "stands as an eternal rule to all men," its obligations not ceasing in society, but if anything only being "drawn closer" by having "known penalties annexed to them" (II, 135). Natural property rights are retained on entrance into civil society. While law or social convention may introduce new, positive rights to property to "draw closer" the bonds of natural right (i.e., to add legal clarity and force to them), this does not mean (as Tully claims) that property *becomes conventional* in civil society. For nothing in the text suggests that members have surrendered their natural rights. They retain their rights, and the law must merely craft legal rights to better secure those natural rights to property. Positive rights do not here replace natural rights, but are merely tools to better protect them.

Locke does, of course, say repeatedly that governments have a role in regulating, determining, and settling the property of individuals in political society; and this may appear to suggest a more substantial job for government than simply preserving natural

[12] As Waldron notes, the passages cited by Tully in defense of his position are both primarily parenthetical in Locke, and do not really support his position ("Locke, Tully," 100–101). It should be added that while only land is actually "joined" to the state in Locke, this fact does not support Macpherson's contention that only landowners are full (voting) members of Lockean civil society (see *Possessive Individualism*, 221–52; see also Cohen, "Structure, Choice," 301–6; and Andrew, *Shylock's Rights*, 141–42). All who give their consent to government submit *all* of their property (in person, money, moveables, freedom, land, etc.) to the government to whatever extent is necessary for effective government. This extent simply differs for the different kinds of property. There is no real support in Locke's texts for Macpherson's reading. For other critiques of Macpherson's position on this question, see Shapiro, *Evolution of Rights*, 137–38; White, *Philosophy*, 53–60; Dunn, "Consent," 39–40; Tarcov, *Locke's Education*, 170; Aaron, *John Locke*, 362–63; Von Leyden, *Hobbes and Locke*, 106.

property claims and exercising jurisdiction over the land. But that appearance is misleading. Governments exercise jurisdiction by enforcing the law, a central part of which is concerned with securing the natural rights of its subjects. But to enforce such laws and secure these rights, a government must first judge who has a right to what (having received the right to make such judgments by the citizens' having transferred to it their natural executive rights). When Locke says that governments "determine" property (II, 30, 50, 136), he means simply that they must judge (i.e., determine) who has a right to what.[13] Government must "determine the rights and fence the properties of those that live under it" by framing "standing rules to bound [property], by which everyone may know what is his" (II, 136). Judging and securing property rights in this way is a far cry from creating, redistributing, or reconstituting property rights; it is rather a matter of discovering and enforcing existing rights. Similarly, "settling" the properties of members is most naturally understood as the process of resolving controversies (i.e., settling disputes) and securing the resultant "determined" rights (see, e.g., II, 38, where "settled" seems to mean "set out the bounds of" property). Finally, the "regulation" of property (II, 3, 45, 50, 139) that is government's right (and duty) merely refers to the process of determining and settling property, and exercising jurisdiction over it. Locke never bothers to distinguish among regulating, determining, and settling (substituting freely among them) precisely because all simply refer to the same process of judging and securing (*not* reconstituting) property rights.

Some of the claims to property that citizens bring with them to political society will be clear and uncontroversial. Others will not be. As we saw in 5.4, a central aspect of government's regulation of property will be its job of settling "controversies" and "quarrels" caused by real or apparent violations of the fair share limit. When the large appropriations of some deny to others independence and self-government, those appropriations are illegitimate; governments must insure that remedies are available (that each person has access to a living), either by returning some holdings to common or by requiring a restructuring of employment opportunities to guarantee a chance for each person to lead an independent, moderately (not necessarily equally) comfortable existence.[14]

[13] Waldron, "Locke, Tully," 103; Den Hartogh, "Tully's Locke," 667–68.

[14] Another cause of obscurity in and controversy about titles to property is the systematic abuse of language by humankind: "language, which was given to us for

The job of government is to settle such controversies and obscurities and to enforce the resulting order of rights. It must make "good and equitable laws" governing property (II, 138), decide contested titles, rectify past injustices, and preserve every citizen's property. In short, government must clarify and enforce the requirements of natural law with respect to property, just as it must generally clarify and enforce the duties and rights defined by the law of nature. In the same way that the "several states and kingdoms" must "settle the bounds of their distinct territories" (i.e., render clear and uncontested the natural boundaries of their domains), individual political societies must "settle the property which labour and industry began" *within* their domains ("within themselves") (II, 45). In neither case is the "settling" a matter of redefining or reconstituting property. International boundaries are primarily determined by the properties of the individuals who incorporate themselves into the community and join their land to it (although states must also decide contested claims and how they will deal with unowned [common] land). The boundaries of individual titles within states are primarily determined by "labour and industry," that is, by the natural law rules for and limits on appropriation. To settle property is thus not to abandon, but rather to clarify and enforce the principles of property we examined in chapter 5.

Exactly how governments should go about settling controversies over property and what the result of this settling is likely to look like are far less clear in Locke. On the first of these questions, there seem to be two obvious possibilities, each with some support in Locke's texts: (a) When governments settle property, they should just do what individuals in the state of nature *could* have done themselves (but were too biased, passionate, or muddled to do in fact). Governments should settle quarrels and contests by simple, direct appeals to the particulars of the law of nature, which law provides a clear answer to every contested moral question. The government's job, then, is simply to be rational and unbiased, and so to see clearly the rights of persons as they are determined by natural law (remember that "the particulars of the law of nature"

---

the improvement of knowledge and bond of society, should not be employed to darken truth and unsettle people's rights; to raise mists and render unintelligible both morality and religion" (E, 3.10.13). The law of nature (which defines property rights) is especially vulnerable to the "mists" of linguistic abuse, for it is "unwritten, and so nowhere to be found but in the minds of men, . . . who through passion or interest . . . miscite or misapply it" (II, 136).

are "as intelligible and plain to a rational creature and a studier of that law as the positive laws of commonwealths" [II, 12]). (b) A second possibility is that "the particulars" of natural law do *not* determine a unique solution to every controversy (or that even a rational, unbiased student of that law cannot *see* all of its particulars [see 1.4]), so that governments must often just decide or legislate solutions to such controversies. This will amount to a positive (or conventional) determination of some property claims *within* the broader rules of property set by natural law. As we have seen (in 2.3), Locke seems sometimes to allow that the *content* of some of the rights and duties of natural law may be "filled in" by positive law or practice. Even if this is true, however, governments remain obligated to settle property (to decide controversies) in ways dictated by the spirit of natural law—that is, in the fairest, most equitable fashion.

What is the outcome of this settling likely to look like? According to Tully, governments will reconstitute property by a radical redistribution of holdings, returning us to a condition more in line with God's intentions. Now it seems clear that governments will have to do some redistribution of holdings, in order to rectify clear injustices (thefts, fraud, etc.). But Locke's language certainly suggests that he is not primarily concerned with the size of people's holdings, but with their origin in "labour and industry" (notice Locke's praise of the "prince who shall be so wise and godlike as by established laws of liberty to secure protection and encouragement to the honest industry of mankind" [II, 42]). It may be no coincidence that the "quarrels and contentions" (of II, 31) that arise when enough and as good is *not* left for others by the appropriations of some, seem related to the "quarrelsome and contentious" (of II, 34), of whom Locke (and God) seem to disapprove. This would appear to equate the industrious (including those who have not left enough for others) with those whose claims are just, even when those claims are contested by others whose positions have been "prejudiced" by the resulting scarcity. Locke says none of this explicitly (nor, as we have seen, *should* he have said this); but his language is hard to ignore.[15]

Locke seems, then, to expect that a just government will not have to limit or redistribute even the large holdings of the working rich (e.g., the estates of the landed gentry, the wealth of the bour-

[15] It comes as no surprise, as a result, that Locke's economic writings stress the limits on the government's ability to regulate economic activity. See Vaughn, *John Locke*, 115, 118–21, 134–35.

geoisie—i.e., those engaged in commerce, finance, manufacturing, etc.).[16] Some redistribution may be required by natural law, but nothing resembling a wholesale restructuring of holdings or the replacement of natural property with a new structure of conventional rights. Locke seems to tell his readers that clear titles (based in honest industry and continued use) to even quite large holdings should be in no danger, from king or church, under a just government (which is, of course, exactly what his readers *wanted* to hear). Even clear titles, of course, are subject to legitimate taxation for the support of society (including, as we will see in 6.3, the support of the needy). But clear titles must still be secured and defended by government, which must establish "guards and defences" to such property (II, 222). Government's proper function is *not*, I should stress, to simply preserve the existing order of property relations, although Locke (unwisely) supposes that the order of his *own* society should in most respects be preserved. Government's function is to insure that only naturally legitimate holdings are permitted and enforced and to secure for all the opportunity for self-preservation and self-government: the "duty of the magistrate" is primarily one of "preserving men in the possession of what honest industry has already acquired, and also of preserving their liberty and strength, whereby they may acquire what they further want" (L, 152). Violations of these duties by government may justify popular resistance to government.[17]

As we have seen (in 5.4 and 5.5), this position is neither a perfectly conservative defense of existing property relations, a free market, and rights of unlimited accumulation, nor a radically redistributive, leveling, egalitarian stance.[18] Locke's position is a moderate, intermediate one, as we should by now not be surprised to discover (see 6.3 below for further defense of these claims). We have also seen, however, that Locke's position is not, for a variety of reasons, the *best* Lockean position—that is, fully descriptive of the Lockean theory of rights. Locke's position *should* be less conservative than his texts suggest, both because he underestimates the inevitability and unfairness of poverty for many, and because labor and industry do not (as Locke sometimes seems

---

[16] Ibid., 100. Note, however, that this position implies that *idle* landowners may face such inroads. See Ashcraft, *Revolutionary Politics*, 246–52, 264, 267–70; and Winfrey, "Charity versus Justice," 427, 433.

[17] See Seliger, *Liberal Politics*, 173–74.

[18] Dunn has effectively defended the reading of Locke that places him between these extremes. See *Political Thought*, especially 214–16, 239–40, 265–66.

to suggest) give title in political society regardless of their effects on others. The "consent" to money that permits labor to produce larger holdings does not in fact justify all of the results of a money economy (as we saw in 5.5). Labor gives title to property in the first place only because each person has a prior right to take by labor up to a fair share of humankind's common resources, to use for self-preservation and self-government. Where appropriation by others has *denied* these goods to some, it will not be enough for governments simply to protect us in our possession of the products of "honest" industry. Changes in property relations will be necessary, even if these changes will not constitute a replacement of the rules of natural property.

It is possible that Locke is sometimes misled by his own arguments concerning natural property rights. The mixing argument (5.2), for instance, can appear to justify property in the products of our labor independent of any effects on others these appropriations might have. I have already argued (in 5.3) that this is *not* the best way to understand the mixing argument; but it remains a good place to look for the source of Locke's confusion. Not surprisingly, it is the same confusion that often leads libertarian followers of Locke to their distinctive, quite spartan conceptions of distributive justice.

6.2. Justice

Locke refers to justice as a "great social virtue" (*Education*, 110) and the "first and general rule of our happiness."[19] For it is justice that "gives every man a title to the product of his honest industry and the fair acquisitions of his ancestors descended to him" (I, 42). Justice is, for Locke, a property of distributions of external goods; specifically, Locke says here that justice is the property of everyone possessing what they have clear title to.[20] Those who mix their labor with external goods, according to the rules of and limits on natural appropriation, have a claim based on justice to possession of (and security in) them. Similarly, persons have a claim based on justice to those inherited goods which were acquired fairly (i.e., by following the same rules of appropriation) by their ancestors.

Locke's remarks in I, 42 also suggest (but do not entail) the fol-

---

[19] "Morality" (MS c28, fol. 140). Justice is also called here "the greatest duty," although "justice" in this essay seems to concern first the keeping of compacts, and only derivatively respect for property.

[20] Dunn, "Justice," 76–77.

lowing: (a) goods taken unfairly (illegitimately) by our ancestors and left by them to us cannot be claimed by us as just holdings (no matter how "clean" our possession appears to us; injustice does not "wear off" over time); (b) fairness (as we saw in 5.4) does not require redistribution of goods as more people come into the world. If an acquisition was fair at the time it occurred, it can be transferred and held justly later, even if at that later time such an acquisition would not have been fair; and (c) by extension, goods fairly acquired by others that we receive in fair trades, as gifts, and those that are fair reparation for injuries, are also ours as a matter of justice. In short, justice is that virtue or principle[21] according to which persons are entitled to their property, what Locke occasionally calls their "just possessions" or "just property" (e.g., II, 46)[22]—that is, not what persons *claim* as theirs or what the civil law *says* is theirs, but what natural law determines to be their property.[23]

Locke's theory of justice is thus what David Miller has called a "proprietary theory of justice."[24] Property is the fundamental notion in terms of which justice is defined. This is, if anything, even clearer in Locke's *Essay*, where the link between property and justice (or injustice) is drawn as directly as possible: injustice is "taking from others, without their consent, what their honest industry has possessed them of" (E, 4.4.9). And Locke also famously claims there that

"Where there is no property there is no injustice," is a proposition as certain as any demonstration in Euclid: for the idea of property being a right to anything, and the idea to which the name "injustice" is given being the invasion or violation of that right, it is evident that these ideas, being thus established, and these names annexed to them, I can as certainly

[21] Locke refers to justice in both ways. Presumably the *virtue* of justice is that trait of character that inclines one to respect the property of others (i.e., to respect that which the *principle* of justice determines is theirs). See *Education*, 110; and Tarcov's discussion of this passage in *Locke's Education*, 145–49.

[22] Dunn notes that the expression "just property" is an odd or empty one for Locke, since true property just *is* what justice assigns to each ("Justice," 80). I assume Locke has in mind the fact that "property" is frequently used to describe both what we merely *possess* and what civil law *protects* us in our possession of, neither of which necessarily corresponds to titles based in justice. "Just property," then, means here "true property" or "property under natural law."

[23] The connection between justice and law noted by Locke in the *Essay* (E, 3.11.9) is this connection with natural law. Justice may also, however, give to us what civil law assigns us in those areas (if any) where natural law is silent.

[24] "Justice and Property," 1–2. See also Cox, "Justice," 254.

know this proposition to be true, as that a triangle has three angles equal to two right ones. (E, 4.3.18).[25]

This passage suggests a more general definition of justice in Locke than we have thus far considered: *Justice is each person's having what that person has a moral right to, or doing only what that person has a moral right to do* ("the administration of justice" is for "the securing of men's rights" [II, 219]). The just is what is rightful, lawful, or legitimate in this sense of according with our moral rights (i.e., with our property in the *general* sense of the word). Justice, then, will be an applicable concept in (and justify our claims in) many areas of life other than the distribution of external goods.[26]

Where justice in possessions is concerned, it seems important to notice two preliminary points. First, justice has no necessary connection with desert, equality, or any other basis for a morally interesting "pattern" of distribution.[27] Fortune, good or bad, will determine many aspects of distributive justice on Locke's account— for instance, whether one's "honest industry" bears fruit (i.e., yields any products, or yields any particular quantity of them), whether one's ancestors leave one their fair acquisitions (or have any to leave), and so on. Desert and equality do not vary similarly with fortune. Second, having more than one has a moral right to in Locke invariably involves violating the rights of others, even if it does not involve having what they had a prior right to have. If I take more than my rightful share of resources, this need not involve taking anyone else's property; it could involve only taking more than my share from the common (and the common is not anyone's private property). But even just taking more than my

[25] "For what justice is there where there is no personal property" (ELN, 213); "Children cannot well comprehend what injustice is, until they understand property and how particular persons come by it" (*Education*, 110).

[26] Just punishment, for instance, is that which we have a right to inflict, which is the punishment appropriate to another's guilt (E, 4.17.4). Justice in the keeping of contracts (E, 1.2.2; "Morality") is all parties getting their rights as determined by the agreement. Just wars are those fought in defense of our rights, against the "unjust [i.e., not rightful] use of force" (II, 85, 176–83). Justice is in these passages equated with defending or "recovering" (e.g., II, 176, where it means securing reparation) one's right; and the unjust use of force is characterized as either "the invasion of another man's right" (II, 176) or the threat-backed refusal to repair injuries done another by prior unjust uses of force (II, 181). There can, of course, be conflicts of right (see 2.3 and 6.3), and justice in these cases is presumably on the side of the greater, more imperative, or overriding right.

[27] Contrary, for instance, to Winfrey's claim that justice for Locke is closely connected to getting one's "just deserts" ("Charity versus Justice," 423–24).

share of the common violates the rights of others, for it limits their rights to take their share of whatever is rightfully common. This is why waste is a kind of "robbery" for Locke, even though it does not involve taking anything that belongs to another (as private property).

If justice in its most general sense is our having what we have a right to (etc.), we can distinguish between *natural* justice in Locke (conformity to or corrections to satisfy the prepolitical and enduring requirements of natural law) and *civil* justice (conformity to natural law demands for the rightful ordering of states and rightful treatment of citizens).[28] Civil justice is done when governors do only what they have rights to do (when they exercise only their "just powers") and provide for citizens what citizens have a right to. While civil justice has different particulars than natural justice, since consent and trust have conferred new rights on governors, both kinds of justice still consist of all having (or doing) only what we have a moral right to have (or do). And while the central feature of civil justice is juridical equality under general laws and impartial judges ("one rule for rich and poor" [II, 142]), there is also a sense in which *all* justice involves a kind of equality—not equality of possessions, but equal standing under one common set of rules. As Locke says, "justice has but one measure for all men."[29]

Characterizing Locke's theory of justice in this way as centrally concerned with property and right-satisfaction, of course, inevitably suggests comparisons with contemporary "historical" theories of distributive justice, such as Nozick's "entitlement theory."[30] Characterized in its simplest terms, the entitlement theory holds "that a distribution is just if everyone is entitled to the holdings they possess under the distribution." More specifically, "the holdings of a person are just if he is entitled to them by the principles of justice in acquisition and transfer, or by the principle of rectification of injustice (as specified by the first two principles). If each person's holdings are just, then the total set (distribution) of holdings is just."[31] The principle of justice in acquisition must, for Nozick, be something at least analogous to Locke's labor theory of appropriation (while Nozick criticizes Locke's theory, it is not clear that he can replace it with anything fundamentally different). Sim-

[28] A similar distinction is drawn in Polin, "Justice."
[29] "Venditio," 85.
[30] This is defended by Nozick in chapter 7 of *Anarchy*. For a concise, clear summary of Nozick's theory, see Kymlicka, *Contemporary Political Philosophy*, 96–98.
[31] Ibid., 151, 153.

ilarly, the principles of justice in transfer and rectification that
Nozick has in mind look broadly Lockean, identifying as just (re-
spectively) free alienation or inheritance of property and fair reparation for injuries (including return of stolen goods).

The entitlement theory of justice is initially motivated by some
apparently modest and appealing claims: "a distribution is just if
it arises from another just distribution by legitimate means. . . .
Whatever arises from a just situation by just steps is itself just. . . .
That from a just situation a situation *could* have arisen via justice-
preserving means does *not* suffice to show its justice. . . . Justice
in holdings is historical; it depends upon what actually has happened."[32] For Nozick, of course, the defense of the entitlement
theory of justice is one step in his defense of the minimal state—
the state that secures our rights (protects and punishes) and does
nothing not required by that task. For if justice consists in our having what we are entitled to (what we have a moral right to), any
agency that secures our rights will insure that justice has been
done (against the view that a more extensive state is necessary to
do justice by, e.g., redistributing holdings as justice requires).
Justice will, of course, even for Nozick involve some required redistributive activity, as dictated by the principle of just rectification. If you steal my bicycle and sell it to Jones for a fair price, I'm
still *entitled* to the bicycle, even if Jones reasonably takes himself to
be (he was, say, entitled to the money with which he purchased
it). Injustice taints goods on this theory; they remain unjustly held
no matter how well-traveled they are after the initial injustice (this
is part of what it means to claim that justice is historical).

What Nozick objects to, then, is not compulsory redistribution
per se, but redistribution where no apparent wrong has been done
by any individual. When everyone just has the products of their
own "honest industry," redistribution of holdings simply for the
purpose of preserving or establishing some favored pattern of
distribution[33] would violate people's rights to their holdings. In

[32] Ibid., 151–52.

[33] Nozick distinguishes both between *historical* principles of justice (according to
which the justice of a distribution depends on how that distribution came about)
and *end-state* principles (which make justice depend on current, structural features
of a distribution), and between *patterned* principles (according to which justice var-
ies with some "natural dimension" or combination of dimensions) and *unpatterned*
principles (which deny that justice is a matter of conforming to any pattern). Of
the four possible classes of principles of justice—patterned end-state, unpatterned
end-state, patterned historical, and unpatterned historical—the second is empty,
and the first and third are supposed to be eliminated by the argument against pre-

any event, simple free alienation between rational persons will quickly upset any pattern of distribution one imposes on society. To preserve this pattern will involve either constant interference with apparently harmless activities (such as gifts, trades, and sales) or constant redistribution of the results of such activities. In either case, Nozick holds, the interference constitutes a kind of tyranny and a clear violation of individual rights.

There is, of course, a vast literature produced in response to Nozick's defense of his entitlement theory, indicating a wide range of problems with Nozick's arguments.[34] For our purposes here, however, the most important point is this. Suppose that justice is simply a matter of us having (or doing) what we have a moral right to have (or do), as both Locke and Nozick seem to say. Suppose desert, equality of holdings, and utility (etc.) are all irrelevant to social justice. Given this, we *still* do not know that justice will not demand massive and continuous redistribution of holdings, even where the rectification of obvious wrongs like theft and fraud is not at issue. We do not know this *until* we know the specifics of the principles of justice in acquisition and transfer (which Nozick declines to provide). Suppose, for instance, that justice in acquisition (or transfer) allows my taking the product of another's labor when I am in dire and unavoidable need. Or suppose that transfers that produce dire and unavoidable need for others are not just, even if freely consented to by all parties to the transfer (Nozick allows, remember [from 5.4], that free transfers *can* violate the

serving patterns (see below). The entitlement theory utilizes the only plausible member of the sole surviving class—the unpatterned historical principles.

[34] For a sample of this literature, see *Reading Nozick*, from which a number of papers are cited below. A brief, representative list of some of the key problems Nozick's theory faces would include: (1) Is the attack on patterned principles an attack on a straw man? Does anyone really favor absolutely *strict* preservation of patterns? (see, e.g., Scanlon, "Nozick on Rights," 4–5; Goldman, "Entitlement Theory," 834; Hodson, "Nozick," 224). (2) The concept of property itself (or the value of self-government that justifies it) may impose clear limits on holdings and transfers, so that apparently harmless activities are in fact contrary to what justifies property in the first place (see Scanlon, "Nozick on Rights," 11–12, 17). (3) The rectification of injustice required by Nozick's theory may be impossible to accomplish (Davis, "Comments," 840–42), and vast and complicated redistributions of holdings may in any event be necessary to reach an *initially* just distribution (as specified by Nozick's theory). (4) The importance of honest industry and free transfer only seems clear where we imagine all as *equals* in the marketplace; but differential natural endowments and social starting places typically make us very far from equal. (5) Nozick's arguments rely on an implausible atomist or "isolationist" conception of rights, according to which all basic rights are not only logically prepolitical (which seems acceptable), but also logically presocial or precooperative (which does not).

CHAPTER SIX

Lockean proviso). To believe Nozick, we must have good reason to believe that honest industry, inheritance, and free transfer are just grounds of property in a fashion sufficiently strong to exclude conflicting or limiting grounds of other sorts. Do we find reasons for such beliefs in Nozick?

At a reasonably basic, intuitive level, of course, it seems easy to defend our rights to labor's products as absolute in the face of petty demands to strictly equalize holdings or to "forbid capitalist acts between consenting adults."[35] But at this same level it is harder to see redistribution as objectionable interference with our rights, when our rights amount to rights to enjoy luxuries and accumulate vast wealth while others starve. Further, the violation of property rights allegedly involved in all (nonrectificatory) forced redistribution is only a conclusive moral objection to such redistribution if (a) there is no more to morality than rights (so that other moral values cannot outweigh rights), and (b) rights are absolute and can never conflict (so that violation of one right cannot be justified by appeal to others). If either (a) or (b) is false, mere rights-violation involved in a policy is not necessarily a conclusive moral objection to the policy. While Nozick seems to embrace both (a) and (b) in *Anarchy, State, and Utopia*,[36] both (a) and (b) seem false. Neither (a) nor (b) is a part of Locke's theory or is essential to the Lockean theory of rights (as we saw in 1.5 and 2.3); for rights can still function as "trumps" or "side constraints" in a reasonably robust sense without being absolute. And Nozick himself no longer seems to hold either (a) or (b).[37]

The one time Nozick directly confronts the question of rights that might conflict with or limit his favored free market rights, his remarks are, I think, entirely unpersuasive:

[35] Nozick, *Anarchy*, 163.
[36] On Nozick's apparent commitment to (b), see Nagel, "Libertarianism," 196, 199; and Thomson, "Some Ruminations," 50–52.
[37] Even in *Anarchy, State, and Utopia*, Nozick's commitment to (b) was clearly in doubt (see 30n, 41). In *Philosophical Explanations* (479) it seems to have vanished altogether. On Nozick's apparent current rejection of (a), see *Philosophical Explanations*, 495–96, 503. For his even more recent (and much more general) rejection of libertarianism, see *Examined Life*, 30, 286–90, 292. With respect to (a), Nozick does say that a concentration only on rights is appropriate in projects in political philosophy, since rights are all that is relevant there (*Philosophical Explanations*, 503). But one may reasonably ask why this should be the case. If our question is when social policy can legitimately infringe rights, we must consider *all* of the values relevant to legitimation. Even if we confine our attention to (b), however, and consider only the possibility of conflicting or limiting rights, Nozick provides little real support for his anti-redistributive stance.

324

The major objection to speaking of everyone's having a right *to* various things such as equality of opportunity, life, and so on, and enforcing this right, is that these "rights" require a substructure of things and materials and actions; and *other* people may have rights and entitlements over these. . . . There are particular rights over particular things held by particular persons, and particular rights to reach agreements with others. . . . No rights exist in conflict with this substructure of rights. Since no neatly contoured right to achieve a goal will avoid incompatibility with this substructure, no such rights exist. The particular rights over things fill the space of rights, leaving no room for general rights to be in a certain material condition.[38]

But surely Nozick here begs the interesting questions. His remarks will convince only us if (1) we are sure there can be no conflicts of rights, (2) we are sure that particular rights to particular things cannot be grounded in, say, need, and (3) we are sure that it is easier to show that unlimited individual rights of appropriation exist than it is to show that general welfare rights exist. But these points are precisely what need showing; appealing to their obvious truth will not do. And there is little reason to accept any of them as obvious, as we will see in section 3 below, and as Nozick now seems to concede.[39]

The need for Nozick's concession should not surprise us, for the general moral theory to which Nozick appeals in *Anarchy, State, and Utopia* seems ill-suited to the defense of his libertarian principles. This theory is (as we saw in 1.3) Kantian in character: "Side constraints upon action reflect the underlying Kantian principle that individuals are ends and not merely means; they may not be sacrificed or used for the achieving of other ends without their consent. Individuals are inviolable."[40] But we know that Kant himself took this "Kantian principle" to entail not just negative rights of nonaggression and noninterference (the free market rights), but positive rights to aid as well (see 1.3 and 6.3). Treating others as ends involves not just not interfering with them, but taking their ends as (to some extent) our own ends. And we see similar claims about the inviolability of persons (and similar rejections of moral teleology) in Rawls, who reaches conclusions dramatically differ-

[38] *Anarchy*, 238.
[39] *Philosophical Explanations*, 498–501.
[40] *Anarchy*, 31.

ent from Nozick's after apparently employing a similar starting point. Where, exactly, does Nozick diverge from Kant and other Kantians?

We know that for Nozick "a person's shaping his life in accordance with some overall plan is his way of giving meaning to his life."[41] When we make impossible a person's free formulation and pursuit of a life plan, we cut that person off from what is essential to a meaningful life. Our moral rights, for Nozick, express our moral inviolability as a function of the importance of individual self-government (and to this point, Rawls and Locke could for the most part agree with Nozick). But the direct interference of others with our plans (from which our moral "inviolability" protects us) is, of course, only one kind of obstacle to self-government and a meaningful life. Equally important obstacles are the lack of resources or the denial of opportunities, overcoming both of which is typically necessary to self-government. Insofar as negative rights are justified by appeal to the Kantian principle or by the importance of allowing each to have a meaningful life, then, they can at best be justified as presumptive or prima facie constraints on the conduct of others. For where the exercise of our negative rights frustrates the efforts of others to govern themselves, those rights must be seen as limited, conditional, or at the very least in conflict with the competing rights to self-government of others.[42] It is not enough for Nozick simply to appeal to the value of our freedom to formulate and pursue a life plan. Freedom as noninterference with plans is no more basic or required (given a plausible reading of Nozick's own moral foundations) than freedom as opportunity or ability to realize plans. Of these two related conceptions of freedom, Nozick defends the value of only one;[43] but he defends it by appeal to the foundations that clearly establish the value of both.[44]

I have argued that both conceptions of freedom are at work in Locke. The right of self-government, so central to Locke's moral theory, includes not only rights of noninterference, but also rights to make for oneself (within one's fair share) that property which

[41] Ibid., 50.
[42] See, for example, Scheffler, "Natural Rights," 158–59; Scanlon, "Nozick on Rights," 13; Hodson, "Nozick," 53–55; Goldman, "Entitlement Theory," 829–30.
[43] Held, "John Locke and Robert Nozick," 176–80.
[44] See Kymlicka, Contemporary Political Philosophy, 120–23, 147–48, 152; Cohen, "Self-Ownership," 135.

allows independence from the will or dictates of others.[45] True freedom, for Locke, is not just being "free from restraint and violence from others." True freedom is also for each "a liberty to dispose and order, as he lists, his person, actions, possessions, and his whole property, within the allowance of those laws under which he is; and therein *not to be subject to the arbitrary will of another, but freely follow his own*" (II, 57; my emphasis). (The magistrate must not only protect our possessions, but must secure those conditions that allow citizens to "acquire what they further want" [L, 152].) Because true freedom is more than just noninterference by others, "we must not content ourselves with the narrow measures of bare justice; charity, bounty, and liberality must be added to it" (L, 132). The Lockean theory of rights must accept some fuller notion of justice than Nozick's, or defend competing considerations that limit or override the claims of justice.

6.3. Charity

God, Locke writes,

> has given no one of his children such a property in his peculiar portion of the things of this world, but that he has given his needy brother a right to the surplusage of his goods; so that it cannot justly be denied him, when his pressing wants call for it. . . . Charity gives every man a title to so much out of another's plenty as will keep him from extreme want, where he has no means to subsist otherwise. (I, 42)

Given the clarity and directness of these claims in the *First Treatise*, the persistence of the view that Locke denies or is uninterested in rights and duties of charity can only be described as odd.[46] Perhaps its persistence is due to Locke's not mentioning charity in chapter 5 of the *Second Treatise*. But even the *Second Treatise* elsewhere contains clear references to our positive rights and duties.[47]

---

[45] See also Grant, *Liberalism*, 91–93; Replogle, *Recovering the Social Contract*, 166–67; Windstrup, "Freedom and Authority," 253. For a contrasting view, see Shapiro, *Evolution of Rights*, 128–29.

[46] Those who defend this (odd) view of Locke include Strauss, *Natural Right*, 221n, 236–39, 242–44; Macpherson, *Possessive Individualism*, 221; Cox, *Locke on War and Peace*, 170–71, and "Justice," 255–56; Goldwin, "John Locke," 484–85; Andrew, *Shylock's Rights*, 56–65; Pangle, *Republicanism*, 143–44, 161, 306–7; Cohen, "Marx and Locke," 382–83.

[47] II, 5 mentions our duty of charity; II, 6 suggests a duty at least as strong as that specified in I, 42 ("when his own preservation comes not in competition, [he ought], as much as he can, to preserve the rest of mankind"); II, 70 notes that we

Locke's other works, of course, are liberally peppered with similar references. We all have a duty to console our distressed neighbors, to give "relief" to "one in trouble," and to "feed the hungry" (ELN, 195). It is "a virtue and every particular man's duty" to "relieve with an alms the poor" (ECT, 182). Locke's educational writings stress the importance of teaching our children liberality—the willingness to part cheerfully with what we have.[48] Even in his notorious "Proposal for Reform of the Poor Laws" (which I discuss more fully below), Locke clearly assumes a natural right to food and shelter (etc.).[49] In short, a substantial right and duty of charity and liberality are affirmed throughout Locke's works.[50] We all have a right to the surplus goods of another to satisfy at least our basic needs, if we are not able to satisfy them ourselves, and others have a duty to supply such goods. This conception of charity seems to approximate the familiar Thomistic conception.[51]

How shall we understand the nature and extent of the right and duty of charity?[52] The right to charity seems in I, 42 (lines 1–8) to function as a limit on the rights of property or justice: rights of charity either conflict with rights of justice and always override them, or else simply define a limit to the possible extent of rights of justice.[53] Either way, of course, this reading creates an immediate problem for my understanding of Locke's view of justice (in 6.2). For if justice is our having what we have a right to, how can rights to charity override or limit the demands of justice? Is charity one kind of justice, in conflict, perhaps, only with a lower "bare

---

owe "relief and support to the distressed"; and II, 93 mentions the "true love of mankind and society, and such charity as we owe all to one another."

[48] See *Education*, 110, where liberality is discussed immediately *before* justice; and Tarcov, *Locke's Education*, 141–45. Locke finds liberality as well to be one of the virtues taught in the Sermon on the Mount, and quotes approvingly from Luke 11:41 ("Give alms of such things as ye have") (R, 141 [188], 143 [195]). And *A Letter Concerning Toleration* (as we have just seen) mentions the need to go beyond "bare justice" to charity and liberality.

[49] "Proposal for Reform of the Poor Laws," 382–83.

[50] See especially Ashcraft, *Revolutionary Politics*, 272–73n, and *Locke's Two Treatises*, 127.

[51] See Dunn, "Justice," 81–82. Contrast with the claims of Andrew (*Shylock's Rights*, 30–31, 56–65).

[52] Locke does not always speak of charity as a right or duty. Sometimes he speaks of it as a feeling (compare with "gratitude," which can be either a duty or a feeling). Here I am concerned only with the relevant rights and duties; but see in 6.4 how a confusion of these two senses of "charity" can create a misleading impression of Locke's position.

[53] See Dunn, "Justice," 74, 81–82; Parry, *John Locke*, 90; Winfrey, "Charity versus Justice," 436. This conflict is part of what Mack regards as an irreconcilable tension in Locke's works ("Distributive Justice," 133, 150).

justice" (which position would approximate one standard medieval view)? Or is charity a limit to justice, the realm of justice not including all rights (but only, say, negative ones)? Locke is not very clear on this point and, as a result, leaves his concept of justice to this extent unclear as well. At bottom, however, this is only a verbal problem. The important point for Locke is that the needy can have a right to the property of others (or what was formerly their property—i.e., the fruits of their honest industry). But to what extent and in what circumstances do they have this right?

The most important qualifications on this right mentioned by Locke in I, 42 are as follows. (1) The needy are entitled to charity only where they have "no means to subsist otherwise." Locke seems to mean by this that only those who can't work to support themselves and their families—the disabled, sick, elderly, or those genuinely unable to secure employment—are entitled to relief. Locke wrote to Molyneux, for instance, that "everyone, according to what Providence has placed him in, is bound to labour for the public good as far as he is able, or else he has no right to eat,"[54] and on another occasion wrote that "the true and proper relief of the poor . . . consists in finding work for them."[55] Locke also wrote, of course, that the poor "must" have food, clothing, and shelter "whether they work or not";[56] but it is unlikely that he regarded able-bodied vagabonds and beggars as entitled to charity in the same way as were those who had "no means to subsist." Everyone is entitled only to access to a living, to the opportunity to preserve, govern, and improve themselves by their own labor. If one cannot use this opportunity (because one cannot labor), then one is entitled to charity. It seems clear that Locke regarded charity as inappropriate for able-bodied adults (although it seems just as clear that he failed to appreciate fully the many ways in which factors beyond their control could put even able-bodied adults in positions of need and dependence).[57] In any event, Locke is clearly committed to at least the minimal position that those in need who really are unable to work have a right to the (former) property of others.[58]

[54] Fox Bourne, *Life*, 2:281.
[55] "Proposal for Reform of the Poor Laws," 383.
[56] Ibid., 382.
[57] See Parry, "Individuality," 175–77.
[58] Shapiro attributes to Locke a "negative libertarianism" (*Evolution of Rights*, 100), apparently on the strength of his belief that Locke requires only that the needy be put to work, not be fed (ibid., 93, 127, 142). As we have seen, however, this is at best true only of the able-bodied needy. And it is not clear, at any rate,

(2) The needy have a right only to be kept from "extreme want" so that they may "subsist." Charity only requires that we satisfy the basic needs of the poor[59] (presumably consisting of "meat, drink, clothing, and firing"). We may not withhold what the poor need, and we may not exploit the market in such a way as to put them (or others) in danger of perishing.[60] But we *may* satisfy our duty of charity simply by providing needed goods for the poor at lower-than-usual prices, if the poor are able to afford the lower prices.[61]

(3) Charity gives the needy a right only to the "surplusage" or "plenty" that others possess. Those who labor to make property for themselves are entitled to keep at least a "liberal allowance of the conveniences of life" (I, 41) for the "*comfortable* preservation of their beings" (I, 87; my emphasis). Each has a right to "subsist and enjoy the conveniences of life" (I, 97).[62] The "surplusage" Locke has in mind as vulnerable to the claims of charity is probably whatever possessions are beyond the requirements of comfortable preservation—that is, our luxuries and unused wealth. Property owners may justly keep what is required for their own needs (and for the present and future needs of their dependents) plus a reasonable "cushion" of modest comforts (see 4.4 and 5.4). Beyond this, they may justly keep only that which is *not* required to satisfy the needs of the poor (who cannot work). Locke, however, seemed to believe that efficient management would leave most of even this surplusage untouched by the legitimate claims of the poor. Locke apparently regarded most of the poor as capable in some way or to some extent of supporting themselves, so that not many would really require charity.[63] Since, in many cases, charity can consist of putting the poor to work, any initial investment from the surplus-

---

why the right to employment should not also be regarded as a positive right, inconsistent with "negative libertarianism" (since a free market need not produce employment for all who want it).

[59] See Parry, *John Locke*, 90–91; Winfrey, "Charity versus Justice," 436–37.

[60] "Venditio," 86–87. See Dunn's discussion of this point in "Justice," 73–74.

[61] "Venditio," 85.

[62] There are, as we have seen, many similar passages in the *Second Treatise*. Notice also Locke's emphases elsewhere on "ease, safety, and delight" or "ease, plenty, and variety" for all ("Knowledge, Its Extent and Measure," 164, 166, 168), and on government's securing "those things that are necessary to the *comfortable* support of our lives" (L, 152; my emphasis).

[63] "Could all the able hands in England be brought to work, the greatest part of the burden that lies upon the industrious for maintaining the poor would immediately cease" ("Proposal for Reform of the Poor Laws," 378). See also Waldron, "Locke's Account," 45n; and Parry, *John Locke*, 90.

age required to create employment for the poor will eventually be
returned by their labor.

Regardless of how likely it is that the surplusage will be drawn
upon, however, it is not at all clear why Locke should take this
surplusage as the only property vulnerable to the claims of charity,
or take subsistence as the only content of the rights of charity. If
all persons have a right "to subsist and enjoy the conveniences of
life," why do not the needy have a right to conveniences, in addition to subsistence? Conversely, if persons really only have a
right to what they need to subsist, why should the wealthy be
entitled to keep their comforts safe from the demands of the poor?
Each person *is* entitled, on Locke's view, to show a certain preference for self over others in matters of property (as we will see below in 6.4); and the laborer who produced them clearly has a different kind of claim on goods than others who simply need them.
But it is hard to believe that Locke really means that the wealthy
may without impropriety keep their comforts and conveniences if
others will die from need as a result (through no fault of their
own). It seems more likely that Locke's claims about the "surplusage" reflect two other beliefs. First, since some comforts and conveniences (beyond our basic needs) may be essential to self-government (i.e., pursuit of our own projects), our claims to that
property will at least be much stronger than claims to luxuries or
great wealth, even if these more limited claims are also vulnerable
in extreme cases to the demands of need. Second, Locke's remarks
on the "surplusage" reflect his perception of the actual condition
of the world in his day: since very few of the poor are in fact unable to work (in Locke's view), no more than the surplus of
wealth, and probably less, will in fact have to be given over for
charity.

As a matter of theory, however, it seems clear that the Lockean
theory of rights (the *best* Lockean position) must include a stronger
right to charity than the one literally described by Locke. We must
preserve others wherever our own preservation (or that of our
families) is not thereby put in jeopardy (II, 6), so long as this does
not involve surrendering our comforts when others have a genuine surplus to give. The fundamental principle of natural law (of
God's will) is that mankind is to be preserved (1.4). The derivative
rights to self-preservation and self-government entail limits on
property, since these rights are held equally by all. But if I cannot
hold property that infringes your right of self-preservation, I cannot keep comforts and conveniences while you starve (at least if

you have no other remedy); your needs must trump my comforts.[64] Strong rights of charity, then, are required by the equal rights of self-preservation. They are required as well by our equal rights of self-government (our natural freedom). Since the right to free formulation and pursuit of our life plans (which justifies our making more property than we need merely for subsistence) requires that we have the opportunity to support ourselves and manage our lives in an at least minimally free fashion, it requires as well that at least our basic needs be satisfied (when we cannot satisfy them ourselves).[65] Charity (with the rights of self-preservation and self-government) requires that our basic needs be met, and that the property of others be correspondingly limited or overridden. The fair share limit (and the right of self-government) requires that we have the opportunity to do more by our labor than simply meet our basic needs, and that the holdings of others be restructured to make this possible. The right of self-government may make our comforts immune to charity when there is a surplus (of luxuries) on which to draw. But only what we need for preservation is in principle immune to the claims of need. The limits on property are thus importantly related to Locke's attacks on dependence, slavery, and absolutism. Rights to charity are necessary, for instance, so that need is not allowed to make us subject to others' wills, make us dependent on them, or make us their vassals.[66] The same reasoning in Locke that justifies rights of property or justice, then, also justifies rights of charity.[67] It should not surprise us, as a result, that Locke approvingly quotes Hooker in II, 5, noting that Hooker "derives the great maxims of justice and charity" *together*, from the same line of reasoning about the "equality of man by nature."

Suppose we have accepted (some version of) Locke's right to

[64] See Plamenatz, *Man and Society*, 1:247–48; and Parry, *John Locke*, 40–41.

[65] See Lomasky, *Persons, Rights*, 126–28; and Gewirth, *Reason and Morality*, 218.

[66] As Locke makes especially clear in I, 42–43. See also Tuck, *Natural Rights Theories*, 172.

[67] Tully argues that property entails charity rights, because property is *for* preservation; once our preservation is secure, then, further holdings must be conditional on the preservation of others (*Discourse*, 132). My objection to Tully's claims here is only to his contention that property is *for* preservation in Locke. Property is also *for* self-government in Locke, which gives claims to a comfortable quantity of property priority over claims to luxuries or great wealth. There is, then, a hierarchy of property claims, descending in strength from needs to comforts to luxuries. Charity's first claim is on the luxuries (surplusage) held by others, and its ultimate limit is the needs of others; the comforts of others are relatively but not absolutely secure from our claims to charity.

charity for the genuinely needy. What, we may ask next, are the consequences of this for those individuals who have consented to be members of some political society? We know that individuals who enter legitimate civil societies surrender some of their rights to the community (and, ultimately, to its government); specifically, they surrender those rights whose surrender is necessary for effective government (II, 99, 129) (see 6.1). It is hard to see how rights to charity could be taken to be among the rights that must be given up, for their surrender hardly seems necessary to morally secure any essential functions of government. Further, we know that we cannot give to others (nor can civil law create for them) rights to do what destroys or tends to destroy us (see 5.1). Since lack of access to essential goods threatens our lives, we cannot give up the right to charity that could be our only moral guarantee of access to these goods in hard times. It seems likely, then, that Locke would hold that persons in society retain their rights to charity, and that even in civil society charity rights either limit or override some of the property rights of those with a "surplusage" (and perhaps, in extreme cases, the rights to comforts as well).

Governments, of course, are trusted to, and hence "obliged to secure everyone's property" (i.e., rights) (II, 131). Governments must, then, secure relief for those in need who are unable to provide for themselves: "common charity teaches that those should be most taken care of by the law, who are least capable of taking care for themselves."[68] Governments may secure rights to charity by taxing the surplus of property to provide relief for the poor who have not been helped privately. And they may mandate a restructuring of employment opportunities to make access to a living available to all. Indeed, governments may prohibit certain (or all) forms of private charity and instead secure rights to charity centrally (as we will see in 6.4). For if all of the needy are provided for by government services, the individual's private duty of charity will never find any objects for required performance. However it is accomplished, though, Locke's position seems to require some form of "social welfare" program, given that private giving is likely to be insufficient to the task and rights of "seizure" for the poor invite chaos.[69]

---

[68] *Some Considerations of the Consequences of the Lowering of Interest and Raising the Value of Money*, 11.

[69] Governments must give citizens what they have a right to and so must be redistributive at least to this extent (contrary to Dunn's apparent suggestion in *Political Thought*, 36n). This is *not* to say (with Tully) that Locke favors a "revolution

Even this position may seem to involve a substantial "moral parochialism," however, for Locke writes as if charity is a duty in civil society owed only to the poor of one's *own* country. While Locke never explicitly denies that there are international duties of relief, his tone certainly does not encourage one to believe that he considered them very seriously. But of course the needy everywhere have rights against all persons to what is needed to keep them from extreme want. Our government, of course, is only entrusted with securing *our* rights, not those of the poor abroad. But our duty of charity toward the needy in other countries (or areas) would seem to be unchanged by our entry into civil society. Can the distance of these needy people from us, and the proximity of "our own" poor, make our duties to the former class so far less imperative than our duties to the latter that they hardly matter at all? I will suggest below (in 6.4) some ways in which "distance" *is* morally relevant; but these will not be sufficient to eliminate altogether Locke's problem in this area.

We have available to us, of course, some indications of what Locke might have taken to be the best way for a government to secure the charity rights of the local poor—in the form of Locke's well-known proposal for the Board of Trade on the reform of the Poor Laws.[70] While Locke's principles seem to allow a much more extensive and rather different program than the one he proposes,[71] there is no denying that Locke's actual program is a hard, unpleasant one that shows an almost astonishing insensitivity to the true causes and extent of poverty in his day (I say only "almost" astonishing, given the quite similar insensitivity of so many others). In his "Proposal," poverty is blamed largely (although not exclusively) on vice and idleness: the "growth of the poor," Locke claims, is largely caused by "the relaxation of discipline and corruption of manners" (378). Virtuous (honest, industrious) citizens seem to prosper; the poor, then, must be mostly vicious (dishon-

---

to reconstitute society" on Leveller principles (*Discourse*, 174). None of Locke's claims requires redistribution of land rather than welfare programs or the provision of economic opportunities (see Horne, "Review of Tully," 454; and Vaughn, *John Locke*, 100). Locke probably favored the least government interference necessary to secure the rights of the poor. But some such interference is necessary. Among those who have seen this are Seliger (*Liberal Politics*, 174–76, 179), Waldron ("Locke's Account," 45; "Enough and as Good," 327), Lemos ("Locke's Theory of Property," 236–37; *Hobbes and Locke*, 150–52, 159), and Ashcraft (*Revolutionary Politics*, 272–73n).

[70] Which Cranston refers to as "this appalling document" (*John Locke*, 425) and Parry as "Locke's draconian proposals" ("Individuality," 175).

[71] Seliger, *Liberal Politics*, 179.

est, lazy).[72] For the able-bodied poor, as a consequence, Locke makes harsh provision. Children as young as three will be separated from their mothers (so the mothers can work freely) and put in working schools, fed on bread (and, if necessary, gruel) (384). Locke proposes severe punishments for unlicensed beggars and vagabonds or repeat offenders, and notes that the poor may be put to work at less than the usual wage. But even while making his unsympathetic proposals, Locke still insists that if poor people die for want of relief, their parishes should be held responsible and fined (390).

Whether Locke's proposal accurately reflects either his personal dispositions or his philosophical principles is, of course, a separate question. Locke's proposal was, after all, obliged to be practicable and acceptable when viewed against the existing harsh background of the Elizabethan Poor Laws—what Paine later called "instruments of civil torture."[73] We know that in his philosophy, and apparently in his personal life as well, Locke was much more sympathetic to the plight of the helpless poor than the "Proposal" would ever lead one to believe. Lady Masham reports that Locke was "naturally compassionate, and exceedingly charitable to those in want. . . . People who had been industrious, but were, through age or infirmity, past labour, he was very bountiful to; and he used to blame that sparingness with which such were ordinarily relieved, 'as if it sufficed only that they should be kept from starving or extreme misery; whereas they had,' he said, 'a right to living comfortably in the world.' "[74] This suggests, of course, that Locke believed the helpless poor to have a right to considerably more than mere subsistence, although one would never guess this from reading his "Proposal."

But whether we take Lady Masham's report or Locke's own proposals as evidence of his personal feelings, we must in any event

---

[72] Macpherson, of course, rests much of his case for the "differential rationality" of social classes in Locke on these claims (*Possessive Individualism*, 222–23, 244–45). See also McNally, "Locke, Levellers," 33; Wood, *Capitalism*, 74–76, 78–79, 106–9, and *Politics*, 35; Dunn, *Political Thought*, 227–28, 251; Parry, *John Locke*, 91. As Tarcov points out (against Macpherson), however, while Locke may assume that the idle poor are vicious and that the virtuous prosper, this does not entail that the prosperous are all virtuous (*Locke's Education*, 104, 238), nor is there any evidence that Locke believed this (despite Macpherson's reliance on it). Indeed, Locke writes elsewhere that virtue and prosperity seldom accompany one another (R, 182 [245]). Further, there is no reason at all to believe that the idle poor are "excluded" by Locke "from the human species," as Polin suggests ("Justice," 275).

[73] *Rights of Man*, 270.

[74] Fox Bourne, *Life*, 2:535–36.

be extremely wary of inferring too much from evidence of Locke's personal conduct about the proper interpretation of his philosophy.[75] I take Locke's considered views on rights to charity to be those outlined above (and *not* those we might creatively infer from either his Poor Law proposal or evidence of his personal conduct). Rights to charity will limit or override the claims of property or justice. Locke's theory of justice, as a result, must not be taken to be a purely historical theory of acquisition, transfer, and rectification. Historical claims to property are limited in at least three ways: (1) by the waste limit, which requires continuous use of property; (2) by the fair share limit, which requires that all have opportunities to acquire or access to their share of God's bounty; and (3) by rights to charity, which require that the surplus (and perhaps the comforts) of others be available to guarantee the preservation of the helpless or working poor.

6.4. Positive and Negative Rights

We can begin to better understand the place of positive rights (to charity) within Locke's overall theory of rights, by taking up again a question first raised in 1.5: why does Locke allow a moral asymmetry between self and others? Charity limits the claims of property and justice, but it still allows us to give priority to our own needs over those of others; we need only preserve others when our own preservation is not thereby risked (or perhaps even when our own comfort is not risked). And this may seem odd, given that the fundamental principle of natural law is that mankind is to be preserved and that all persons are equally parts of mankind. Further, respect for persons (taking them seriously) seems to require taking their plans and ends to have the same kind of moral importance as our own. But Locke seems to allow each to exercise not only a preference for self, but also a preference for family over others, and for local poor over other poor. Indeed, one senses in Locke a "scale" of the moral priority of needs and plans that is strictly relative to their "closeness" to oneself—roughly, self, family, local poor, others (in descending order of priority). Can "close-

[75] To cite another example, Locke's personal involvement in the slave trade should not be a decisive factor in our reading of his philosophical position on the morality of slavery. Not many of us always live up to (or even "talk up to") the moral principles that we defend in more reflective moments, and in some sense genuinely believe to be valid. Locke's greatness as a philosopher in no way guarantees that his personal conduct or practical proposals always accurately reflected his philosophical principles.

ness" to self be morally important in this way within Locke's (universalist) natural law deontic theory?

A "yes" answer seems possible along the following lines. Take first the asymmetry between self and others. We know that God wills the preservation of mankind, and that God's will is law for us. But I have argued (in 1.4) that what this law in fact requires is that we follow the best set of rules for preserving mankind. Now all persons are equally "men" in Locke's sense (they are equally God's creatures, equally priceless, equally made in His image, etc.). But persons also tend to care most about their (own) well-being, know themselves and their needs best, and are least likely to be meddlesome in or to frustrate their (own) plans (as Mill famously argued in *On Liberty*). As a rule, then, each person will be the one best suited to look to self-preservation and personal happiness.[76] Mankind will be most effectively preserved, then, if each tends to self first, and only afterwards to the needs and plans of others. (By similar reasoning, those close to us should be tended to before those farther from us.) And since God has entrusted each person with a life to care for (as we saw in 5.2), we have additional special obligations with respect to care of ourselves that we lack in the case of caring for others. The strength of our duty to preserve mankind, then, can be expected to diminish as the distance from ourselves (of the "man" in question) increases, despite the fact that we are all equally persons.

Similarly, while all persons must be equally respected, respecting oneself and others would seem to involve quite different kinds of conduct. Respecting others involves treating them as what they are—that is, caring for them if they are *not* persons (and need care), but treating them as autonomous individuals if they *are* persons. Treating another as an autonomous person requires maintaining a certain distance, allowing another to formulate and pursue personal plans, make mistakes, lead a separate life. We should prevent that person's misery and death (at least where that person *wants* us to) and make sure that the opportunity for self-government is available. But respect requires nonpaternalistic attitudes and conduct (4.5). None of these reservations is necessary where respecting oneself is at issue. It follows that one is entitled (in-

---

[76] Remember that the particular counterinstances are not objections to this claim, and that by "persons" or "men" Locke means only rational individuals, who are given the moral law, can control their desires by reason, can formulate plans and pursue values. The case here, then, is similar to Locke's case against paternalism (which I examined in 4.5).

deed, obliged) to concentrate on oneself (over other persons) in
the formulation and pursuit of plans and the provision of comforts. In matters of life and death, where others will likely want
our help, preferring ourselves (feeding myself rather than another,
say) is permissible (where other things are morally equal), because
the choice between equals is morally indifferent. Each may per-
missibly choose self, without denying the equal personhood or importance of others.

These arguments have primarily concerned the moral asymmetry of self and others. But we have also seen that one argument
(the rule-consequentialist one) seems to yield as well a conclusion
concerning the relative strengths of our various duties toward others (namely, that they are weaker toward those "farther" from us).
It would be helpful to see if this suggestion can be sustained more
systematically; and it would be useful as well to have some sense
of the relative strengths of positive and negative duties in Locke.
But there is only one place in Locke's writings where he has anything substantial to say about the stringency of duties—in essay 7
of the *Essays on the Law of Nature*. I turn briefly to that essay, to see
what light it might cast on our present concerns.

Locke tells us in essay 7 ("Is the Binding Force of the Law of
Nature Perpetual and Universal? Yes") that while "the binding
force of the law of nature is permanent" and "continuous," this
does not mean that we are "bound at all times to perform everything that the law of nature commands." We are allowed to
"sometimes stop acting according to the law . . . ; rest is sometimes allowed" (ELN, 193). By way of explanation, Locke distinguishes four categories of duty (according to the ways in which
acts are forbidden or required) defined by natural law.

(1) Acts that are absolutely forbidden (e.g., murder or theft).
These acts we are never at liberty to do (ELN, 193–95). Locke
seems to have in mind here the class of *perfect negative duties*.[77]

[77] Here, as elsewhere in this work, I use the negative duty/positive duty distinction to refer to the loose, intuitive distinction between duties to forbear and duties
to perform positive actions (*without* assuming that this distinction can be drawn in
an especially rigorous way). By perfect duty I again intend the standard account:
perfect duties are those which require a strict, uniform adherence because they
correlate with others' rights (we are unimpressed if the murderer points to all the
other times he *didn't* murder, pleading that he only did it "just this once"; there is
no "quota" of not-murdering that can be filled, after which we are free to decide
whether to murder or not). Imperfect duties, by contrast, allow some measure of
discretion by actors in how and when they perform the required actions, for the
duties in this case do not correlate with any other persons' rights that would be
breached by nonperformance on particular occasions.

(2) Required sentiments or attitudes (such as reverence toward and fear of God, affection for parents, love of one's neighbors). One must always maintain these sentiments, so as to be properly "disposed toward" the objects of duty (ELN, 195). Here Locke describes what were earlier called by others (e.g., Hobbes) obligations *in foro interno*. I am skeptical about the possibility of having obligations or duties to have certain feelings or attitudes, since these may often be matters beyond our control;[78] and Locke's later writings on toleration display a related doubt that religious conviction can be forced on people, by law or by a sense of obligation. But given that we also have duties to act toward God, parents, and neighbors, and not just to feel certain things with respect to them, there is, I suppose, nothing wrong with saying that we have a duty to be prepared to act as required (if such preparation is necessary to so acting). We must try to remain "disposed toward" them in certain ways so that we will be able to act as required (which may be all that obligations *in foro interno* really amount to[79]). As Locke says elsewhere, "all negative precepts are always to be obeyed," but "positive commands only sometimes on occasions. But we ought always to be furnished with the habits and dispositions to those positive duties in a readiness against those occasions."[80] This last remark by Locke refers not only to our "required sentiments," but also to the third class of duties discussed by Locke in the *Essays*.

(3) Acts where "the outward performance is commanded," but where "we are not under obligation continuously, but only at a particular time and in a particular manner." Locke's examples are the outward worship of God, consoling the distressed, relieving the troubled, and feeding the hungry (ELN, 195). This may seem at first to be an attempt to define a class of imperfect duties, duties that do not correlate with the rights of others and consequently allow the actor to decide when and where to perform. But when Locke explains his remarks further, he says: "For we are not obliged to provide with shelter and to refresh with food any and every man, or at any time whatever, but only when a poor man's misfortune calls for our alms and our property supplies means for charity" (ELN, 195). This, however, is not an account of imperfect duty, but only of the conditions on our positive duties. I am bound to give to others not always, but only when their needs and my

[78] See my *Moral Principles and Political Obligations*, 166–67.
[79] See, for example, Hobbes, *Leviathan*, chapter 15, paragraphs 36–39.
[80] Letter to Grenville, in Fox Bourne, *Life*, 1:393.

means require it. But when these conditions are satisfied, charity is absolutely required. I cannot decide *not* to give it on that occasion, preferring to wait for some future needy person to appear, for the needy person has (as we saw in 6.3) a right to charity (and nothing Locke says here contradicts that point). Locke's third category of duty, then, is that of *conditional (perfect) positive duties*. There are no imperfect duties in Locke's moral theory (as I suggested in 2.1); all duties correlate with the rights of others. Notice in passing, however, that Locke's comments on this third category do seem to suggest that the "proximity" or "special placement" of the needy "calls for our alms" (an issue to which we will need to return).

(4) "Cases where the action in itself is not commanded but only circumstances accompanying it" (ELN, 195). Locke seems to have in mind here cases in which one is not bound to do A, but if one *chooses* to do A, one has a duty to do A in a certain fashion. Thus, one is not bound to "hold a conversation about his neighbor"; but if one chooses to do so, one is duty-bound to converse in a "candid and friendly" fashion (ELN, 195).

Locke draws two main conclusions from this classification of duties. First, while some duties are *constant* (those in categories [1] and [2]) and some are *conditional* (those in categories [3] and [4]), the binding force of natural law is perpetual and universal in all of these cases (despite initial appearances to the contrary). Second, while some duties (and rights) are special, arising out of "the various relations between men" (such as the duties of princes, subjects, generals, soldiers, and parents), and others are general (binding "any and every man"), this also in no way contradicts the claim that the binding force of natural law is perpetual and universal (ELN, 195–97). Both of the points Locke is making seem to me to be fair and important. Natural law (natural morality) constantly binds all who either are naturally or who make themselves subject to its provisions. That duties are conditional or special does not argue against their following from a universally applicable moral law, or argue in favor of a "partialist" moral theory (see 4.1 above). Locke's systematic defense of impartialism (or universalism) in moral theory, in the face of his recognition that duties can be conditional or special, is, as far as I know, the first explicit defense of its kind.

Locke's arguments also suggest, however, two ways in which some duties might be more stringent than others (to return to the point from which we began our examination of Locke's classification of duties). First, duties to those "closer" to us are often stronger than duties to others, because we often have additional special obligations or duties to those close to us (and they have special rights against us). While we have general duties to all other persons (e.g., to help the distressed), we enter into additional special relations with spouses, partners, children, and friends, which ground further duties and thus make our duties to them more imperative (as I argued in 4.1). Second, even those with whom we have no ongoing or voluntary special relations may in some cases be specially placed with respect to us, making our duties to them especially imperative. This point bears both on the relative stringency of positive and negative duties and on the relative stringency of different kinds of positive duties.

The difficulties here can probably be best understood when viewed in the context of a certain class of objections to governmental or legal enforcement of positive duties (in the form of welfare programs, Good Samaritan laws, etc.). The objections I have in mind come from two sources: one is the view we can call "minimalism," while the other is a particular form of "liberalism." The minimalist argument, in its simplest form, runs as follows: civil society, including its legal system, is in the best interests of every individual; but there is an individual price in liberty that must be paid for living in society. We must each refrain from doing those things that make the orderly functioning of society impossible. But this price should be kept as low as possible, or people will rightly feel oppressed by it. Since directly harming one another by murder, assault, theft, and the like, makes peaceful pursuit of our interests impossible, the law may legitimately proscribe such actions. But being charitable and rescuing one another from perilous situations, the argument continues, are not similarly necessary for an orderly society. It might be nicer if we all helped one another, just as it would be nicer if everyone raised pretty flower gardens in their front yards; but neither activity is necessary for an orderly society, and thus neither should be a concern of the law. The burden of participating in a scheme of mutual assistance should not be forced on anyone; it should be assumed voluntarily, if at all.

One conception of liberalism yields a different (but obviously related) ground for opposing the enforcement of positive duties. The essence of liberalism, on this view, is a special kind of neutrality. According to this liberal, governments and laws must remain scrupulously neutral among competing moral, religious, or other personal or sectarian conceptions of the good life; the law must favor no one view over any other. The liberal's reasons for insisting on neutrality may be either theoretical or "practical." On the theoretical side, the liberal may be motivated by skeptical doubt about the possibility of showing any one view of the good life to be uniquely justifiable, that is, rationally preferable to alternative views. In the face of such doubts, the law's decision to enforce any particular conception of the good looks hopelessly arbitrary. On the practical side, the liberal may simply look at how deeply entrenched and firmly defended our particular moral and religious views tend to be, and despair of ever having a free, cooperative society while at the same time enforcing duties that conflict with the deepest convictions of many. The only practical stance on such difficult matters is one of neutrality.

What kinds of laws satisfy this requirement of neutrality? Our legal system should, on this conception of liberalism, allow each person the greatest possible freedom to pursue a personal conception of the good, consistent with allowing everyone this same freedom. This seems to indicate that the law ought to concentrate first (and, perhaps, last as well) on preventing aggressive, coercive exercises of liberty, those which limit another's freedom to pursue a personal life plan. So once again, the direct harming of others will be the law's primary focus. From the theoretical perspective, our duties not to directly harm others may seem the most defensible, the most nearly objective duties. From the practical viewpoint, the duties not to directly harm others will be the "lowest common denominator" of competing ethical and religious views; they will be the duties in which people of diverse persuasions can all voluntarily acquiesce. By contrast, the duties to give charity or to rescue those in peril appear, on the one hand, to be theoretically controversial, and on the other hand, to be duties that form a part of only some, not all, ethical views. To allow the law to enforce such duties would be to take precisely the kind of stand on difficult theoretical and practical problems that the liberal is committed to avoiding.

The minimalist and liberal rejections of the enforcement of positive duties share several features, but for my purposes the one to emphasize is the most obvious: on both views, the negative duties we have to refrain from directly harming others are viewed as somehow more basic than any positive duties we might have to prevent harm from befalling them. On the minimalist view, they are more basic because more essential to the orderly functioning of society; on the liberal view, they are more basic because less controversial.

How ought a Lockean to respond to these charges? It may seem that Locke's own position has much in common with both the liberal and the minimalist views, particularly the latter, and particularly when we emphasize various remarks made by Locke in his writings on toleration. In *An Essay Concerning Toleration*, for instance, Locke argues that the magistrate's job is simply to preserve the peace ("quiet and comfortable living of men in society"). Giving alms to the poor is a virtue and every person's duty, Locke claims, but the magistrate may still lawfully prohibit the giving of alms (ECT, 181–82). Locke only says that it is *permissible* for the magistrate to prohibit this, not that requiring the giving of alms would be wrong. But the two paragraphs together seem to at least suggest that charity is a duty having no intimate connection to the "public weal," and so a duty that the magistrate ought not to enforce. This will seem especially true if we read the *Essay* in light of Locke's later *A Letter Concerning Toleration*, where he makes claims that sound even more strongly minimalist. "Uncharitableness," Locke says there, is a "sin"; but it is not "to be punished by the magistrate," since it is not "prejudicial to other men's rights" nor does it "break the public peace of societies" (L, 148). This passage suggests not only that government is for preserving property, not enforcing virtue or religious doctrine;[81] it even seems to suggest that charity is not a right.

How are we to square this evidence with Locke's assertions that charity is a right of those in need (if they cannot provide for themselves), that the refusal to aid them (when we have the means) is "prejudicial to their rights"? And how can we reconcile this apparent minimalism with my claims that for Locke governments must enforce the charity rights of the poor? Notice, first, that the passage cited from Locke's 1667 *Essay* does not say that the poor have no right to relief; it says only that the magistrate may forbid giving alms to beggars (for which policy it is not hard to think of good supporting reasons). If the magistrate makes other provisions for the relief of the poor (e.g., by taxation and poor laws), prohibiting only this one means of relief, then the duties of individual citizens will not require the giving of alms, nor will the poor have a right to alms (since the poor can then be provided for through the legal system). Society's right (and duty) to coordinate

---

[81] See Cox, "Justice," 252; and Polin, "Justice," 276.

efforts to secure the charity rights of the needy is thus perfectly consistent with its prohibition of specific (and, in this case, counterproductive) uncoordinated or private forms of charity.

Locke's *Letter* is the harder case, for here Locke *does* seem to say specifically that no rights are breached by lack of charity. It is important to see, however, that Locke seems in the cited passage to mean by "charity" something rather different than the duty to aid the needy. Locke, remember, talks about charity in the very first paragraph of the *Letter*; and there "charity" seems to mean feelings of love for others and toleration of their views and (harmless) practices (L, 123–24). But having those kinds of feelings is required only in Locke's second category of duties (the duties of required sentiment), which is specifically distinguished by him from the (third category) duties to perform acts of charity (consoling, relieving, feeding). "Uncharitableness," then, can mean either failing to have the requisite feelings of charity (we must keep these "warm in our hearts"[82]) or failing to actually give aid to the needy. And it is entirely possible that Locke means in the *Letter* only that uncharitableness of the first kind is not prejudicial to our rights (and should not be forbidden by law). Indeed, it seems quite plausible to maintain that my failure to have certain feelings toward you cannot breach your rights.[83] But this would be perfectly consistent with claiming that uncharitableness of the second kind (the kind with which we are here concerned) does prejudice our rights— namely, the rights of the genuinely needy to the surplus of others' property—and ought to be prohibited by government.

Magistrates should not (because they cannot) legislate feelings. We should not be (cannot be) forced to be charitable in our hearts (to love and be tolerant of others), for to lack such feelings in itself does no injury to any other. These claims, as I have already suggested, are related to central themes in Locke's writings on toleration—that force cannot compel belief (or feelings), and that care of each person's soul is a personal matter. But magistrates can compel acts, and should do so where failure to act breaches the rights of others. This is the case in instances of morally required charity. On the reading urged here, Locke is no minimalist (of the

[82] We must keep "love to God" and "charity . . . warm in our hearts, and sincerely practice what they upon occasion suggest to us" (Fox Bourne, *Life*, 1:391).

[83] This would, of course, commit Locke to a class of duties that do not correlate with the rights of others, a conclusion I have suggested he wished to avoid. This is a further reason to be suspicious of the second category of duties discussed by Locke in the *Essays* (in addition to those reasons noted above).

sort described above). He can point to the arguments he uses to justify rights to charity to show that duties of charity are as basic and strong as negative duties of forbearance (even if the former are more "conditional" than the latter). Failure to give aid in some cases does harm others and prejudice their rights; indeed, rights to charity override the negative duty to refrain from taking or using another's property without consent. For the property of all is not secure where some are denied the opportunities for self-preservation (and self-government).

This Lockean position, however, is seldom taken seriously, nor are the arguments Locke uses to defend it very often accepted. The standard view seems to be that duties to assist others are obviously less basic and less imperative than duties not to directly harm others (and may not be "real" duties at all). This makes government enforcement of positive duties a questionable practice. Why, we might ask, do defenders of these claims take them to be so obviously true?

One reason is certainly the appeal of commonsense moral arguments of the following sort. Suppose that I stand to lose $10,000 if I do not use a mob hitman (who owes me a favor) to kill one of my business competitors (a perfect stranger); and suppose as well that I learn of another stranger who will certainly die if I do not give him $10,000 for an operation (other sources of funds are out of the question). In either case, I will be out $10,000 unless some stranger dies. But surely, we argue, my duty not to kill my business competitor is far stronger and more basic than my duty (if any) to save the sick stranger, even though the stakes for me are precisely the same in the two cases. Many would argue that I have no duty at all to save the sick stranger, but none would argue that I may legitimately order the murder of a business competitor. This seems to show that duties not to harm others are stronger and more basic than duties to help them (as the minimalist and the liberal both claim).

Rather than conducting a lengthy analysis of this example, I will simply oppose it with another that seems to point in precisely the opposite direction. To use a variation on one of Bentham's favorite examples,[84] imagine an evil babysitter, bathing his charge, an unruly infant girl. Annoyed by the baby's constant screaming, the babysitter gives her a tiny shove, then watches gleefully as she

[84] This example also closely approximates one used in Rachels, "Active and Passive Euthanasia," 493–94.

slides slowly under the water and drowns. Contrast this case with one in which the babysitter, again annoyed to the point of having only the most malicious intentions toward the child, watches as the child causes *herself* to slide under the water. He does nothing but watch her drown, gleefully omitting the tiny effort that would save the child. Has the babysitter clearly done a worse thing in the first case, where he directly harms the child, than in the second, where he merely refuses to help her? If you are inclined to respond that a "no" answer is appropriate only because the babysitter owed a special duty to this child (or to the child's parents), replace the child with a perfect stranger, drowning in a lake near the babysitter's boat. Does the babysitter clearly do better when he lets the stranger drown a few inches from his boat without making any effort to help, than when he pulls the line to which the stranger is clinging from his hands? The moral difference between harming and failing to help is in many contexts not a substantial difference at all (or so it seems at this purely intuitive level). And it is easy to imagine cases where the failure to help another in need seems far worse morally than the direct causing of a minor harm to another (by punching him in the arm, say, or by stealing a dollar). Such cases should make us initially skeptical of claims that negative duties are more basic or imperative than positive duties could be. But many are not appropriately skeptical. One likely reason for this is a confusion about the possibility of correlative rights for the two kinds of duties.

When one begins trying to give examples to illustrate the distinction between perfect duties (those with correlative rights) and imperfect duties (those which lack them), it is common to notice the following: the clearest examples of perfect duties (e.g., not to murder, not to steal) all seem to be negative duties to refrain from directly harming others, while the clearest examples of imperfect duties, if any (e.g., general duties of beneficence, or broad duties to share one's wealth), all seem to be positive duties to assist others or to prevent harm from befalling them. If duties to help those in need can as a class be dismissed as merely imperfect duties, then no one has a right to be helped, no matter how small an effort by others this help would involve. No person has a claim to press against you for simply "minding your own business."[85] If positive duties correlate with no person's rights, this would seem to sug-

[85] See Buchanan's similar remarks in "Competition, Charity," 133, and "Justice and Charity."

gest that such duties are not as basic or imperative as negative duties. It would certainly indicate that such duties are less likely to be matters of consensus between competing ethical and religious views. And all of this seems to point naturally (again) to the conclusion that governments should not enforce positive duties.

That conclusion would obviously contradict Locke's claims for duties of charity and for government enforcement of those duties, given that the job of Lockean government is to secure and protect rights (property). We can, however, resist this conclusion about correlative rights at several levels. Consider this also first at a purely intuitive level, taking as our example a specific positive duty: the duty to rescue those in peril. Are we really confident that Kitty Genovese's neighbors (in Kew Gardens in 1964) did not wrong her by failing even to call the police when they heard her screams (leaving aside the further fact that none tried to interfere themselves with her prolonged and brutal murder)? Is the duty they had to render at least this minimal aid really controversial, weak, or insignificant? It is hard to believe that anyone takes it to be obvious that the patrons at Big Dan's Tavern (in New Bedford) had a clear duty not to actively assist in raping the helpless woman, but had no duty at all to even summon help, instead of cheering on her attackers. More to the point, it seems not at all implausible to suggest that rights were at issue in the cases just mentioned, that Kitty Genovese and the woman raped at Big Dan's had a right to at least the minimal aid involved in summoning help. Kitty Genovese's neighbors certainly acted wrongly, but this was not just some abstract wrong with no victim. Surely she was wronged by them. She had a claim against her neighbors, based in the minimal respect owed a person, that they take her seriously enough to act. They wronged her, just as the babysitter wrongs the child when he lets her drown, and I wrong Bentham's drunk (lying face down in a puddle) when I do not even bother to lift his face from the water.

Where, then, did the argument that all positive duties are imperfect go wrong? It went wrong chiefly, I think, in its assumption that all positive duties must be of a single kind. The argument I mentioned moved smoothly from the fact that the clearest cases of imperfect duties are also positive duties, to the conclusion that all positive duties are imperfect. Not only does this conclusion not follow logically, I have offered reasons at an intuitive level for supposing that it is false. Some kinds of assistance to other people are morally more basic or imperative than others.

We can press this point at a slightly deeper level. One reason, we might believe, why negative duties of forbearance are stricter or more perfect than positive duties of aid, is that it is so easy to refrain from harming others. It seems no great moral burden on a person not to murder, assault, or steal from others. Nearly all of us are, at any given moment, doing all of these things without noticing. So we can reasonably expect uniform adherence to negative duties. But if this is part of the rationale for regarding negative duties as strict, then surely some positive duties should also be counted as strict duties. Some rescues, for instance, are very easy to accomplish. It is no great moral burden on a person to have to call the police, shout a warning, throw a rope to a drowning man, or turn the head of Bentham's drunk. Nor is it very hard for most of us to give some money or food to the poor. These activities interfere with our autonomous pursuit of our life plans no more seriously than refraining from harming others. Indeed, lest we mistakenly assume that not harming others is virtually automatic, and so no strain at all, we would do well to remember just how difficult it can be to refrain from striking one who angers or insults you, to refrain from stealing what you badly want but cannot afford, and so on.

If these observations are sound, we should expect some positive duties to be as strict as familiar negative duties, and to correlate with rights in the same way, while other positive duties will seem less strict. Indeed, it seems possible to distinguish various kinds of positive duties and to rank them according to strictness or "perfection." At the top of the scale would be those positive duties that are in fact now recognized and enforced by Anglo-American legal systems—that is, the duties to help others that are grounded in a contractual relationship (such as the duty of a paid nurse or lifeguard) or in a special status relationship (such as the duty of a parent toward a child). But if my examples above were at all convincing, there would seem to be other clear cases of strict, perfect, but nonetheless positive duties. In some circumstances, we are "specially placed" to give aid to others. Kitty Genovese's neighbors, but not the other residents of New York, were specially placed to help her. The people who walk past Bentham's drunk or who are in Big Dan's when the rape occurs are specially placed to render aid. Whether or not we find ourselves specially placed to help is normally, of course, purely a matter of luck; but it seems clear that whether or not we *are* specially placed is a matter of considerable moral importance.[86] Kitty Genovese's neighbors were blameworthy in her death in a way that I was not. Of course, even when we *are* specially placed to assist another in need, other variables will still seem to affect the strength of our duty, such as the degree of need at issue, and the amount of risk, cost, or inconvenience that the one giving aid would suffer (as Locke saw in specifying the conditions on duties of charity).

Our duty to assist others will clearly seem strictest in those cases where no, or virtually no, risk, cost, or inconvenience is involved. In other cases, there may be minimal risks, costs, or inconvenience, which have no interesting effects at all on our free pursuit of our own plans and projects, on our own abilities to preserve and govern ourselves. In all such cases, I contend, the duty to give aid to those genuinely in need (at least where we are specially placed to do so) is a *perfect* duty; not only would I act wrongly in ignoring the needs of others in such cases, but they have a *right* that I not so act.[87] It further seems entirely appropriate that the law should enforce our positive duties in such circumstances, and that those who fail to extend themselves should be punished in a fashion serious enough to indicate the conduct's degree of wrongfulness.

Where serious risk, cost, or inconvenience would be involved, of course, even those who are specially placed to help will normally have less extensive duties toward those in need, and may have no duties at all. Some help is simply beyond the call of duty. So special placement is not all that matters in determining the strictness of our positive duties. But that special placement is relevant in central ways to the stringency of positive duties seems clear; and it is, if anything, made even clearer by considering more specifically the Lockean duties of charity with which we began. Most will agree that we are bound in some way (at least by an imperfect duty) to help those in dire need even when we have no direct contact with them, and when they will require longer term support than is given in typical "rescue" situations.[88] But we also

[86] On the relevance of "distance" to duties of rescue, see Woozley, "a Duty to Rescue," 1284. See also Daniels' claim that being in a special position to give aid turns an imperfect duty into a perfect one (*Am I My Parents' Keeper?* 33).
[87] See Feinberg, *Harm to Others*, 130–34, 143–50.
[88] It is clear that considerations of fairness will have to be in some way invoked to deal with questions about the distribution of the burdens of such positive duties. I do not attempt here to deal with those questions. But it is plainly part of the job of government in Lockean civil society to insure that the burdens of supporting the

tend to feel a stronger duty toward the poor we see, toward those who live around and with us, toward the local needy, toward "our" poor, than toward needy persons abroad (charity, they say, "begins at home"). Locke, as we have seen, seemed to share this feeling. But can the "scale of stringency" suggested by my remarks here really support these feelings in any systematic way? Better still, can this really be defended in a systematic way that could be accepted by Locke (and Lockeans)? I believe that both rule-consequentialist reasoning about the best preservation of mankind and secular, (roughly) Kantian reasoning about respect for persons will in fact support the scale of stringency for positive duties, as I have defended it (in loose, intuitive terms) above. In other words, both styles of systematic moral reasoning to which Locke subscribes will support the views on positive duties that he expresses.

Rule-consequentialist reasoning will support Locke's views as follows: mankind will be best preserved if positive duties are strongest (i.e., least likely to be legitimately overridden, hence least likely to be ignored) where the risks and costs of doing one's duty are minimal or acceptable (e.g., where we give only from our surplus, or at least give only where we do not risk our own preservation). Otherwise, we add the costs of transfer of resources and risks of mistaken or misguided charity to an exchange of resources, which in effect simply saves one from peril at the expense of putting another in peril. Further, mankind will be best preserved if positive duties to others vary in strength with others' proximity to us. Our aid to others is likely to be most efficient (because we are in these cases best informed and most concerned) where those others have special relationships with us or where we are specially placed to give aid. More generally, as their emotional, geographical, and cultural distance from us increases, so does the likelihood that our efforts to help them will be inefficient or counterproductive.

Kantian reasoning will, I believe, support similar conclusions. Recall (from 1.3) that the basic requirement of Locke's "Kantian" reasoning (where it concerns duties toward others) is that we respect others and their ends (that we take, in some respects, "their ends as our own"[89]). Now one common measure of respect for

genuinely needy are distributed fairly among the more affluent citizenry. This is clear even in Locke's proposal for poor law reform (discussed in 6.3 above).

[89] On how to take others' ends as our own, see Herman, "Mutual Aid," 600–601.

others and their ends is how much we are willing to give or give up in order to advance their well-being. If we are willing to make not even a small sacrifice to assist others, it shows that we do not much respect them or their projects. If we are unwilling to advance their interests when it costs us virtually nothing to do so, we show complete contempt for their interests, and show that we do not take them or their interests to be in any way as important as us or ours. If respecting others is important to moral conduct, then, we should expect what I have already urged—that the most basic and serious kinds of breaches of positive duties will be those where we refrain from acting to help another, where we could do so with minimal or acceptable risks, costs, or inconvenience. It is hard to imagine a better way of failing to show respect for others than by refusing to save their lives when it would cost us nothing of significance. When the risk, cost, or inconvenience is more significant, of course, reluctance to help may be based in justifiable fear or reasonable preference for self, rather than in a failure to respect the other. This suggests a scale of stringency on which positive duties are stricter as their breach constitutes a more straightforward failure to show respect for others.

Similarly, being specially related to or specially placed with respect to another would seem on this account directly relevant to the strictness of our duties. Being specially placed to give aid makes the failure to do so a particularly clear and dramatic way of not respecting another. While others besides those who are specially placed may have knowledge of the plights of the needy, when those specially placed refrain from giving aid it becomes dramatically less likely that aid will be given. One who is directly confronted with, and therefore fully aware of, another's plight has no excuses. The man who callously lets Bentham's drunk drown in his puddle treats him like a *thing*, like a mere lump in the road, not like a being worthy of respect, whose life has value. As those in need are farther and farther removed from our lives, however, the more plausible it becomes for us to claim that our awareness of their plight lacked a certain immediacy, that our failure to help was not so much a failure of respect as a failure to take what we "know" to heart. But the specially placed or specially related person can make no such claim.[90] This is not to argue that we have no duties toward those distant from ourselves, but only that (as

[90] For another discussion of the relevance of distance to Kantian moral reasoning, see O'Neill, "Moral Perplexities," 288–90.

Locke's remarks suggest) distance diminishes the strictness (or perfection) of positive duties.

My conclusion, then, is that Locke's moral theory (and, to the extent that we are Kantians or rule-consequentialists, *our* moral theory) provides ample material for the defense of most of Locke's claims about positive duties and their enforcement, as well as for those hints he gives of his views on the relative stringency of duties (and the relevance of "distance" to it).[91] Our positive duties can be as fundamental as negative duties, derive from the same roots as negative duties, can override negative duties, and can correlate similarly with the rights of others. If our negative duties ought to be viewed by law and government as important enough to be worthy of earnest enforcement, our duties of rescue and charity ought to be so viewed as well. Governments have the duty (and right) to secure *all* of our rights, positive rights included.

[91] I will not attempt here to deal with any other of the standard objections to the legal enforcement of positive duties, but will merely mention the most prominent of them (and suggest where to look for effective replies). To one such objection, the "slippery slope" objection (best defended in Epstein, "a Theory of Strict Liability"), I have already provided the material for a response. This objection claims that enforcing any positive duties really commits the law to a full sharing of society's wealth, positive duties needing in consistency to be either enforced or ignored as a class. I have already argued that there are clear, principled differences among various kinds of positive duties, which gives the law adequate basis for more discriminating enforcement. See also Feinberg, *Harm to Others*, 150–59; and Smith, "Duty to Rescue." Other popular objections include trying to cast positive-duty-specification as a variant of the Sorites problem (see Feinberg, *Harm to Others*), and denying that those who fail to aid others cause any harm to others (see Mack, "Bad Samaritanism"; Harris, "Bad Samaritans"; Husak, "Omissions"; Gewirth, *Reason and Morality*, 221–26; Feinberg, *Harm to Others*, 165–85).

CONCLUSION

The usual view of Locke's political philosophy seems to be that while it may be appealing and suit the liberal temper, it is utterly unfounded in Locke, underargued, and unconnected with any serious, systematic philosophy.[1] It is only as an epistemologist (if at all) that Locke is to be taken seriously as a philosopher. His moral and political writings are more like attractive rhetoric than philosophy. I have argued, by contrast, that there is much to be taken seriously in Locke's theory of rights (the theory that directly underlies his political philosophy). First, I have claimed, Locke's scattered remarks on rights do in fact deserve to be taken seriously as a theory. Studied carefully, they can be seen to point to a coherent, if irreducibly pluralistic, body of theory (which includes a convincing defense of impartialism for moral philosophy). Second, we have seen that Locke's work anticipated (even if not always altogether self-consciously) a host of important points and distinctions emphasized in contemporary philosophical literature on rights. Finally, I have defended many of Locke's arguments for specific natural rights (and properties of rights) as far more interesting and persuasive than is commonly supposed.

We have seen that Locke's writings suggest a plausible conception of the right to punish and of that right's significance for political philosophy. Indeed, they suggest as well ways in which Locke's views on punishment can be defended in secular terms (either by rule-consequentialist reasoning or through a fairness theory of forfeiture). Similarly, Locke's remarks on familial morality point us to defensible positions on the moral dimensions of marriage, the rights of natural (and other) parents, the duties and rights of children, rights of and limits on inheritance, and the rejection of paternalistic government. In Locke's theory of property

---

[1] A good recent example of this view can be found in Andrew's *Shylock's Rights*, where it is maintained that Locke's "politics have no demonstrable relation to his philosophy" (146). For similar claims, see also Medina, *Social Contract Theories*, 33. Dunn takes the more reasonable, but still related position that while we have "come to accept in the broadest terms the politics of Locke," we have also "firmly discarded the reasons which alone made them seem acceptable even to Locke" (*Political Thought*, 267).

we were able to find the groundworks necessary for articulating a convincing labor-mixing theory of original acquisition, carefully conditioned by a "fair share limit" on the extent of legitimate appropriation. And, finally, we have seen that from Locke's few and scattered remarks on the subject can be drawn plausible views of social justice and of the rights and duties of charity and rescue, including plausible views of government's proper roles with respect to property. Throughout Locke's theory of rights expresses a moderate individualism, neither radical or revolutionary nor conservative or apologetic in its social implications. Locke's is an individualism that springs from disparate sources, both teleological (consequentialist) and deontological, both theological and secular. And it is because of this pluralism in Locke's moral and political philosophy that we can build upon (and beneath) Locke's own theory to erect an interesting and persuasive Lockean theory of rights.

Locke's political philosophy, far from being unrelated to any systematic philosophical position, rests directly on a developed and consistent theory of rights. Not only, then, does *Locke's* theory of rights serve as a viable foundation for *his* political philosophy. The Lockean theory of rights may serve as a viable foundation for *ours*. For the logical detachability of much of Locke's theory from his theology allows it to function as a consistent development of secular moral theory (either Kantian or rule-consequentialist). Locke's arguments from the values of self-government, fairness, and common humanity "fit" contemporary secular moral philosophy. Anyone, then, who does not utterly reject the idea of natural rights (as I defined and defended that idea in chapter 2) is obliged to take seriously Locke's theory of rights and the project of reconstructing and revising it here undertaken. The Lockean theory of rights cannot, I think, be responsibly rejected by the casual dismissal of Locke's theology, which is so common in contemporary discussions of Locke. Nor should we any longer ignore the many significant ways in which Locke's insights can today continue to illuminate the liberal rights theories to whose original inspiration Locke contributed so much.

WORKS CITED

Aaron, Richard. *John Locke*. Oxford: Oxford University Press, 1971.

Abrams, Philip. "Introduction" to Locke, *Two Tracts on Government*. Cambridge: Cambridge University Press, 1967.

Alston, William P. (and Jonathan Bennett). "Locke on People and Substances." *The Philosophical Review* (January 1988).

Altham, J. E. J. "Reflections on the State of Nature." In *Rational Action*, ed. R. Harrison. Cambridge: Cambridge University Press, 1979.

Andrew, Edward. "Inalienable Right, Alienable Property and Freedom of Choice: Locke, Nozick and Marx on the Alienability of Labour." *Canadian Journal of Political Science* (September 1985).

———. *Shylock's Rights: A Grammar of Lockian Claims*. Toronto: University of Toronto Press, 1988.

Anscombe, Elizabeth. "On the Source of the Authority of the State." *Ratio* (June 1978).

Arnhart, Larry. *Political Questions*. New York: Macmillan, 1987.

Arnold, Christopher. "Analyses of Rights." In *Human Rights*, ed. E. Kamenka and A. E. Tay. London: Edward Arnold, 1978.

Arthur, John. "Resource Acquisition and Harm." *Canadian Journal of Philosophy* (June 1987).

Ashcraft, Richard. *Revolutionary Politics & Locke's Two Treatises of Government*. Princeton: Princeton University Press, 1986.

———. *Locke's Two Treatises of Government*. London: Allen & Unwin, 1987.

Baier, Annette. Review of Colman (1983). *Philosophical Review* (October 1984).

Baldwin, Thomas. "Toleration and the Right to Freedom." In *Aspects of Toleration*, ed. J. Horton and S. Mendus. London: Methuen, 1985.

Bandman, Bertram. "Do Children Have Natural Rights?" *Philosophy of Education* (Proceedings of the 29th Meetings) (1973).

Barker, Ernest. "Introduction" to *Social Contract*. New York: Oxford University Press, 1962.

Bayles, Michael (and Kenneth Henley). *Right Conduct: Theories and Applications*. New York: Random House, 1983.

Beccaria, Cesare. *On Crimes and Punishments*. Indianapolis: Bobbs-Merrill, 1963.

Becker, Lawrence. "The Labor Theory of Property Acquisition." *Journal of Philosophy* (October 21, 1976).

————. *Property Rights*. London: Routledge & Kegan Paul, 1977

————. "The Moral Basis of Property Rights." In *Nomos XII: Property*, ed. J. Pennock and J. Chapman. New York: New York University Press, 1980.

————. "Individual Rights." In *And Justice for All*, ed. T. Regan and D. VanDeVeer. Totowa: Rowman & Littlefield, 1982.

———— (and Kenneth Kipnis) (eds.). *Property: Cases, Concepts, Critiques*. Englewood Cliffs: Prentice-Hall, 1984.

————. *Reciprocity*. London: Routledge & Kegan Paul, 1986.

Beitz, Charles R. "Tacit Consent and Property Rights." *Political Theory* (November 1980).

Belliotti, Raymond. "Honor Thy Father and Thy Mother and to Thine Own Self Be True." *Southern Journal of Philosophy* (Summer 1986).

Benditt, Theodore. *Rights*. Totowa: Rowman & Littlefield, 1982.

Benn, S. I. (and R. S. Peters). *Social Principles and the Democratic State*. London: Allen & Unwin, 1959.

Bennett, John G. "A Note on Locke's Theory of Tacit Consent." *Philosophical Review* (April 1979).

Bentham, Jeremy. *Pannomial Fragments*. In *A Bentham Reader*, ed. M. Mack. New York: Pegasus, 1969.

————. *Anarchical Fallacies*. In *Human Rights*, ed. A. Melden. Belmont: Wadsworth, 1970.

————. *Of Laws in General*, ed. H. Hart. London: Athlone Press, 1970.

Best, Judith A. "The Innocent, the Ignorant, and the Rational: The Content of Lockian Consent." In *The Crisis of Liberal Democracy*. ed. K. L. Deutsch and W. Soffer. Albany: State University of New York Press, 1987.

Blum, Lawrence. "Gilligan and Kohlberg: Implications for Moral Theory." *Ethics* (April 1988).

Blustein, Jeffrey. *Parents and Children*. New York: Oxford University Press, 1982.

Bogart, J. H. "Lockean Provisos and State of Nature Theories." *Ethics* (July 1985).

Bok, Sissela. *Lying*. New York: Random House, 1978.

Bosanquet, Bernard. *The Philosophical Theory of the State*. 4th ed. New York: St. Martins, 1965.

Brandt, Richard. *Ethical Theory*. Englewood Cliffs: Prentice-Hall, 1959.

———. "The Concepts of Obligation and Duty." *Mind* (July 1965).

———. "The Concept of a Moral Right and Its Function." *Journal of Philosophy* (January 1983).

Brogan, A. P. "John Locke and Utilitarianism." *Ethics* (January 1959).

Buchanan, Allen. *Marx and Justice: The Radical Critique of Liberalism*. Totowa: Rowman & Littlefield, 1982.

———. "What's So Special about Rights?" *Social Philosophy & Policy* (Autumn 1984).

———. "Competition, Charity and the Right to Health Care." In *The Restraint of Liberty*, ed. T. Attig, D. Callen, and J. Gray. Bowling Green: Bowling Green Studies in Applied Philosophy, 1985.

———. "Justice and Charity." *Ethics* (April 1987).

———. "Assessing the Communitarian Critique of Liberalism." *Ethics* (July 1989).

Cherno, Melvin. "Locke on Property: A Reappraisal." *Ethics* (October 1957).

Christman, John. "Can Ownership Be Justified by Natural Rights?" *Philosophy & Public Affairs* (Spring 1986).

———. "Self-Ownership, Equality, and the Structure of Property Rights." *Political Theory* (February 1991).

Clark, Lorenne. "Women and John Locke; or, Who Owns the Apple in the Garden of Eden?" *Canadian Journal of Philosophy* (December 1977).

Cohen, G. A. "Marx and Locke on Land and Labour." *Proceedings of the British Academy* 71 (1985).

———. "Self-Ownership, World Ownership, and Equality." In *Justice and Equality Here and Now*, ed. F. S. Lucash. Ithaca: Cornell University Press, 1986.

Cohen, Joshua. "Structure, Choice, and Legitimacy: Locke's Theory of the State." *Philosophy & Public Affairs* (Fall 1986).

Colman, John. *John Locke's Moral Philosophy*. Edinburgh: Edinburgh University Press, 1983.

Copp, David (and David Zimmerman) (eds.). *Morality, Reason and Truth*. Totowa: Rowman & Allanheld, 1985.

Cox, Richard. "Justice as the Basis of Political Order in Locke." In *Nomos VI: Justice*, ed. C. Friedrich and J. Chapman. New York: New York University Press, 1963.

———. *Locke on War and Peace*. Washington, D.C.: University Press of America, 1982.

Cranston, Maurice. *John Locke: A Biography*. Oxford: Oxford University Press, 1985.

Daniels, Norman. *Am I My Parents' Keeper?* New York: Oxford University Press, 1988.

Davis, Lawrence. "Comments on Nozick's Entitlement Theory." *Journal of Philosophy* (December 2, 1976).

Davis, Nancy. "Using Persons and Common Sense." *Ethics* (April 1984).

Day, J. P. "Locke on Property." *Philosophical Quarterly* (July 1966).

De Beer, Esmond S. "Locke and English Liberalism: *The Second Treatise of Government* in Its Contemporary Setting." In *John Locke: Problems and Perspectives*, ed. J. Yolton. Cambridge: Cambridge University Press, 1969.

Den Hartogh, G. A. "Tully's Locke." *Political Theory* (November 1990).

D'Entreves, A. P. *Natural Law*. London: Hutchinson University Library, 1951.

Drury, S. B. "John Locke: Natural Law and Innate Ideas." *Dialogue* (December 1980).

———. "Locke and Nozick on Property." *Political Studies* (March 1982).

Dunn, John. "Justice and the Interpretation of Locke's Political Theory." *Political Studies* (February 1968).

———. *The Political Thought of John Locke*. Cambridge: Cambridge University Press, 1969.

———. "Consent in the Political Theory of John Locke." In *Political Obligation in Its Historical Context*. Cambridge: Cambridge University Press, 1980.

———. "What Is Living and What Is Dead in the Political Theory of John Locke?" In *Interpreting Political Responsibility*. Princeton: Princeton University Press, 1990.

Dworetz, Steven M. *The Unvarnished Doctrine*. Durham: Duke University Press, 1990.

Dworkin, Gerald. "Paternalism." In *Morality and the Law*, ed. R. A. Wasserstrom. Belmont: Wadsworth, 1971.

Dworkin, Ronald. *Taking Rights Seriously*. Cambridge, Mass.: Harvard University Press, 1975.

———. "Rights as Trumps." In *Theories of Rights*, ed. J. Waldron. Oxford: Oxford University Press, 1984.

Ellerman, David P. "On the Labor Theory of Property." *Philosophical Forum* (Summer 1985).

English, Jane. "What Do Grown Children Owe Their Parents?" In

Having Children, ed. O. O'Neill and W. Ruddick. New York: Oxford University Press, 1979.

Epstein, Richard. "A Theory of Strict Liability." *Journal of Legal Studies* (January 1973).

Farrell, Daniel. "Coercion, Consent, and the Justification of Political Power: A New Look at Locke's Consent Claim." *Archiv fur Rechts- und Sozialphilosophie* 64/4 (1979).

———. "Legitimate Government and Consent of the Governed." In *The Restraint of Liberty*, ed. T. Attig, D. Callen, and J. Gray. Bowling Green: Bowling Green Studies in Philosophy, 1985.

———. "Punishment Without the State." *Nous* (September 1988).

Feinberg, Joel. "Duties, Rights, and Claims." *American Philosophical Quarterly* (April 1966).

———. "The Nature and Value of Rights." In *Rights*, ed. D. Lyons. Belmont: Wadsworth, 1979.

———. *Social Philosophy*. Englewood Cliffs: Prentice-Hall, 1973.

———. "Voluntary Euthanasia and the Inalienable Right to Life." *Philosophy & Public Affairs* (Winter 1978).

———. "The Child's Right to an Open Future." In *Whose Child?*, ed. W. Aiken and H. LaFollette. Totowa: Littlefield, Adams, 1980.

———. "The Rights of Animals and Unborn Generations." In *Rights, Justice, and the Bounds of Liberty*. Princeton: Princeton University Press, 1980.

———. *Harm to Others*. New York: Oxford University Press, 1984.

———. *Harm to Self*. New York: Oxford University Press, 1986.

Filmer, Robert. *Patriarcha*. In Locke, *Two Treatises of Government*, ed. T. Cook. New York: Hafner, 1947.

Finch, R. P. "An Alternative to Claim-Theories of Rights." *Journal of Value Inquiry* (Winter 1977).

Finnis, John. *Natural Law and Natural Right*. Oxford: Oxford University Press, 1980.

Fishkin, James. *The Limits of Obligation*. New Haven: Yale University Press, 1982.

Foot, Philippa. "Morality as a System of Hypothetical Imperatives." *Philosophical Review* (July 1972).

Fox Bourne, H. R. *The Life of John Locke*. London: Henry S. King, 1876.

Frankena, William K. "On Defining and Defending Natural Law." In *Law and Philosophy*, ed. S. Hook. New York: New York University Press, 1964.

Frankfurt, Harry. "Freedom of the Will and the Concept of a Person." *Journal of Philosophy* (January 14, 1971).

Freeden, Michael. "Human Rights and Welfare: A Communitarian View." *Ethics* (April 1990).

Fressola, Anthony. "Liberty and Property: Reflections on the Right of Appropriation in the State of Nature." *American Philosophical Quarterly* (October 1981).

Fried, Charles. *Right and Wrong*. Cambridge, Mass.: Harvard University Press, 1978.

Gauthier, David. "The Role of Inheritance in Locke's Political Theory." *Canadian Journal of Economics and Political Science* (February 1966).

———. "Why Ought One Obey God? Reflections on Hobbes and Locke." *Canadian Journal of Philosophy* (September 1977).

———. *Morals by Agreement*. Oxford: Oxford University Press, 1986.

Gewirth, Alan. *Reason and Morality*. Chicago: University of Chicago Press, 1978.

———. "Are There Any Absolute Rights?" In *Human Rights*. Chicago: University of Chicago Press, 1982.

———. "The Basis and Content of Human Rights." In *Human Rights*.

———. "Ethical Universalism and Particularism." *Journal of Philosophy* (June 1988).

Gibbard, Allan. "Natural Property Rights." In *Readings in Social and Political Philosophy*, ed. R. Stewart. New York: Oxford University Press, 1986.

———. "What's Morally Special about Free Exchange?" *Social Philosophy & Policy* (Spring 1985).

Gierke, Otto. *Natural Law and the Theory of Society*. Cambridge: Cambridge University Press, 1934.

Gillespie, Norman (ed.). *Moral Realism. Southern Journal of Philosophy*, vol. 24, supplement.

Glenn, Gary D. "Inalienable Rights and Locke's Argument for Limited Government: Political Implications of a Right of Suicide." *Journal of Politics* (February 1984).

Golding, Martin. "Towards a Theory of Human Rights." *Monist* (October 1968).

———. "The Primacy of Welfare Rights." *Social Philosophy & Policy* (Spring 1984).

Goldman, Alan. "The Entitlement Theory of Distributive Justice." *Journal of Philosophy* (December 2, 1976).

————. "The Paradox of Punishment." *Philosophy & Public Affairs* (Fall 1979).

Goldwin, Robert. "John Locke." In *History of Political Philosophy*, ed. L. Strauss and J. Cropsey. 3d ed. Chicago: University of Chicago Press, 1987.

Goodpaster, Kenneth. "Morality as a System of Categorical Imperatives." *Journal of Value Inquiry* 15/3 (1981).

Gough, J. W. *John Locke's Political Philosophy*. Oxford: Oxford University Press, 1950.

Gould, Carol C. "Contemporary Legal Conceptions of Property and Their Implications for Democracy." In *Philosophical Issues in Human Rights*, ed. P. Werhane, A. Gini, and D. Ozar. New York: Random House, 1986.

Grady, Robert C., II. "Obligation, Consent, and Locke's Right of Revolution: 'Who Is to Judge?' " *Canadian Journal of Political Science* (June 1976).

Grant, Ruth. *John Locke's Liberalism*. Chicago: University of Chicago Press, 1987.

Green, T. H. *Lectures on the Principles of Political Obligation*. Ann Arbor: University of Michigan Press, 1967.

Grotius, Hugo. *De Jure Belli ac Pacis Libri Tres*, tr. W. Kelsey. Oxford: Oxford University Press, 1925.

————. *De Jure Praedae Commentarius*, tr. G. Williams and W. Zeydel. Oxford: Oxford University Press, 1950.

Gutmann, Amy. "Children, Paternalism, and Education." *Philosophy & Public Affairs* (Summer 1980).

————. "Communitarian Critics of Liberalism." *Philosophy & Public Affairs* (Summer 1985).

————. *Democratic Education*. Princeton: Princeton University Press, 1987.

Hacker, Andrew. *Political Theory*. New York: Macmillan, 1961.

Haksar, Vinit. "Excuses and Voluntary Conduct." *Ethics* (January 1986).

Hancey, James. "John Locke and the Law of Nature." *Political Theory* (November 1976).

Harris, John. "Bad Samaritans Cause Harm." *Philosophical Quarterly* (January 1982).

Harrison, Ross. *Bentham*. London: Routledge & Kegan Paul, 1983.

Hart, H. L. A. "Are There any Natural Rights?" *Philosophical Review* (April 1955).

————. *The Concept of Law*. Oxford: Oxford University Press, 1961.

————. "Prolegomenon to the Principles of Punishment." In

Punishment and Responsibility. Oxford: Oxford University Press, 1968.

———. "Bentham on Legal Rights." In *Oxford Essays in Jurisprudence*, ed. A. W. B. Simpson. 2d ser. Oxford: Oxford University Press, 1973.

———. *Essays on Bentham*. Oxford: Oxford University Press, 1982.

———. "Utilitarianism and Natural Rights." In *Essays in Jurisprudence and Philosophy*. Oxford: Oxford University Press, 1983.

Haslett, D. W. "Is Inheritance Justified?" *Philosophy & Public Affairs* (Spring 1986).

Hegel, G. W. F. *Philosophy of Right*, tr. T. Knox. New York: Oxford University Press, 1969.

Held, Virginia. "John Locke on Robert Nozick." *Social Research* (Spring 1976).

———. "Introduction" to *Property, Profits, and Economic Justice*. Belmont: Wadsworth, 1980.

Henley, Kenneth. "The Authority to Educate." In *Having Children*, ed. O. O'Neill and W. Ruddick. New York: Oxford University Press, 1979.

Herman, Barbara. "Mutual Aid and Respect for Persons." *Ethics* (July 1984).

Herzog, Don. *Without Foundations*. Ithaca: Cornell University Press, 1985.

Hill, Thomas E., Jr. "Servility and Self-Respect." In *Rights*, ed. D. Lyons. Belmont: Wadsworth, 1979.

Hobbes, Thomas. *Leviathan*, ed. C. B. Macpherson. Harmondsworth: Penguin, 1975.

Hodson, John. "Nozick, Libertarianism, and Rights." *Arizona Law Review* 19/1 (1977).

———. *The Ethics of Legal Coercion*. Dordrecht: D. Reidel, 1983.

Hoekema, David. "The Right to Punish and the Right to Be Punished." In *John Rawls' Theory of Social Justice: An Introduction*, ed. H. G. Blocker and E. H. Smith. Athens: Ohio University Press, 1980.

Hohfeld, W. N. *Fundamental Legal Conceptions as Applied to Judicial Reasoning*. New Haven: Yale University Press, 1964.

Honderich, Ted. *Punishment: The Supposed Justifications*. Harmondsworth: Penguin, 1971.

———. "Punishment, the New Retributivism, and Political Philosophy." In *Philosophy and Practice*, ed. A. P. Griffiths. Cambridge: Cambridge University Press, 1985.

Honoré, A. M. "Ownership." In *Oxford Essays in Jurisprudence*, ed. A. Guest. Oxford: Oxford University Press, 1961.

———. "Property, Title and Redistribution." In *Property: Cases, Concepts, Critiques*, ed. L. Becker and K. Kipnis. Englewood Cliffs: Prentice-Hall, 1984.

Hooker, Richard. *Of the Laws of Ecclesiastical Polity.* Cambridge, Mass.: Harvard University Press, 1977– .

Horne, Thomas. Review of Tully (1980). *Political Theory* (August 1981).

Hospers, John. "Property." *Personalist* (Summer 1972).

Hume, David. *A Treatise of Human Nature*, ed. L. Selby-Bigge. Oxford: Oxford University Press, 1978.

Hurka, Thomas. "Rights and Capital Punishment." *Dialogue* (December 1982).

Husak, Douglas N. "Omissions, Causation and Liability." *Philosophical Quarterly* (October 1980).

Ingram, Peter. "Natural Rights: A Reappraisal." *Journal of Value Inquiry* 15/2 (1981).

Jecker, Nancy S. "Are Filial Duties Unfounded?" *American Philosophical Quarterly* (January 1989).

Jenkins, John J. "Locke on Natural Rights." *Philosophy* (April 1967).

Kant, Immanuel. *Foundations of the Metaphysics of Morals*, tr. L. Beck. Indianapolis: Bobbs-Merrill, 1959.

———. "On a Supposed Right to Tell Lies from Benevolent Motives." In *Kant's Critique of Practical Reason and Other Writings in Moral Philosophy*, tr. L. Beck. Chicago: University of Chicago Press, 1949.

———. *Lectures on Ethics*, tr. L. Infield. London: Methuen, 1930.

———. *The Metaphysics of Morals*, part 1, tr. W. Hastie (as Kant, *The Philosophy of Law*). Edinburgh: T. & T. Clark, 1887.

Kelly, Patrick. " 'All Things Richly to Enjoy': Economics and Politics in Locke's *Two Treatises of Government*." *Political Studies* (June 1988).

Kendall, Willmoore. *John Locke and the Doctrine of Majority-Rule.* Urbana: University of Illinois Press, 1959.

———. "John Locke Revisited." *Intercollegiate Review* (January–February 1966).

King, Peter, Lord. *The Life of John Locke.* London: Henry Colburn & Richard Bentley, 1830.

Kleinig, John. *Paternalism.* Totowa: Rowman and Allanheld, 1984.

Kymlicka, Will. "Liberalism & Communitarianism." *Canadian Journal of Philosophy* (June 1988).

Kymlicka, Will. *Contemporary Political Philosophy: An Introduction.* Oxford: Oxford University Press, 1990.

Laski, Harold. *A Grammar of Politics.* 5th. ed. London: Allen & Unwin, 1977.

Laslett, Peter. "Introduction" to Locke, *Two Treatises of Government.* Cambridge: Cambridge University Press, 1963.

Lee, J. Roger. "The Arrest and Punishment of Criminals: Justification and Limitations." In *The Libertarian Reader,* ed. T. Machan. Totowa: Rowman & Littlefield, 1982.

Leites, Edmond. "Locke's Liberal Theory of Parenthood." In *John Locke: Symposium Wolfenbuttel 1979,* ed. R. Brandt. Berlin: Walter de Gruyter, 1981.

Lemos, Ramon. "Locke's Theory of Property." *Interpretation* (Winter 1975).

———. *Hobbes and Locke.* Athens: University of Georgia Press, 1978.

———. "The Concept of Natural Right." In *Midwest Studies in Philosophy VII,* ed. P. French, T. Uehling, Jr., and H. Wettstein. Minneapolis: University of Minnesota Press, 1982.

Lenz, John W. "Locke's Essays on the Law of Nature." *Philosophy and Phenomenological Research* (September 1956).

Locke, John. *Two Treatises of Government,* ed. P. Laslett. Cambridge: Cambridge University Press, 1963.

———. *An Essay Concerning Human Understanding,* ed. P. Nidditch. Oxford: Oxford University Press, 1975.

———. *Essays on the Law of Nature,* ed. W. Von Leyden. Oxford: Oxford University Press, 1965.

———. *A Letter Concerning Toleration.* In *The Second Treatise of Civil Government and A Letter Concerning Toleration,* ed. J. Gough. Oxford: Basil Blackwell, 1947.

———. *Two Tracts on Government,* ed. P. Abrams. Cambridge: Cambridge University Press, 1967.

———. *An Essay Concerning Toleration.* In Fox Bourne, *The Life of John Locke.* London: Henry S. King, 1876.

———. *The Reasonableness of Christianity,* ed. G. Ewing. Washington, D.C.: Regnery Gateway, 1965.

———. *Some Thoughts Concerning Education,* ed. J. W. Yolton and J. S. Yolton. Oxford: Oxford University Press, 1989.

———. *A Second Letter Concerning Toleration.* In *The Works of John Locke,* vol. 6. London: Thomas Davison, 1823.

———. *Some Considerations of the Consequences of the Lowering of In-*

terest and Raising the Value of Money. In *The Works of John Locke*, vol. 5.

———. *Further Considerations Concerning Raising the Value of Money.* In *The Works of John Locke*, vol. 5.

———. "Some Thoughts Concerning Reading and Study for a Gentleman." In *The Educational Writings of John Locke*, ed. J. Axtell. Cambridge: Cambridge University Press, 1968.

———. "Of Ethics in General." In King, *The Life of John Locke*, 2:308.

———. "Ethica B." Bodleian MS c28, fol. 141.

———. "Morality." Bodleian MS c28, fol. 139–40.

———. "Obligation of Penal Laws." In King, *The Life of John Locke*, 1:114.

———. "Thus, I think." In Fox Bourne, *The Life of John Locke*, 1:164.

———. "Knowledge, Its Extent and Measure." In King, *The Life of John Locke*, 1:161.

———. "On the Difference between Civil and Ecclesiastical Power, Indorsed Excommunication." In King, *The Life of John Locke*, 2:108.

———. "Proposal for Reform of the Poor Laws." In Fox Bourne, *The Life of John Locke*, 2:377.

———. "Venditio." In Dunn, "Justice and the Interpretation of Locke's Political Theory," 84.

Lodge, George Cabot. "The New Property." In *Philosophical Issues in Human Rights*, ed. P. Werhane, A. Gini, and D. Ozar. New York: Random House, 1986.

Lomasky, Loren. *Persons, Rights, and the Moral Community.* New York: Oxford University Press, 1987.

Louden, Robert. "Rights Infatuation and the Impoverishment of Moral Theory." *Journal of Value Inquiry* 17/1 (1983).

Lyons, David. "The Correlativity of Rights and Duties." *Nous* (February 1970).

———. "Rights, Claimants, and Beneficiaries." In *Rights*, ed. Lyons. Belmont: Wadsworth, 1979.

———. "Mill's Theory of Morality." *Nous* (May 1976).

———. "Rights Against Humanity." *Philosophical Review* (April 1976).

———. "Human Rights and the General Welfare." *Philosophy & Public Affairs* (Winter 1977).

———. "Utility and Rights." *Nomos XXIV: Ethics, Economics, and the Law*, ed. J. R. Pennock and J. W. Chapman. New York: New York University Press, 1982.

Mabbott, J. D. *John Locke*. London: Macmillan, 1973.

McCloskey, H. J. "Rights." *Philosophical Quarterly* (April 1965).

MacCormick, D. N. "Rights in Legislation." In *Law, Morality, and Society*, ed. P. M. S. Hacker and J. Raz. Oxford: Oxford University Press, 1977.

MacDonald, Margaret. "Natural Rights." In *Theories of Rights*, ed. J. Waldron. Oxford: Oxford University Press, 1984.

Machan, Tibor. *Individuals and Their Rights*. La Salle: Open Court, 1989.

MacIntyre, Alasdair. *A Short History of Ethics*. New York: Macmillan, 1966.

———. *After Virtue*. Notre Dame: Notre Dame University Press, 1981.

———. "Philosophy and Politics." In *Philosophy and Human Enterprise* (USMA Class of 1951 Lecture Series, 1982–1983).

———. *Whose Justice? Which Rationality?* Notre Dame: University of Notre Dame Press, 1988.

Mack, Eric. "Locke's Arguments for Natural Rights." *Southwestern Journal of Philosophy* (Spring 1980).

———. "Bad Samaritanism and the Causation of Harm." *Philosophy & Public Affairs* (Spring 1980).

———. "Distributive Justice and the Tensions of Lockeanism." *Social Philosophy & Policy* (Autumn 1983).

Mackie, J. L. Review of Tully (1980). *Philosophical Quarterly* (January 1982).

———. "Can There Be a Right-Based Moral Theory?" In *Theories of Rights*, ed. J. Waldron. Oxford: Oxford University Press, 1984.

McNally, David. "Locke, Levellers and Liberty: Property and Democracy in the Thought of the First Whigs." *History of Political Thought* (Spring 1989).

Macpherson, C. B. *The Political Theory of Possessive Individualism*. Oxford: Oxford University Press, 1962.

———. "Natural Rights in Hobbes and Locke." In *Democratic Theory*. Oxford: Oxford University Press, 1973.

———. "Servants and Labourers in Seventeenth Century England." In *Democratic Theory*.

———. "Human Rights as Property Rights." In *Property: Cases, Concepts, Critiques*, ed. L. Becker and K. Kipnis. Englewood Cliffs: Prentice-Hall, 1984.

Mansfield, Harvey C., Jr. "On the Political Character of Property in Locke." In *Powers, Possessions and Freedom*, ed. A. Kontos. Toronto: University of Toronto Press, 1979.

Marx, Karl. *On the Jewish Question*. In *Karl Marx: Selected Writings*, ed. D. McLellan. Oxford: Oxford University Press, 1977.

———. *The Communist Manifesto*. In *Karl Marx: Selected Writings*.

———. *Critique of the Gotha Program*. In *Karl Marx: Selected Writings*.

Mattern, Ruth. "Moral Science and the Concept of Persons in Locke." *Philosophical Review* (January 1980).

Mautner, Thomas. "Locke on Appropriation." *American Philosophical Quarterly* (July 1982).

Mavrodes, George I. "Property." *Personalist* (Summer 1972).

Medina, Vincente. *Social Contract Theories*. Savage: Rowman & Littlefield, 1990.

Meilaender, Gilbert. "A Little Monarchy: Hobbes on the Family." *Thought* (December 1978).

Melden, A. I. *Rights and Right Conduct*. Oxford: Basil Blackwell, 1959.

———. "Olafson on the Right to Educate." In *Educational Judgments*, ed. J. F. Doyle. London: Routledge & Kegan Paul, 1973.

———. *Rights and Persons*. Berkeley: University of California Press, 1977.

———. "Do Infants Have Moral Rights?" In *Whose Child?*, ed. W. Aiken and H. LaFollette. Totowa: Littlefield, Adams, 1980.

Mendus, Susan. *Toleration and the Limits of Liberalism*. Atlantic Highlands: Humanities Press, 1989.

Mill, J. S. *Utilitarianism*. In J. S. Mill, *Utilitarianism and Other Writings*, ed. M. Warnock. New York: NAL, 1962.

———. *On Liberty*. In Mill, *Utilitarianism and Other Writings*.

Miller, David. "Justice and Property." *Ratio* (June 1980).

Miller, Fred D., Jr. "The Natural Right to Private Property." In *The Libertarian Reader*, ed. T. Machan. Totowa: Rowman & Littlefield, 1982.

Miller, Richard. "Rights and Reality." *Philosophical Review* (July 1981).

Minogue, Kenneth R. "The Concept of Property and Its Contemporary Significance." In *Nomos XII: Property*, ed. J. Pennock and J. Chapman. New York: New York University Press, 1980.

Monson, Charles H., Jr. "Locke's Political Theory and Its Interpreters." In *Locke and Berkeley*, ed. C. Martin and D. Armstrong. Notre Dame: University of Notre Dame Press, 1968.

Morris, Herbert. "Persons and Punishment." *Monist* (October 1968).

Murphy, Jeffrie G. "A Paradox in Locke's Theory of Natural Rights." *Dialogue* (September 1967).

Murphy, Jeffrie G. "Three Mistakes about Retributivism." *Analysis* (April 1971).

———. "Rights and Borderline Cases." *Arizona Law Review* (1977).

———. "Cruel and Unusual Punishments." In *Retribution, Justice, and Therapy*. Dordrecht: D. Reidel, 1979.

Nagel, Thomas. "The Fragmentation of Value." In *Mortal Questions*. Cambridge: Cambridge University Press, 1979.

———. "Libertarianism Without Foundations." In *Reading Nozick*, ed. J. Paul. Totowa: Rowman & Littlefield, 1981.

Narveson, Jan. "Commentary." *Journal of Value Inquiry* (Winter 1970).

———. "On Honoring Our Parents." *Southern Journal of Philosophy* (Spring 1987).

Nelson, William. "On the Alleged Importance of Moral Rights." *Ratio* (December 1976).

Nickel, James. *Making Sense of Human Rights*. Berkeley: University of California Press, 1987.

Nielsen, Kai. "Some Remarks on the Independence of Morality from Religion." *Mind* (April 1961).

Nozick, Robert. *Anarchy, State, and Utopia*. New York: Basic Books, 1974.

———. *Philosophical Explanations*. Cambridge, Mass.: Harvard University Press, 1981.

———. *The Examined Life*. New York: Simon & Schuster, 1989.

Olafson, Frederick. "Essence and Concept in Natural Law Theory." In *Law and Philosophy*, ed. S. Hook. New York: New York University Press, 1964.

———. "Rights and Duties in Education." In *Educational Judgments*, ed. J. F. Doyle. London: Routledge & Kegan Paul, 1973.

Olivecrona, Karl. "Appropriation in the State of Nature: Locke on the Origin of Property." *Journal of the History of Ideas* (April–June 1974).

———. "Locke's Theory of Appropriation." *Philosophical Quarterly* (July 1974).

O'Neill, Onora. "Begetting, Bearing, and Rearing." In *Having Children*, ed. O. O'Neill and W. Ruddick. New York: Oxford University Press, 1979.

———. "The Moral Perplexities of Famine Relief." In *Matters of Life and Death*, ed. T. Regan. New York: Random House, 1980.

———. "Nozick's Entitlements." In *Reading Nozick*, ed. J. Paul. Totowa: Rowman & Littlefield, 1981.

Oppenheim, Felix. "The Metaphysics of Natural Law." In *Law and*

Philosophy, ed. S. Hook. New York: New York University Press, 1964.

Paine, Thomas. *Rights of Man*, ed. H. Collins. Harmondsworth: Penguin, 1969.

Paley, William. *The Principles of Moral and Political Philosophy*. Boston: David Carlisle, 1806.

Pangle, Thomas L. *The Spirit of Modern Republicanism*. Chicago: University of Chicago Press, 1988.

Parry, Geraint. "Individuality, Politics, and the Critique of Paternalism in John Locke." *Political Studies* (June 1964).

———. *John Locke*. London: Allen & Unwin, 1978.

Parsons, J. E., Jr. "Locke's Doctrine of Property." *Social Research* (Autumn 1969).

Pateman, Carole. *The Problem of Political Obligation*. Berkeley and Los Angeles: University of California Press, 1979.

———. "Women and Consent." *Political Theory* (May 1980).

Pettit, Philip (and Robert Goodin). "The Possibility of Special Duties." *Canadian Journal of Philosophy* (December 1986).

——— (and Chandran Kukathas). *Rawls*. Stanford: Stanford University Press, 1990.

Piper, Adrian. "A Distinction Without a Difference." In *Midwest Studies in Philosophy VII*, ed. P. French, T. Uehling, Jr., and H. Wettstein. Minneapolis: University of Minnesota Press, 1982.

Plamenatz, John. *Man and Society*. London: Longmans, Green, 1963.

———. *Consent, Freedom and Political Obligation*. 2d ed. Oxford: Oxford University Press, 1968.

Polin, Raymond. *La Politique Morale de John Locke*. Paris: Presses Universitaires de France, 1960.

———. "Justice in Locke's Philosophy." In *Nomos VI: Justice*, ed. C. Friedrich and J. Chapman. New York: New York University Press, 1963.

Postema, Gerald. "Nozick on Liberty, Compensation, and the Individual's Right to Punish." *Social Theory and Practice* (Fall 1980).

Pufendorf, Samuel. *De Jure Naturae et Gentium Libri Octo*, tr. C. Oldfather and W. Oldfather. Oxford: Oxford University Press, 1934.

Quinn, Warren. "The Right to Threaten and the Right to Punish." *Philosophy & Public Affairs* (Fall 1985).

Rachels, James. "Active and Passive Euthanasia." In *Moral Problems*, ed. Rachels. 3d ed. New York: Harper & Row, 1979.

WORKS CITED

Railton, Peter. "Alienation, Consequentialism, and the Demands of Morality." *Philosophy & Public Affairs* (Spring 1984).

Rapaczynski, Andrzej. "Locke's Conception of Property and the Principle of Sufficient Reason." *Journal of the History of Ideas* (April–June 1981).

———. *Nature and Politics*. Ithaca: Cornell University Press, 1987.

Raphael, D. D. *Problems of Political Philosophy*. London: Macmillan, 1976.

Rawls, John. *A Theory of Justice*. Cambridge, Mass.: Harvard University Press, 1971.

Raz, Joseph. "Right-Based Moralities." In *Theories of Rights*, ed. J. Waldron. Oxford: Oxford University Press, 1984.

———. *The Morality of Freedom*. Oxford: Oxford University Press, 1986.

Reeve, Andrew. *Property*. Houndmills: Macmillan, 1986.

Reich, Charles A. "The New Property." *Yale Law Journal* (April 1964).

Replogle, Ron. *Recovering the Social Contract*. Totowa: Rowman & Littlefield, 1989.

Richards, B. A. "Inalienable Rights: Recent Criticism and Old Doctrine." *Philosophy and Phenomenological Research* (March 1969).

Richards, David A. J. *Toleration and the Constitution*. New York: Oxford University Press, 1986.

Richards, Judith (Lotte Mulligan, and John K. Graham). " 'Property' and 'People': Political Usages of Locke and Some Contemporaries." *Journal of the History of Ideas* (January-March 1981).

Riley, Patrick. *Will and Political Legitimacy*. Cambridge, Mass.: Harvard University Press, 1982.

Roemer, John. "A Challenge to Neo-Lockeanism." *Canadian Journal of Philosophy* (December 1988).

Rogers, G. A. J. "Locke, Law, and the Laws of Nature." In *John Locke: Symposium Wolfenbuttel 1979*, ed. R. Brandt. Berlin: Walter de Gruyter, 1981.

Rorty, Richard. "Postmodernist Bourgeois Liberalism." *Journal of Philosophy* (October 1983).

Ross, W. D. *The Right and the Good*. Oxford: Oxford University Press, 1930.

Rothbard, Murray. *The Ethics of Liberty*. Atlantic Highlands: Humanities Press, 1982.

Ruddick, William. "Parents and Life Prospects." In *Having Children*, ed. O. O'Neill and W. Ruddick. New York: Oxford University Press, 1979.

Ryan, Alan. "Locke and the Dictatorship of the Bourgeoisie." In *Locke and Berkeley*, ed. C. Martin and D. Armstrong. Notre Dame: University of Notre Dame Press, 1968.

———. "Utility and Ownership." In *Utility and Rights*, ed. R. Frey. Minneapolis: University of Minnesota Press, 1984.

———. *Property and Political Theory*. Oxford: Basil Blackwell, 1984.

———. *Property*. Minneapolis: University of Minnesota Press, 1987.

Sabine, George H. *A History of Political Theory*. New York: Henry Holt, 1937.

Sandel, Michael. *Liberalism and the Limits of Justice*. Cambridge: Cambridge University Press, 1982.

——— (ed.). *Liberalism and Its Critics*. New York: New York University Press, 1984.

Sarkar, Husain. "The Lockean Proviso." *Canadian Journal of Philosophy* (March 1982).

Sartorius, Rolf (ed.). *Paternalism*. Minneapolis: University of Minnesota Press, 1983.

———. "Persons and Property." In *Utility and Rights*, ed. R. Frey. Minneapolis: University of Minnesota Press, 1984.

Sayward, Charles. "Anarchism and Rights Violations." *Critica* (April 1982).

Sayre-McCord, Geoffrey (ed.). *Essays on Moral Realism*. Ithaca: Cornell University Press, 1988.

Scanlon, Thomas. "Thoughts about Rights in a State of Nature" (unpublished).

———. "Nozick on Rights, Liberty, and Property." *Philosophy & Public Affairs* (Fall 1976).

———. "Liberty, Contract, and Contribution." In *Readings in Social and Political Philosophy*, ed. R. M. Stewart. New York: Oxford University Press, 1986.

Scheffler, Samuel. "Natural Rights, Equality, and the Minimal State." In *Reading Nozick*, ed. J. Paul. Totowa: Rowman & Littlefield, 1981.

———. *The Rejection of Consequentialism*. Oxford: Oxford University Press, 1982.

Schmidtz, David. *The Limits of Government: An Essay on the Public Goods Argument*. Boulder: Westview, 1991.

Schochet, Gordon. "The Family and the Origins of the State in Locke's Political Philosophy." In *John Locke: Problems and Perspectives*, ed. J. W. Yolton. Cambridge: Cambridge University Press, 1969.

WORKS CITED

Schochet, Gordon. *Patriarchalism in Political Thought*. Oxford: Basil Blackwell, 1975.

Schrag, Francis. "Rights over Children." *Journal of Value Inquiry* (Summer 1973).

———. "The Child in the Moral Order." *Philosophy* (April 1977).

———. "Children: Their Rights and Needs." In *Whose Child?*, ed. W. Aiken and H. LaFollette. Totowa: Littlefield, Adams, 1980.

Schwarzenbach, Sibyl. "Locke's Two Conceptions of Property." *Social Theory and Practice* (Summer 1988).

Scott-Craig, Thomas. "John Locke and Natural Right." In *Natural Law and Natural Right*, ed. A. L. Harding. Dallas: Southern Methodist University Press, 1955.

Seliger, M. "Locke's Natural Law and the Foundation of Politics." *Journal of the History of Ideas* (July–September 1963).

———. *The Liberal Politics of John Locke*. London: Allen & Unwin, 1968.

Shapiro, Ian. *The Evolution of Rights in Liberal Theory*. Cambridge: Cambridge University Press, 1986.

———. "Resources, Capacities, and Ownership: The Workmanship Ideal and Distributive Justice." *Political Theory* (February 1991).

Shoeman, Ferdinand. "Rights of Children, Rights of Parents, and the Moral Basis of the Family." *Ethics* (October 1980).

———. "The Social Theory of Rights." In *Social Justice*, ed. D. Braybrooke and M. Bradie. Bowling Green: Studies in Applied Philosophy, 1982.

Sidgwick, Henry. *The Methods of Ethics*. New York: Dover, 1966.

———. *Outlines of the History of Ethics*. Boston: Beacon Press, 1960.

Sigmund, Paul E. *Natural Law in Political Thought*. Cambridge: Winthrop Publishers, 1971.

Simmons, A. John. *Moral Principles and Political Obligations*. Princeton: Princeton University Press, 1979.

———. "Inalienable Rights and Locke's *Treatises*." *Philosophy & Public Affairs* (Summer 1983).

———. "The Obligations of Citizens and the Justification of Conscription." In *Conscripts and Volunteers*, ed. R. Fullinwider. Totowa: Rowman & Allanheld, 1983.

———. "Consent, Free Choice, and Democratic Government." *Georgia Law Review* (Summer 1984).

———. "Locke's State of Nature." *Political Theory* (August 1989).

———. "Locke and the Right to Punish." *Philosophy & Public Affairs* (Fall 1991).

Singh, Raghuveer. "John Locke and the Theory of Natural Law." *Political Studies* (June 1961).

Skinner, Quentin. *The Foundations of Modern Political Thought*. Cambridge: Cambridge University Press, 1978.

Slote, Michael. "Obedience and Illusions." In *Having Children*, ed. O. O'Neill and W. Ruddick. New York: Oxford University Press, 1979.

Smith, Patricia. "The Duty to Rescue and the Slippery Slope Problem." *Social Theory and Practice* (Spring 1990).

Snare, Frank. "The Concept of Property." *American Philosophical Quarterly* (April 1972).

Snyder, David. "Locke on Natural Law and Property Rights." *Canadian Journal of Philosophy* (December 1986).

Soles, David E. "Intellectualism and Natural Law in Locke's *Second Treatise*." *History of Political Thought* (Spring 1987).

Sommers, Christina Hoff. "Filial Morality." *Journal of Philosophy* (August 1986).

Spencer, Herbert. *Social Statics*. New York: A. M. Kelly, 1969.

Steiner, Hillel. "The Natural Right to the Means of Production." *Philosophical Quarterly* (January 1977).

——. "The Structure of a Set of Compossible Rights." *Journal of Philosophy* (December 1977).

——. "Slavery, Socialism, and Private Property." In *Nomos XII: Property*, ed. J. Pennock and J. Chapman. New York: New York University Press, 1980.

——. "Justice and Entitlement." In *Reading Nozick*, ed. J. Paul. Totowa: Rowman & Littlefield, 1981.

Stell, Lance K. "Dueling and the Right to Life." *Ethics* (October 1979).

Strauss, Leo. *Natural Right and History*. Chicago: University of Chicago Press, 1953.

Sumner, L. W. "Rights Denaturalized." In *Utility and Rights*, ed. R. G. Frey. Minneapolis: University of Minnesota Press, 1982.

Tarcov, Nathan. "A 'Non-Lockean' Locke and the Character of Liberalism." In *Liberalism Reconsidered*, ed. D. McLean and C. Mills. Totowa: Rowman & Allanheld, 1983.

——. *Locke's Education for Liberty*. Chicago: University of Chicago Press, 1984.

Taylor, Charles. "Atomism." In *Powers, Possessions and Freedom*, ed. A. Kontos. Toronto: University of Toronto Press, 1979.

Thomson, Judith Jarvis. "Property Acquisition." *Journal of Philosophy* (October 21, 1976).

Thomson, Judith Jarvis. "Some Ruminations on Rights." *Arizona Law Review* 19/1 (1977).

―――. "Self-Defense and Rights." In *Rights, Restitution, & Risk.* Cambridge, Mass.: Harvard University Press, 1986.

Tuck, Richard. *Natural Rights Theories.* Cambridge: Cambridge University Press, 1979.

Tully, James. *A Discourse on Property.* Cambridge: Cambridge University Press, 1980.

―――. "Political Freedom." *Journal of Philosophy* (October 1990).

Tyler, E. L. G. *Family Provision.* London: Butterworths, 1971.

VanDeVeer, Donald. *Paternalistic Intervention.* Princeton: Princeton University Press, 1986.

Vaughn, Karen I. *John Locke: Economist and Social Scientist.* Chicago: University of Chicago Press, 1980.

Vlastos, Gregory. "Justice and Equality." In *Social Justice*, ed. R. B. Brandt. Englewood Cliffs: Prentice-Hall, 1962.

Von Leyden, Wolfgang. "Introduction" to Locke, *Essays on the Law of Nature.* Oxford: Oxford University Press, 1954.

―――. "John Locke and Natural Law." *Philosophy* (January 1956).

―――. "Locke's Strange Doctrine of Punishment." In *John Locke: Symposium Wolfenbuttel 1979*, ed. R. Brandt. Berlin: Walter de Gruyter, 1981.

―――. *Hobbes and Locke.* New York: St. Martins, 1982.

Waldron, Jeremy. "Enough and as Good Left for Others." *Philosophical Quarterly* (October 1979).

―――. "Locke's Account of Inheritance and Bequest." *Journal of the History of Philosophy* (January 1981).

―――. "Two Worries about Mixing One's Labor." *Philosophical Quarterly* (January 1983).

―――. "Locke, Tully, and the Regulation of Property." *Political Studies* (March 1984).

―――. *Nonsense upon Stilts.* London: Methuen, 1987.

―――. "When Justice Replaces Affection: The Need for Rights." *Harvard Journal of Law & Public Policy* 11/3 (1988).

―――. *The Right to Private Property.* Oxford: Oxford University Press, 1988.

―――. "Rights in Conflict." *Ethics* (April 1989).

Walzer, Michael. *Just and Unjust Wars.* New York: Basic Books, 1977.

―――. "The Communitarian Critique of Liberalism." *Political Theory* (February 1990).

Warrender Howard. *The Political Philosophy of Hobbes*. Oxford: Oxford University Press, 1957.

Wasserman, David. "Justifying Self-Defense." *Philosophy & Public Affairs* (Fall 1987).

Wasserstrom, Richard. "Rights, Human Rights, and Racial Discrimination." In *Rights*, ed. D. Lyons. Belmont: Wadsworth, 1979.

Wellman, Carl. "Upholding Legal Rights." *Ethics* (October 1975).

Wheeler Samuel C., III. "Natural Property Rights as Body Rights." In *The Main Debate: Communism versus Capitalism*, ed. T. Machan. New York: Random House, 1987.

Whelan, Frederick G. "Property as Artifice: Hume and Blackstone." In *Nomos XII: Property*, ed. J. Pennock and J. Chapman. New York: New York University Press, 1980.

White, Alan. *Rights*. Oxford: Oxford University Press, 1984.

White, Morton. *The Philosophy of the American Revolution*. Oxford: Oxford University Press, 1978.

Wicclair, Mark. "Caring for Frail Elderly Parents: Past Sacrifices and the Obligations of Adult Children." *Social Theory and Practice* (Summer 1990).

Wilkes, Kathleen V. *Real People*. Oxford: Oxford University Press, 1988.

Williams, Bernard. "The Idea of Equality." In *Problems of the Self*. Cambridge: Cambridge University Press, 1973.

Windstrup, George. "Locke on Suicide." *Political Theory* (May 1980).

———. "Freedom and Authority: The Ancient Faith of Locke's Letter on Toleration." *Review of Politics* (April 1982).

Winfrey, John C. "Charity versus Justice in Locke's Theory of Property." *Journal of the History of Ideas* (July–September 1981).

Wong, David. "On Moral Realism Without Foundations." *Southern Journal of Philosophy*, vol. 24, Supp. (1986).

Wood, Allen. *Hegel's Ethical Thought*. Cambridge: Cambridge University Press, 1990.

Wood, Neal. *The Politics of Locke's Philosophy*. Berkeley: University of California Press, 1983.

———. *John Locke and Agrarian Capitalism*. Berkeley: University of California Press, 1984.

Woozley, A. D. *Law and Obedience*. London: Duckworth, 1979.

———. "A Duty to Rescue: Some Thoughts on Criminal Liability." *Virginia Law Review* (October 1983).

Yolton, John W. *Locke and the Compass of Human Understanding*. Cambridge: Cambridge University Press, 1970.

———. *Locke: An Introduction*. Oxford: Basil Blackwell, 1985.

——— (and Jean S. Yolton). "Introduction" to Locke, *Some Thoughts Concerning Education*. Oxford: Oxford University Press, 1989.

Young, Robert. "Dispensing with Moral Rights." *Political Theory* (February 1978).

———. "In the Interest of Children and Adolescents." In *Whose Child?*, ed. W. Aiken and H. LaFollette. Totowa: Littlefield, Adams, 1980.

Yutang, Lin. "On Growing Old Gracefully." In *Vice and Virtue in Everyday Life*, ed. C. H. Sommers. San Diego: Harcourt Brace Jovanovich, 1985.

INDEX

Aaron, Richard, 18n, 19n, 56n
Abrams, Philip, 55n
absolute authority (right), 172, 172n,
178, 197n, 216, 216n, 224n, 230,
230n, 233n, 261–63n, 332. *See also*
despotical rights
absoluteness of rights, 93–94, 94n, 94–
95n, 111–12, 324, 324n
alienation of rights, 122–24, 164n, 178–
79, 179n, 204–11, 211n, 225, 229–32,
230n, 232n, 261, 261–63n, 268, 279n,
311–13, 321–22. *See also* inalienability;
transfers
Altham, J.E.J., 139n, 160n
anarchism, 163n, 165–66
Andrew, Edward, 77n, 119n, 269n,
313n, 328n, 353n
animals, 193–95, 197n, 203–4n, 236–
37, 239, 262
Aquinas, Thomas, 96, 96n, 99, 177,
187, 188n
archetype, 20, 25n
Aristotle, 180, 188n
Arnold, Christopher, 117n
Arthur, John, 280n, 294n
artificial power, 90, 123–24, 129–30,
130n, 167, 173–74
Ashcraft, Richard, 9, 9n, 11, 19n, 65n,
66n, 75n, 76n, 77n, 79n, 85–86n,
127–28, 177n, 208n, 225n, 226n,
233n, 236n, 245n, 246n, 253n, 260n,
272n, 278n, 317n, 328n, 334n
atheism, 39, 39n
authority. *See* absolute authority; authority to punish; right of creation
authority to punish, 122–24, 142–48

Baier, Annette, 25n
Beccaria, Cesare, 139n
Becker, Lawrence, 70n, 81n, 83n, 89n,
92n, 169n, 171n, 183n, 187n, 191n,
192n, 198–99n, 223n, 241–42n, 242n,
246n, 271n, 276n, 291–92n, 292n
Beitz, Charles, 312n
Belliotti, Raymond, 188n
benefit theory of rights, 93, 93n, 97n,
117, 203, 203–4n

Benn, S. I. and Peters, R. S., 201n
Bentham, Jeremy, 71n, 93n, 97n, 107–
9, 107n, 109n, 116–17n, 140–41n,
248, 345, 347, 348, 351
bequest, rights of. *See* inheritance,
right of
Best, Judith, 16n
Blum, Lawrence, 168n
Blustein, Jeffrey, 167n, 168n, 181n,
182n, 185n, 189n, 190n, 198–99n,
199n
Bok, Sissela, 65n
Bosanquet, Bernard, 110n
boundary problem, 268, 270, 276–77
Brandt, Richard, 70n, 94n, 118n
Brogan, A. P., 57n
Buchanan, Allen, 83n, 94n, 107n, 111n,
112n, 170n, 346n
Burke, Edmund, 110n

capital punishment, 139, 139n, 149,
196n
categorical imperative, 39–42, 39–40n
charity rights, 87–88, 90, 221, 225n,
278n, 291, 327–36, 332n, 339–40,
341–42, 343–45, 346–47, 349, 350–
52, 354. *See also* positive rights
Cherno, Melvin, 226n, 228n, 242n
children's duties. *See* filial duties
children's rights. *See* filial rights
choice theory of rights, 92–93, 93n, 203
Christman, John, 246n, 255n, 271n,
277–78n, 302n
civil justice. *See* justice
civil law, 27, 89
civil rights, 87–91, 308–10
civil society, 127–29, 146–48, 161–66,
212–15, 270, 304–5n, 307–17, 341
claim right, 70, 71–74, 71n, 72–73n,
74–75n, 92n, 97–98, 125n, 142n,
154–55, 182–84, 182n; mandatory,
74–79, 76n, 85, 87, 182, 245; optional, 73–79, 73n, 76n, 77n, 85, 85–
86n, 87
claiming, 97–99, 98n, 119–20
Clark, Lorenne, 171–72n, 173n, 205n

The Princeton University Press series "Studies in Moral, Political, and Legal Philosophy" is under the general editorship of Marshall Cohen, Professor of Philosophy and Law and Dean of Humanities at the University of Southern California. The series includes the following titles, in chronological order of publication:

Understanding Rawls: A Reconstruction and Critique of A Theory of Justice by R. P. Wolff (1977). Out of print

Immorality by R. D. Milo (1984)

Politics & Remembrance: Republican Themes in Machiavelli, Burke, and Tocqueville by B. J. Smith (1985)

Understanding Marx: A Reconstruction and Critique of Capital by R. P. Wolff (1985)

Hobbesian Moral and Political Theory by G. S. Kavka (1986)

The General Will before Rousseau: The Transformation of the Divine into the Civic by P. Riley (1986)

Respect for Nature: A Theory of Environmental Ethics by P. W. Taylor (1986). Available in paperback

Paternalist Intervention: The Moral Bounds on Benevolence by D. VanDeVeer (1986)

The Longing for Total Revolution: Philosophic Sources of Social Discontent from Rousseau to Marx and Nietzche by B. Yack (1986)

Meeting Needs by D. Braybrooke (1987)

Reasons for Welfare: The Political Theory of the Welfare State by R. E. Goodin (1988)

Why Preserve Natural Variety? by B. G. Norton (1988). Available in paperback

Coercion by A. Wertheimer (1988). Available in paperback

Merleau-Ponty and the Foundation of an Existential Politics by K. H. Whiteside (1988)

On War and Morality by R. L. Holmes (1989). Available in paperback

The Rhetoric of Leviathan: Thomas Hobbes and the Politics of Cultural Transformation by D. Johnston (1989). Available in paperback

Desert by G. Sher (1989). Available in paperback

Critical Legal Studies: A Liberal Critique by A. Altman (1989)

Finding the Mean: Theory and Practice in Aristotelian Political Philosophy by S. G. Salkever (1990)

Marxism, Morality, and Social Justice by R. G. Peffer (1990)

Speaking of Equality: An Analysis of the Rhetorical Force of "Equality' in Moral and Legal Discourse by P. Weston (1990)

Friedrich Nietzsche and the Politics of the Soul: A Study of Heroic Individualism by L. P. Thiele (1990). Available in paperback

Valuing Life by J. Kleinig (1991)

The Lockean Theory of Rights by A. J. Simmons (1992)

Liberal Nationalism by Y. Tamir (1993)

On the Edge of Anarchy by A. J. Simmons (1993)